HOME DESIGN GUIDE

HOME DESIGN GUIDE

Barty Phillips

SOMA
san francisco

First published in 1997 by Bloomsbury Publishing plc. American Edition published 1998 by SOMA Books by arrangement with Bloomsbury Publishing Plc.

SOMA Books is an imprint of Bay Books & Tapes, Inc. SOMA Books may be purchased for education, business, or sales promotional use at attractive quantity discounts. For information, address: Bay Books & Tapes, Inc., 555 De Haro Street, No. 220, San Francisco, CA 94107.

for SOMA Books:
Publisher: **James Connolly**
Art Director: **Jeffrey O'Rourke**
Design: **React**
Production: **Cabra Diseño**
American Editor: **Judith Dunham**
Proofreader: **Marianna Cherry**

Library of Congress Cataloguing-in-Publication Data
Phillips, Barty
      Home design guide / Barty Phillips
             p.   cm.
      1. Interior decoration. I. Title
      NK2110.P49 1998
      747--DC21   97-53195
                                              CIP

ISBN 1-57959-008-x

Printed in China

10 9 8 7 6 5 4 3 2 1

Distributed to the trade by Publishers Group West

ACKNOWLEDGMENTS

A book like this is a big undertaking and I could never have managed it without the help and goodwill of many professionals and organizations, and an enormous amount of support and advice from friends and family. In particular, I would like to thank Bill Blake, Rosamund and Eion Downs, David and Judy Afia, Sarah Tisdall, Shiu-Kay Kan, Bruce Gornick, Philippa Watkins, Leslie Hoskins, Paul Priestman, Jo Steel, John Tchalenko, Judith Turner, Graham Hopewell, Mary Mullin, Alf Martensson, Jane Priestman, Peter Peretti, Brian Dawson of H & R Johnson, Sanderson's Made-to-Measure Service, Neil Broomfield, Coles of London, Roger Dyson of Pendle Heritage Centre, Melvyn Seddon of Bultitude & Duncan, The Glass & Glazing Federation, The Georgian Group, The Victorian Society, the Paint Research Association, The National Trust, The Building Centre, the RIBA and all the people who have so generously allowed us to use their transparencies, in particular Perstorp and Fired Earth. I would also like to thank Elisabeth Rickard, Jane Donovan, Liz Boggis, Terry Evans, Paul Marshall and Peter Dyer at React and everyone at Bloomsbury for their advice, editing, general support and a very good-looking book.

Contents

AROUND THE HOUSE

FOREWORD & INTRODUCTION
8
Using Your Space
10
Clothing the Spaces
30
Living Rooms
50
Kitchens & Dining Rooms
68
Children's Rooms
98
Bedrooms & Bathrooms
114
Workrooms
134
One-Room Living
150
Attics, Warehouses & Basements
164
Outside Meets Inside
174
A Short Guide to Interior Styles
184

CHOOSING AND USING

Wood
210
Plaster, Brick & Stone
222
Paint
230
Wallcoverings
242
Textiles
252
Floor Coverings
266
Lights, Glass & Mirrors
278
Heating
292
Furniture
298
FACTS & FIGURES
308
GLOSSARY & ADDRESSES
309
CREDITS & INDEX
315

FOREWORD

In the very early seventies, Libertys mounted the willfully incorrect launch of Ringo (Starr) and Robin's furniture that was made from British steel. Barty Phillips' lovely and serious piece in the *Observer* lent cred in the all-too-prevalent hype. The morning after the party, at opening time, the late, stupendous Keith Showering (cashmere coat, velvet collar, giant cigar and all), bought a steel table and four chairs for his poolside and paid in cash. These were about the only items we sold and they are still stainless, I'm sure.

Many books, programs and projects, but also twenty-five years on, Barty has written the *Home Design Guide*. Beautifully conceived, photographed and produced, the *Home Design Guide* holds its own on any coffee table. Much more importantly, though (particularly if you're anything like me and always dragging a miscellany of collected items from encampment to encampment), it is a book to which you should pay heed. This is a practical almanac for enhancing your life at home: you can use it and retailers can certainly learn from it, too.

Richard Stewart-Liberty

INTRODUCTION

You are poised to decorate your new home, or perhaps to renovate your existing home. It is one of the most rewarding projects you can do and full of possibilities. So full of possibilities, in fact, that it becomes almost impossible to make decisions. Where do you start? You want your home to be warm, comfortable, welcoming and attractive. Should you choose a particular style or hope that your own taste will automatically create its own fascinating interior? Should you call in experts or will it be cheaper to do it all yourself? Can you find what you want in local stores or is it worth shopping around to get something more interesting, and will that bump the cost up enormously?

This book will lead you through the labyrinth of design decisions which confront all those who want to make the most of their home. You can read it from cover to cover if you wish, or you can concentrate on a particular section. It is a readable encyclopedia. Complete beginners can use it as a guide through the complicated process of turning ideas into reality, but it is also for those with more experience, who will find it useful to have a reference book on hand. It is easy to use because of the way it is divided into sections that enable the reader to tackle the home methodically.

Section One takes a look at the house and the various rooms in it, checking that best use is being made of the space and the various ways of arranging furniture and fittings. At the end of this section is a chapter describing the most popular styles, and guidelines on achieving the look of particular styles are included throughout the book. A new interest in historic styles is backed up by a wide body of research and an availability of fabrics, wallpapers and paints based on old colors and designs, and this can give a very exciting extra dimension to designing your home.

Section Two, called Choosing and Using, is all about materials and what you can do with them, what sort of effects you can produce with them and a number of projects that most people could attempt without difficulty. Wood, plaster moldings, textiles and wallpaper are covered in this section and so is heating and – particularly important when designing a home – lighting.

Section Three is full of factual information and includes a glossary, a bibliography and an address list of useful organizations, stores and suppliers, as well as measurement conversions and a chronological list of the styles covered in Section One.

This book is jam-packed with inspirational ideas and hard information, checklists, cheap solutions and practical projects. It is liberally illustrated with photographs that are not just pretty to look at, but have something to say as well. This is a book to enjoy and a book to use constantly.

Using Your Space

Space is the magic ingredient in any interior. The shape of rooms, their height and width and the way they connect offer plenty of scope for different uses. You can make new door openings, open up the roof spaces, remove walls to create a large, open room or add walls to create smaller ones. In practice, too much structural work is expensive and time-consuming, and you can often create spaces simply by rearranging furniture or using the height of a room.

Don't think about each room or the function of a room in isolation from the rest of the house. Be aware of the way rooms open onto and give a vista of each other or a hall or passageway. Be clear about your own tastes and requirements. It may be fashionable to add an extra bathroom, but if you don't need or want one, use that valuable space for something you do want. Don't alter the set pattern of a house, however, without good reason. It is a pity to change the use of satisfactory spaces, and drastic solutions will alter the way the rest of the house works.

Work with the character of the architecture, not against it. For example, a nineteenth-century terraced house will not respond well if its walls are knocked down to try and provide a large, open space, thereby losing all the Victorian detailing, which is part of its charm. In this chapter we will look at the various ways in which small and large spaces can be adapted or arranged to give most use and pleasure.

Who Will Live in the House?

(previous page)
A wide, curving staircase,
carefully chosen colors and
golden wood strip flooring give
this narrow hall an open,
spacious feeling.

(above)
Downstairs, upstairs: the
circular window at the top of the
stairs (previous page) brings
light into both areas, and this,
together with the woodstrip
floor, unifies the two areas.

Before you move into a new home, think through all the things you want it to provide. A family is a moving, changing entity, and a certain amount of flexibility should be designed into the spaces so that as children grow older, their new hobbies and interests can be incorporated. Single people or couples can, perhaps, design more specifically and on a more permanent basis, since their requirements are unlikely to change so quickly or drastically.

Make a checklist of the people who will live in the house and their various requirements. The following sample checklists may be useful as guides. Do adapt these to make them your own, adding or altering items as you require. Anything considered important by anybody in the house should be incorporated, so think it through carefully. If your own interests demand specialized equipment or space, add these to the list, for example, room for an exercise bike; storage for serious sports equipment such as tennis racquets, skis, footballs, etc.; space large enough to house a pottery wheel and kiln; space for carpentry or other do-it-yourself tools; space for permanently setting up a sewing machine. You may want to have a tenant to help pay for a mortgage, or you may want to offer accommodation to a student, provide a home for an elderly relative, run a bed-and-breakfast business or simply enjoy having visitors. If you are going to let rooms or provide an in-law apartment, then the space should be as self-contained as it can possibly be made. A separate front door is ideal, but if that's impossible, an entrance which does not involve running the gauntlet of the rest of the house is best. A separate bathroom is ideal for tenants, or at least their own washing facilities and their own cooking arrangements, even if it's just a microwave. For all of these structural alterations, you'll need to plan very carefully indeed and will probably have to conform to local planning regulations and building codes.

CHECKLIST FOR A FAMILY OF FOUR

- Double bedroom
- Children's room
- Spare room
- Living room
- Space for play
- Home office space
- Family kitchen/dining room
- Laundry/utility room
- Sewing area
- Large storage area
- Bathroom
- Downstairs half bath
- Toy storage
- Book, tape and compact disc storage
- Stroller storage
- Coat/boot storage.

If there are teenage children, how about adding space for games, storage for outdoor games equipment, for bicycles and perhaps for any interest or hobby?

CHECKLIST FOR A TENANT'S ROOM OR IN-LAW APARTMENT

- Separate entrance, if possible
- Separate electricity and gas meters, if possible
- Level living area, particularly for an elderly person
- Storage for clothes, shoes and accessories: easy to see, easy to reach
- Writing table or desk
- Easy-clean surfaces
- Warm, nonslip floors, perhaps fitted carpeting
- Efficient heating system, separate from rest of house
- Separate telephone line, if possible
- Own bathroom, if possible
- Washing facilities
- Simple cooking facilities
- Efficient lighting: bedside lamp, desk lamp, good general lighting.

CHECKLIST FOR AN OLDER COUPLE MOVING INTO A SMALLER HOME

- Bedroom large enough to house a bed or beds comfortably, as well as clothes that have been accumulated over the years
- Living room large enough to hold dining table with ease (and also to take furniture brought from previous home, of which there will almost certainly be too much at first)
- No tricky steps or steep stairs
- Sunroom/garden
- Small, labor-saving kitchen with carefully planned space
- Convenient bathroom with shower and fitted with grab rails
- Pleasant view, whether of houses or country. Low windows, so that you can see out while sitting down
- Space for leisure activities and equipment: painting and paints, bird watching and binoculars, gardening and boots, tools, etc.

(above)
This storage cart, fitted on casters, is versatile and can hold any number of different objects, from games equipment to clothes.

(above)
This custom-designed and built work space takes up one end of a batchelor's attic flat.

CHECKLIST FOR A YOUNG COUPLE WITH BABY

- Large double bedroom with room for the baby's crib for the first months
- Small bedroom for the child as it grows older, but big enough to adapt later on
- Useful open-plan living space with room for toys on the floor
- Living room/kitchen so parents can cook and supervise at the same time — with a room divider to keep the baby out of the dangerous area
- Plenty of high storage to keep precious or dangerous things out of reach
- Ample storage for baby clothes and other equipment
- An efficient and safe heating system
- A stairway that is not too steep and allows a safety gate
- Nonoperable bottom windows with bars or safety glass
- A spacious hall for the stroller and other paraphernalia
- Electrical outlets at work-surface height.

CHECKLIST FOR A ONE-PERSON APARTMENT WITH HOME OFFICE

- Single/double bedroom with room for wardrobe and general storage (failing a second bedroom, it should be big enough to use as a bedroom at one end and a workroom at the other)
- Ideally, a spare bedroom/workroom: desk space for computer; storage for office and other essentials
- Fold-out bed, sofa bed or divan
- Small, but convenient bathroom
- Interior space for general storage
- Tiny ship's galley kitchen
- Living room — workroom (if the bedroom won't allow this)
- Very organized storage
- Perhaps a trestle table to double up as a dining table
- Balcony or small patio to add to the illusion of space
- Hallway, or any wall space for added storage.

CHECKLIST FOR A PROFESSIONAL COUPLE
- Double bedroom
- Well-organized living room for relaxation
- Labor-saving kitchen, possibly with space for informal eating
- Dining room for formal entertaining
- Spacious bathroom, possibly two sinks, bath and shower
- Half bath
- Plenty of clothes storage
- Utility room
- Library/study
- Small garden or patio with sunroom.

Which Room Is Which?

You don't have to accept the real estate agent's assessment of which rooms should be used for what. It might be more convenient to use the rooms differently, and you may be able to change the use of certain rooms without too much disruption. A bathroom can sometimes be moved from a large room to a smaller one (or a larger one), for example, provided the drainage is nearby and the work does not involve a lot of extra plumbing. This would then leave the larger space free for living or sleeping purposes.

Bedrooms are mainly empty during the day but, with careful planning, a larger bedroom can be given a double purpose and can act as a sewing room, a sitting room, a music room or even an office without the loss of the peace and tranquility that most people feel their bedroom should have. You could decide to have the bedroom downstairs and the living room upstairs. This makes good use of the better light that is usually available in the upstairs room, which often looks out onto a more interesting view.

As for the kitchen, which is generally regarded as one of the most important rooms in the home, some people prefer a ship's galley kitchen of great neatness, while others want to have a family farmhouse kitchen. Smaller kitchens can be created with partition walls or room dividers and, with careful planning (see page 70), medium-sized rooms can make good family kitchens with plenty of room to eat and chat, as well as for cooking meals. Any of these options should be easy to provide without too much adjustment of space. Whether the kitchen is separate or part of a bigger room, the dining area must be near the cooking area, both for the convenience of the cook and so that the food arrives at the table while it is still hot.

Even a garage can be given a useful living function if it is turned into a children's playroom or teenager's games room. Most garages would need to be insulated and heated, and to have some sort of flooring, such as quarry, ceramic or vinyl tiles, or linoleum to create a more pleasant surface. Garages may also be turned into satisfactory workshops or studios, provided you install good fluorescent or "day" lighting to work by, a good working table and convenient storage.

(above)
This dining room/kitchen makes a pleasantly integrated single space using a similar wood for both cabinets and table.

(above)
This small, square addition
opens straight onto the garden
through French windows.

Altering the Space

Opening up two rooms to make one larger space is tempting and often creates an attractive room. This can be good for parties, for stylish furnishings, for socializing and for children's play. However, you do lose a room and you may find it more convenient to keep the two rooms separate. One solution can be to create wide doors in the arch between the rooms, which can be closed. This means that one half of a living room could still be used as a separate bedroom or for board games, but it can still be opened out, if necessary.

Rooms can be divided as well as opened up, of course, but this is where the proportions often go wrong, providing two rooms that are each too narrow and too tall, so that it is difficult to furnish them with comfort and elegance. A suspended ceiling may help: apart from creating a more pleasant space, it can provide concealed storage and also concealed lighting. Suspended ceilings may be solid-looking, to take the place of the existing ceiling, and moldings similar to the originals can be fixed where the new ceiling meets the walls. However, a slatted ceiling would be possibly more useful in a kitchen where it could be fitted with hooks and used as hanging storage. In a room where the ceiling is already very low, slats will be less claustrophobic. Remember that a suspended ceiling can act as a sound chamber of resonance and, where this would cause annoyance, the ceiling should be insulated against noise. A word of caution here: Altering the spaces structurally may affect the resale value of your home, so if you don't intend to remain in the house for long, don't do anything too unconventional.

Extending the Space

Adding on, building up and burrowing down can all provide useful extra space in your home, but again, careful planning is required.

(left)
An attic space can be put to good use as a playroom or, as shown here, a guest bedroom.

If you want to combine two rooms, brick up a chimney or open up a fireplace, you will have to take into account whether the walls are load-bearing, what sort of work will be involved, how much it will cost and how it will affect the rest of the house. This is a good time to bring in an architect or an interior designer to work out the possibilities, the costs and the proportions. A professional's training in visualizing spaces will result in interesting and practical solutions. (Refer to the back section for information.)

EXTENDING UP

Opening up the attic space or adding an extra story in the roof can offer scope for new, habitable rooms. Some homes are not built to carry the extra weight. You could use the space for storage, but not for living. Adding extra strength in the form of steel beams and joists used to support a floor or roof will be expensive. Always get the advice of an architect. There are building codes concerning height, windows, and whether you will have to encroach on your neighbors and fire security. Stairs, even if they have to be steep, are more inviting and safer than a ladder, and will encourage people to use the room. It is

of heat in summer. Double-glazing or some form of insulated barrier between the sunroom and the house is essential to protect the rest of the home from these extremes.

In narrow houses, particularly in poor conversions, you may find you have to go through one room in order to get to another: for example, it's quite common to have to go through the kitchen to get to the bathroom. A small addition at the side of the house can create a hallway to link the two rooms.

EXTENDING DOWN

Many houses have basements: they may be rabbit warrens of little poky rooms, which can be converted into spacious areas opening out onto a garden or small courtyard. Often basements suffer from excessive moisture, and a skin of concrete needs to be applied over the interior walls, and a moisture barrier needs to be inserted to make sure that they remain dry. Apart from the normal professional advice you should always obtain from architects and surveyors before undertaking structural work, you should also check the water table and make sure there is no danger of flooding in the basement area.

Imaginative Use of Space

Many excellent reference books are widely available from specialist building and architectural bookstores and suppliers, which nonprofessionals can find helpful when designing a home. These books are invaluable as they give accurate measurements and show in clear diagrams exactly how much space is needed to accommodate various pieces of equipment and all kinds of activities in the home, depending on your needs. For example, there are calculations that illustrate just how much space a person needs when bending down to get something out of the oven, or how much comfortable headroom is actually required in an attic.

(above)
A basement has been imaginatively turned into a kitchen.

obviously important to get professional advice, and there are many companies specializing in roof additions, who will take responsibility for the plan, the permits and the work; an architect may produce a design with more imaginative use of the space and can also take responsibility for obtaining the necessary permits and completing the work to a satisfactory standard with the help of a team of outside contractors.

EXTENDING OUT

The most obvious way of extending is out onto the garden, creating a larger kitchen, perhaps, and there is even the possibility of building on top of the original addition to give an upstairs addition as well. A popular form of garden addition is the sunroom, which helps to ensure that there is light in the interior rooms, while making a pleasant transition between the garden and the house. Remember that sunrooms can bring a lot of cold into the house in winter and an uncomfortable amount

Using the Height

If the available space is restricted, then make use of the height of the room. Wall cabinets or shelves will keep things off the floor and can create room for a surprising number of belongings, thereby avoiding clutter. A raised platform can provide an extra living, playing or sleeping space, as well as adding an interesting feature to a room. The idea of using the height of a room for adding bunks to children's rooms can be extended to building an adult bed on a platform, with cabinets fitted underneath. Various forms of storage can be used under the bed. If it's a double bed, pull-out storage will be more easily accessible. The higher the platform for the bed, the more scope for imaginative storage there will be underneath, and the space could also be used to house a desk. Obviously, a very tall bed is only suitable for older children, and there should always be a sturdy rail to prevent the child from falling out of bed. A balcony or narrow mezzanine floor can provide a separate area for cooking and eating in large, tall rooms, with a separate workspace or room for a bed. This is especially useful in a loft or warehouse conversion, where the difference in height can act as a psychological barrier between what goes on elsewhere in the room.

Lofts and warehouses provide great opportunities for open-plan living. People unaccustomed to large rooms may find so much open space awe-inspiring at first. However, the largest rooms can be effectively divided by large pieces of furniture. Enormous sofas or seating units that form an L shape can be backed by large, freestanding storage pieces, which also provide some privacy and mark out areas designated for different activities: quiet relaxation, desk work and computer games, for example. In these huge spaces, you can wall off a comparatively tiny area for the essential privacy of bathroom and bedroom.

Pockets of Space

In many houses, there are pockets of unused space, perhaps on a landing or where a sloping roof adjoins a room, or in a loft or basement and especially under the stairs, which can be put to good use as telephone, dining and utility areas, making ordered storage space (rather than existing chaos), depending on the available space.

THE ENTRANCE HALL

This space is often underused because it seems too narrow, or because it is shared by a number of apartment dwellers, or simply because nobody has thought about what to do with it.

If it is a narrow space, you can fix narrow shelves to the walls and put a console table underneath to provide useful storage without gobbling up too much space. This is the place where it is most convenient to hang coats, leave gloves, peer into a mirror, and keep letters waiting to be opened or posted.

(above)
A built-in platform, which houses a pull-out bed, makes ingenious use of the height in this tall room and allows room for the comfortable seating area placed above it.

CORRIDORS AND LANDING

A typical leftover space is the landing at the top of the stairs. Here you might be able to fit a set of floor-to-ceiling shelves forming a personal library or even a small shower stall. A framework of architraving can give the plainest shelves a "library" look. A landing can become a well-equipped area for sewing or be used as the shoe-care centre of the home, with cleaning equipment kept neatly stored in a narrow cabinet and hanging pockets for the shoes. It could become a phone bay or even a place to do homework. Make sure that there is good lighting and that the space is warm, because no one will want to use an ill-lit and chilly corner.

BASEMENTS AND ATTICS

An attic can be a useful extra space for children's floor activities, such as playing with train sets or building blocks. If the children are likely to be running around, you must make sure there's enough headroom to ensure they don't bang their heads on the beams. Your architect can advise you on this. Attic beds can be pushed under the angle of the roof (and pulled out at night for sleeping, if necessary). During the day you can gain at least 19.3 square feet (1.8 square meters) of space (the area of a bed), for more general activities. Be warned, however, that many houses are not strong enough to support any extra building upward and the cost of strengthening may make the exercise not worthwhile. Always get professional advice.

UNDER THE STAIRS

The amount of space available will depend on the angle of the stairs and their width, and whether they are open or closed off, but a telephone area doesn't need much elbow room. You might be able to squeeze an extra half bath under a steep staircase, with a tiny sink for hand washing. There are tiny "sit-in" baths that will fit under some staircases and are then conveniently placed for a neighboring bedroom. All sorts of storage devices can be fitted under stairs, from pull-out drawers to staggered shelves: you might even be able to house the washing machine there.

Space-Saving Equipment and Furniture

Beds: Hinged beds can be useful where there is not much space. For example, a whole wall of shelving and cabinets can incorporate a section which pulls down, revealing a bed. Sheets and blankets can be strapped into place while the bed is in the upright position. A bed like this can be useful where a workroom is also the spare bedroom, or in a teenager's or student's room.

Baths: Small, but deep sit-in baths, the modern equivalent of the old "Sitz" bath, can be squeezed into very small spaces and semi-circular baths will fit into the corner of a small bathroom, thereby saving a lot of space. A shower takes up less space than a bath and less hot water too (unless it's a massaging shower head). You could certainly add a shower cubicle to a bedroom in cases where an en suite bathroom would not fit.

Table: Hinged tables, which pull down from the wall, can provide a little breakfast bar or dining area in a tiny kitchen and, together with folding chairs or chairs hung from pegs on the wall, a satisfactory seating area can be created without making the cooking space too cramped.

Screens

Screens can be used to cleverly divide up living spaces, to demarcate or conceal parts of a room and to keep out cold air, particularly in rooms where open fires, which encourage drafts, are used. In traditional Japanese houses, sliding screens were used instead of fixed walls to divide the home into flexible living spaces. These screens were made from a lightweight, wood framework covered in translucent paper to let in light.

Fixed screens, such as sliding, folding doors, can be used to divide two rooms, but the choice must be carefully made since some are downright ugly and others take up too much space when they are opened out.

Another form of screen is the room divider. This can take many forms, from a narrow set of shelves reaching up to the ceiling, to a projecting work surface with cabinets fitted underneath.

Portable folding screens can be useful for hiding unsightly bits and pieces and for preventing drafts, and they can be decorative in their own right. These are versatile pieces of furniture: they can be large or small, made of solid wood panels hinged together, or with a framework of wood or metal finished in many different ways, from the traditional Victorian screen collage of printed cut-outs created especially for the purpose, to fabric, paper, glass or hand-painted finishes.

Stairs

Built in most town houses since the eighteenth century, the conventional staircase takes up a major part of the available ground floor space and redesigning it can add greatly to the usable space in such houses. You may be able to remove a wall and open up the staircase to become part of the living room. An alternative treatment is to install a spiral staircase. These have disadvantages, in that it can be difficult to get large pieces of furniture up the stairs, and they can be dangerous to negotiate, particularly for young children and elderly people, because of the narrowness of the treads at the centre. Nevertheless, they can be elegant and may open out the space, particularly in loft areas or basements.

Fireplaces

Today, because of central heating, a fireplace is an optional feature of the home, but rooms still need to have a focus. For many rooms, this is provided by a television set, but

choose from. In a traditional house, a fire-place in a similar size and style to that which would have been in the house originally will probably look best. Scale is an important factor. In a small basement room, which was perhaps once part of the servants' quarters, a grandiose, marble fireplace will look ridicu-lous, but a small Victorian cast-iron fireplace will fit in well. The width and height of the fireplace should fit in with the proportions of the room. In modern houses, rooms tend to be lower and the fireplace should be proportion-ately lower to allow for this, which means the mantel shelf will also be set quite low. Installing a nineteenth-century French marble fireplace, for example, in an English home is silly and out of place. Check that the flue is clear and the linings are fireproof and not cracked, that the mortar is intact and that the chimney is not sealed at the top.

Windows

Although, in the first place, windows exist to let in light and air, they are also important architectural features. They are part of a house with a specific architectural style, and the house may look best when fitted with the windows it was born with. If you want to add windows, try to add them to the sides or the back of the house, so that they do not alter the main facade. Aim to match the proportions and sizes of the panes with the existing ones, and try to get the tops and sills of the new and the existing windows lined up.

a fireplace is a much more comfortable centerpiece. Even if you don't intend to light a fire in it, a fireplace can be used to frame a single object or even a collection.

Fireplaces can be fitted with healers or the more efficient types of wood burning stove (except where prohibited), so it is important to keep the flues intact. In some older terraced houses, the flues interconnect with those of the neighboring house, so you may not be allowed to remove any of the brickwork at all and, in any case, the flue plays a useful role in the ventilation of the house.

If you have decided to remove a fireplace, perhaps in a small bedroom or bathroom, you can often leave the two side piers of brickwork and extend the chimney opening upward to the same height as the doors of the room. This can then become a valuable space for a cabi-net, or even a niche to display a piece of sculpture or a vase of flowers. If you are replacing a fireplace that was removed some time ago, there are many different kinds to

It is sometimes possible to extend a flat window a very small amount, perhaps only the depth of the wall, to make a small bay. In a very small kitchen, for example, this can add enough room to have a small table and window seat as a breakfast space for one or two people.

French or patio doors, looking out onto the garden, are usually at the back or side of the house where they will not be so noticeable. Adding French or patio doors can make your house vulnerable to break-ins, so always get professional advice on the type of door, the type of glass and the best locks to install.

Inside the house, you can make the most use of small or inconvenient windows. A small window, when positioned off-centre in the wall, can be matched by a corresponding "mock" window to make a pair. Windows whose sills are slightly too high for visual comfort can be made much more friendly by building a "frame" of shelves around them and adding a window seat.

Doors

A door in the wrong place, which opens the wrong way, can cause constant annoyance. You may find that simply hinging it on the other side may make it more convenient. (This is often true of closet doors, as well.) A door in the corner of a room should be placed so that you can open it at least a little more than 90 degrees.

If you have a doorway that you would like to block off, don't remove it; simply alter the door on the room side. That is, take off the moldings and treat the door as part of the wall. You can even fit a full length sheet of mirror over it, which will help to brighten and seemingly widen the space.

Sliding doors are often installed as space-saving devices, but they do require careful detailing to ensure a good, soundproof fit, and conversions from hinged to sliding doors are seldom satisfactory. An alternative to a sliding door is a bi-folding door; one which is split in half and hinged in the middle, as well as at one edge and sometimes controlled by a guide in a track at the top. This type of door can be useful, for example, if you have a cramped bathroom or lavatory, or as cabinet doors.

Bi-folding, louvered doors can provide a barrier between two rooms, but only if sound-proofing is not important. If you are adding a new door to a room and blocking off another (for example, to gain access to a bathroom

from a landing or hallway, rather than through another room), you can also have a smaller-than-standard door specially made to fit a small opening so that it won't take up all the hall space, when open.

EXTERIOR DOORS

Like windows, exterior doors are an important part of the architectural style of a house. It's a mistake to try and put over-large and over-ornate doors that are far more suitable for a large mansion onto a small terraced house and unnecessary, since smaller, wood doors come in a wide range of suitable sizes and styles.

In a kitchen, where you may have a door opening into a garden or courtyard, or into a dining room, a Dutch door is often a practical feature. This is a door split horizontally in half, enabling the bottom part to be closed when the upper half is open. A Dutch door is useful for keeping children and animals in or out, or under your eye while you are working.

(above)
New windows have been installed under the roof to create a new built-in bathroom with a view.

Bills, school notes and other paperwork, toys, kitchen equipment and so on, which you need every day, should be stored within easy reach. Things used once a year may be stored high up or in less accessible places, while heavy items, such as sewing machines, are best kept where they can be easily lifted, unless they are kept out on a tabletop ready for use. Visually attractive items can be given permanent display storage with special lighting to show them off, and keep them safe.

Shelves

Shelves are among the most versatile methods of storage. One obvious place for them is in the alcoves created by a chimney. The side walls provide ready supports for simple bookshelves and built-in bookends. You can carry the shelves right up to the ceiling or just as far as you wish, perhaps leaving a shelf in the middle for a display. Make the shelves narrower as they go up, or they may appear top-heavy. Shelves with slightly deeper cabinets below look good and provide closed storage for untidy things like magazines and games.

The simplest type of shelving is created by shelves fixed onto individual brackets on the wall. There are many types of bracket available, from plain, wood ones to elaborate wrought iron. If you want more shelves, a system of uprights, with brackets slotted into them to support the shelves, would be sturdy, convenient and adjustable. Choose shelves that are strong enough not to sag under the weight of books and other heavy objects, such as music centers and television sets (see chart, opposite). When fitting shelves, don't assume that your walls are straight: they seldom are. Measure the back and the front of the alcove and get the wood cut to size.

Freestanding shelves are now available in many different sizes and finishes, some as part of modular storage systems, which can include cabinets, chests and tables.

(above)
A custom-designed narrow storage unit for a hall, which would go equally well in a living or dining room.

Patio doors can bring the garden into the house in a dramatic way, while providing much more light and enabling the garden to be enjoyed, even when the weather is foul.

Glass doors, made from a single sheet of safety glass that is either plain, tinted or frosted, can be fitted into an ordinary door opening and will help to bring in light.

Storage

It's impossible to exaggerate the importance of storage in any home. It should be one of the first things you think about when walking through your home with your tape measure and notebook. Everything in a home, whether it is large or small, needs its own place. The only real way to provide the correct sort of storage for your own home is to make a detailed list of what you own, with measurements of unusually shaped and sized items, and then provide cabinets and shelves to make everything simple to find, easy to get at, and kept out of the way when not needed.

SHELVING GUIDELINES

The load that your shelves are able to carry depends on the strength of the wall, the strength of the supports, the distance between these supports, and the strength and thickness of the shelves themselves.

- *Good choices for shelving materials include 2/3 in (15 mm) melamine-covered chipboard, hardwood, plywood, medium-density fiberboard (known universally and referred to throughout this book as MDF) or 3/8 in (10 mm) thick glass.*
- *Melamine-covered chipboard can work out more expensive in the long run for heavy items because it needs more support, therefore extra uprights and brackets.*
- *Use trim in front of thin shelves to give a more substantial look.*
- *You can buy individual freestanding shelves as pieces of furniture or as modular units. Buy the latter if you want to extend the shelves later on.*
- *The cheapest freestanding shelving available is secondhand, metal office shelving, which can be sprayed in any color, using automobile spray paints for durability.*
- *Smaller-sized, pine shelving sets can be fixed onto a small wall area in the kitchen or bathroom for decorative items. Add hooks to the fronts of the shelves, if you want to hang things from them.*
- *In the case of partition or hollow walls, the load-bearing points are studs, which are usually placed 16–18 in (40–45 cm) apart and covered with plasterboard. Attach track or brackets to these. You can find out where they are located by tapping gently with a hammer.*
- *Use special wall plugs or togglebolts to attach shelves to plasterboard. However, don't use the shelves for heavy objects as they will pull the plasterboard away.*
- *If you are attaching brackets or uprights to brick or plaster walls, use fiber or nylon anchors, which give the best grip.*

MAXIMUM DISTANCES BETWEEN SHELF SUPPORTS		
	Shelf Thickness	Distance Between Uprights
Hardwood	2/3 in (15 mm)	20 in (50 cm)
	7/8 in (22 mm)	35 in (90 cm)
	1 1/8 in (28 mm)	3 ft 4in (105 cm)
Plywood	1/4 in (18 mm)	30 in (80 cm)
	1/2 in (12 mm)	18 in (45 cm)
	1 in (25 mm)	3 ft 3 in (1m)
MDF	3/4 in (18 mm)	27 in (70 cm)
Melamine-covered chipboard	2/3 in (15 mm)	16 in (40 cm)
	3/4 in (18 mm)	20 in (50 cm)
	1 1/4 in (32 mm)	35 in (90 cm)
Glass	3/8 in (10 mm)	27 in (70 cm)

MOUNTING SHELVES

Draw a plan to scale on paper first before you start putting up shelves. Mark the position on the wall with a pencil. Make a note of light switches and electrical outlets, and make sure you are not going to drill into them. There is a useful gadget that is available from electrical stores which lights up whenever you approach electrical wires in the wall.

Cabinets

If you build cabinets on two sides of a wall, you can leave space in the middle to create an alcove. This could be used to make a dressing table with a mirror, or for a desk with fitted shelves positioned above. The effect is less dominating than a wall-to-wall closet or a large, freestanding wardrobe or armoire.

Deep cabinets are not as convenient as they may at first seem, unless they are very carefully designed. Shallower cabinets are more accessible and their contents can be seen at a glance. If you do have a deep cabinet, try fitting pull-out shelves on runners wherever you can and install a light inside so that you can see exactly what's what. The best one is operated by the opening and closing of the door.

CABINET GUIDELINES
- *Use fitted, modular cabinets for flexibility and to give plenty of space. These consist of prefabricated parts of a particular width or multiples of that width, lined up along a wall, and are commonly used as bedroom and kitchen storage.*
- *Don't take cabinets right up to the ceiling because they can make a room look much smaller.*
- *Cabinets with folding or sliding doors are useful in a small space, where a standard door may not be able to open fully, if a large piece of furniture is in the way.*
- *Buy cabinet units with adjustable shelves to make planning the interior easier.*

Important Practical Considerations

DO YOU NEED PERMITS?
If you intend to do anything to change the structure of your house, such as altering load-bearing walls, pulling down chimneys or building additions, you will need permission from your local building department. There are regulations to ensure that a so-called habitable room has adequate natural light and that the ventilation is good enough to ensure that danger from faulty drains is at a minimum. For example, there are regulations covering the way a bathroom is linked to other rooms, on lowering ceilings and creating balconies, on reducing window areas, reducing the area of a room and creating internal rooms without windows. (These window-less rooms must be non-habitable, i.e., used as storage space or bathroom space or as a service area, but not as bedrooms or living rooms.) You cannot add

a window that will look out onto an adjoining house, and in an internal bathroom with no window, an automatic fan must be connected to the light switch. In short, if you intend to do any serious alterations to the structure of your home, you should always get professional advice and building permits from the relevant authorities.

If the house is registered as being of historic interest, it is even more important to get permission. The authorities may insist on particular materials and even certain building techniques being used, in keeping with the original architecture of the house. You may be able to get a grant for work on historic buildings. Living in a registered house may have advantages in that you may be exempt from tax on certain materials and building work, and you may even be eligible for a grant. The drawbacks are that you will have to get permission for every alteration you want to make, and you may be restricted to certain materials and building techniques.

Measuring and Documenting

If you can, measure the rooms before you move into a new house. Wishful thinking has been the downfall of many a hopeful new home owner, who then finds the sofa won't fit through the front door and there never will be enough room for even half the chairs and furniture, which keep emerging from the moving van.

Real estate agents will give dimensions, but these usually lean toward the rather over-optimistic, so measure out the space yourself, including door openings and windows, power outlets, gas meters and anything else that may affect the use of the spaces. If you can't do this at the first viewing, try to do it while the place is still empty. Always carry a tape measure with you; you need to know the measurements of particular spaces and the items you hope to install in them. Write down all the measurements or you will surely forget

them. Provide yourself with a personal "house book" in which you document everything about your home, from your original ideas and sketches to the details of the work. Remember to include names and telephone numbers of any people involved in the work so that you can contact them again, if necessary. Make a careful note of any drawbacks to be eliminated, advantages to be made the most of, and what furniture will go where.

Making a Plan

A plan can be invaluable when trying to work out how furniture, cabinets and appliances will fit in, yet still leave pleasant and practical spaces for living. Remember that you have to be able to bend down to get things out of the oven and to reach things in low cabinets, and that chairs have to be pulled away from a table in order for people to be able to sit down. You need to be able to move between pieces of furniture without knocking into them and it's surprising how much space this takes

up. A plan need only be a rough sketch, provided you get the dimensions right. First, you should draw the space as you find it, and then you can make several copies of the drawing and use it as a basis for working out how you want to change it. You can make as many drawings as you like and will almost certainly have to do several before you begin to get the solution you want. You do not need to have had any previous practice in technical drawing, provided you work on graph paper and measure carefully.

You will need: a long metal tape measure or a folding rule; a pad of tracing paper; a pad of graph paper; pencils and eraser; colored felt-tip pens to mark exactly where pipes and electrical wiring circuits run and to emphasize areas of particular importance in your design scheme. Consider using some standard architectural symbols as these may be useful to show, for example, exactly where windows and doors are positioned within the living space.

(above)

A wall has been knocked through to provide a spacious kitchen, giving a view of co-ordinating colors through the arch, and these are all held together by the pale, hardwood floor.

Drawing a Plan

1. Fix the tracing paper to the graph paper with masking tape, using the cardboard backing of the pad or a piece of board to hold it firm. Use a scale rule – a scale of 1:50 should be suitable for a plan of a room 27 x 17 ft (8.2 x 5 m) to fit on a sheet. Alternatively, you could simply decide that 10 ft 7 in (1 square meter) will be equal to, say 3 square inches (2 square centimeters) on an ordinary ruler. Measure the walls, starting from the corner to the left of the entrance door. Draw in pencil. Measure right up to the wall, ignoring baseboards, and measure right into any bays and alcoves. Draw to scale.

2. Measure the projections and openings, chimneys, doors and windows and also baseboards and radiators. Show which direction the doors open onto and which way the windows are hinged. Mark where the floor changes level, or where it changes from one material to another. Include notes of measurements on your drawing, as a check against inaccuracy and to give information about smaller details.

The plan needs to be easy to understand, so incorporate all important information. At this stage don't put in unnecessary extras. This is enough for a builder to understand in general what you require. The plan shows you floor space and how things are arranged. An elevation does the same for walls.

Drawing an Elevation

1. Make use of the position of the openings or alcoves. Take the plan and draw the line that indicates where the floor joins the wall. Measure the height of the room and draw lines up at each corner to the ceiling. Complete the rectangle. Show the depth of any coves. Now you can draw in the vertical lines that show the corners of alcoves and bays, and the sides of doors and windows. Complete these rectangles, showing moldings, baseboards and sills.

Planning the Work

Make sure you get the work sequence right. It is worth waiting for basic improvements and projects to be completed before embarking on the secondary work, such as decorating and laying flooring. Insulating and protecting against moisture should all be tackled now.

SOUND INSULATION AND ELECTRICITY

Whenever you create a new partition, use insulating material. There are special partitioning materials designed to reduce noise.

Make sure you put in enough electrical outlets: (the rule is to count the number of sockets you think you will need and then double the number, so that you don't overload sockets or have cords trailing around the house. Sockets should be fitted flush with the wall.

WHAT WILL GO WHERE?

Planning should also include leaving spaces for future items. Fill these spaces with temporary cabinets and provide a running work surface over the whole lot. You can make paper cut-outs of the most important items of furniture and equipment, measured to the same scale as your plan. Check that items will go through the doorway or up the stairs, or whether they can be dismantled. Grand pianos and giant-sized sofas usually make their entrance into a house through a window.

Any rewiring, adjustments to the heating system, alterations in the water system and plumbing should be done before anything else, otherwise you'll have to take up the carpets, and paint or paper again after the work has been completed. Radiators, in particular, are often put in the most inconvenient places, where much of the heat may be lost out of a window, or where they take up valuable wall space or are hemmed in by furniture, and the heat cannot get through to the room. This is quite unnecessary because

radiators are available in a wide range of shapes and sizes, from baseboard strips running along the bottom of the wall, to tall, elegant structures running from floor to ceiling. Even if you can't change the radiator itself, a shelf running above it will help to direct the heat into the room and provide a little extra storage space as well.

Good ventilation is particularly important for eliminating smells and steam from cooking, but also to ensure that there is enough fresh air in the place to breathe. If you are insulating, make sure that air bricks are kept clear to let in air, which will reduce condensation and help the walls to dry out in damp weather.

Basic planning should include working out exactly what you can afford – only you really know. Make sure you've done the budget right and you know just how much the monthly payments will be. It may be worth taking out insurance in case the regular source of money dries up. Do many budgets and, when considering any scheme, work out the hidden costs,

for example, work being delayed or unforeseen problems arising, such as dry rot, which will need to be attended to. Allow for the complications that so often occur in remodeling work. Suggestions for budgeting will be given throughout this book, and remember that your choice of materials can affect the budget considerably. Buying good quality materials and paying to have good work done will give you pleasure and satisfaction for many years to come. Sometimes it is worth having less work done, but having it done beautifully.

Many jobs can be done on a do-it-yourself basis, but don't underestimate the amount of time (and money) involved, and it is essential for some jobs to be done by professionals. Draft-proofing and ceiling insulation are cheap, simple and quick: they immediately make a home feel comfortable and lower the fuel bills. A certain amount of carpentry is suitable for DIY, if you have basic skills, but wiring should always be done by professionals, as should heating and plumbing work.

(above)
Buying good quality materials, such as this wood block floor, will save you money in the long run and will always look good.

Clothing the Spaces

Choosing decorations and furnishings is adventurous and exciting. For many people, it's the most enjoyable part of designing a home, but it is also the most fraught with possibilities and decisions. It really is worth thinking the whole thing through before getting down to the actual act of buying paints, wallpapers and fabrics.

If you are seduced by, and bring home, a marvelous carpet in green and pink before making any sort of color decisions, you will be confined to colors that will go with green and pink for that room. These may not be compatible with already existing curtain materials and upholstery that you intended to use, and the whole scheme will turn out wrong or else it will be very expensive to put right.

Many people already own a certain amount of furniture before moving into a new home. If you do and it's family furniture, you probably want to hang onto it, which also means spending less money than if you were to buy new. This may mean sacrificing any ideas you may have for a lean, sleek look, but it can also be an interesting challenge. Seating can change character completely with new covers or throws, and tables and chairs can be transformed by a coat of paint.

Respecting the Architecture

(previous page)
Even the plainest room can be made to look warm and interesting by the careful choice of furniture and colourful fabrics.

(above)
Plain, undecorated plaster walls, with rounded corners and tall ceilings, lend themselves to an Art Deco interior, which would have been quite wrong in, for example, a Neo-Classical building.

Many buildings, large and small, old or new, fall far short of being great architecture, but each has an intrinsic character of its own, either because of the materials or techniques used in its construction, or because of some particular effect desired by the architect. It is much better to acknowledge this special character and to make the most of it, rather than to try and turn your home into something else.

Traditional homes, with their particular use of space, proportion and detailing, respond well to the sort of furniture and furnishings that would have been used in them during their heyday, while modern "box"-like rooms can often respond better to an up-to-date approach with the use of contemporary materials, colors and textures.

Large eighteenth-century homes, built in the Italian tradition with classical proportions, are asking for impressive-looking fireplaces and plaster moldings; the more ponderous and rather grandiose styles of the nineteenth century look well with heavy, carved oak furniture and large Gothic motifs. In the tiny homes that were built in rows for laborers and factory workers, the spaces are much smaller in scale, and a simpler treatment is required. Millions of "between-the-wars" semi-detached houses were built in the twenties and thirties, which have a clearly recognizable style, and these will respond best to Arts and Crafts or Art Deco style, high-rise blocks have uncompromising geometric and symmetrical forms that lend themselves well to a modernist look, while modern subdivisions, which often seem to concentrate on small homes with very small rooms, call for order and simplicity, whatever the chosen style. You may not have in-depth knowledge of architectural styles, but you can still get a lot of pleasure from being aware of the type of building you are dealing with and a little of its history; you can then use this awareness to make the most of the good qualities of the interior and to conceal what is ugly.

If you are not particularly interested in re-creating a historical style, but just want to create a good-looking, comfortable and practical environment fairly cheaply, there are some general guidelines which can be helpful for the beginner or as a useful checklist for those with more experience. We will look first at some basic guidelines and then see what the possibilities are for creating an "authentic" period style, or simply the impression.

Creating a Harmonious Environment

The inside of a home will depend very much on the tastes and lives of its inhabitants. Some people are happy to live with what seems like no order at all, surrounded by books and papers or the collected paraphernalia of a lifetime. Others are completely organized, with every chair and picture in its allotted place, every inch of space, every color and fabric variation carefully planned. Somewhere

in between is what most of us would like: an organized interior where things can be easily found, where decorative objects are shown off to their best advantage, where there is encouragement to entertain, to read or work, with pleasing colors and textures, and a generally comfortable ambience.

Finding Inspiration

Inspiration rarely comes immediately to mind. By carefully noting down ideas, cutting out pictures from magazines, taking photographs and sketching out interiors that you like, you will begin to see what you want, and a design will gradually take shape in your mind until you have a pretty good idea of exactly what you want. There are good sources of inspiration wherever you look, from innumerable glossy magazines to other people's homes, museums and exhibitions. Upscale stores and fabric shops often have interesting room displays to show off their new collections, which can be an invaluable source of inspira-

tion as they are full of ideas and flair and have been specially created by professionals. Your local library will have a whole section of books on interior design, and everywhere you look there are exciting color combinations and textural contrasts. Auction houses often have exhibitions of furniture, carpets and textiles, and sometimes of contemporary paintings of interiors, which can be rich sources of inspiration. Their catalogues can be helpful. Use your camera for photographing shapes and colors (for example, doorways, window treatments, colors of fishing boats in a harbor). They can all add to the file of ideas for the home. Build up your own library of information and keep it in box files, with one for each important room or function of the home, i.e., a file each devoted to Kitchen / Bathroom / Flooring Materials / Fabrics / Wallcoverings / Paints. Always try and remember to include important addresses, contact names and telephone numbers of your chosen suppliers.

(above)
Mediterranean skies and sunshine were the inspiration for this cheerful kitchen.

Guidelines to Color

Color is probably the first thing that most people notice when they come into a room, and it greatly affects the moods and feelings of people in the house. Colors have certain characteristics, which you need to know about before you can use them to their best effect, and the color wheel (see opposite page) is a good way to demonstrate them.

All colors originate from the three primary colors: red, yellow and blue. Mixing two primary colors together in equal parts creates a secondary color. For example, yellow and blue create green; yellow and red make orange, and blue and red give purple. If you mix a primary color with the secondary color next to it, you get a more subtle, tertiary color. The color wheel shows the primary colors and the secondary and tertiary colors in the correct sequence. These colors can be mixed ad infinitum to create hundreds of subtle shades and tones.

Complementary colors (as their name implies, those which go particularly well together) are opposite each other on the wheel. Reds, oranges, tans, golds, pinks and yellows are warm or hot colors. They are known as dominant or "advancing" colors and give the impression of being nearer than cool ones. Such colors can be used to make cold, north facing rooms much warmer and cozier. At the other end of the scale are the cool and cold colors: the blues, greens, lilacs, purples, some greys and turquoise. The cooler colors are often easier to live with, giving even small rooms a spacious look. Warm or cool colors nearly always need to be balanced by a third group of "neutral" colors: the greys, beiges, creams and off-whites. They can also be used as a balance between several strong and contrasting colors. Used by themselves, they can create a spacious, elegant look that is best used on south facing rooms, when sunlight will provide warmth.

When colors are described as "light" or "dark," this is an indication of how much white or black has been added to the basic color. Light colors reflect light and make a room seem lighter and brighter, whereas darker ones absorb light.

The wheel shows only a few examples of the colors, tones and shades available. Take the color green, for example: there is grass green, hospital green, holly-leaf green, goose turd green (as Samuel Pepys described one of his wife's dresses in his diary), gray-green, sunny green, sea green and greens that veer toward orange or dead grass. This is true of all the colors. Brown, for example, runs the gamut of sandy browns, buff browns, coffee bean browns, mahogany, chestnut, boot polish or burgundy. Even white is by no means always the same color, and there are many different shades of black, from blue black to brown black. Each one looks different, produces another mood and reacts differently with other colors, in various lights and depending on how large an area it covers.

The quality of light is particularly important when choosing a dramatic color scheme (i.e., black, red or midnight blue walls). The effect can be fabulous in artificial light, but dreadful in the harsh reality of daylight. The expanse of the room has to be considered too. North facing rooms call for a warm color scheme and south facing ones for a cool one, particularly in hot countries where the aim is to get away from the sunlight and heat.

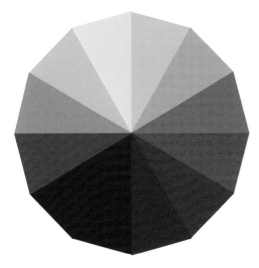

Harmonious Colors

Attractive color schemes can be devised by using one of the "color harmonies," which can be seen on the color wheel. For example, you might choose three colors that are positioned an equal distance apart (red-orange, yellow-green and blue-violet, say, or red, yellow and blue). Or you might choose two colors that lie directly next to each other (for example, yellow and yellow-green or purple and a shocking shade of pink). Alternatively, you might choose one color and its complementary color — the one directly opposite it on the wheel.

A completely monochromatic scheme, using only one color, but in varying degrees of strength and tone, would need some positive "complementary" accents to prevent it from becoming boring.

Following the Rules

There are really only two ways to tackle the color scheme. The first is to follow certain well-tried rules or guidelines, and the second is to break the accepted rules, experiment, choose colors that please you and be prepared to change them if they don't work. If in doubt, follow the rules until you feel more confident. The basic accepted rules for color run more or less like this:

1. First choose a main color for each room. It helps to coordinate a home if the main color in a principal room is extended out to the hall or passage, and even into other rooms. White is much favored among architects and is certainly effective in dark homes, where it will reflect much more light than any other color, but many people find white rather bleak and prefer one of the many whites with a tinge of some warmer color, such as apricot. Some rooms will benefit from good, bold colors. Russian kitchens were often painted a really deep, rich red, which emphasized the feeling of warmth in a cold climate and didn't show the smoke from the stove.

2. In many countries (for example, in Great Britain, North America and Australia), the convention is to paint the woodwork, including the window and door frames, white. This gives a framework to a room. White looks good with any color and emphasizes the shapes of banisters, covings, moldings, arches, baseboards and other architectural details. In a traditional French house, however, subtle variations of greys would be used.

3. Choose a secondary color for floors and ceilings to complement the main color. This can be a paler or darker version of it, or a complementary one.

Trust your instinct and your own taste, and be imaginative and bold. You can create wonderful, jewel-like colors as inexpensively as you can choose safe, understated ones, and you can always paint over them if they don't

much in fashion, all over the house. It will demonstrate a lack of imagination. In much the same way, concentrating on a particular pattern such as stripes or floral patterns all over the house can become both tiring and boring. Remember where your house is situated. A Mediterranean color scheme, using vibrant colors and deep indigo blues, may look completely out of place in an English house, although glorious in a Greek villa, because of the different quality of the light. In old houses, acrylic paints look somehow too flat. Several paint companies are reintroducing whitewashlike paints, which create a more powdery finish, don't show up defects on the surface and create a more authentic finish. **(See Paint, page 233.)**

Color as Camouflage

- *North facing and gloomy rooms, where daylight is excluded by trees or buildings, should be decorated in warm colors such as yellows (avoid the green-tinged ones) and oranges.*
- *Mirrors will help to double any natural light if they face a window and will double the amount of color you have chosen, too.*
- *Cold rooms, particularly basements with their susceptibility to dampness, can be given an added warmth by using reds and oranges. Use brownish or orangish reds, rather than the harsher blue-tinged ones. Modern subtleties of color mean that reds do not have to dominate.*
- *Vertical stripes can make a room look taller, but will also make it look narrower. They have an aura of Regency style and stateliness, so take care, in a small room, that you do not give a mistaken impression of the room being too big for its boots.*
- *Horizontal stripes can make a room look wider, but will also make it seem lower, which may be a good thing in enormous rooms where the height dwarfs both furniture and people, and it is difficult to give*

(above)
Colored cushions will enliven an interior, which might otherwise be rather bland in appearance.

work, to make changes much more cheaply and easily than in many other forms of decoration.

Be courageous. A room painted entirely in deep blue, with white or grey woodwork, is much easier to live with than a mishmash of "safer" colors put together without rhyme or reason. So decide on a color, stick to it and carry it through. Personal taste is all-important, but there is no doubt that colors go in and out of fashion just as clothes do. In the approach to the millennium, there has been a move toward fresh, natural fabrics and colors: unbleached linens and cottons, muslin, fabrics made of hemp and horsehair, and pale paints and fabrics are used in friendly, informal settings, set off by white.

Whatever your taste, carry the main color over walls and floors, everywhere from the hallway to the bathroom. Use it plain in paint, or patterned on wallpaper and fabric, but stick to it. Beware of producing a boring result by using your favorite color, or a color very

human dimensions. A popular way of creating this effect is to have a dado rail fitted about 3 ft (91 cm) from the floor and to paint the wall below it in a different color.

- Small-patterned wallpapers can make a room look larger and can certainly hide any defects in the wall finish. They look pretty and fresh, and will not detract from any pictures you want to hang on the wall.
- Large-patterned designs are more difficult to get right and can positively overwhelm a small room, making it look even smaller. It is important to get the main pattern positioned in the right place, and it may take more wallpaper. What's more, large patterns usually dominate any pictures or objects hung on them. Keep large patterns for large rooms.
- Large-patterned flocked wallpapers were introduced in the late eighteenth-century and became a cheap alternative to wall hangings. These and similar large-patterned papers can look impressive in nineteenth-century interiors.

- Busy rooms, like kitchens or workrooms, which are full of equipment, will look tidier and more businesslike if the main color is a plain one. If you like the idea of a distressed paint finish, the warm, subtle, faded colors of Italian stucco are both evocative and interesting.
- Remember, too, that walls and floors are only one way of adding color to a room. Lampshades, tablecloths, fruit, flowers, objects, wall hangings, brightly colored storage units or shelves, painted furniture and upholstery can all provide extra interest. To take an exaggerated example: a completely monotone grey would be totally transformed by adding just a few touches of poppy red.
- In simple, uncluttered rooms, really deep colors are exciting to use and can do an excellent job of camouflaging the problems of too much height or awkward shapes, and give an effective background to boldly shaped objects.

(above)
A bold, blue scheme avoids the bland look that afflicts so many bathrooms and gives a holiday, seaside look.

Pattern

There is such a wealth of marvelous patterns to choose from in both wallpapers and textiles, it is tempting to choose too many and to have them all vying with one another. Pattern, after all, is provided by everything in a room: furniture, books, pictures, papers, objects and rugs. However, pattern specifically chosen for walls and floors can often determine a particular style, as well as being a very useful way of covering up eyesores. A Regency stripe will immediately set the scene for a rather grand interior of a particular type, whereas a tiny, floral wallpaper will indicate a cottage room.

Painting is one of the easiest decorating jobs and also one of the cheapest. To add subtle pattern with paint is not difficult and can be satisfying. You can get interesting effects simply by using a large natural sponge, wrung out in a contrasting paint to the base coat, pressing it onto the walls at regular intervals. This adds depth, covers up blemishes, and is much cheaper than buying wallpaper. There are many different paint techniques, from simple ones like stippling, sponging, dragging and "distressing," which most people can tackle with a little practice, to the more complicated effects of marbling and wood graining, which need expert skills **(see Paint, page 240)**.

A cheap, effective and more personal way to add pattern to a room is with stencils. There are many stencil kits on the market, ranging from the neat and pretty to the bold and beautiful, and from traditional designs to modern. The motif that you choose can influence the whole look. Armed with one of these, a can of spray paint, or a bucket of paint and a brush, you can create wonderful effects along the dado line or as a frieze positioned about two-thirds of the way up the wall, around the doorways, on cabinets, doors, curtains and cushions, or as a small, all-over pattern on the wall. For a minimal cost, you can give a room a light-hearted feeling.

One of the most effective ways of providing pattern is with wallpaper and fabric. Patterns can range from the neat and pretty floral patterns, once used for boudoirs and maids' rooms, and repopularized by Laura Ashley in the 1970s, to florid florals beloved by nineteenth-century home-makers, formal Regency stripes, often in rich tones of red or green, less formal, narrower stripes with floral accompaniment, flocked wallpapers, "tapestry"-weave fabrics and hand-woven kilims or dhurries. Today, there is truly an embarras de choix. The choice can be made easier if you remember that certain textiles belong very much to particular periods, and that if you are trying to achieve a particular "look" or if you have period furniture, you should not create the incorrect context for it by choosing the wrong fabrics. Modern furniture will look odd in a room where the very French, eighteenth-century Toiles de Jouy

patterns are used; Art Deco furniture will not work with nineteenth-century fabrics and wallpapers as its background; and minimalist metal tables and chairs will look silly with overblown, floral chintzes. If you are unsure of what would be suitable, get professional help or go to an upscale specialist fabric shop, where you will be likely to get helpful advice.

Juxtaposing and overlaying patterns can be effective if done with skill, and there is a particular art in putting different floral or geometric designs next to, and on top of, one another, yet still keeping an overall sense of unity. Many chain stores and department stores now sell whole ranges of wallpapers with matching or related fabrics, using the same design in different forms, or putting patterns with plain colors, which can be used together to make an elegant whole.

Staircase walls and landings benefit from the consistent use of one color or pattern throughout to make them appear less incohesive and therefore part of a harmonious whole.

Patterned floors are popular, partly because they are supposed not to show the dirt, but a dirty floor will show through anything. You can add pattern to a plain floor by using woven rugs, and stenciled floors can be effective in certain rooms, provided you use a tough paint. Different patterns and textures are often mixed in today's interiors, with layered velvets, tapestries, needlework and jacquard weaves to create an overall Gothic impression. Another, rather lighter mixing and matching technique is to use large and small floral prints in one room, not necessarily matching, but with a definite main color that is common to them all.

If you want a coordinated home, it is helpful to think of the house as a whole, rather than to take each room in isolation, using one pattern or color of carpet running right through the house or at least on each floor.

In small houses, different schemes in each room can jar. Let the scheme flow into the next room, with corridors and common parts serving as transition areas.

(above)
An attic space has been used here to create a suprisingly roomy bathroom.

Texture

(above)
Matte, warm and rough textures are set off by light filtering through a filigree screen.

Texture is an important contributory factor to the comfort of the home, both visually and physically. This can be rough or smooth, shiny or matte, warm or cold, dense or delicate. Tactile qualities transfer themselves to the eye and make an enormous visual impact on an interior. Smooth surfaces will provide a sleek, businesslike and hygienic background for the home office and for bathrooms and kitchens, in particular. They can also, in the form of glass-topped tables and polished surfaces, give a satisfying contrast to the warm, soft textures of carpets, upholstery and curtains. Textiles themselves can offer diaphanous see-through gauze, smooth, glazed chintzes, the rough textures of hand-woven rugs, the luxurious feeling of silk and the sensuous softness of velvet pile. Velvets are coming back into fashion in an infinite variety of colors and textures, with crushed, embossed designs being created by varying the length of the pile.

Below are some qualities to look out for in different textures.

- *Shiny/smooth/cold: Glass, mirror, highly polished furniture, polished floors, plastic laminate; marble, alabaster, silk, satin, brass, copper, silver and ceramic tiles are all cold to the touch and, as a result, bring a cool atmosphere into any room where they are used, in much the same way as the cooler colors on the color wheel. They also help to create a feeling of spaciousness, particularly when used in pale colors.*
- *Matte/warm/rough: Tweeds, whilewash, brick, stone, insulating cork, matting, unpolished wood, woven fabrics, pile carpets, sisal, jute, coir and rush matting, burlap, linen, wool and embossed wall-coverings are all warm textures and, like the warm colors of the spectrum, help to create an intimate feeling and make a room seem welcoming.*
- *Dense: Brick, stone, ceramic tiles and metal.*
- *Delicate: Voile, lace, muslin, net, flimsy cottons, china and glass ornaments.*

Texture and Light

Texture is affected by color and light, and the same color will appear to change in different textures. Some colors will look dull on a flat surface, but then spring into life on a rough one. Smooth surfaces reflect light and dull ones absorb it, so the same color may look lighter on an emulsion-painted wall than it would appear on a carpet or on textured upholstery. Shadow tends to accentuate texture, so a heavily textured wall covering will show up better next to a window, rather than opposite it. A textured fabric will look more exciting against the light, for instance in the form of a curtain.

Getting a Balance

It is important to achieve a balance between the different textures used in a room. If all the surfaces were of the same texture, the final effect would be dismally bland. The contrast between cold and warm, sleek and stubbly, smooth and rough, helps to give excitement and uplift to a scheme. Avoid clashing contrasts. The shiniest surfaces, such as mirror, glass, high gloss paint and polished furniture, can create such an illusion of space as to make a room seem twice its actual size: a large, polished table can reflect almost the whole room. These cool, shiny materials must be balanced by some contrasting warm ones from the warm, matte group. Dark, matte surfaces absorb light and will make large rooms seem smaller. Light, matte surfaces reflect and diffuse light, and enhance both natural and artificial light. However, some shiny textures would be essential in such a scheme to give some contrast.

Even homes that are centered around computers, televisions and music systems, and which concentrate on smooth, hard surfaces, will benefit from being softened by a tapestry on the wall, a luxurious rug or some other form of soft, textured surface.

Door Treatments

Doors are an important feature in the decorating scheme and take up a considerable amount of wall and floor space. Old-fashioned, paneled doors don't require a great deal of special treatment. They can be painted in two tones, with the panels a slightly paler or darker version of the main color if you wish to add definition.

If you are considering installing sliding doors, to save space, for example, do be prepared to spend money on getting sturdy and well-constructed doors and track. Inefficient sliding doors are a constant irritation and will not provide a barrier (this is especially important if they are doors to a bathroom); they will also look much better. This is one item where extra money spent will pay for itself in looks and convenience. Be wary of buying cheap, pine doors and storage fittings, which will shrink and warp when the central heating is turned on because the wood has not been dried.

(above)

A combination of rough, hard textures, shiny sleek textures and the soft textures of the rugs and chair covers gives an interesting, enlivening quality to this interior.

Doors

You can make a door into a focal point with ornate curtaining, which will also help to insulate the room against drafts. The curtain can be draped in a grand fashion from a pole above the door and held back with a tie, or it can be attached to the door itself so that it opens and closes with the door. If you do it this way, you will need the pleated or gathered part to end slightly above the top of the door to prevent drafts coming in at the top. Make sure the curtain covers the bottom of the door without dragging over the floor.

In hot countries, where doors are normally kept open during the day, bead curtains are attractive and help to keep the flies out. There are many versions of these, from very delicate and pretty glass bead curtains, which have an attractive, "weighty" quality, to lightweight beads or seeds, and even colored plastic strips.

If you have patio doors, choose curtains that will cover the whole wall and pull right back to the corners when open, for a unified and stylish look and also for convenience.

Ugly or unsuitable door handles can spoil even the most splendid door. There are a great variety of door handles now available, from old-fashioned brass and ceramic ones to enameled metal or plastic versions in chunky, modern designs. Hardware stores and upscale do-it-yourself and furniture stores often have a good selection.

Traditional paneled doors look best with traditional rounded door handles in brass, china or wood. If they have lost their original handles, you can find reproduction or second-hand ones quite easily. There are many ranges to choose from.

Cheaper doors with flat surfaces can be cheered up by the use of bold, well-designed, modern door handles. Choose something positive and well-made, which will add a touch of class to even a cheap door.

Ideas for Doors

- *Mailboxes on exterior doors should be generous enough to take large envelopes, but not wide enough to let in a burglar's arm. Many mailboxes have integral draft-proofing: if yours is not draft-proofed, you can fit a box inside for the letters to fall into.*

- *New and second-hand brass and cast-iron mailboxes are available in a variety of period styles, also door knockers, handles, house numbers and enameled plates.*

- *A stained glass panel in an interior door can be very pretty in a bathroom or hall.*

- *Painted chinoiserie panels can brighten up the door to a breakfast room, living room, bedroom or bathroom.*

- *Shapely doors can be accentuated by stenciling a frame all round, while heavy doors can be enhanced by painting a bold frame, perhaps with an Egyptian theme in cream, red and black.*

- *Cut out plywood or MDF panels to the same width as the door, and fix them above the*

door then paint them in the same color to give an impression of a loftier room.

- Have a Gothic arch or frame cut out in MDF and fix it above or around a door, then paint it in a limed oak color for a period effect.
- If the original fanlights have been removed from Georgian front doors, you can get a skilled restorer to replace them.
- Don't make the mistake of buying a modern door that incorporates a fanlight in its top panels. The proportions are wrong.
- Wood plank doors look right in country cottages where you want a "peasant" look and also in traditional American country houses. They nearly always look better painted, rather than being left in their raw pine state. For these doors, use heavy metal hinges, latches and handles.
- If you are happiest living in a bohemian atmosphere, paint every single door panel (including the cabinet doors), in freehand using the abstract or stylized motifs and slightly muddied, bright colors.

- Minimalist living looks best with unpaneled doors. You could give a door extra chic by putting the door handle a little farther down than usual (although still within easy reach), giving a sense of extra height.
- Paint a flat door in a glowing color to give it the same sort of importance as a panel in a Mondrian painting.
- Glass fitted into a door adds light and space to a room. The size and shape of the glass panels create their own decorative effects.
- You can cover the wood panels in some doors with stained glass or mirror panes, which will bring extra light into the room.
- A flat door can be lined with felt and covered in green baize (like the traditional door to the servant's quarters), for privacy and quiet. (This is a good solution for workrooms, if you share the house and need to concentrate without being disturbed.)

(above)

In 1939, architect Erno Goldfinger designed and built his own home in Hampstead, London, England. The front door is painted in a deep red, giving it a minimalist, almost Japanese, lacquered look that is enhanced by the glass window.

Window Dressing

There are so many different sizes, types and arrangements of windows, and so many different ways of treating them, that it might be a good idea to make several sketches of the windows in a particular room, and then try out different treatments until you decide what looks best. Curtains frame the view, protect you from the outside world, help to insulate the room and to reduce noise.

When decorating in a particular style, proportion is all-important. If your rooms are too small, or the wrong shape for a particular style, don't try to squeeze that style in — choose a style which can be adapted for the space. Window treatments should be compatible with the size and shape of the window. It's no good trying to create stately home drapes, originally intended for tall windows, on a one-paned picture window built in the sixties. The proportions are all wrong and the result will be unsatisfying.

Curtain Styles

In the eighteenth century, windows were often left uncurtained, and waxed and printed linen was frequently used to make economical Roman blinds. Shutters gave warmth and privacy, and were designed as integral parts of the architecture. They were decorated with as much care as the walls and ceilings, and often carved and embellished with motifs and moldings that were in keeping with the classical style. Occasionally, balloon shades might also be used and, in grander homes, huge draperies would hang over the top of a window, with heavy curtains falling in elegant folds to the ground.

A Gothic look can be achieved with curtains hung over a wood or metal curtain pole. These can be plain, rich fabrics such as velvet or heavy, plain cotton with contrasting lining or borders, or in rich ecclesiastical-style patterns with heraldic devices such as ever-popular

fleur-de-lys, Tudor roses, lions, griffins or a mille-fleurs tapestry material.

Victorian bedrooms used lots of lace draped casually from a simple rod over a sheer fabric or pretty, dimity-patterned cottons. Main rooms were heavily hung with velvets in a variety of styles, from Gothic to Neo-Classical. In the early days of colonial America, curtains were unpretentious, usually short and used primarily to retain heat in cold winters. They would be hung from curtain rings over a simple rod and were usually made of simple, printed cottons and lined, perhaps with a valance hanging over the top. Curtains were often combined with rattan blinds or louvered shutters.

In Scandinavian countries, curtains are usually left very simple in appearance to let in the maximum amount of daylight, and blinds are often the preferred choice. These colors are usually rather uninhibited, but patterns are restrained: simple stripes or checks, or bold, stylized prints. The eighteenth-century Gustavian style might use white net curtains with a matching, swathed valance mounted on a white or brass pole, or simple curtains, perhaps in blue-and-white checks.

Curtain fashions and styles during the twentieth century have been, for the most part, mainly simple (unless recreating a period look), relying on the strong colors and patterns of the fabrics to reflect the latest style; pure white or bold, jazz fabrics for the thirties, for example. A notable characteristic of the architecture of the fifties and sixties was the introduction of enormous "picture" windows that took up a whole wall. These windows were not always easy to dress, and curtains usually hung from track running right across the top of the window, from wall to wall and ceiling to floor, with a simple plywood valance covered in the same fabric. Pinch-pleat tapes were available on the market for the first time in 1958 and immediately became popular.

(opposite)

Window treatments should suit the window for which they are intended. Here, the taller parts of these splendid windows are left uncurtained, and a simple style has been chosen, with gathered fabric hanging from a metal pole.

Curtain Guidelines

- *Heavier curtains hang better than light ones, so for formal curtains, choose from velvets and velours, richly colored brocades, watered silks, heavy cottons, wools and linens, and you could consider interlining them. Heavily lined, glazed chintz will also hang well.*
- *Curtains help to give a room a "dressy" look, so don't skimp on them. They should reach to the ground unless they are covering a tiny window and should pull right back from the window frame, when open.*
- *For formal curtains, make the most of valances, fringes and tie-backs of the same fabric or twisted silk rope.*
- *Semi-transparent muslin or other light-weight fabric can be over-draped to spread out onto the floor – an elegant type of curtaining, which requires a well-ordered and very clean home.*
- *Curtains that match pale walls will give a lighter look to a room, whereas contrasting curtains will frame the window more dramatically.*
- *Lined curtains not only hang better than unlined ones, but do a more effective job of insulating. On the other hand, if you live in a house with large windows where there is really very little space to pull the curtain back from the window, you might prefer to have sheer curtains, which don't need lining and are not bulky, and therefore take up the minimum of space.*
- *Rather than using nylon net curtains, consider getting some really pretty lace and using that instead. On the European continent, there is a tradition of cotton lace curtains with very defined patterns of elegant birds or small houses, which present a positive attraction to the viewer, rather than the negative anonymity of net.*
- *Blinds can be used in conjunction with curtains to give greater privacy.*

There is practically no window which cannot be satisfactorily curtained with rods or track of varied degrees of sophistication.

Manufacturers now produce comprehensive color brochures with many ideas and color schemes, and details of tracks, rods and fixtures to help you choose. There is a track to fit every sort of window, even deep bays, arches and hinged rods for very deeply recessed windows. (For details of tracks and rods, see pages 257–259.)

Shutters

On windows where you might want to keep out the sun, you could combine shutters with plain roller or Roman blinds. Today, shutters can also contribute to the security of the home. If you live in a traditional house, which still has its original wood shutters, keep them. As well as being historically interesting, they will go with the house and provide good insulation and security. If the house has lost its shutters, you can get them replaced.

Blinds

Blinds help to control heat, reduce noise and provide privacy. They tend to work better on small windows and in small rooms because of their simplicity. Blinds look best when longer in length as opposed to greater in width. It is better to hang several narrow blinds on a large window, than to hang one huge one. Using several blinds also gives more flexibility in controlling light. They are relatively inexpensive because most types need the minimum of fabric. Narrow, slatted blinds are particularly suitable for a Japanese-style interior, perhaps surrounded by simple red or black curtains on a metal rod. If you cannot afford the curtains you would like, use blinds instead as they accentuate the shape of well-proportioned windows, and can be made of any fabric or even designed to order. There are many different kinds to choose from, including the trusty roller blind, slatted blinds,

pleated blinds and the elegant, unobtrusive, modern/classic Roman blind. (See page 262 for making up different styles of blinds.)

The Personal Touch

Of course, your home is going to reflect your interests. If you often travel and like to bring back souvenirs from your trips, you will want to display it. On the other hand, if you concentrate largely on sports, you may need an uncluttered environment, which will allow room for an exercise bike and weights. People who entertain formally will want a well-equipped kitchen, a dedicated dining room and a living room that is, at the same time, both elegant and welcoming. Most styles will probably fit into one of four general categories, which could be classified as formal, informal, rustic and modern.

Formal

Formal interiors, in which symmetry is important and in which aesthetics often come before comfort, lend themselves to various period styles and will suit people who want to entertain with some ceremony, or those who like things "just so" and appreciate fine detailing. They are often based on the decoration of the great houses and palaces of the past, and require sumptuous fabrics and materials, good workmanship and careful attention to detail, and will reflect a sound knowledge of art history and period styles. If you are unsure of your knowledge in this respect, it will be worth getting the advice of a professional architect or interior designer.

Informal

An informal style implies practicality and versatility above all, and a relaxed attitude to living. This style can be found in most family homes, where the lives of various people of different ages, with a wide range of interests and tastes, make formal interiors impossible to achieve. Here the emphasis is on practicality and comfort rather than symmetry, and a

(above)
This bright and cheerful living room has been given a personal touch with primary colors, comfortable furniture and woodstrip flooring, which is good for children's play.

Modern

Modern styles are usually disciplined and often sparse. They may incorporate high tech (items designed for industrial use, which are incorporated into domestic interiors), angular, geometric shapes, smooth metal and plastic surfaces and blocks of bold color, together with greys or black and white. The modern look includes the minimalist (anticlutter) school of interior design, which is basically a style of the utmost sobriety, where everything that is not in use is put away (including beds), and function is not allowed to intrude into a given space. Most homes will incorporate elements from all of these styles.

What is important for most people is not whether something is authentic or in fashion, but whether it is comfortable and suited to the life they lead. Antiques can sit comfortably with contemporary art and furniture, provided the scale and style don't clash. Most of us will judiciously put together a mixture of furniture and decoration based on more than one style to achieve the result we want, as people have done throughout the centuries. What matters most are that the proportions and scale are right, that the colors and patterns are harmonious, and that the lighting is efficient and comfortable.

Evolving a Design

Whether you want to create an informal, highly personal design of your own or aim for a particular historical or other style, one way of sorting out an idea is to make up a collection of paints, wallpapers, fabrics and floorings, and then to experiment with different combinations of these until you get a scheme you like. This is absorbing and helpful in sorting out ideas and establishing color preferences. Choose the basic colors for the largest areas first and then add the rest. Find a piece of hardboard or cardboard and pin small pieces of your samples onto it. Make sure they are big

(above)
A modern design, which makes good use of a tall building with clean, spare lines and natural materials, without lingering in the past.

successful result depends on strong personal tastes to ensure cohesion and harmony. Furniture will not be matching, or even necessarily of the same period, but it will be in proportion to the house and in materials that complement each other. Color harmonies are particularly important in such an environment, and even if lots of different fabrics are used, they must have qualities of pattern, color and scale in common.

Rustic

This is the country look, found in country cottages, farm and barn remodels, and it is based on simplicity, practicality, natural materials and hand-made artifacts; Wood-burning stoves (or their electric and gas conversions), large kitchens with generous dining tables pine cabinets, tongue-and-groove paneling and wood flooring with rag rugs all imply a sympathy with the country and its pursuits. A porch is essential to keep the weather at bay.

enough for you to get a realistic idea of the patterns and textures. You can rearrange the pieces as much as you like, but the basic color must dominate so that you get the proportions right. It's best, as pointed out earlier, to choose one basic color and one secondary color, which either contrasts or matches, and then to add touches of brighter colors to these. Look at the colors on the board in both natural and artificial light, and do the same when you are actually purchasing the materials.

If you are unable to get samples of the real thing, substitute something that has a similar color and texture. A sanded and sealed floor, for example, can be represented by wood grain paper, which will give you more or less the correct idea of what it will look like.

Re-creating a Specific Style

If you want to follow a particular style more precisely, there are specialized companies that make wallpapers, paints, plaster moldings and reproduction chairs. They use the same materials, pigments, patterns and manufacturing techniques as the originals from the seventeenth and eighteenth centuries and many papers and fabrics from the various styles of the twentieth century or those that can help to evoke a particular period. Recent research into both fabrics and wallpapers found in old houses has meant there is now a body of information to help you achieve an authentic look. Here, we can take a quick glance at some of the most influential architectural and interior styles that have affected the way we approach our homes today.

House interiors have never been static, so in most homes there is little virtue in trying to reproduce exactly the interior of any particular period. This is well demonstrated in Sutton House, a house in the East End of London, built in the early sixteenth century, when it consisted mainly of the Tudor great hall. When it was divided in 1750, the great hall was lost. The parlor, one of the finest Tudor rooms still

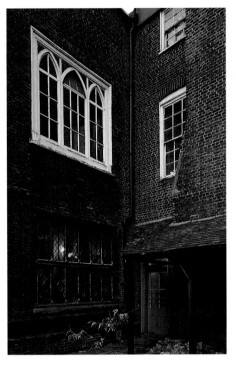

(left)

The exterior of Sutton House, owned by the National Trust and open to the public, showing the Armada window below and a contrasting Gothic window above.

in existence, has wood panels that were thought to have been installed in 1550, and these were subsequently rearranged to allow for changes to the windows and doors. The so-called Armada window in the lobby dates from 1535, but the glass and lead work are probably nineteenth century. The stairway, inserted in 1630 to give a grander entrance, has elaborate seventeenth-century paintings of faces, coats of arms and animals, but seventeenth-century style balusters were added in 1904. All through history, people have altered and adapted the interiors of their homes in this way to suit their own lives.

It is useful to be able to relate particular styles to the architecture for which they were originally intended because the proportions, materials and colors were designed for particular types of buildings. They worked well in terms of balance and proportion, so it makes sense to think in these terms when furnishing a traditional home today.

Living Rooms

The living room probably has more functions than any other room in the house. It's where people go to relax, read a book or write letters, where visitors are entertained or games are played, where television is watched and music or radio is listened to. The room must be welcoming and warm, comfortable, presentable and practical. It must have comfortable chairs, efficient storage, tables for games or coffee, a pleasing combination of colors and textures, and good lighting. The important thing is that people should enjoy it and use it to the full.

If you want to open up a fireplace, knock down a wall or move a door to lengthen a wall, do this before you get too settled in. Such projects always create dust and havoc, and it is much easier to do them early on. If the room doesn't need any drastic alteration but you are finding it difficult to decide on its decoration, paint it white initially and live with it for a while to give you time to work out exactly what you want.

Lighting is an aspect of the living room that is often not taken seriously enough. Yet it is such an important factor in creating a good-looking room, which is pleasant to be in. The secret is having several different light sources, creating pools of light in strategic areas, highlighting the best aspects of the room and creating working light for those who want to read, while providing a soft background light for watching television.

What's Required?

(previous page)
A comfortable living room designed for warmth, relaxation, entertaining or reading.

(above)
A large, well-lit living room, furnished in an almost eighteenth-century style, with the furniture arranged against the walls, leaving plenty of open space.

The special requirements of a living room are:
1. *Location:* Which room should you choose? Should it be upstairs or downstairs? Should it be the largest, smallest or the grandest in the house?
2. *Arrangement of the room*: How can you best arrange the room so that it looks inviting, while incorporating diverse leisure activities?
3. *Comfort*: How can you provide an ambience which is relaxing, comfortable, stylish and inviting?
4. *Children*: Will they be welcome in the room or be expected to stay in their own playroom?

Location

The choice of which room to use as a living room depends very much on who is going to use the room and what rooms are available. If the present living room opens out onto the garden, it might be preferable (particularly for those with young families), to plan a large family kitchen/living room which takes over this space and to have a quieter, more peaceful living room, perhaps upstairs, looking out onto the garden.

An upstairs bedroom can often be turned into a living room, or even a second living room, so that anyone using a computer, playing games or entertaining schoolfriends can remain separate from others, who may want to listen to music or to quietly read a book. An upstairs living room will receive better light than a downstairs room, which may be shaded by trees and other buildings.

Arrangement of the Room

The first thing is to arrange the room so that there is comfortable space for all the activities that will take place in it. Formal living rooms are more for show than for "living." They are often showpieces, ideally intended for entertaining in a formal manner, and should not cater to other activities, such as dining, studying or pets. The look is of primary importance. Traditionally, formal living rooms never had comfortable chairs: hard chairs designed for sitting bolt upright with never a crease in their firm upholstery were the norm. They were designed for social intercourse. This is because people were expected to socialize, converse, take tea and not to lounge around or go to sleep in them! Nowadays it is quite possible to create a sense of formality with some comfort. Formality is normally associated with symmetry and the disciplined placing of furniture, and the furniture itself tends to be of a very disciplined design. Objects will be expensive and displayed on large tables or in cabinets. Never be such a slave to formality that the room is cheerless or lacks interest. Rooms are meant to be used. Too perfect an environment looks dreadful when untidy.

Informality indicates a feeling of comfort and relaxation, and a somewhat haphazard approach, with freestanding and nonmatching furniture, floral prints and uninhibited

colors. A well-designed informal room must be able to absorb newspapers, books and cast-off jackets with good humor. Chairs are chosen for lounging, rather than for grandeur. An informal interior will have comfortable chairs and settees, in arrangements that may be altered at the whim of the owner. Asymmetrical groups of pictures and paintings will be hung on the wall, which may itself be papered or painted, plain or patterned. Furniture will seldom match and will be covered in good fabrics, which can be allowed to fade and become worn without losing their charm. There will be plenty of surfaces for working or playing, and any objets d'art will be arranged on a mantelpiece or shelf, rather than taking up valuable space on a tabletop.

If you have a young family, be prepared to live in a fairly haphazard and relaxed way for the first few years. Informal cheerfulness is much more welcoming and acceptable to visitors than a stiff formality, which is impossible to live up to.

In most living rooms, chairs and sofas take pride of place. There should be comfortable seating for listening to music or reading books, grouped so that people can sit and chat. The choice of seating and the way it is arranged are vital to the success of the room as somewhere to relax and entertain. A low table in front of a group of chairs or sofas can be used for drinks, tea plates, jigsaw puzzles and/or magazines.

In small living rooms, this sociable seating will take up most of the space. It may consist of a large or small sofa with a couple of armchairs, either matching as a complete set or a collection arranged in a semi-circle, facing a fireplace. Fireplaces can make particularly successful centerpieces, not only because they are the traditional source of warmth, but also because they are as imposing and interesting as pieces of sculpture. If there is no fireplace, the television may be used as a central focus, but many people prefer to keep it somewhere less obtrusive, in

(above)
This bright red sofa makes a positive focus for the modern, simple but comfortable room. The open shelves are sculptural and effective.

(above)
Low seating lends itself to attic living and to low-level lighting too. Here, Skylights have been used to advantage by placing the seating directly beneath them.

which case two rows of seats facing each other in the center of the room would be appropriate, each giving a focus for the other.

In a living room which has views from large panoramic windows, you can arrange the seating to face a window, making the view the focal point, at least during good weather. Here, it pays to have furniture which can be moved around easily so that in winter you can make the most of a cozy interior instead. Make sure the seating area is not in the way of people passing through the room. If it is, you might be able to block up a door or move it. It is very irritating to have people using the living room as a passageway.

ARRANGEMENT: SEPARATE ACTIVITIES
Large households, incorporating a wide range of interests, could usefully set two rooms aside for use as living spaces. In smaller homes, you can often create separate spaces for different activities in one room. The way to approach such an arrangement is to have not

just one central seating arrangement, but to divide the room up into small activity areas with groups of tables and chairs, and small areas of seating with perhaps two armchairs on either side of a fireplace. Obviously, larger rooms lend themselves best to this sort of arrangement, but it does enable all sorts of different interests to be catered to. For those who are musical, a small piano could be placed against one wall, a circular or semi-circular table could provide a base for playing games or writing letters, and a two-person sofa could be placed by the fireplace or under a window, perhaps with a narrow table behind it to hold magazines and books waiting to be read. Even in a small room, you should be able to find wall space for a small writing table. Sliding partitions, folding doors and portable screens should not be overlooked as ways of dividing a room, because they allow distinct areas to be created without making the sub-divisions too obvious.

Make sure there is plenty of room to move

between pieces of furniture, without knocking into things, and that the furniture itself has a unifying quality, all being made of the same materials (i.e., wood or glass-and-metal), in proportion and in style, and any fabrics should coordinate in colors and in style, otherwise the end result could be far from relaxing.

Another approach is to make the most of the feeling of space by keeping the furniture more or less to the sides of the room, so as to leave the central space free. In the eighteenth century, this was the accepted way of arranging a room and was one of the reasons for the dado — so that when the furniture was pulled up against the wall it would not damage the woven tapestries that were hung on it. This sort of arrangement is useful if you give large parties or for children, who need plenty of floor space for play. If the room has a small alcove or bay, you could have a small, tailor-made study space built in.

ARRANGEMENT: LARGE SPACES

In enormous rooms, such as lofts, warehouses and barns, the space may seem rather daunting at first, but do resist the temptation to divide it up into human-sized cubicles by adding too many dividing walls. Make the most of the rare luxury of such a large area by dividing it by the arrangement of the furniture, so that bookcases, cabinets or giant-sized settees act as room dividers without blocking the view of the whole room. Different activity areas work well in such large spaces, but they do need massive pieces of furniture. Here is where you can install a giant upholstered sofa or L-shaped arrangements of modular seating, enormous refectory tables using solid planks of wood or great slabs of slate or glass on trestles: monumental spaces require monumental treatment. Extremely tall rooms should be furnished with a few impressive and carefully chosen pieces of furniture, which will anchor the room and balance the height with their weight.

ARRANGEMENT: L-SHAPED ROOMS

These provide good opportunities for creating two different moods or uses in one room: one area for quiet relaxation, another for playing, eating or working. You can achieve a contrast in the mood by using slightly altered, but compatible colors, fabrics and lighting without losing the overall unity of the space.

Comfort

SEATING

Living room seating should, of course, be comfortable. It is a waste of money to buy chairs or sofas that look devastatingly chic, but whose seats are too short for people's legs, or which throw the sitter right back so that he or she has no control and feels ill at ease. Seating at a table should be upright and supportive, with or without arms.

Some people like to sit on the floor and for those, big floor cushions or low, wood chairs with low tables can be comfortable, so that the whole orientation is toward floor level. A low orientation to the room lends itself to a style based on the Japanese plan of futons (folding mattresses), floor cushions, soft floor mats, interior screens and sparse furnishings, which focus on just one or two decorative elements, such as one painting or a sculpture being given much prominence and to soft, diffused lighting, also positioned near the floor. It lends itself also to nomadic, tentlike interiors with cushions on the floor, lots of boldly colored, woven patterned fabrics and also woven rugs.

Children in the Living Room

If children are going to be using the room, it's usually much easier in the long run to install the sort of sturdy furniture that will look just as good rumpled, carpets that won't show up every scuff mark and washable wallcoverings. Try to leave enough space for floor play. The more contented children are, the less they will trouble you for attention.

somewhere to display things or even a way of letting light in from another room. Japanese sliding screens, which run in grooves fixed to the floor and ceiling, can divide a room effectively in two and so can folding doors. Portable folding screens are less private, but more flexible. These can be made in many different ways, but basically, they consist of panels, hinged together. These may be of a wood or metal frame filled with gathered fabric or glass, they may be of solid wood or MDF panels, stained, painted or covered in collages or fabric. MDF has the advantage of not becoming distorted, but it can be quite heavy. It is now available in various thicknesses, and the thinner ones are relatively lightweight. If the chosen materials of a screen make it very heavy, you can fix casters to the base.

Storage

The most vital items to find homes for are those that you use every day, such as the television, radio, sound system, and tapes, records, compact discs, books and magazines.

If you don't want to keep books in alcoves created by a chimney, a pair of decorative mirrors can be placed there to enhance both the space and the light in the room. Small tables placed in alcove spaces can hold flower arrangements, lamps and other objects. If there is no alcove, you can build a frame (about the size of a door frame), against the wall and build narrow shelves within it. A mirror in the back will make it appear deeper and alcove-like. Don't assume that walls are straight: they seldom are. Measure the back and front of any alcove, or your shelves may fit at the back and be too wide at the front.

In a formal setting, i.e., where the room is used mainly for polite entertaining and where symmetry is important, day-to-day storage is best kept behind closed doors. Freestanding cabinets in a Neo-Classical style can look imposing in a large room and glass-fronted cabinets will display and protect books or

Don't go for white or pale upholstery or carpet if children are going to play in the room (or dogs or cats for that matter). Make sure there is suitable storage for their toys, either in closed cabinets, or in good-looking boxes, or under a window seat, so that you can put them away quickly when the children have gone to bed and you want to feel civilized. Make sure that precious ornaments, books and other treasures are on display where the children can't reach them, so you don't have to be constantly on the lookout for trouble. Young children love to play with the controls for television sets and videos, so put those out of reach as well.

Furniture

SCREENS
Screens come in many different shapes, sizes and designs. They can often provide a certain amount of privacy, a psychological barrier between one part of a room and another, a way of concealing things you don't wish to be seen,

collected treasures.

In a more informal setting, the storage can be both versatile and attractive. Modular storage combining closed cabinets and open shelves will be useful for many households. Work out what will fit where, how much you need and in what arrangements. You can install a window seat and use it to conceal a low radiator. Design the front with a radiator grille, so the heat can still get into the room. Shelves for displaying objects should be top- or back-lit to get the best effect.

Built-in storage has the disadvantage that you can't take it with you if you contemplate moving eventually, but from a practical point of view, it has many advantages. It can be specially made to measure and created in a particular style. Built-in storage can fit into alcoves, under stairs, into odd corners and awkward spaces. It can cover a whole wall from end to end with no gaps, or it can fit around a small window, and above all, it can be designed to hold the particular belongings of you and your family.

Some Common Problems

SQUARE "BOX" ROOMS

When a room has little architectural interest or merit, visual satisfaction must be introduced. In large rooms, a bold pattern may be the answer. Very large-scale, floral paper, with an enormous gilt-framed painting, will immediately distract the eye from a low ceiling. In smaller rooms, strong wall colors and a white ceiling will help.

- *Low ceiling: Consider installing a low, wide fireplace whose proportions will be better for the height of the room than a tall, stately one.*
- *A mirror placed above the fireplace can help to add interest by reflecting the opposite wall. (Take care that it reflects something of interest and not just plain paint with a crack in it.)*
- *Elaborate, or just larger-than-usual, base-*

boards and cornices can help to give weight and height to a room, and so can paneling (whether real or trompe l'oeil).

- *The same basic rules apply to modern, as well as to traditional design: the grouping of furniture, choice of colors, patterns and textures: in short, the overall balance is just as important to modern interiors as to eighteenth- or nineteenth-century homes.*
- *Use the geometry of such spaces, make use of vistas, angles and curves by emphasizing them with paint colors, or picking them out in white or a contrasting color, or a whitewash finish. Create curves with upholstery, softness with textiles.*
- *Echo the geometry in furniture, which should be low, simple, squared and angled. Soften angles with sculptural indoor plants and the occasional tufted rug or kilim.*
- *Single, large paintings can take on greater significance and can be a major contributory factor to the interior scheme.*

(above)
Box-like rooms look best when the aim is not to be too elegant. This square stove has style, if not elegance.

(above)
This room has been made to look dramatic with the two stately lamps, the sophisticated background lighting and the generous arrangement of fresh tulips.

Making the Most of Particular Features

HEIGHT

A tall, generously proportioned room needs well proportioned and meticulous detailing. You could install a gallery at one end and use it as a library, with books displayed from top to bottom and a sliding ladder hooked onto a track. In period houses, though, you may not want to alter the proportions of the room. Library shelves can be given added style with the introduction of a series of mock columns, which will emphasize the elegance of a tall room. A taller-than-normal baseboard with decorative detailing at the top edge will give the room more presence, in keeping with its height. Draw attention to any molded plasterwork, ceiling roses and cornices by painting them white or the ceiling a slightly different color. If you are installing a new ceiling rose, make sure that it is in scale with the room. Those purchased in decorating stores are often too small and will look inappropriate in a large room.

There are all sorts of tricks with color and paint, which can be used to divide the wall vertically and to break up large expanses. A dado rail marks a line usually about 3 ft 3 in (1 meter) from the floor. You can panel or paint a different color under the rail, adding interest and making the height more friendly. Large paintings, pictures and wall hangings (such as rugs or tapestries) will all help to fill the height. Enormous pieces of furniture will help to put the height of the room into scale.

Treatments for Arches

When two rooms have been knocked into one, the square arch that has been created between them often requires some sort of treatment or definition. One way of dealing with this is to build a deeper arch by adding buttresses to the sides and a beam across the top. The alcoves created by the buttresses can

be used for storage and/or display, and the shelf created by the beam is often useful for displaying sculptures and indoor trailing plants, and should be lit from the back (see page 291). If the platform created is large enough and there is enough height, it can even form a balcony for a spare bed.

Alternatively, the opening can be "framed" on either side with some form of trompe l'oeil, giving it a positive identity and leading through into the other part of the room. If the arch has been given some interesting detailing, such as columns on either side topped with curved capitals, pick out this detail in a different color.

Focal Points

If you have no fireplace, you can avoid the blandness of a blank wall by providing something else as a centerpiece or perhaps more than one centerpiece. Indoor plants are excellent as "soft" focuses. They give life to a room without dominating. One imposing plant or groups of different-colored and shaped foliage can be lit at night to provide a refreshing and mysterious focus. Remember that plants can survive only if they have an adequate amount of light and the right temperature and humidity. Special light bulbs are now available to make up for light deficiency for plants (see page 291), and you can create humidity by

(above)

This room has a splendid fireplace and mirror as its focal point, but the gallery and the central table also provide points of interest.

(above)
An old fireplace has been used to frame a modern stove in a comfortable, cottage style, with wicker chairs and a large basket for logs.

Decorating

There are endless choices of fabrics, paints, floorings, ideas, combinations and styles today, so it is not difficult to hit on a decor which will suit any home, whether it is traditional or modern, large or small. The most successful living rooms are those that gather together a variety of unique ideas, colors, shapes and patterns, which, in proportion, tone and scale, complement each other and which suit the shape, scale and interior measurements, and detailing of the room. Always respect the architecture.

Don't try for grander decoration than your home, lifestyle or budget merits. The grander your aspirations, the worse the finished result will be, if it is not done well enough or set in an unsuitable environment. Remember, too, that comfort, convenience and a relaxed atmosphere are what most people remember best about a home. Comfort includes visual comfort, as well as physical. The glossary of styles on page 184 gives details of some of the most popular and well-known styles of the past and present, with ideas on how to achieve the effect.

Most of us are drawn to particular styles, perhaps for quite undefined reasons, and certain homes, particularly ones built within a particular historical tradition, seem to ask for particular styles to be applied to them. Most of us, however, will adapt and combine the historical with the modern, the existing and the new to create an entirely personal style which fits in with our way of life, personality and budget.

The living room is usually the showpiece of the home and is the obvious room to dress in a particular style. Only the perfectionist will attempt to slavishly re-create the exact style belonging to a particular period and certain place, and, indeed, specialists often disagree about what would be correct and in keeping with the whole feel of the room.

setting plant pots in a tray of pebbles, which you keep topped with water. Arrangements of dried or fresh flowers, in enormous decorative vases, jars or pots, will provide good points of focus and will be even more imposing in front of a large, ornate mirror. A mirror itself can be a focus, particularly if it is very ornate and placed fairly low on the wall, perhaps with a table in front of it.

A room does not need to have just one eye-catching angle. If you are arranging it in areas of different activity, you can introduce several focal points. A light fixture can, in itself, be attractive to look at, provided the shape is interesting and the light does not glare into the eyes. Low, sculptural lamps, which diffuse the light, can be very attractive. Individual small tables covered with pretty cloths are attractive and useful for displaying framed photographs or collections of objects (but do leave enough space for a visitor to put down a glass or a coffee cup). Small, unused corners are the places for these details.

In the past, the style of decoration was created by the architect to complement a particular architectural style. The tall ceilings of seventeenth- and eighteenth-century grand homes enabled a wall to be divided into three: dado, middle and frieze or cornice. However, dividing a square room with a low ceiling in this way will only emphasize the smallness of the room and seems to bring the ceiling even lower. The enormous fireplaces installed in the time of Louis XIV in the seventeenth century would not fit into a small, modern home, and scaled-down versions of these grand fireplaces will be out of proportion and look wrong. Something less pretentious is required in a small space, and there are many modern designs of stoves and fireplaces, which offer scope for other sorts of decoration.

If you are deeply in love with eighteenth-century classic styles and live in a small home, go for the look of the less grand rooms – the boudoir, rather than the drawing room. Boudoirs were used for entertaining on a small scale and were, in fact, small reception rooms, rather than simply bedrooms. They were frequently decorated with smaller prints and patterns than more grandiose rooms, and with a more informal feeling altogether.

One useful way of producing a harmonious, easy-to-live-with environment is to provide consistent decorative elements. Paint color is an easy way to do this: all walls one color, all woodwork white. Wall color can be made more interesting with the use of decorative treatments (for example, color washes, stippling and marbling), but the basic color is used throughout. If the idea is to hang a number of paintings on the walls, then the pattern or paint effect should not be too dominant. Matching or coordinating upholstery, curtain and cushion fabrics can also create harmony. When coordinating, a wide variety of colors and patterns can be used, but one color should predominate throughout, and patterns should have some shared quality of either scale, color or shape.

(above)
This living room with its cool blues and whites and simple furniture has Scandinavian leanings..

Do get the scale of furniture right for a particular style and for the size of your room. And do make sure that the lighting, though almost certainly brighter than it would have been in the past, corresponds in feeling to what the lighting would have been like during the period in question.

Inspiration

Inspiration can come from anywhere. Other people's living rooms often incorporate ideas that are satisfying and work. There is nothing wrong with noting arrangements, colors, combinations and details that you like. By the time you have put these ideas together with your own furniture, your own living room, your own belongings, interests, tastes and way of life, they will have subtly altered and become your own. Being open to ideas is one of the joys of decorating. There are hundreds of books, magazines, products and information sources that can help here. Many local historical societies will be happy to show photographs or documents relating to your street or even your house.

Any color combination that catches your fancy, whether you are indoors or out, should be photographed and used as a reference. Libraries are a good source of information. Some will specialize in books on interior design, which will have bibliographies.

Decorating Tips

Modern "square" architecture lends itself to modern styles better than to traditional: modern paintings, bold, bright colors and sharper forms suit the more angular, boxlike spaces of high-rise apartments and other contemporary buildings.

- *For an informal atmosphere, follow through with the basic color or pattern you have chosen, which gives unity to a room, but don't have too much matching furniture, or too perfect a finish. A color wash applied over the original paint can help to give it a subtle color and a softer finish.*

Old furniture can go with new, provided they have a common scale and are made of compatible materials: for example, glass and metal tables go better with modern metal furniture than with eighteenth-century mahogany; pale Scandinavian furniture with its simple lines can complement sleek, modern pieces or some of the simpler pieces of traditional furniture: for example, a traditional Jacobean carved oak corner chair will not look out of place with modern craftsman made furniture, provided that the style is strong and solid.

- *Checks and stripes can complement floral patterns, provided neither dominates the other, and there is a strong color choice.*
- *Fabrics in different-sized checks and plaids can be mixed, but there should be a predominating color, and they are best seen against a plain background.*
- *Floral fabrics can be used with other florals in a different scale, provided there is a unifying element in the colors.*
- *Too much pattern in curtains, carpets and upholstery limits flexibility in the decoration, whereas if you add color and pattern in the form of cushion covers, you can change the look of a room immediately.*

The same basic thinking applies as much to modern as to traditional designs: the grouping of pieces of furniture, choice of colors, patterns and textiles, and the overall balance are applicable to modern interiors, just as well as to eighteenth- or nineteenth-century ones. Use the geometry of spaces; make use of vistas, angles and curves. Where there are none, create them with screens, furniture and trompe l'oeil painting.

Rooms for Different Purposes

ROOM FOR ENTERTAINING

- *Make sure the furniture is arranged to encourage sociability: for example, that it is not too far apart and not too reclining.*
- *Make sure there are plenty of tables or*

stools on which to place drinks and nibbles: for example, a low coffee table by the sofa, nests of tables that don't take up space when not in use, or tiny, folding tables that can be hung onto the wall.
- *An inglenook provides a framework for a grand fire screen and somewhere to sit when cold visitors first arrive. This should be complemented by a fire screen to prevent sparks and embers from falling on the floor.*
- *A series of low or diffused wall lights or a halogen uplight will provide efficient, but friendly lighting and create an atmosphere of relaxation and comfort.*
- *Paintings, drawings, posters or prints should be carefully framed and displayed, either individually or in groups, to provide interest (see page 306).*

FAMILY ROOM

- *You cannot have too much organized storage in a family room. Plan it carefully.*
- *Comfortable, old chairs covered in attrac-*

(above)
Checks and a floral pattern in complementary colors produce a semi-formal interior of traditional comfort.

(above)
A Scandinavian touch for a modern town house, with long curtains, draped valances, a crystal chandelier and simple, but elegant painted furniture.

- Be bold with color. Large walls can take color well. If you don't want to commit yourself to painting whole walls in vibrant colors, paint them white and buy huge paintings to go on them.
- Use the available space to make the most of paintings and sculpture.
- Have the same flooring throughout, whether it is industrial materials, wood or carpet.
- Make use of the height and add an extra dimension by creating a mezzanine floor, or a gallery or tiered section. You can build cabinets underneath and make a feature of the stairs that lead up to it.

COTTAGE

- Try to choose furniture and fabric that are not too large or out of scale with the surroundings.
- There is always a temptation to make small cottages too cluttered. Leave room to move around easily. If necessary, get rid of furniture that doesn't fit, even if you are fond of it.
- Choose classic, traditional furniture such as Windsor chairs or other plain, wooden chairs, a simple writing desk, perhaps a footstool in needlepoint or a small embroidered fire screen.
- Individual upholstered chairs and sofas are usually better than a traditional three-piece set, which would be too overwhelming in a small cottage.
- Stained or dark woods can be more sympathetic to a cottage look than pine, which is fine for vacation homes, but has a rather raw look when used in a traditional house unless it is painted or stained.
- Fabrics should be flower prints or natural-colored, or even white linen or cotton. Curtains can be short, rather than floor length.
- Always go for a comfortable style, rather than impressiveness.

tive rugs or throws are more sensible than smartly upholstered ones, which you will worry about.

- You will need a table large enough to eat at, play games around, and do homework on (especially if the kitchen is small).
- It's important that the different areas of the room should be well lit, with working lights by tables and reading chairs, and pleasant, general light. A tungsten halogen standard lamp, which reflects light off the ceiling, gives an efficient and very pleasant light (see page 287).
- If you want the floor to be carpeted, choose short or uncut pile or matting, which is tough and easily cleaned, and can be covered with small rugs.

LOFT/BARN

- Do have a few enormous pieces of furniture to provide the main focus within the room, rather than an untidy clutter of small, half-hearted pieces.

TOWN HOUSE

- *Town houses respond to a more sophisticated look.*
- *Roman blinds at the windows will look rather elegant.*
- *A Neo-Classical style will suit most town houses, with freestanding furniture, which should be elegant and can be ornate.*
- *Use plain, but sumptuous fabrics such as velvet, or fabrics where the pattern is in the weave, such as woven silks, rather than being printed.*
- *Curtains can be given draped headings and use tie-backs to finish off.*
- *Floorboards are quite suitable for a town house, but they should be covered in Persian rugs.*
- *Use fitted cut pile carpet, with borders in either plain or traditional designs.*
- *Stair carpet is back in fashion and should match carpet on landings and in formal rooms. Borders on stair carpets can also be fitted around edges of landing carpets.*
- *Made to measure storage, running directly from floor to ceiling, can be extremely elegant in a tall room.*
- *Radiators can be hidden behind specially fitted grilles.*

ALTERNATIVE TOWN HOUSE

- *If you want a minimalist look, keep the interior very simple.*
- *Use metal and glass furniture or very understated modern, wood furniture to vary the look.*
- *Freestanding pieces of storage are often asymmetric and sculptural: sculptures in their own right.*
- *Use plain surfaces, simple fabrics and bright colors on a white or black background.*
- *Make a feature of the sound system.*
- *Keep unnecessary belongings and paraphernalia to a minimum.*

(above)
A beautiful rug can often lift the most ordinary interior into something quite luxurious. This hand-tufted rug was designed in Great Britain and woven in the Caucasus by traditional family weavers.

Budget Ideas

(above)
This versatile, adjustable
shelving system can be added
onto, as required, and moved
around and adapted to
different circumstances.

(opposite)
Fabric and cushion prints in
bright, cheerful colors.
Try combining various
colors together until you
achieve the look you like.

- *If you cannot afford new upholstery, buy fabric and tie or drape it around the chairs and sofas, or cut it to fit over the backs and arms: make the pieces long enough to tuck in wherever possible and just lay them over.*
- *If you are clever with the sewing machine, you can quite easily make loose covers for most upholstered furniture: it takes time and is bulky to sew, but not difficult.*
- *Use muslin or cheesecloth, instead of expensive curtain fabrics or lace to screen windows. Muslin is so fine, it can simply be draped over a curtain rod and tied back.*
- *Spend money on small amounts of special fabric used as cushion covers or throws and settle for plain and simple materials for use as background fabrics. One or two pieces of carefully chosen, expensive fabric can lift a room from being ordinary to being stylish.*
- *Forgo expensive wallcoverings until you can afford them. In the meantime, marvelous effects can be achieved with paint. The renewed interest in whitewash, as well as the use of natural-colored pigments and glazes, has encouraged manufacturers to produce specially formulated paints, very similar in texture and color to those used in the eighteenth and nineteenth centuries. For modern interiors, there's practically no end to the colors and finishes available, and water-based paints, in both gloss and matte finishes, have made painting much easier for the home-maker.*
- *Make a color board. This is probably more important for the living room than any other room, because of the versatility it needs to have. Pinning paint, fabric or flooring samples onto a board about 10 or 15 square feet (1 or 1.5 meters square) is rather like doing a jigsaw puzzle, and you can change and alter what's on it until you have a result you like. This can save a great deal of time by avoiding expensive mistakes. An even simpler exercise is to use the wall itself as a sample board.*

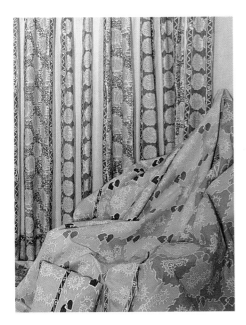

- Use an upright and bracket shelving system, which is adjustable and which you can fit with cheap shelves to begin with, progressing to more expensive ones, if you wish to, later on. You can also add sides and architraving at the top, and cabinets at the very bottom.
- Use the cheapest shelving and surround it with colonnades of cheap battens with Victorian-style bosses at the corners, and paint or stain it so that it matches the floor or furniture.
- Look in thrift stores and raid garage sales for secondhand items, which you can paint and/or alter. Architectural salvage yards often have interesting and useful items that you won't find elsewhere, although they are not necessarily cheap.
- Use secondhand rugs, many of which acquire a more interesting quality with age.
- Save your money to buy one really expensive piece of furniture or textile that you have set your heart on.

Design Checklist

- Have you decided what kind of storage you will need for books, collections, magazines, sound system, tapes, compact discs, sewing/knitting equipment, games, toys, musical instruments and other items particular to your family? Where will it all go?
- Have you decided where the radiators will go and what kind of radiators will best fit into your design?
- Have you made sure there are enough electrical outlets? They should be fitted flush with the wall so that they won't prevent furniture from butting up to them.
- Carefully measure out the arrangement of the seating areas and make sure there is enough room to walk comfortably around the furniture.
- If you want to incorporate a work area, make sure it fits in with the style of the rest of the room and that you have enough room to pull the chair out and sit in comfort.
- Make sure the flooring is suitable for all likely activities and in keeping with the rest of the room. Don't go out and buy a carpet you like, and then try and fit the rest of the decor in with it.
- Make sure all your wallcoverings and ceilings are compatible with the style you have chosen. Visualizing what wallpaper patterns will look like when on the wall is difficult. Always try to see a photograph of a room set with the paper shown: patterns that seem inoffensive in a sample book can be very dominating in a room.
- Mirrors must be hung in the right place if they are to have any impact, so that they reflect something interesting and make the most of any available light.
- Make sure there is enough lighting with the use of natural daylight, general artificial lighting, reading lighting, "mood" lighting and mirrors.
- Consider the size, style and amount of furniture.
- For window treatments, remember that window trim comes in different widths. Get one big enough for what you want; the wider, the better as a rule.
- Don't allow any piece of furniture to take too dominant a position in the room.

Kitchens & Dining Rooms

The kitchen is the very core of the home, so it must be efficient, convenient and pleasant to work in. Some cooks would like a small ship's galley, where everything is within arm's reach, some enjoy a disciplined cooking laboratory with highly polished surfaces and catering quality equipment, while others prefer a country-style kitchen with wood surfaces and a traditional wood-burning stove, where friends and family can congregate and the cook can participate in whatever is going on.

If your house has only a small kitchen, you might be able to move it from its present place to a larger room. Parents may prefer to use a room facing the garden, where small children can run in and out and be easily supervised. If you don't enjoy cooking and rarely eat in, you could move the kitchen into a smaller space and use the larger room for leisure activities. Moving a kitchen means moving the plumbing and installing extra electrical outlets, so check on the cost of such a move and always get professional advice before you go ahead. Moving a door or cutting back a partition are relatively easy alternatives that may, by themselves, make a major improvement to the kitchen layout. Kitchen planning is complex: always get professional advice before replanning or altering the room.

What's Required?

Of all the rooms in the home, the kitchen is the one where planning will really pay off and make the difference between a room where cooking is made pleasurable and one where it is a chore because you are constantly bending down to reach things, negotiating awkward corners and also knocking your head against jutting cabinets. There are many specialized kitchen companies that will design and install an attractive and efficient kitchen for you, but they are usually created to a formula and will lack your personal individuality. An architect or interior designer may design a kitchen with more flair.

If you are going to do the planning yourself, take time to consider all your requirements. Juggling all the elements is the difficult part. Both the planning and the style need clear thinking and disciplined choices. Visit the most upscale kitchen showrooms with a small notebook in your hand and record clever design features or solutions as a source of inspiration. You will find you can adapt many of these ideas to your own circumstances. Try to follow a sensible plan of design – based on how you live. If you go through a day's kitchen activities in your mind, you will soon see the way things will be most conveniently placed. These are the immediate priorities:

1. *Work sequence:* What order do you work in, and what appliances and equipment do you need?
2. *Layout:* Having decided on the equipment, how can you make it work most efficiently?
3. *Safety:* Build safety into your kitchen, especially if you have young children or elderly people in the house.
4. *Lighting:* Since this is a workroom, efficient lighting is a priority.

The Work Flow

A good design should minimize anything interfering with the ongoing work and prevent unnecessary fatigue. Cooking involves three basic kitchen operations, sometimes called

the work triangle (although they may take place in a straight line, rather than in triangular formation). They consist of:

1. Food storage (for example, refrigerator and pantry).
2. Food preparation (for example, sink, chopping board and work surfaces).
3. Cooking (stove and microwave).

Of course, you still have to consider storage space for pans, equipment, plates and cutlery, but these three operations are crucial. The ideal work triangle includes adequate working space in a reasonably compact area: the total length of the sides of the triangle should be between 11 feet (3.5 meters) and 23 feet (7 meters). Define the different zones of activity you want to include in your kitchen: for example, food preparation, washing and cooking. Some cooks find it useful to have a little office corner with a wall-mounted telephone. Make sure you allow enough circulation space to move about comfortably, efficiently and (most important) safely.

Whatever the size of the kitchen, your basic aim should always be to have the sink and stove fairly near to one another with plenty of work surfaces between them, so that there will always be room for chopping, for rolling pastry and for general food preparation, when it is required. Sometimes a large refrigerator-freezer seems to dominate a small kitchen and, if there's space, you might prefer to have a separate refrigerator and freezer under the work surfaces. Fresh vegetables can be stored in a cabinet or rack near the sink. Ideally, a dishwasher should be placed close to the sink, with the trash bin under the sink unit, but where it won't interfere with the loading of the dishwasher. In many homes, the washing machine is in the kitchen, but this is not really the best place for it. It gets in the way of the work sequence, takes up valuable space and mixes up dirty clothes with food. It may even be possible for you to fit the washing machine under the stairs, in a corridor or in a separate utility room.

(above)
This springlike kitchen is a good example of the work triangle, with the stove placed next to the sink and food storage nearby.

Try to have a counter dividing the sink from the stove, where you can do any slicing and chopping, and the stove should have a heat-resistant surface on either side. Sugar, salt, pepper, herbs and spices used every day in cooking should be kept on a narrow shelf near the stove. If you want to put in extra electrical outlets, do this at an early stage. They should be installed at the back of the counters, where they can be conveniently reached and are out of the way of children, and you will need several: for food processor, toaster, coffee-maker, mixer, radio, possibly a television, microwave and the unexpected.

Make a list of the appliances you are going to require and where they will go. A microwave can take up a lot of work surface; perhaps you could fit it in on the wall instead? Always measure the spaces and the appliances carefully. If something is a fraction of an inch too large for a space, no amount of optimism will enable you to squeeze it in. Electric mixers and food processors all need space (and electrical outlets).

Layout

The following kitchen layouts can all provide satisfactory working conditions and can be adjusted ad infinitum to fit into almost any size and shape of room. How much and how little you want — or can fit in — is an individual choice. Every room will have its own problems: windows in different places, more or fewer doors and uneven walls, but the basic requirements can nearly always be accommodated, even if some juggling has to be done.

ONE-WALL KITCHEN

In very narrow rooms, a one-wall arrangement can work well. This is sometimes known as a single galley kitchen. A room that is 6 ft 6 in (2 meters) wide is the narrowest you could hope to use and, of course, this would be purely a working kitchen; you couldn't eat in it. You can run your kitchen along one wall in a large room too, leaving a spacious area free for socializing, eating or working. Depending on the length of wall, you could incorporate a stovetop and oven, refrigerator and dishwasher, and a single sink and drain board, with cabinets above and below. Or you could turn the whole wall into a large built-in unit with open shelves, fitting the stovetop and sink into the counter. If the house has a garden, you can fit the sink in front of the window, looking out onto it.

You can add to the impression of width in a narrow kitchen by having built-in, open shelves, rather than cabinet doors, which bring the room forward. Good lighting will help too, particularly lighting strips fitted under cabinets and shining onto the counter. This sort of kitchen works well for a large family, because it leaves the rest of the room open for a large table and comfortable seating.

DOUBLE GALLEY KITCHEN

If the room is slightly wider (not less than 7 ft 2 in (2.2 m), you could create a double

galley with units running along opposite walls. The passage between the units should be large enough for two people to pass through fairly easily, and there must be room to bend down and get things out of the refrigerator and oven without knocking into the opposite units. This sort of kitchen can usually fit into a long, narrow space and is best for the use of one cook or two very neat cooks. If there's a window at one end, a small, folding or hinged table can provide enough space for meals. The area will not work so well if it is interrupted by doors, and if there is a door, out into a garden, say, try to find some other route.

U-SHAPED KITCHENS

These are similar to double galley kitchens, but the units are carried around the far end of the room in a horse-shoe shape. This is a satisfactory general layout, which allows maximum work area within a compact space. The U-shape means that a smaller length of the room can be used for the work area, which may leave enough space at one end for a dining table. Tall appliances (for example, a freezer or built-in oven) should fit at the end of the row of units. Many of your decisions concerning how to arrange appliances will be determined by the position of windows and doors. This layout could work well in an area separated from a large, converted warehouse or loft space. It could also be used for a one- or two-person household, where the kitchen space is small and square.

L-SHAPED WORK STATION

This is a useful layout, where a kitchen is placed in the corner of a room. For efficiency's sake, the stove, sink and refrigerator should be positioned as near to the center of the L as possible. Tall refrigerators, or eye-level ovens and other tall units, should be kept at the end of the run of work units so as not to interrupt the work surfaces. This shape is often useful

(above)
A glass-fronted cabinet is a good display feature in a customized and beautifully crafted kitchen, with meticulous detailing.

(above)
The curvaceous blue wave
on these stylish ceramic
tiles picks up the color of
the stove and the painted
cabinets and drawers in a
charming and practical
blue-and-white kitchen.

be reached from both sides, which is convenient for setting and clearing away the table—
a very practical feature. It is another good
solution for a studio apartment, providing
storage space and a barrier to the rest of the
room.

ISLAND WORK STATION
A separate work unit sitting in the middle of a
kitchen sounds appealing, but seldom works
well. It takes up a lot of space and can leave
other parts of the room with no particular
purpose. However, in a large room it can be
useful in providing a great deal of cabinet
space for gadget-minded cooks or for those
cooking for a large number of people and
needing lots of plates and cutlery, possibly a
wine rack and much more. Because it is
detached from the standard units, an island
work station can be made to any height or
depth and can incorporate useful features,
such as a chopping block. Central island
stations have great appeal where space is not
at a premium, but remember, if the stovetop
is within the unit, it will also require special
ventilation arrangements: either an overhead
range hood with ducting exposed or concealed
behind a false ceiling. Racks of slatted
shelves can be installed overhead to conceal
this ducting and can be used for hanging or
stacking large cooking utensils. This can give
a very professional look to a kitchen.
Otherwise, under-floor exhaust ducts will need
to be installed near the stovetop, but that's a
solution strictly for fat budgets.

KITCHEN IN AN ALCOVE
Kitchens that consist of a small, closet-like
space off a main room are not uncommon,
particularly in custom-built retirement homes
and in some house remodels. Often at first
glance, it is difficult to see how you can make
such a kitchen either convenient or attractive,
but if it is well planned, the idea can work
well. The advantages are that although the

in the corner of a studio apartment. One leg of
the L is a good place to have a table, so that
you could create a slightly separate environment for eating.

PENINSULA WORK STATION
This layout can provide a convenient work
surface by projecting into the room at right
angles to a kitchen counter, with cabinets
fitted underneath. The extension can be short
enough for just an eating counter with stools,
or it can run across three-fourths of the
room's width providing a safe play or a separate eating area. Unless you have some practical reason (for example, the need for a
breakfast area), always think twice about
dividing the space in this way. Sometimes a
table can provide the only division you need,
whereas a work station partition can alter the
proportions of the space, making the room
seem cramped. This can be a useful layout for
a young family. The cabinets of a peninsular
extension have the advantage that they can

kitchen is joined to the main room, it is still separate and doesn't interfere with the decor of the room, and the cook can still be in contact with visitors. The main problems are storage and countertop space, but since such kitchens are usually designed for a single person, minimum storage is necessary. It is useful with such tiny kitchens to make a list of the things you don't need and to exclude them from the house. Don't forget to incorporate an exhaust fan; otherwise steam and cooking smells will be very unpleasant and can spoil the decor in the main room very quickly.

Planning for Comfort and Efficiency

Mass-produced kitchen cabinets and equipment are designed for the "average"-sized person. If you are very much taller or shorter than most people, then it would be best to have a kitchen especially built for your height. Most mass-produced items are standard all

over the world (though some American-made and industrial appliances are larger). All base units are designed to be 35 in (900 mm) high, though this height can be raised or lowered slightly by altering the height of the base on which they sit. Most units and appliances are made to a depth of 23 1/2 in (600 mm). The countertop height should be varied according to your needs to avoid backache. Some people like a high work surface of, say 3 ft 3 in (1 m), for chopping and carving and a lower one of 30 in (760 mm) in height for rolling out pastry. A low-level work surface is best for a stovetop as it is easier to see what's cooking on the back burner and to reach out to stir it. (Remember, however, that the lower the stovetop, the easier it will be for children to reach it.) From the aesthetic point of view, you could probably get away with using different work heights in a large kitchen, but it's probably better to stick to one level in a small one, to give a more coherent look.

A minimum of 19 1/2 in (500 mm) is usually

(above)

This sort of unfitted kitchen is both relaxing and friendly, but it will only work well in a large room. The style suits the charming, individual items of furniture and the large kitchen table.

Remember that it often pays to buy a small number of good quality items and to save up for the rest, rather than to get a complete set of tacky cabinets whose doors will drop, drawers stick and veneer peel away, so look for good structural design, well-fitted joints, braced corners and sturdy hinges, a hard surface finish which will stand a certain amount of scratching, heat and acids, and strong handles and catches.

Some Common Problems

DOORS

Too many doors or doors fitted in the wrong places can badly affect the smooth running and comfort of a kitchen, getting in the way of the work flow, as well as encouraging people to use the room as a throughway. If there is a door that you don't need, you can either ignore it, treat it as part of the wall, or block it up and build the kitchen as though it wasn't there. This may make it easier to accommodate a dishwasher. Removing a door is a relatively easy alteration for any do-it-yourself enthusiast to do.

Most kitchen cabinet doors are designed so that they either hinge on the left or right hand side, so make sure they open in the most convenient way for you and that they don't get in the way of other doors or open out against a wall.

Double doors, opening out onto a terrace or garden, are an excellent way of joining both home and garden, especially where there are young children. It can be argued that they take up valuable wall space, but if you can plan your kitchen to run along one wall, you may be able to put a new door in the other wall. If there's no space for a double door, a single door can be attractive and could incorporate a small porch to store muddy boots. A Dutch door is often a practical solution, and this serves a dual purpose: it will keep dogs and children out (or in), while letting in fresh air and sunshine.

(above)
The space between two windows can often be rather overbearing, when fitted with conventional cabinets, but here a set of boxed-in shelves provides both storage and interest.

the standard depth of work surfaces, where shelves or cabinets are to be fixed above them. If there is enough space, it is more useful to have deeper work surfaces. The fronts of appliances can then be flush with the units and there will still be plenty of room at the back of them for plumbing and ventilation. Often the space behind a stovetop is a useful place for allowing hot pans to cool down, and otherwise wasted space hidden behind the sink can store dishwashing accessories, such as detergent. Taps are best fixed to the wall, if possible, as this avoids a pool of water collecting at the base and prevents the build-up of mineral deposits.

The deeper the countertop, the harder it will be to reach tall cabinets above it. When fixing wall-hung cabinets, remember for your own convenience, that they should be high enough to allow you to keep some items (for example, a mixer or coffee maker), on the work surface underneath them and also, so high that an open door will not swing back and knock you in the eye.

Alcoves

Sometimes a straight run of wall is interrupted by an alcove created by an old fireplace. It may be best to ignore this and treat the whole wall as one – perhaps using the alcove for a deeper counter or breakfast bar, with a painting or decorative dish on the wall behind it. The chimney opening should always be blocked off at the bottom to prevent old soot and birds' nests from dropping down. Alternatively, this could be the place to install a wood-burning stove, where the chimney could be used to house an exhaust fan. Or you could build a tall cabinet in the space, with glazed doors at the top to show off china.

Partition Wall

Kitchens in remodeled houses are often divided from the rest of the home by a partition wall, rather than a load-bearing one. Cutting back an unwanted partition wall is easy and fairly inexpensive, and may open up the space to provide one generous room,

rather than two uncomfortable ones. However, obtain an expert's advice first before going ahead. Load-bearing walls cannot be moved so easily and the wall above will need extra support, which will necessitate the fitting of a steel beam. Always get a specialist's advice, and you may also need to seek a building permit for this.

Windows

Windows can be expensive to move because it may be difficult to match the lintels, which hold up the wall above the window. Always get professional advice for this. If the window is above ground floor level, you would need scaffolding as well, which would greatly add to the cost as you would need to get in professionals. However, you may be able to extend the window out by a few inches to give a slight bay, just enough, even in a small kitchen, to allow a circular or semi-circular folding table, where friends or children can sit and eat breakfast or chat to the cook over a drink.

(above)

A tiny window in this Mexican-style kitchen has been treated like a small painting, being framed in the same green as the open shelving and surrounded by ceramic tiles.

Irregular Walls

These walls make it difficult to be accurate when measuring. Get countertops specially cut and measure the wall in two places, where the top and bottom of the units and appliances have to fit. Or stop the units several inches short of the corners, leaving enough space for a chopping block, chair or vertical tray storage, to make sense of the gap.

Don't try to use every square inch of an awkwardly shaped or oversized room. It is much better to concentrate on making the neatest and most convenient kitchen without slavishly following the lines of the existing wall. Any wall you don't use will have another use – if only as space for an armchair.

Bathroom Through Kitchen

This is a surprisingly common problem in remodeled houses because it is convenient to have the bathroom and kitchen plumbing close together. It means the bathroom user has to run the gauntlet of the kitchen and the kitchen itself is diminished by people walking through. The best thing is probably to resite the bathroom, perhaps directly above, where the plumbing may have the shortest distance to run. Alternatively, if both kitchen and bathroom open out onto the same passage or corridor, the bathroom could be rearranged so that a small door could be knocked through from the passage, or you could extend the house slightly to create a new corridor. As mentioned previously in this chapter, always seek professional advice before going ahead with major alterations and check whether you need to obtain permits.

Columns

If the room has a column supporting the roof or ceiling structure, it will be cheaper to try and incorporate this into the design of the room rather than to change it, because expensive structural work would have to be carried out by professionals to provide alternative support for the roof. Try to arrange things so that the column does not interrupt the work triangle. It might be incorporated into a room divider, with the cooking area on one side and the eating or playing area on the other. Turn it into a feature with decorative painting.

Safety

The kitchen is potentially one of the most dangerous rooms in the house. When planning, make sure that safety thinking is integral to the design.

- *Plan so that you don't have to walk across a thoroughfare to drain off hot pans into the sink.*
- *Don't put the stovetop under a window, where a draft might cause curtains or fat to catch fire or right next to a door, where someone might knock into it as they come in.*
- *Ceramic stovetops that take a long time to cool down are very dangerous when toddlers can get to them. Get stove guards, and these will also prevent children from grabbing hot saucepan handles.*
- *Put a knife rack at the back of the countertop where children can't reach it.*
- *Place small appliances and equipment near an outlet, so there are no trailing wires and you don't have to reach awkwardly to get at them.*
- *There should be a heat-resistant countertop on each side of the stovetop, such as an inset of ceramic tiles or a trivet.*
- *Storage of everyday items should be within easy reach.*
- *Keep high cabinets for things you only use very infrequently and for people who find bending down difficult. Low cabinets, too, should only be for things used infrequently. For tall storage, make sure you have sturdy steps to reach items. Lightweight, folding steps take up little space.*
- *Make sure you plan out the storage so*

A long, narrow kitchen opens out onto a light and spacious dining room. The countertop is subtly lit at the back, while the dining room has natural light coming in from the tall windows.

(above)
Kitchens don't need to have cabinets hanging from every wall. Here the brick wall has been painted white and left bare.

• Safety catches for low cabinet doors will stop children opening the cabinets.

Planning for the Elderly and Disabled

• Each person's needs will be a little different, but here are some general hints that should be helpful. Within most standard kitchen designs, there are features that are particularly suited for people with disabilities (and often good for able-bodied people too).

• D-shaped handles on cabinets and drawers are easier to grasp than knobs.

• Narrow shelves are more convenient than deep ones.

• A separate oven and stovetop can be placed at the most convenient heights for each.

• An oven door that pulls down is often a better option than a side-opening one and provides something to slide dishes onto.

• Many standard kitchens have pull-out work surfaces, which can be convenient for people in wheelchairs.

• Waste bins with automatic lifting tops and tip-out drawers can store anything from vegetables to plates.

• Electric appliances, such as can-openers and sharpeners, can be useful for the weak-wristed, but must be placed where they are easily reached and most often used.

• Some faucets are better than others for those with a weak grip. Cross-top taps are better than bulbous ones, and those with a lever are best of all. A tap with a tall, swivel spout is good for filling pans and kettles from the countertop, rather than having to put them in the sink.

• Shallow sinks are easier to reach into from a wheelchair.

• If you are designing a complete kitchen for a disabled person, it's best to get professional advice because, for wheelchair users in particular, experience and expert knowledge are vital.

everything has a user-friendly place, work surfaces are free for work, and the floor area is clear for moving around safely.

• Lighting is important. You should be able to see your work without shadows, especially over the stove, sink and countertops.

• Hang a fire blanket next to the stove and keep a fire extinguisher nearby – but not in a place where children can play with it. Get professional advice on the best type of extinguisher and where to keep it. A smoke alarm is recommended too. Everyone in the house should know where they are and how to operate them.

• Set aside an area where young children can play safely. Put up a safety gate or some kind of solid barrier to keep them from under the cook's feet and away from the cooking area.

• Keep household cleaners and chemicals on a high shelf – not under the sink, which is the most tempting place to store them.

• Buy products with child-proof lids, if possible.

Kitchen Storage

Providing convenient and suitable storage for small, large and variously shaped kitchen tools and equipment is one of the most important aspects of kitchen planning. Whether you choose to have fitted cabinets, open shelves or custom-built storage, the important thing is that everything should be easily seen, accessible and in the most convenient place.

Shelving

Open shelving is cheap and easy to install, and suits people who like the look of their kitchen equipment and use it often. Shelves can be fitted where cabinets cannot, (for example, in front of windows, on the backs of cabinet doors, under sloping ceilings and in small recesses). An "up-and-over" shelf can also be fitted so that a heavy piece of equipment, such as a food processor, can sit in a cabinet and swing out, when required. Shelves can also be of different depths. Wider shelves are good for large plates, pitchers and bowls,

but it is useful to have some narrow shelves. One narrow shelf, running along the wall about 12 in (30 cm) above the countertop and above any electrical outlets, is indispensable for jars of herbs and spices and any other small items, which would get lost on deep shelves.

In standard cabinets, fit a deep shelf below, with a half width one placed above, so that you can more easily reach and see what's at the back of the bottom shelf.

Cabinets

Enclosed cabinets can be very dominant in a kitchen and will usually set the style for the whole room. You can choose the simplest wood, Shaker-style design and paint it, or you can have an elaborate, molded wood kitchen in a dark stain, and in between these, there are many variations of wood, veneered or plastic-finished kitchens to choose from. If you plan carefully, you should not have to cover every wall with cabinets. It is often more

(above)
This dining room/kitchen is well equipped for serious cooking; utensils hang from a metal bar and still more from a circular rack hung from the ceiling. Most items are openly displayed and easy to reach.

Drawers

Drawers are among the most useful forms of storage. They can be any depth and size: shallow for linen, table mats and cutlery, square for dry staples and smaller items such as string and labels, and deep for upright bottles, saucepans, a laundry basket or waste bin, and children's toys.

You can buy standard drawers and design the interior for a specific purpose (for example, fill them with wire baskets for vegetable storage, bottles and jars or laundry). Very narrow drawers, fitted with wire shelves, are available as part of some types of kitchen units, which can store nearly all your cans and dry ingredients in a very compact space. Such units can be short in height to fit next to an under-the-counter refrigerator, or tall to fit next to a large refrigerator-freezer or, indeed, into any spare, narrow space in the kitchen.

pleasant to have some open wall space to hang a picture on, or to act as your home office. Having too many cabinets simply means you can shove things into them, which you don't need and never even glance at. For a narrow kitchen where cabinet doors may open straight into your face, you can get units with sliding doors, but these can be irritating to use and small things can often get hidden behind them.

Plan the interiors of cabinets carefully. A narrower shelf fitted inside a cabinet will mean that you have room to hang a set of shelves on the back of the cabinet door, which can be a more convenient way of storing small items. Low cabinets are easier to use if the shelves pull out on runners, so you can see what's on them. Wire basket shelves will prevent things from rolling off. If the kitchen is next to the eating area, equipment for eating and setting the table can be kept in a double-sided peninsula unit, to make more efficient use of the area.

Food and Drink Storage

Ideally, all vegetables and dairy products should be kept in a well-ventilated, unheated pantry. Wine should always be stored in a cool, dry atmosphere and laid on its side. Some refrigerators incorporate a useful "pantry" section, but there's nothing like a real pantry to keep food in good condition.

Compact pantry storage can be bought as standard units from some kitchen companies, but any large, walk-in closet can be turned into a pantry, provided it is built against an outside (preferably north facing) wall, so that it can be ventilated and cool. Pantry shelves should have cool surfaces (marble, slate, quarry tiles or white glazed tiles are all good) and, failing that, a wood shelf covered with laminate is perfectly serviceable. They should be within reach and easy to clean. Arrange them in a U shape so you can see to the back and in the corners. Higher shelves should be narrow for cans and bottles, but a deep shelf positioned at counter height is useful for storing cheeses, eggs, butter and other dairy products and bread. The top shelf should be only about 5 ft 10 in (1.8 m) above the floor, with another at about 4 ft 9 in (1.5 m) and at this height, it should not be any wider than the depth of two standard jars. Fix hooks to the ceiling or under these high shelves for hanging meats or dried herbs.

There should be a ventilation hole or at least one air brick in the outside wall. A built-in electric ventilator system will ensure that air circulates freely to keep everything fresh and cool. Install a light that will automatically switch on whenever you open the door, and fix door handles that allow you to open the door with your elbow when carrying trays of food.

Storage Ideas

There are many other and far more convenient ways of storing kitchen items than covering every inch of available wall space with built-in kitchen units. In a small kitchen, too many units can gobble up kitchen space, leaving a rather cramped result.

- *Some of the wall area can be covered in 1 in or 1½ in (2.5 cm or 3.8 cm) horizontal slats fixed to upright battens. S hooks can be bought or made out of an old wire clothes hanger to hang over the back of the slats, and these can store a multitude of small items, from pastry brushes to small saucepans, instead of the drawers in which they nearly always get lost.*
- *A narrow, metal rod with sliding hooks, fixed in the space above the countertop, will hold ladles, nutmeg graters and tea strainers. Use this to keep things which you use quite often or they will collect dust.*
- *If you have a narrow space between an appliance and a cabinet or wall, fit it with pull-out rods for tea towels.*
- *Attach a thick, metal rod or bar about three-fourths of the way up the wall and hang it with butcher's hooks to hold large pans. Alternatively, mount a circular metal*

bar to the ceiling above the stove to do the same job. These are available from professional catering equipment shops.
- *Fit a waste bin to the inside of a cabinet door so that it will swing out whenever you open the door.*
- *A plate rack fixed to the wall above the draining board will dry and store plates at the same time.*
- *Cup hooks under shelves are invaluable for mugs, cups and small pitchers.*
- *There are many variations of plastic-covered wire storage devices, including pull-out wire drawers and small holders to fit on the back of cabinet doors to hold tricky items, such as cloths and shoe cleaning equipment.*
- *A colored metal rack, about the size of a bulletin board, is useful for holding oddly shaped and ungainly objects.*
- *Saucepans can be kept in a deep drawer at low level.*
- *If pans are kept inside a cabinet, a lid rack*

(above)
A neat little butcher's block can serve several functions in a kitchen. This one is mobile and has two shelves, a drawer and a rail from which to hang a tea towel.

A quarry-tiled floor always looks
marvelous in a traditional
kitchen. These are old terracotta
tiles and every one is slightly
different and full of character.

can be installed inside the door of the unit.
- *A freestanding saucepan rack is often a useful form of storage, if you have the space available.*
- *If you have a separate oven and stovetop, a pull-out rack can go under the latter.*
- *If drawers are intended to be used for holding heavy objects, fit them on filing cabinet runners, which are smooth and robust and can stand the weight.*
- *A large expanse of cabinet doors will make it difficult for you to remember exactly what's behind them. Glass doors are the obvious solution (though these are strictly for the very tidy).*
- *All cleaning equipment should hang, if feasible, from brackets, preferably in a closet. Keep cleaning products and cloths in separate wire baskets at the top of the closet where children can't get at them. Keep everything off the floor, if possible.*

Flooring

Kitchen flooring must be good-looking, tough, easy to clean and in sympathy with the style of the kitchen. Many floorings can be bought, either as tiles or sheets. Tiles are easier to lay and many people like their versatility. Others prefer the smooth look of sheet flooring and it is marginally easier to clean. The different options for kitchen flooring include:
- *Ceramic, quarry and slate tiles: These are good-looking and reliable, but hard and ungiving, deliciously cool in hot countries and can be both cold in winter and for children's play. You can cover them with rugs and matting but these tiles must have some form of backing or underlayment to prevent slipping and creasing. All tiles should be either secured with suitably strong adhesive onto plywood, or bedded into a solid subfloor, such as concrete, for example. Tiles are heavy, so always check their overall weight before laying them in an upstairs room.*

- *Stone, brick: Stone is available in similar thicknesses to tiles, but traditional flagstones are likely to be much thicker. Finish with a wax polish. Not ideal for those who have children. If you like brick, use paving bricks or brick tiles. Check whether the bricks you choose need any special treatment. Your local tile supplier will be able to advise you on this.*
- *Linoleum: Comfortable, hardwearing material, made from natural products including wood, linseed oil and cork. Agreeable feel and texture; good for children's play. Sheets or tiles; good colors available; not difficult to cut and lay.*
- *Vinyl: This is the most common of all the kitchen floorings that are now available and comes in a wide variety of finishes, colors and textures. Can imitate almost any sort of flooring, from brick and wood to tiles. Some vinyls are cushioned. Good for children's play. Available in tiles or sheet. Easy to cut and lay.*
- *Wood: Excellent for kitchen floors, provided you look after it. The surface should be thoroughly sealed. You can use a polyurethane for a high shine, or shellac and wax for a more natural look. Wood floors can be painted with special floor paint (with additional varnish, this can last a long time). Stencil designs and colored stains can be used as well. Hardwood is expensive, but more durable than softwood.*
- *Cork tiles: Good material because it is soft and comfortable, but tough. Available in different colors and textures. Good for children's play. Must be sealed; can be damaged by sharp objects; should be laid on hardboard or plywood. Cork is good insulation material.*
- *Carpet and matting: Standard man-made fiber carpets and carpet tiles are suitable for kitchens. Carpet tiles are probably the best choice because you can wash them individually and lift and replace them when*

they get stained or when damaged. Matting can be comfortable in kitchens, but is not as easy to clean as the smoother floorings. It nearly always has a rubberized backing to stop it from buckling and can be painted, or stenciled, or you can even add decorative borders, if you wish.

(above)
As well as being an ideal flooring for the kitchen, slate is a practical, hardwearing and stylish material for work surfaces.

Work Surfaces

Base units are usually supplied without a top so you can put a continuous counter over the whole length. Into this will go the sink, faucets and stovetop. The surface must be able to cope with pastry-making, chopping and holding hot pans. (Ideally, you would have a different surface for every task, but that would be very expensive and visually distracting. One answer is to have separate pastry and chopping boards, and a trivet by the side of the stove.) When choosing a counter, a square edge is better than a rounded one, which allows spilled water to fall onto your feet. Some well-finished counters include a

groove along the edge to avoid this. Remember that shiny surfaces (especially stainless steel), show up finger and hard water marks. Good counter materials include:

- *Laminates: Smooth, hygienic, fine for pastry, but will get scratched and ruin knives if used for chopping. This material won't withstand heat.*
- *Stainless steel: Expensive and needs to be constantly wiped to look good. For the dedicated cook who likes a restaurant look.*
- *Ceramic tiles: Durable and attractive; will withstand heat and acid; shouldn't be used for chopping.*
- *Slate: A long slab of slate would be expensive, but slate floor tiles make an attractive countertop; will withstand heat and acid, but don't use them for chopping.*
- *Corian: Synthetic material which looks like marble, but is lighter and warmer to the touch; virtually scorch- and stain-proof.*
- *Hardwood: Excellent material for a traditional kitchen; must be saturated with*

linseed or teak oil to avoid water damage; won't withstand hot pans; can be used as a chopping board, if you don't mind it acquiring a lived-in look.

Lighting

Good lighting is as important in a kitchen as in any other workshop. Each working zone should have its own lighting treatment. Halogen lighting is inconspicuous and much cooler than conventional light bulbs, and can look very stylish. When choosing halogen light bulbs, make sure they include an additional glass filter (most do not), to protect against ultra-violet emissions. Halogen bulbs are expensive, but will last much longer than conventional bulbs.

Heating

Ideally, the kitchen should be on the main central heating system, as some form of constant heat helps to prevent condensation. A kitchen needs about half the radiator area as compared with a similar space elsewhere in the house. Modern radiators come in a variety of shapes, and there are fan convector heaters which can fit into odd spaces, such as the foot of a base unit. Radiators are often placed in the most inconvenient positions, but you needn't be limited to the existing heating layout. Compact radiators, which run along the floor at baseboard level, might be used instead, and radiators with rungs exist, which can double up as towel racks, while others are very tall and narrow to fit into awkward spaces, and others still can be made to follow the shape of a curved wall.

If you have a traditional, wood-burning stove, you will require no extra heat. For kitchens that are used mainly morning and evening, and on weekends, a quick-boost form of heating is best, such as a gas or electric wall heater. The kitchen is a busy room so don't have a heater on the floor; otherwise it will get in the way. Electric storage heaters are not recommended for kitchens because they are bulky, dispense heat when it is least needed, and don't provide the room with instant heat.

Ventilation

The kitchen produces steam and smells, which often turn into condensation on walls and windows. The only way to prevent this is to provide three things: continuous warmth, good ventilation and warm surfaces.

Exhaust fans are the most efficient ventilators, drawing steam and smells through a fan in a window pane or external wall, or the roof. They should be positioned as high as possible on the wall and near to the source of steam.

Range hoods use charcoal filters to eliminate cooking smells and steam. They must be placed directly over the stovetop. You can get exhaust or recirculating hoods in a wide range of shapes and sizes. Make sure they are fitted at the recommended height.

Choosing a Style

You should decide on the style you want for your kitchen before choosing any appliances, floor, wall and work surfaces, or units or forms of lighting.

Dedicated Cook's Kitchen

If you are passionate about cooking, you will want a true workshop. A galley or a U-shaped layout, or an island kitchen, would be very convenient. All materials should be practical: countertops and sinks of stainless steel with possible insets of marble for pastry making and wood surfaces for chopping. A double sink will allow for food preparation and washing up, and there should be a garbage disposal. The floor can be white ceramic tiles or vinyl, and the wall behind the stove could be tiled.

For the other walls, you could choose white latex paint. Equipment and units will be solid, simple, black or white laminate. Pans will hang from butcher's hooks above the stove. Catering equipment will be kept on

(above)

A sleek, no-nonsense kitchen is given added warmth by the rich tones of the wood, and there is a professional, high-tech quality in its metal hanging storage, quality stainless steel sink, wall of glass bricks and heavy work surface.

open shelves where it is easy to reach. If true catering materials are too expensive, standard units can be used to create a highly efficient cook's environment. The dominant color in the streamlined kitchen is likely to be white, offset by black or navy blue. Pale gray is a popular color for understated sleekness. Keep the kitchen simple and uniform. Suspended track lighting will ensure efficient working light over each work surface.

High-Tech Kitchen

High-tech kitchens use products of modern technology, usually designed specifically for industrial or commercial use. The robust, ad hoc style goes well in large, open spaces such as warehouses and lofts. High tech in a kitchen means using metal office shelving, flooring materials normally used in factories or airports, exhibition lighting systems, catering equipment and appliances.

If you have time to research and source materials, you could easily make up a kitchen

relatively cheaply. You can use paint or enamel, or automobile spray paints in bright primary or metalic colors to create a unified or a bright, lighthearted look. Remember, because they are built to be robust, the components may not be so very cheap. Try to find secondhand office equipment, exhibition flooring and equipment.

A Small, Personal Kitchen

This is the very opposite of the dedicated cook's kitchen and will reflect your personality, rather than your interest in cooking. It may be an alcove kitchen within a larger room, or a small room in a variety of convenient or inconvenient proportions. Give yourself just enough working and cabinet space for your needs. Concentrate on base cabinets and try to leave some wall free for a feeling of space and some scope for versatility of use. The layout will depend on the shape of the room. (See page 70.) When you have a satisfactory plan, you can impose your own style onto it.

If you live in a minimalist environment, then you can extend the floor covering into the kitchen: choose the sleekest kitchen units in colors that match those in the other room and choose the minimum of equipment and appliances, which are sculptural in their own right. You can choose individual Gothic-style wall lights, or a hanging lamp with a frilly shade, but make sure the lighting enables you to see what you're doing or supplement it with working lights.

If your chosen style is softer, your kitchen can reflect this look with fewer built-in cabinets and more freestanding furniture. Choose cabinets with beading or architraving at the top and paneled doors, giving a hand-made look, and you could paint them in a limewash for a traditional look. A round or semi-circular table under the window will allow you to sit and enjoy the room while you eat, read or write, and a telephone on the wall will reinforce the feeling that this room is more than just a kitchen. Leave enough wall room for

pictures and shelf space for pretty pieces of china you may have collected. Stencil around the door and at counter height. There are lots of stencil styles to choose from, and your colors can be as bold or as delicate as you like. Curtain the window with a floral chintz or café-curtain gingham, or use a roller or Roman blind.

Once you have completed the initial installation, you can build up your stock of china and equipment at your leisure. All equipment should be chosen for your own visual pleasure: you may decide to choose a practical style with traditional mixing bowls and wood bread boards, a feminine style with floral pitchers and decorated china or a modern style with brightly colored dishes or an eclectic mixture. Add any small touches that you like to make the room personal to you: a small, wood shelf for cook books, porcelain or brass handles on cabinet doors to replace the manufacturers' originals, a lace tablecloth or an espresso machine.

(above)
This kitchen has been treated in café style, with a circular metal table and prettily covered chairs for sharing breakfast or coffee with a friend.

Efficiency Kitchen

This is suitable for a single person or a couple who work all day, eat out a good deal and don't want to spend too much time cooking. The kitchen should be minimal and basic, with a microwave oven for convenience. It can be a one-wall, and have an L-shaped or U-shaped layout. Surfaces should be easy to clean, for example, a Corian or laminated counter, a vinyl floor and smooth cabinet surfaces. One part of the counter can be left without cabinets to create a breakfast area with stools kept underneath. Work space should be as generous as possible to allow for labor-saving equipment, such as coffee makers, toasters, juicers and coffee grinders. There should be plenty of electrical outlets at counter height for these appliances and also for both a radio and a television.

Child-Proof Kitchen

It's not easy to make a kitchen child-proof. In a small kitchen, it's better to keep children out altogether with a safety gate. If children are going to be in the kitchen, try to see that there is enough space for them to have their own play area on the floor, where they will be safe. The floor itself should be of some sympathetic and warm material such as cork or linoleum. Put everything that is poisonous or potentially dangerous (for example, all cleaning products, knives and sharp objects, and all breakable items) out of reach. Fit safety catches on all the cabinet doors and make sure all electrical outlets are fixed at counter height, not at floor level, or fit plug guards. Remove all chairs, which can be climbed onto, and install stovetop guards so that children cannot reach pans and burners.

Family Kitchen

The traditional family kitchen is based on the idea of the old farmhouse kitchen being the center of the household: the dining room,

work-room and meeting place. The essence of this sort of kitchen is spaciousness, combined with practicality and natural materials. You can have a one-wall layout, an L-shaped layout or a peninsula kitchen. Traditionally, there would have been a wood-burning stove, and you can choose from a number of modernized versions of these, which will keep the room just as efficiently warm as several radiators. Suitable materials are quarry tiles or brick flooring, wood for the counters and furniture, porcelain for the sink, wood paneling or paint on the walls and ceramic tiles that can be used as a back splash behind the sink. Complementary furniture would be a big dresser for storing and displaying china, a large, wood table with Windsor chairs and wood base units. That's the feeling to aim for. Within this, there are many variations. You can choose simple, painted Shaker-style units or pine units with some decorative detailing finished with a matte varnish and tongue-and-groove paneled units painted white. The table can be varnished pine, scrubbed fir or oak refectory. Remember that the size of a refrigerator should be related to the number of people living in the house. It's never big enough! If you don't want an enormous refrigerator dominating the whole room, you might

(opposite)

A double-size stove and generous built-in cabinets make a good basis for a family kitchen.

(above)

This kitchen makes full use of the original brick fireplace and adopts a wholehearted traditional farmhouse look, with willow baskets and dried flowers hung from the ceiling and utensils on show and easy to reach.

be able to fit in two much smaller-sized ones instead into the space.

Don't overdo the country feel by introducing too much fancy decorative paneling to units. Traditionally, most country kitchens were plain and utilitarian. But don't feel obliged to get a traditional sink if what you would really like is one made of Corian, provided it has the right sort of shape. Add hooks to the beams for dried flowers, strings of onions, useful baskets or the odd ham. If the room is used for homework, make sure there's shelf space for notebooks, pens and other necessary paraphernalia. You could put up a bulletin board for lists, appointments, reminders and bills to be paid. Ideally, such a kitchen would have a utility room leading off it and a walk-in pantry. If there is a garden, the door leading to it can be a basic plank or a Dutch door, which opens in two halves. Make sure you have an enormous doormat and, if possible, a porch where people can leave their wet coat, muddy boots, etc.

Cottage Kitchen

This is a smaller version of the family kitchen. The same materials and layout apply, but the look is rather more basic. The handmade look is very appropriate to this sort of kitchen, and individual wall cabinets and base units could be put together from secondhand furniture, although they should all be given a unity by following the same style and being given a matching finish, basically of paint or varnish. If the cottage is a vacation home, pine would be acceptable, although it often looks rather raw in its natural state and its appearance can be improved when painted. In smaller rooms you might not have space for a large table, but a small, square or oblong one could probably be fitted under a window.

Budget Kitchen Ideas

• *Make a list of the appliances and fixtures you will need now and in the future, and note any cheaper alternatives in case you overspend your budget.*

- Select kitchen units from three or more brochures so that you have a chance to choose the cheapest from similar designs. Check that hardwares, such as hinges and drawer runners, are sturdy and of good quality.

- Remember to allow for countertops, which are not always included in the price of the base units.

- Take time to shop around. Some cheaply made standard units are expensive to buy, without looking any better than cheaper ones.

- Allow for the installation of the units in your budget, and for electrical and plumbing alterations. Use reputable people for this work, particularly from the safety point of view. A local builder should be able to give you an estimate for carpentry, plumbing and electrical work based on a sketch, if you are not getting a custom kitchen supplier to do the scheme.

- Include the cost of any decoration, tiling, floor coverings and light fixtures.

- If you employ a designer or architect, allow 10 – 15 percent on top of the total cost to cover his or her fees.

- Do the work in stages. Start with the essentials and fit in other items when you can afford them. Leave spaces under the counters for appliances you plan to buy, but can't yet afford.

- Tile seconds are often excellent buys, but if you miscalculate the quantity you might find there are none left to finish the job, so make sure you order enough (and don't rely on the supplier to do the calculations for you). When you know the tile size, count how many tiles are needed to fill a horizontal row from wall to wall, and how many rows are needed to tile the wall to the desired height. Order extra tiles to allow for breakage when cutting and count part tiles as whole ones for estimating purposes. If you are creating a definite pattern, with tiles of different colors and designs, do a scale drawing so that you can count how many tiles of each color you need.

- Go for an "unfitted" style with, for example, secondhand cabinets and individual chests of drawers. For the sake of a unified look, choose things which will go together, for example, all pine or oak, or all pieces from the 1940s. Unfitted kitchens need more space: if your kitchen is small, a fitted style is essential, although if you are good at do-it-yourself projects, you could even create your own fitted kitchen by adapting individual pieces.

- Open shelves are not only cheaper, but sometimes better in a small kitchen, where they take up less space than cabinets. If cleverly designed, they can be used as the top half of a sideboard, and a floor cabinet can be placed beneath them to add to this impression. Remember that what you put on these shelves will get dusty, if they are not in constant use.

(above)
This is the dining room end of a workman-like kitchen. The garbage can, pots and pans are all proudly displayed against an Italianate sun-bleached, plaster wall.

(above)
The dining room half of this kitchen/dining room leads into the living room and the colors have been chosen to be inviting and exciting. The dining room sits conveniently between the kitchen and living room.

- *Give old units a fresh look by installing new doors, or by painting the old ones. Provided the basic frame is solid and sturdy, this can transform a kitchen very cheaply.*
- *Accept offers of old chairs or buy chairs in junk shops and flea markets. If they are sturdy, they can be revamped with cushions or paint. They don't have to match each other. Paint each chair in a different color for an individual look. Use transfer patterns for quick and easy decorations.*
- *Basic swivel faucets, if made by a reputable manufacturer, are just as good as more ornate versions and are much cheaper.*

Dining Rooms

A dining area must provide a pleasant setting for meals and must also be arranged so that food can be served quickly and conveniently. With the present interest in cooking and entertaining at home, a separate dining room has great appeal. However, it is important that it should be cook-friendly, as well as eater-friendly. Ideally, there will be a communication door between the dining room and the kitchen and possibly a pass-through as well. Pass-throughs need not look ugly and are invaluable. The shelf part should be wide and deep enough to hold plenty of dishes. It will look better and be more convenient if it has built-in cabinets fitted underneath. If you want to conceal the kitchen from the dining room, use sliding doors.

Comfortable seating is vital, as is a table placed at the right height for sitting. There should be enough room to fit your legs under the table, and chairs should have supple seats and give good back support. In small rooms, a round table will be easier for everyone to fit round than a rectangular one, and an expandable table will be the best solution. A long, narrow room may also require a long, narrow table.

If you have special occasion tableware, you can store it in narrow, glass-fronted cabinets or on a sideboard. Everyday china and glass is best kept in the kitchen, where you can put it away easily after washing up. If you don't have a sideboard, a chest of drawers or built-in cabinets will be invaluable for table linen, table decorations and other items special to the dining room. Make sure that such pieces of furniture don't take up so much space that people can't easily get around the table or pull out the chairs enough to sit comfortably. Dining rooms are often small in size, with little natural light. If this is the case, go for paler colors and mirrors to enhance the feeling of light.

Formal dining is ceremonious. The room should be used for dining and nothing else. It should be disciplined: no word processors, sewing machines or drawing boards lurking behind the scenes. Lining one wall with library shelves and well-ordered books can look in keeping, however. Polished wood surfaces, well-displayed china and glass, ornately decorated candlesticks, elegantly draped curtains and crisp linen all add to the formal atmosphere.

The table should be the center of attention. Formal dining does not necessarily mean a nineteenth-century overblown look with plush maroon curtains and elaborately carved chests. A Neo-Classical look will suit formal dining and so will a modern or minimalist look. It is important to choose a style and stick to it; otherwise the result will be unsettling and detract from the purpose of the room, which is to concentrate on the table, what's on it and who's sitting round it. Choose your colors carefully. A deep color that looks rich and opulent at night may look tawdry by day.

Lighting is particularly important for a feeling of well-being. You need to create a feeling of intimacy, but also to see what you're eating. Candles give a particularly enchanting and becoming light, but you will need brighter light at times. An adjustable light over the table is a good idea because you can raise it to illuminate the whole table, or lower

it to give a glow, making sure the bulb is not visible from any chair. Wall-mounted uplights can add pleasant illumination.

A sunroom is one of the most charming places to eat, with views of the garden and potted plants all giving a relaxed atmosphere. However, because there's so much glass, you will need to protect it from the sun in summer and from the cold in winter. Double-glazing is ideal, of course, but special sunroom blinds will help. In winter, curtains will insulate the room against drafts and expanses of cold glass, and will also keep the dark at bay and create a cozy atmosphere. Heating can be provided by narrow radiators running along the floor. Hanging oil-type lamps will be appropriate, with an adjustable overhead lamp above the table. In this sort of room, a lighter look will be best, with sunny-colored curtains decorated with floral prints or a chinoiserie look.

(above)
This narrow basement area is lightened in mood by placing the table next to the window and using lightweight metal furniture, which does not look bulky and also reflects the light.

Kitchen/Dining Room

(above)
A very attractive and stylish design makes this kitchen a pleasant room to eat in.

(opposite)
Narrow units, hanging storage and storage on casters can all be useful in a kitchen.

If there is no separate dining room, the eating area is often incorporated into the kitchen, and it is important that the transition from the cooking to the dining area should be smooth and easy to negotiate, and that dining can take place without the cooking process being overpoweringly obvious. You can achieve two quite different effects in a small room without drastically changing the style by subtly altering the decoration and choosing versatile lighting. Look for relatively unused areas in the home, if your kitchen is very small and you prefer to eat away from it. The living room is an obvious place, but a small recess in a hallway might be suitable for eating in. A folding, circular table or any small table that can be pushed into a corner when not in use—together with small, upright chairs that can line up against the wall or folding chairs that can be hung up when not in use—mean that you can eat quite comfortably in a relatively small space. If the room is used to feed a baby, it's better to have an easily cleaned floor, maybe of polished wood, linoleum or vinyl, than to have carpet.

In remodeled houses, the kitchen is often an extension of the house into the garden, often just a brick or concrete box, but sometimes a sunroom. The back of an extended room is liable to be fairly dark. If it has a flat roof, bubble lights, patio doors and glass bricks making up part of one wall, it will all help to bring more light into the space. A modern, low voltage standard or wall-mounted uplight will help considerably, reflecting light off the ceiling and creating an efficient and pleasant white light

Other Uses for the Kitchen

In the normal, small-sized kitchen, it's usually best not to try to fit in other activities. It is not really ideal even as a laundry room, although there may be nowhere else for the washing machine to go. However, even the smallest of kitchens can incorporate a small domestic

office space with a wall-mounted telephone, a bulletin board, a rudimentary filing system for bills, a jar for pens, paper clips and tape, and a stool to sit on. In a larger kitchen, with a big table and space for storage, the kitchen could make a satisfactory sewing room, but you will have to clear everything away for eating.

Budget Ideas

- *If you only occasionally have large dinner parties, put an old door on two sawhorses when you need a larger table, then cover it with a festive cloth.*
- *Folding chairs are cheaper than standard dining chairs and can be hung on the wall or put away in the garage or a closet, when not in use.*
- *Make a sideboard from a set of cheap pine shelves with a small pine cabinet fitted underneath. This can look good in a small dining or kitchen/dining room.*
- *If you have no room for a sideboard, fit shelves and a door under the stairs, where you can store plates, jams, salt and pepper.*
- *If you can't afford a handsome set of boxed cutlery, buy a cheap and cheerful set which hangs on its own stand. Handles are available in several colors and can match the scheme of your room.*
- *An old oak or pine table can be sanded or scraped with a piece of glass and, if necessary, bleached with a wood bleach.*

Design Checklist

- *Plan the space on graph paper, making sure there's enough room for all your needs. Don't underestimate the amount of space needed for a family, say, to eat in comfort.*
- *Check that doorways to nearby rooms and activity areas such as dining rooms, play rooms, laundry and delivery areas are conveniently placed.*
- *Make the most of views from windows, access to the garden and good daylight.*
- *Keep preparation, cooking and washing out of any circulation area.*
- *Make sure you can find useful places for radiators.*
- *Decide whether you want a fitted or freestanding kitchen (more space is needed for freestanding).*
- *Make use of the corners of a room by cutting directly across them, or using a corner cabinet that can incorporate a lazy Susan.*
- *Make sure there's enough clear counter space for food preparation (minimum 3 ft (900 mm) each to allow for preparation and dirty plates; 2 ft 6 in (760 mm) for washed dishes; 2 ft (600 mm) next to the oven and stovetop for serving).*
- *Determine a convenient working height for the main user of the kitchen.*
- *Don't forget to allow for waste disposal.*
- *Try to include storage space for tall or bulky items, such as the broom and vacuum cleaner.*
- *Make a list of all the equipment you want now and in the future, and allow for this in your design. If you can't afford everything at once, leave space for future purchases, filling in with temporary cabinets or shelves.*
- *Check that the stove is not in a drafty place (for example, under a window), where a breeze could easily blow out the gas flame.*
- *Provide a safe play space for children, preferably with a safety gate.*
- *Make sure there are plenty of electrical outlets at counter height.*
- *Arrange for efficient lighting over every work space and for eating.*
- *Plan for efficient ventilation.*

Children's Rooms

Lucky children have separate rooms for sleeping and playing (or escaping from each other), but most have to fit everything into one room that has to incorporate outlets for energy, concentration, visitors, quiet moments, drawing, reading, model making and so much more. The suggestions in this chapter apply to playrooms, bedrooms or combined rooms. In combined rooms, you will have to plan more carefully to make sure the necessary requirements for peaceful sleeping are provided, as well as those for play.

When planning for small babies, it is tempting to design a pretty, frilly room with a tiny crib and a specially designed diaper-changing table. This will look delightful to new parents for nine months and then, suddenly, it will be all wrong for the curious, crawling toddler.

Where children are concerned, planning ahead means looking ten years away and trying to imagine a small bundle in athletic clothes as an energetic youngster with a computer, footballs, tennis rackets and siblings, not to mention friends, that you will need to find room for.

Children should always be allowed a say in how their rooms should be. Little girls don't always necessarily want frilly lampshades and floral duvet covers and small boys may have strong ideas about how they would like their room to be. Since play is a child's way of learning and studying, there must be suitable space for as many activities as possible.

What's Required?

(previous page)
Children can really enjoy attic spaces when there is good light coming in from well-designed skylights and a warm, smooth floor for them to play on.

(above)
Don't be tempted to overfurnish a young child's room. This room has been decorated with nursery wallpaper, which can easily be changed later on for an older child; otherwise it relies on the crib, a hamper and a simple chair so that other suitable furniture can be added as necessary.

Children's needs change rapidly when they are young and growing up, so give the room a flexible plan. Even at the baby stage, the choice of floor and wall coverings, treatment of windows, heating sources, basic lighting and, of course, safety can be just as relevant for children as they grow older. Specifically "baby" colors and patterns can be kept to curtains, fabrics, the crib and other accessorizing items, which can be changed more easily and cheaply. If you design the room with a particular child in mind, you will get clues as to exactly what he or she will need.

Checklist for a New-born Baby

- *A crib or portable bed with its own stand.*
- *A surface for changing. (This can be a table or low chest with a padded mat or the parents' bed.)*
- *Storage for diapers and clothes. (This can be a small chest of drawers, blanket chest or small hamper.)*
- *Baby bath (this can be kept in the bathroom).*
- *Stroller (to be kept in the hall).*
- *Portable car seat (this will be in constant use in all the rooms in the house!)*
- *Soft toys or mobiles (in or near the cot or above it).*

These items do not require a special room to themselves and can be incorporated into the parents' room or around the house.

The Young Child's Room

A young child's room should contain some things which are small scale. One- or two-year-olds tend to feel lost in a room where everything is adult-sized. Choose a low bed and a set of small tables and chairs. Many children like to arrange their room so they can write and draw in the same conditions as when they are at play group or nursery school, with a small desk and places for pens and papers. Children should get into the habit of sitting down properly to write and draw from an early

age. It will help them to enjoy desk work and make homework less of a chore later on.

Young children should sit in chairs that are at the right height for them and at a table which is of related height. Even when they spend most of their time playing in an adult room, a living room or kitchen, for example, it is useful to have a small table and chairs for the children to play at and to have their meals. Sets of plastic tables and stacking chairs suitable for children are available quite cheaply. Although small tables and chairs are appreciated, don't try to scale down all the furniture. Low chests of drawers are irritating to use and don't hold enough. Even a baby has an inordinate amount of clothes and belongings. Changing tables are soon outgrown, then what do you do with them?

A playhouse will help to introduce the small-scale feeling, and later on, a dolls' house can provide extra small-scale for children, which makes them feel omnipotent, and this is something they don't often get a

chance to be. No matter how full of toys the room is, small children are unlikely to play there on their own for long. They will prefer to be with their mother or another grown-up.

Painting and drawing activities are very absorbing and help manual dexterity. They can keep children occupied for long periods, so it's worth providing good facilities for these. One completely white, washable wall, which children are allowed to draw and scribble on, will encourage creativity and can also discourage them from drawing on other surfaces. When it's completely covered with artwork, you can paint it again and let them start from scratch. Or you could fix a white, erasable marker board to the wall, or a piece of hardboard painted with blackboard paint.

If you keep a basket or a box on casters full of toys and blocks in the child's room, you can bring it into a safe area in the kitchen or living room with you so that the child can play near to you. At the end of the day, the toys and blocks can be piled back into their box and

(above)
Children like bright colors, and this cheerful red and yellow room would please little ones in particular.

(above)
Plenty of floor space is essential
for children's play. The matting
used in this room is good for
building blocks and setting
up train sets.

returned to the child's room. You will not then be inundated with a whole cabinetful of toys to tidy up.

Until they are about ten, children will play on the floor. So, for the early years, the floor is one of the most important assets of the room. Allow as much floor space as possible by making do with very little furniture and by storing most things on shelves or in cabinets fixed to the wall. The floor should be easily washable and warm. Cork, linoleum or a cheap carpet would all be suitable surfaces. Matting is good in many respects, but can be hard on bare knees. Carpet tiles can be replaced when they get damaged or dirty, but the color range is a bit muddy.

Windows for children to see out of are a much better choice than those that are too high. If they are on an upper floor, you can fix bars to the bottom half of the windows, so there's no fear of the child falling out. Build a window seat underneath, with storage below for toys or books. Children can spend hours

chatting to each other or playing with dolls on such a seat, enjoying the feeling of space provided by the view of the outside. If there's no window seat, the window is a good place to put a table for painting and playing. Later on this can become a desk used for homework. Windows are not the distraction many people suppose and often act as a refresher for the mind. When the child begins to spend more time sitting at a desk, make sure the chair is comfortable and supportive. A chair with a seat sloping very slightly forward helps to encourage a straight back. The feet should be placed squarely on the floor. Office-type swivel chairs are good for desk work and are available in many stores, and the height can be adjusted as the child grows.

If you are rewiring, install plenty of electrical outlets on each wall. Put them out of reach of young children and cover those not in use with socket guards. Even if you don't use them now, they will be invaluable as the children grow older.

Older Children

Many of the suggestions for younger children's rooms will still apply to a teenager's room. It should be a question of some rearranging and a few additions, rather than a complete remodel. More storage will be necessary as the child grows older and larger. Shelves can be added to existing systems and a deep shelf can be fitted into an upright and bracket system to become a desk. You will need to allow extra storage for collections, such as stamps, model cars, shells or dolls.

By the time your children become young teenagers, they are likely to have a great number of clothes and a personal computer of some kind. Plan the inside of the closet in the same way as you would tackle a military operation. Many children are unlikely to make use of this storage space in the general way of things, but when they do tidy up, they will have some hope of creating order, albeit for ever such a short while.

The work space should be large enough to house a computer and its peripherals, and a suitable area for any writing and reading that the child wants to do. Storage designed for easy reaching distance is essential for reference books and pens. Small shelves or cubby holes are invaluable for specific storage of disks, tapes and other miscellaneous objects.

Schoolchildren who have to share a room should have their own areas carefully demarcated so there's no cause for aggravation. Even in a small studying space, children will appreciate some privacy. Try to arrange the furniture so that one desk is screened off from the other, perhaps facing one another with a partition between, which can also act as another form of storage. Any divider is better than none. You could use a portable screen, a curtain or a bookcase. Make sure the divider is securely fixed so that it won't topple over. Give each child a separate light too, which will help to cut down arguments when one

person wants to sleep and the other doesn't.

Older teenagers probably won't want to be too near their parents. They feel they are growing up and want to test their independence. It is probably in the parents' interests too, to have the child's room a bit farther away from their own room, since there are likely to be visitors, late nights and loud music. This is a good time to build an addition or remodel an attic or a basement. A good remodel can be useful later on for putting up visitors or tenants. If remodeling is not possible and there is no extra room down the corridor, try sound-proofing the walls and door for everybody's peace of mind.

The older teenager's room now becomes more like a studio apartment. You can make the bed into a daybed, to be used as seating during the day, by removing the headboards and putting cushions on top of it. Include more hanging storage because clothes often become an obsession at this age.

You can extend the work surface yet more

(above)
A built-in shelving unit can be designed for a particular child to reflect his or her individual interests. This one has a useful small desk space.

- Carpets should be smooth and flat. Rugs should not be wrinkled and should not curl up at the corners.
- Rugs, matting and carpet, and cork or vinyl tiles should all be kept in good repair.
- Electrical outlets should be fitted flush to the wall, out of reach of young children and fitted with socket guards when not in use.
- Electric cords should not trail all over the floor or become twisted with use.
- Where young children are playing, lamps should be fixed onto the wall, not placed on the floor or a table.
- All electrical equipment should carry an official underwriters' laboratories label which shows that it has been checked and has passed certain safety regulations. If you are using foreign equipment, check that it is suitable for the voltage of the country in which you are living.
- Use a safety gate if the child's room is near the entrance to the stairs.
- Install a protective metal base or a grid or bars to the lower frames of upstairs windows at least.
- Fit windows with safety catches.
- Furniture should not have any sharp corners at child's head-height.
- Make sure bunk bed ladders are secure and that there's a safety rail to stop a child falling out of the top bunk.
- Ensure that large items of furniture and heavy heaters cannot be pulled over onto the child.
- Always choose a sturdy crib and playpen with no protruding parts that could cause cuts or bruises.
- Ideally, spaces between crib or playpen bars should be between $1 1/2 - 2$ in ($38 - 50$ mm). If the crib is drop-sided, there should always be an automatic locking device.
- Never put a child under four years old into a top bunk.

(above)
A personal crow's nest for an older child, this wood platform has sensible stairs with a fitted handrail leading up to it, a padded soft section around the bed and room for storage or seating underneath.

(opposite)
A large play space, lots of bright color and a smooth wood floor: what could be better for an enthusiastic child?

now for serious study and expanding hobbies. This is when all the electrical outlets you thoughtfully installed when the children were tiny will come into their own for the hair dryer, television, sound system, computer and all the other electrical gadgets that teenagers cannot do without.

From now on, the choice of decor should be entirely theirs. Be appreciative and sympathetic, if you want to be allowed in and to have a say. Black and red are popular colors at this age, but you can always paint or paper over the scheme later, when their tastes have moved on.

Safety Checklist

No home can be completely safe but there are some very obvious and easy things to do, which can make a child's room considerably safer.
- Don't use kerosene or oil burning heaters and make sure radiators and open fireplaces have guards.
- The floor should be nonslip.

Decoration

Function and decoration should be combined. Pretty curtains can be fun for a child's room, but for rambunctious children who are tempted to swing from anything that hangs, roller blinds may be a better bet and won't need cleaning so often. They are also less likely to dislodge small collected items, which may be stored on the window sill. Decoration should not be thought of as something tacked onto the room as an afterthought, but should be part of its integral design. If a child is given a pleasant room from an early age, he or she will learn to think about the room, enjoy it and have definite ideas for decorating it later on, which should be listened to. These ideas may not fit in with your own opinions, but then it is not your room. Painted walls are ideal because they can be repainted when the child wants a change of color or pattern. Use water-based paints, which do not smell too strongly and are quick-drying. Don't attempt to introduce nursery friezes and murals unless you are not bothered if they get scribbled over. If you really do mind, varnish the mural with a protective polyurethane matte varnish. Professional murals can be expensive, with the result that they become untouchable, but parents may enjoy painting a wall with characters or scenes from a child's favorite book. Some ideas and guidelines on basic techniques can be found on pages 111–112. The wall next to the child's bed would be best, perhaps, for this treatment, which can give the child something to focus on when going to sleep and waking up in the morning. An alternative to a mural is to stencil a simple motif (perhaps a star or animal, or a butterfly) onto the wall at regular intervals.

For children, walls are not simply surfaces for displaying pretty wallpapers or paint finishes, but a whole dimension with many decorative and practical uses. Whether you have a blackboard or not, they will use a wall to kick against, for bouncing balls off, and even for bouncing themselves off, so the

finish should be durable and easy to clean. You can provide a painting and display area by fixing hardboard onto the lower third of the wall. Nail a batten to the wall. Fix the top of the board to this and the bottom of the board to the baseboard. Apply two or three coats of special blackboard paint over a base coat of latex to give a good surface for chalk. A strip of pegboard or a long, narrow cork-board can run along one wall for pictures and letters. It is more fun for children if their pictures are pinned at eye-level, rather than higher up where only adults can enjoy them.

Floors

Very young children will use the floor to learn to crawl and walk, while preschool children will build on it, play with train sets, do large floor puzzles and many other activities, so it should be warm and easy to clean. The floor should also be smooth enough for block edifices to be built on it, train track to slot satisfactorily together, and so that cars and

trains with small wheels can run smoothly. A train track can be set up permanently on a lightweight board fixed to the ceiling by a pulley system, then wound up and down, when needed. You could use an old-fashioned clothes-dryer pulley for this. Some floorings have games printed on them, but in the long run, a plain surface is probably more satis-factory. You can also buy floor mats with games and streets painted on them, which can be folded up and put away when the child has had enough.

Pile carpet is warm and comfortable, but often too "lumpy" and not always easy to clean. Flat, woven carpet, such as a large Turkish kilim, can be satisfactory, but don't put loose rugs on top of wooden floors, because they may wrinkle, or children may trip over them while running about.

Woodblock and other wood floors are smooth and fairly warm; linoleum and cork are both suitable floor surfaces; and cushion vinyl, though not particularly warm, is soft,

(above)
This architect-designed basement interior has been cunningly divided into two so that the child has separate living and playing areas.

(above)
Plenty of storage is one of the
first priorities in designing a
child's room (for the parents'
sake as much as the children's).
This double bookcase-cabinet
could eventually have a third
section added on.

comfortable and smooth for children's rooms. Matting is another practical, warm alternative for flooring, and there's a wide choice available. Most matting has a backing that stops dust from escaping and also prevents the matting from creasing. Matting is easy to vacuum and to scrub clean, if necessary. Go for a smooth, rather than a ridged surface, because coarse matting can be very uncomfortable to kneel on. It can be stenciled with simple patterns or you can edge it with a decorative border.

In general, it's best to keep the decoration fairly simple so that the child has a chance to develop his or her own individual character.

Lighting

For both safety and health reasons, a child's room must be as well lit as any other room. There should be good overall or general light so that children can see their way about the room, but there should also be good light near the bed so that they can read and play easily,

and above any table so they can see to do their homework or hobbies. Young children should be allowed adequate light at night if they are afraid of the dark. A dimmer switch on the main light will provide comforting illumination at night, and there are many child-friendly lamps specially designed to give a gentle glow. These should be placed out of the way where small children cannot knock into them by accident.

Heating

A baby's room should always be kept at a constant temperature of between 65 and 70 degrees fahrenheit (18 and 21 degrees centigrade) throughout day and night. The best way to maintain the correct heat level is with a thermostatically controlled central heating system. If this is not available, a thermostatically controlled electric heater is a substitute, and a thermostat fitted onto an individual radiator can keep the baby's room at the correct temperature. Electric storage heaters can also work well, but you may have to boost the heat during the early evening, when the heater has used up its stored heat.

Furniture

BEDS AND BUNKS

Children move around a lot while sleeping and they use a wider sleeping area than most adults. In the first year they grow very fast, usually trebling their birth weight. Even their first bed has to be fairly sizable and an expensive cradle can be an unnecessary extravagance unless it is intended to be passed on to family and friends. A portable bed with a stand is often more convenient than a cradle. Check that the portable bed is suitable for use as a permanent one, and not just as a transporter. A drop-sided crib, which can later become a bed may be useful, but most children will be more comfortable in a full-size single bed when they have grown out of their crib. When buying a bed, a firm, flat one is best. Manufacturers tend to use inadequate plywood bases, which may warp with fluctuations in temperature in summer and winter. Slats that are too lightweight may snap if they are bounced upon.

Bunk beds are often the only solution where there are too few rooms and/or too many children. If you are installing two bunks, make sure both children can sit up in bed to read or play without knocking their heads on the bunk or ceiling above. Making the beds can be difficult, but if you use fitted bottom sheets and duvets, there's not really a problem. Hot air rises and the top bunk can get stuffy, so make sure there is adequate ventilation. Bunks are space-saving and fun to use, but they must be robust and have well-secured ladders and carefully fitted safety rails positioned at the right height to suit your child. Some bunks are designed to be taken apart and can be used as single beds. There are also cleverly designed modular units that include everything a child requires, which can be placed in

the middle of a room allowing a great deal of flexibility. These are exciting and intriguing for those children who love anything trendy or avant garde. Even when only one child is using it, a bunk can create extra space in a small room for a desk or play area below.

Storage

Children's belongings are so many and so diverse, from clothes and shoes to books, toys and sports equipment. All their belongings are different shapes and sizes, which means that unless some sort of storage order is devised, half of them will simply never be found or used again and many will get broken.

Storage can vary from a set of baskets, plastic stacking boxes or drawers under the bed to carefully ordered cabinets. Categorize the items and give each category a place of its own so that tiny plastic figures are in one place, blocks have their own bag or box, while writing or painting equipment and paper is stored in separate drawers or boxes. You can

(above)
Stacking storage is ideal for toys. These plastic boxes can be wheeled around or lifted off one another and help to categorize toys and keep them in some sensible order.

then have some control over what is in use at any one time, and the larger things will not conceal or break the smaller ones.

Many modular storage units exist in a variety of different styles, and these combine shelves, cabinets, drawers and surfaces for storing and displaying collections, and small objects. Such units often incorporate beds or bunks. Books are not easy to store, being in all sorts of sizes, and open bookshelves are probably best positioned where they can be seen and easily reached, at least once the child is old enough not to be tempted to tear them apart. Books of a large size are best stored flat. Provide one set of shelves for smaller books and a special, deeper shelf for larger ones. Remember that books are heavy objects and a freestanding book case can seem like an attractive climbing frame to a child and may topple over, causing him or her injury, so make sure you fix any cabinets and bookcases securely onto the wall to avoid causing accidents and injuries.

Quick Ideas for Storage

- *Under the bed: Drawers or boxes. If you are using boxes, fit them on casters.*
- *Internal cabinet organization: Wire basket systems are useful: fit built-in shelves, compartments and drawers designed for individual items, such as soft toys, shoes, hats and gloves.*
- *Stacking plastic boxes; stacking wood boxes; stacking drawers.*
- *A long set of shelves under a window sill for toys and books.*
- *Hooks under shelves to hang scarves, gloves-on-strings, etc.*
- *A wood peg rail mounted halfway up the wall is useful for hanging chairs (and perhaps large toys), in a Shaker-style fashion.*
- *Use biscuit and decorative tins to hold stamp collections and other small items.*
- *A fold-down panel designed to be concealed*

in a cabinet is useful for diaper-changing and can later on be used as a desk top for an older child.

Furniture Ideas

- *There are plenty of mix-and-match nursery furniture styles available, which make designing a child's room both interesting and satisfying. Beds, bunks, under-bed storage, shelves, cabinets, wardrobes, chests, stacking storage in various simple styles, materials and colors can all be chosen to create the ideal combination in a particular room.*
- *Modular systems are normally bought as kits to put together at home. They should be packed complete with screws, handles and instructions. Check that everything is there before you carry it all home and completely secure once you have assembled it.*
- *Remember that for a young child, floor space is playing space, and there's no point in filling the room with unnecessary furniture. Choose what's absolutely essential and keep as much of it off the floor as you possibly can.*
- *Furniture that claims to be dual purpose is often more trouble than it's worth. A bed that flips over to turn into a play table is one that you can't climb into without destroying whatever game you are playing, or breaking up the space ship that you are in the middle of building.*
- *If a crib has several adjustable levels for the mattress, you can raise it to its highest level when the baby is young, which is easier on your own back. The mattress may be lowered as the baby becomes more and more active.*
- *When buying a small table for a child or cutting a larger one down to size, a useful rule of thumb is that the table top should be positioned at elbow height for a child sitting upright with feet on the floor.*

Flexible Ideas

- Paint rather than paper rooms. It's cheaper and, when the time comes to change the room, it will be much cheaper the second time around too.

- Try to keep decoration simple in a young child's room, and add color and pattern with curtains and cushions. These are easily changed later, but if you choose brightly colored abstract, zoo or animal designs instead of ABCs and ducks, the children will not tire of them so easily as they grow older.

- Try your hand at a mural. A young child will enjoy a mural he or she has watched being created and perhaps you could even allow them to help you (under supervision, of course). Older children may even like to create their own design.

- A modular storage system can start with just a few shelves for baby items and then be added to, and adjusted as the child grows older.

- Use large floor cushions or bean bags filled with coated polystyrene granules instead of chairs. If you choose foam-filled cushions, check that they have a "fire-retardent" label on them.

- Paint your own blackboard on the wall. Blackboard paint is available in some decorating shops.

- A tiny baby can sleep in a cheap cradle or bassinet, which you can dress up with muslin. Make sure the muslin is firmly fixed and that the basket has a mattress no thicker than 6 in (150 mm) deep, with an approved filling and washable cover. Look for labels that indicate it conforms to official safety standards, and don't forget to remove the plastic wrapping.

- Once the child has grown out of a barred crib, move on to a bed or bunk – don't waste money on an intermediate child's bed. These can often be very tempting and charming, but a cheap bed can be given a separate head board or you can paint a head board on the wall behind it and, provided it has a firm base and a good

(above)
Children will enjoy fun storage items like this friendly caterpillar.

mattress, this can be the final bed that is necessary for the child before he or she leaves home.

- A good alternative solution to the first crib can be to buy a travel bed, which can also be used, of course, while traveling. Be careful in your choice. Some travel beds are much easier to use than others and much more sturdy. Once outgrown, the bed will take up very little space until the next baby needs it.

- Support a bed frame on an old chest of drawers at one end, with legs or battens mounted at the other to create a homemade bunk. Make sure there is a secure rail and that the steps or ladder leading up to it are firmly attached.

- Buy a basic cabinet or shelving system and install doors that can be easily removed later on if the children want to use the system in some other way.

Budget Ideas

- *Sand and seal an existing wood floor instead of covering it with expensive vinyl or carpet. Make sure there are no splinters or nails sticking out, and that you fill all the gaps between the boards by gluing down slivers of wood or, if they are not too wide, filling them with papier mâché.*

- *Keep baby furniture to an absolute minimum. For small children, this is both cheap and practical because they need floor space to crawl about and to learn to get their balance when they take their first steps and begin walking.*

- *Secondhand furniture can be totally transformed with a lick of paint and can even be cut down to size, if necessary. You can paint flowers, country scenes, cars and astronauts. Get your inspiration from children's books or magazines, or you can use stencil designs. There are many stenciling kits available, which make decorating furniture quite a quick and easy process, and there*

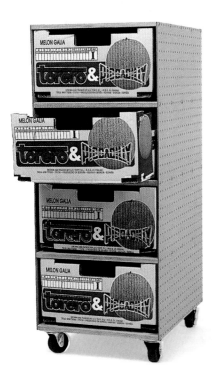

are a variety of books giving inspiration and practical advice for complete beginners. You could also have some fun getting the child to help you decorate furniture with decoupage or transfers.

- You can make a cheap desk by putting a low chest of drawers on either side of a radiator with a flat door or piece of shelving running across. This has the advantage of allowing the heat to come under the table into the room, and it will warm the legs of the child. A thermostat fitted on the radiator will prevent it from becoming so hot as to burn the child's legs, if the work surface is very narrow.
- A piece of hardboard can often be used as a safety gate (provided it is really not removable by the child). Sand and paint pictures onto it to make it more welcoming and user-friendly.
- Sleeping bags can be used instead of duvets if you have a number of young visitors staying.

Design Checklist

- *Place to sleep comfortably and quietly – don't forget the bedside light.*
- *Smooth, yet warm floor covering so that the child can play comfortably on the floor.*
- *Wall space to paint and draw – this can be a whole wall or a board fixed onto it.*
- *Storage for small toys – these are best kept in separate boxes.*
- *Storage for large toys – drawers under the bed may be the answer to this.*
- *Storage for dolls and soft toys – preferably where they can be on show and also where they can be easily reached.*
- *Storage for blocks and other building systems – these can be kept separately or together, depending on their type.*
- *Storage for books – remember that some books are too big to stand upright.*
- *Small table and chairs – cheap, plastic ones will please children just as much as wood ones.*
- *Heavy furniture safely secured to prevent children from pulling it over by accident.*
- *Safe fireplaces with guards – make sure the guard is tall enough so that the child is unable to reach over it.*
- *Good lighting and ventilation – make sure the window opens from the top.*
- *Lighting for bed and desk – this must be secure and preferably wallmounted.*
- *Check Safety Checklist (page 104).*

Bedrooms & Bathrooms

The idea of keeping a room separate for sleeping is a fairly new concept. In the Middle Ages, the whole household slept in the great hall, which was the only warm place. Tapestry screens would be erected to give the lord and lady some privacy. Even when separate bedrooms were introduced in the seventeenth century, wealthy and important people would expect to receive visitors in their bedchambers, and such rooms often had a "secret" entrance/exit by which the occupant could escape from unwelcome visitors. The bed was in an alcove or curtained off to separate it from the rest of the room, and was furnished with comfortably upholstered chairs, small tables and desks. Rooms have only been set aside purely for use as bedrooms in the nineteenth and twentieth centuries.

Bathrooms are an even more recent invention. Affluent Victorians did, indeed, install well appointed bathrooms in their homes, but right up until the 1950s many homes did not have separate bathing or even toilet facilities within the house, and when they were installed, they were, often as not, very small, very cold and very uncomfortable. Happily, today's bathrooms have a more honorable status and can be one of the home's greatest luxuries.

Bedrooms

(previous page)
A lovely, sunny bedroom has been clothed in bright colors that are reminiscent of sea, sky and sand.

(above)
A simple and restrained design in white, with a coronet and mosquito net above the bed, makes a charmingly peaceful room.

PRIORITIES

The main requirements for a bedroom are a comfortable bed, which is convenient to get in and out of, good ventilation and ample storage for clothes. Once these things are established, you can then impose the style you want onto them, whether it's romantic, peaceful, indolent or exotic. If you want to use the bedroom just for sleeping and dressing, don't pick the best room in the house. Any thoughtfully arranged, small room will do for these purposes. However, if you are going to use the room as a quiet retreat to read, sew or write letters, choose a room with good, natural light and enough space for a comfortable easy chair and a small table. A single person might choose the smallest room available and create a "nest" for sleeping, which could be curtained off so that it is snug, warm, compact and secure. If you want to include a sink or shower, choose a room near the kitchen or bathroom, where the plumbing is nearby and it won't be necessary to install a long extra run of expensive pipe.

A room large enough to divide can be turned into a dual purpose sleep-cum-workroom but it is important to make the division solid so that the two uses can be separated from each other. A busy work space is not always conducive to sleep.

The Bed

A bed should be easy to climb in and out of, and simply made from either side. If the bed is a double one, there should be enough space between it and the wall. It should not be positioned so that it is far too close to closets or drawers so that it is difficult to open them.

Shelves or bedside tables should be large enough to hold an alarm clock–radio, reading lamps (if they are not fixed to the wall), magazines and books, a pencil and paper, a glass of water or anything else you might need to reach during the night.

Mirrors should be placed so that you can stand back and get a complete picture of your appearance from top to toe. The light should fall on you and not be reflected in the mirror. There should be double electrical outlets, both by the bed and by the dressing table, adequate general lighting and light to see inside the closet. An interior closet light that switches on when you open the door is a good idea.

Storage

Most of us have far more clothes than we know what to do with and difficulty in finding space for them all. This is where disciplined planning can really make the difference between chaos and control. One closet should be enough for most needs, but a whole wall of storage can be built for those with a bigger collection of clothing.

Divide the closet up into separate compartments, allowing space for the sort of garments that you wear. For example, you will need hanging storage for shirts and blouses, coats and jackets, dresses, suits, pants and skirts. A high-level hanging closet pole for short items, such as shirts, will leave room for another pole below it, or you can put shelves underneath for folded items, socks and belts. You may then need only a very short closet pole for coats and dresses. A narrow shelf at the top of the closet could hold hats and small pieces of luggage.

An efficient way of dealing with the shelf space is to install metal runners for wire drawer-baskets of various depths. This form of storage makes it easy to identify and quickly take out anything you want, and uses the available space efficiently. If you are creating your own customized space, then use an adjustable upright and bracket shelving system into which you can fit wire drawers. There are several modular systems available on the market in kit form, which you can put together at home. Fit a set of pockets or a rack for shoes on the inside wall of the closet: it

(above)
A divan can be given a sense of style with a simple fabric canopy.

(above)
An antique wardrobe can be the perfect foil for a traditional bedroom. This one is mirrored, which helps to bring light into a rather dark section of the room.

does help to have as many objects off the floor as possible. Keep boots upside down over long wood pegs set at an angle. Clothes not wanted for a season can be stored in a blanket chest or an old trunk. You can paint a trunk to give it new life or cover it with an attractive fabric. Don't forget to wash or clean clothes before putting them into long-term storage, and treat them with a moth-proofing product.

Alternative Storage Possibilities

- *A surprising number of garments can be hung on a traditional bentwood hat stand, from coats to dresses, blouses, scarves and a collection of hats.*
- *Coat hangers should be hung on a pole running parallel to the wall about 12 in (30 cm) in from both sides of the closet, so that they hang at right angles.*
- *If your closet is too narrow, you can run the closet pole from back to front, rather than from side to side, which will give the hang-ers more room and prevent clothes from being crushed.*
- *Attic bedrooms have great storage potential. You can screen off the end of the room to give walk-in closet space, or you can build shelves under the lower part of the roof for shoes and boxes.*
- *Hooks can be screwed into sloping beams to take coat hangers.*
- *Old-fashioned chests of drawers can be charming in a traditional home, but in a modern one, you may well prefer to build wall-length storage at dressing-table height with drawers and cabinets below.*

Some Common Problems

IS THE ROOM TOO SMALL FOR STORAGE?
Alas, many bedrooms lack not only built-in cabinet space, but even the necessary alcoves to put cabinets into satisfactorily. Built-in cabinets may be more space-saving than freestanding wardrobes, but this is not always the case. An attractive, smaller wardrobe may

be a less dominant solution in a small bedroom. If the room has an alcove (or even two alcoves on either side of a chimney), you might abandon the idea of enclosed storage, and have hanging poles and shelves fitted instead. If this effect looks too stark, a Roman blind running from floor to ceiling will make an elegant screen and protect the clothes from the dust.

In a narrow room, it may be difficult to open cabinet doors because they knock into the bed. It may help to rehang them so that they open from the opposite side, or to replace them with half-width doors, hinged in the middle. Such doors, in either plain or louvered styles, are available in many stores and are easily installed. Alternatively, you could use Roman or roller blinds.

Many second bedrooms, particularly those in remodeled houses or houses designed for first-time buyers are tiny, boxlike cabinets rather than real bedrooms, and making them pleasant and convenient can be challenging. There will often be room for just a single bed. In that case, it is best to choose a bed that has drawers fitted underneath it. Hanging storage can be housed somewhere else in the home, or it might be provided by a bentwood hat rack placed in a corner of the room. It is best to leave a room of this size as simply furnished as possible and not to try to cram extra uses into it. If the length of the bed runs along one wall, you could make the bed more interesting by creating a narrow canopy along its length using special holders fixed to the wall. Fold the material in half lengthwise. Take the central fold and pull it through the central holder to make a sort of rosette, then stretch out one length of fabric to one side and pull it through the side holder so that it drapes gracefully, leaving a piece hanging. Do the same at the other side. This creates the effect of a narrow canopy, and you can give the most boring bed a stylish look. It is a simple and cheap way to alter the look of the room, giving

it a little depth and dignity, without taking up any room space.

Although the recommended minimum width for a single bed is 3 ft (91 cm), house guests, who will not be using it for long, can sleep perfectly comfortably on a narrower bed, with a width of, say 2 ft 6 in (76 cm). This solution will take up less space and make the room seem larger. There are many modular systems available on the market which can provide both bedding and storage to make best use of the space.

Noise at Night

Traffic noise can be a problem in many homes, where the main bedroom often looks out onto the street. For light sleepers, it would be worth having double-glazing installed, with a wide enough gap to keep much of the noise out of the room. If low-flying aircraft make an unacceptable noise or you live near a factory, you should consider special double-glazing.

(above)
This modern version of a classic American Colonial four-poster bed can be used simply, with crisply starched, cotton sheets, a white lampshade and a handsome rug on the floor.

Awkwardly-Shaped Rooms

The best rooms in the house are usually allocated to the living room, dining room and kitchen, so the unusually shaped ones often end up as bedrooms. Awkward corners can be fitted with tailor-made storage units. A wide, triangular window seat can be built under two corner windows — the sort of windows often found in modern buildings, where little wall space is left for curtains or furniture. You could build drawers into the space underneath the window, or it would be a good place for a radiator. The wide top can act as seating, as well as a place for a vase of flowers.

In a long, narrow room, a bed built across and against the window wall will make the room seem better proportioned. If the bed is raised 3 ft (91 cm) or so, it will allow for storage space underneath and give the occupant a good view out of the window. A step or a small ladder will be needed to get in and out of the bed, and this should be fixed securely in place.

Very Tall Rooms

Build a raised section to make use of the height of the room. If you intend to build an elaborate structure, seek architectural advice. Don't make it too high if the room is very narrow (often the case in remodeled homes where rooms have been divided), and make sure you can stand up and sit comfortably in it. The easiest way to make the most of the height in a small bedroom is to install a simple platform for the bed. A 4 ft (1.2 meter) platform could incorporate spacious drawers or storage underneath it. Taller and larger platforms can have more elaborate storage beneath them, with drawers in the steps leading up to them and a balustrade, if necessary.

A comparatively narrow platform positioned over the entrance door to the room can provide additional sleeping or storage space. It may be curtained off for neatness or have a

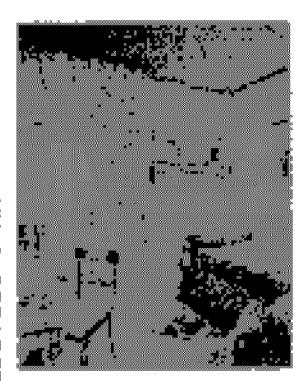

balustrade built round it for purposes of safety. You could create a fabric "tent" over the bed and turn it into a cozy, enclosed area. (Tenting was extremely fashionable in the seventeenth century, no doubt because it kept out drafts.) Make sure any ladder or other means of reaching the platform that you use is sturdy and safely secured.

Very Large Rooms

For those used to thinking small, a very large room can be a daunting prospect. It can be as difficult to deal with a large room as a small one. Clusters of furniture are more pleasant to live with than odd pieces arranged around the room. Try putting the bed in the middle of the room, surrounded by low cabinets. Screens, plants and low storage-seating can help to divide the room off comfortably. You could box in the whole of one end of the room with paneling, leaving a space for a canopied bed in the center. Alternatively, you could use a grand four-poster bed to make a focal point.

(above)
A luxurious town house bedroom in an alcove off the main living room, with rich drapes and a fringed lampshade.

(opposite)
This splendid brass bedstead is set off fabulously by an antique tapestry.

Mirrors

(above)
A classic Victorian bedroom has an elegant brass bed, a comfortable upholstered chair, a cloth-covered table and an old tapestry with a portrait hung over it in time-honored fashion.

Every bedroom should have a full-length mirror. A cheval glass can be moved around and adjusted, and will look elegant in a spacious bedroom, but would be a waste of valuable space in a small room. You can mirror the fronts of plain, built-in cabinets, which will help to give a feeling of space. More simply, you can fix a small mirror to the inside of a closet door, if it doesn't have one already.

Decorating

People often tend to play safe when choosing decorations for the bedroom or go for a very overblown, floral look. However, pale, coordinating fabrics and carpet and standard built-in wardrobes positioned along a whole wall can be as characterless as a hotel bedroom, and there are so many interesting ways of tackling this, the most personal of rooms. Study the range of interesting decorating and design options that follow.

Country House

This style has gradually evolved over several centuries and relies on elegance, spaciousness and an awareness of the countryside and the seasons.

English Country House: The English look is largely achieved by bringing the garden indoors, with floral chintzes patterned in anything from dainty sprigs of wild bluebells and forget-me-nots to enormous cabbage roses. Curtains, sheets and loose chair covers will coordinate in this indoor bower, which can be a model of crispness or have a slightly faded or overblown look.

The bed is placed fairly high off the ground and may be a brass bed, or a simple four-poster or half canopy. The look can be complemented by the popular coronet-style hanging over the head of the bed and is not difficult to make (**see Textiles, page 263**). Flooring can be wood with Aubusson-style rugs, or carpets, or fitted carpet in a pale color. A freestanding, stripped pine wardrobe suits the look best, although you could install really simple, unadorned built-in closets and paint them white, if you need more storage space. Find brass or ceramic handles for the doors. The dressing table can be kidney shaped or oblong and should be covered in chintz. Chests of drawers work well in oak or pine woods. Find an old-fashioned, gilt-framed mirror to position over the fireplace and a couple of ceramic dogs or a shepherd and shepherdess to stand on top of the mantelpiece. Bedside tables are round and covered in chintz tablecloths, on which stand ceramic lamps with pleated or gathered fabric lampshades.

The walls should be covered in a small, floral pattern or a floral with narrow stripes, or a chinoiserie paper. If you have paneled doors, you could fill in the panels with a similar chinoiserie trompe l'oeil. Woodwork would be white. Find room for a small upholstered chair or a neat two-seater sofa.

The American Colonial version of this is more disciplined and more deliberately planned. Several different floral patterns may be used, unified by one predominating color or a plain-colored lining picking out the main color, and festoons held in place by wide ribbons. There will be more valances and frills, all crisply laundered and well cared for. Go for strong colors, such as dark green and bright red, usually on a white ground. Suitably styled pictures would be family portraits, flower paintings, fine watercolors and traditional embroidered samplers.

French Country Look: This is more restrained than English country house, being simple, uncluttered and restful, with plain painted walls and lace curtains for the windows. Finish the walls with a decorative border around the ceiling, doors and windows. Most French country houses would have exposed beams. If there are no beams, you can put up fake ones that have been purchased from an architectural salvage store, or use wood from a local lumberyard and stain it. An iron bedstead or a heavy wood one would have crisp white sheets and a white, crocheted cotton bedspread. Tall armoires, carved and paneled, and wood chests and an upright chair would make up the furniture. The floor would be polished floorboards with a Persian or Aubusson carpet. Lighting would be minimal, with a pull switch by the bed to turn on an overhead lamp with a glass shade and metal wall sconces with candle bulbs fitted inside them.

Farmhouse or Cottage: This look is simple, if not spartan, with a wood or brass bedstead and simple, floral curtains. These could be made of muslin or a pretty cotton print with a small overall motif, and hung from a narrow valance. Furniture is freestanding, wood, natural or stained, solid, no-nonsense and very well made. The floor can be pine boards, sanded and sealed, or stained and sealed, then softened by rag rugs or kilims. An old-fashioned washstand will act as a dressing

(above)
This modern cottage look is created with a simple color scheme using white to hold it together.

samplers would decorate the walls. The curtains would be simply gathered on a rod, reaching to just below the window; you could choose whether to have a small valance or frill above them, or to leave them unadorned. Plain or painted floor boards would be softened with rag or tufted rugs.

Mediterranean: The bedroom is small, stark and bare. Painted walls will be pure white, or possibly a deep sky blue; the floors will be made of stone, ceramic tiles or wood, with a small, woven rug by the bed; the bedis made from simple wood or iron with a bright, woven wool bedcover. There will be a minimum of cabinets and a few iron hooks on the wall. The windows will have shutters, rather than curtains. A tiny washstand under the window can hold a geranium in a pot.

Town House Style: Town house bedrooms disregard the outside world, creating an affluent and sophisticated atmosphere as a calm and sometimes somber escape from a fast pace of life.

Biedermeier is often a good choice for a town bedroom. The attractive, highly polished Biedermeier bed with its lyre-shaped sides, known as the sleigh bed or lit en bateau, is the center of attraction, and it can be used as a good-looking sofa during the day, making the room more versatile. The room could appropriately double as a well-appointed library, with built-in bookcases and a round writing table. The design of the room should be left as uncomplicated as possible. Use plain paint in strong colors on the walls, or a restrained stripe. Balloon shades look good, if they are not too extravagant. The polished wood floor will be complemented by Persian rugs. Appropriate furniture is freestanding, highly practical, and simple but sculptural.

A Neo-Classical style is also a suitable choice for the town house bedroom, provided it is kept dignified. The hallmarks are grandeur, formality and elegance. Strong, vertical lines will make the room look taller.

table and can be modernized with a plumbed-in sink and heated towel rack. A small, wood cabinet acts as a bedside table, with a small ceramic lamp with a parchment shade for reading in bed. (It's more practical today to have an adjustable lamp, but choose the simplest style you can find.) The rest of the room would be lit from simple wall lamps and an overhead light with a frilled shade; the room shouldn't be over-lit; rather, try to create pools of light and dark. A quilted or patchwork spread covers the bed, and the sheets would be floral or white cotton. A small fireplace can be filled with a huge container of dried flowers. Victorian cast-iron radiators would look at home here.

New England Style: This will be similarly sparse, with tongue-and-groove paneling or wainscoting painted a different color from the plain, painted walls above. Freestanding furniture might have small flower motifs painted on it. A wood or cast-iron bed would be covered in a patchwork quilt. Framed

Make the most of plaster moldings by painting them white, or add a mock frieze and Corinthian pilasters highlighted in white. A four-poster bed is the most appropriate choice, canopied and draped in heavy silk, fringed and corded, then held with tasseled tie-backs. Avoid too much pattern and concentrate on color, although you could use a decorative paint finish on the walls and doors. Built-in storage can have the door panels finished in a fine fabric to match the curtains. Gilt mirrors will reflect candelabra and wall sconces. Gilt-framed pictures and neat, upright chairs, upholstered in tapestry or silk, will all emphasize the look. So will a large carpet with a wide border.

Victorian-Style Bedroom: This masculine-room should have an imposing mahogany wardrobe with mirrored doors, striped wallpaper, a heavy, important-looking wood or brass bed, dark fabrics and a fitted carpet or a large square carpet showing dark-stained floorboards at its edges. Curtains should be heavy wool or velvet, and a desklike dressing table would hold a silver brush set. Install brass wall lights on either side of the bed and brass wall sconces.

Traditional Japanese Bedroom: This has a cotton-filled futon mattress unrolled onto the floor for sleeping. A futon with a wood, slat base is probably more suited to Western lifestyles and can be used as seating during the day. If the bed is low, it will look best if all the furniture is placed low. Low cabinets should be arranged around walls; a screen will conceal clothes storage. Similar simplicity could be achieved by positioning a divan in the center of the room. Everything should be deliberate, nothing unnecessary or accidental. Matting makes a suitable floor finish covering, echoing the Japanese tatami mats. Colors are disciplined: gray with touches of red, or red and black.

Design Checklist: Bedroom

- *Is the bed where you can reach all sides easily for making it?*
- *Is there a bedside table and reading lamp for each occupant of the bed?*
- *Is there enough organized storage to keep all your clothes and accessories?*
- *Is there enough organized storage for other items including jewelery?*
- *Is the interior of the closet well lit?*
- *Is there sufficient lighting for somebody looking in the mirror?*
- *Is there a full-length mirror?*
- *Is there room to open the closet doors and chests of drawers fully?*
- *Is there a comfortable chair and other chairs for sitting or putting clothes on?*
- *If there are washing facilities, are the surroundings waterproof?*
- *Is there a shelf near the sink?*
- *Is there a heated towel stand?*
- *Is the bed low enough for an elderly person to climb in and out of it easily?*
- *If the room is not carpeted, is there a warm rug to put your feet on?*
- *If the room is very small, are there drawers or boxes on casters under the bed for storage, or space at the top of the closet?*
- *If the room is for a student, have you allowed enough work and shelf space?*
- *If the room is dual-purpose (i.e., also a workroom), have you enough room for a shelving unit/room divider? If not, a portable screen can provide some privacy instead.*

Bathrooms

The main properties of a welcoming bathroom are enough space to use all the facilities comfortably: warmth, ventilation and hygienic surfaces, with no cracks to harbor mildew. In large bathrooms, these qualities are quite easily provided, but most bathrooms are small, and these do present a design challenge. They must be functional, while still managing to combine comfort and a sense of luxury.

Planning

When planning, remember that there must be enough space surrounding bathroom fixtures to enable you to use them comfortably. It is better to do without an extra shower or a bidet, than to try to squeeze them into too small a space. You will find that it is very helpful to make a scale drawing of the bathroom (see page 27 for details of this) so that you can work out where the fixtures should go, and whether there is enough room to use them conveniently.

How many people are going to want to use the room and what facilities do they require? If it's a very small room, you might consider doing without a bathtub and installing a shower instead. This would leave room for a toilet, and possibly a bidet and a large sink. If you want to change the position of any fixtures, you can run the pipes under the floor to emerge in their new position, provided you make sure there is an adequate drop to make sure the water flows easily. However, this will be expensive and inconvenient while the work lasts. Built-in bathrooms can be very satisfactory solutions. Vertical pipes can often be concealed at the back of built-in cabinets, and horizontal pipes can be boxed in to form seating, if they are positioned at low level, or you could conceal them as a shelf, if they are at waist height. The drains for the bathtub, shower, toilet, bidet and sink should be grouped fairly close together to make planning and building units much easier. Incorporate a built-in laundry hamper (if the

bathtub doesn't take up the whole length of a wall, there is often room for this at one end), plenty of shelf space, a lockable medicine cabinet (rather larger than the minute cabinets available in major stores), a mirror and a bathroom stool or other seat.

The Bath

If several people are going to use a large bathroom, you could install two sinks and a separate shower, or even indulge in a double bathtub. You might even like to add an upholstered armchair by the window. Do this only if the ventilation is good; otherwise the upholstery will become mildewed.

For the right price, you can get really exotic bathtubs: two-person tubs, hexagonal, triangular, circular and sunken tubs, and, of course, massage baths, whirlpool systems and steam baths. You can get modern, sleek baths and also Victorian roll-top baths. Make sure your chosen bathtub will fit through the door and up the stairs before committing

yourself. There are bathtubs in many colors, but the most appealing color is still white as it allows you more freedom with your color scheme. Allow 27 1/2 in (70 cm) floor space by the bathtub, so that you can climb in and out with ease. If the space is very narrow, place the faucets against the outside wall of the room, or install them as separate fixtures into a side wall and step into the bath from the end, rather than the longer side.

Bathtubs are available in many shapes and sizes: there are small, deep baths for sitting, rather than lying in, and many corner bath designs, which take up much less space than standard bathtubs. A sunken tub is the ultimate luxury, giving a heightened feeling of relaxation. The requirements for fitting such bathtubs are not easily met, however, so get professional advice.

Most bathtubs are usually made in one of four different types of materials:
Enameled Cast-iron: This is the traditional material for bathtubs and it is really the most

(above)
The epitome of the modern bathroom: Philippe Starck's monumental suite gives bathing a forgotten long-splendor.

hard wearing and good looking, but it is also very expensive. Heavy impact can cause chipping. Because cast-iron is so thick, it tends to cool the water quickly. You can solve this problem by installing a long, narrow radiator running the full length of the bath, behind a panel along the front. Leave a gap at the top and bottom of the panel to allow the radiator to heat the room as well. The panel can be held in place by invisible, magnetic catches.

Enameled Steel: Looks like enameled cast-iron and is strong and rigid, but less expensive, lighter in weight and easier to install. There are various qualities.

Acrylic: The cheapest material for bathtubs on the market and light enough for one person to carry. These bathtubs are not as rigid as other types and they will scratch. (Scratches can be removed with metal polish.)

Fiberglass-Reinforced Plastic: usually made from cast-acrylic sheet reinforced with fiberglass and polyester resin. This versatile material can be molded to almost any shape and offers a wide range of finishes, including gold, pearl and sparkly effects. Most specialized bathtubs (for example, hip baths, double baths and corner baths) are made of FRP. Molded seats and back rests can be incorporated in this material.

The Shower

A shower takes up less space than a bathtub, uses considerably less hot water (although a massaging showerhead won't save you as much water as you think) and is cheaper to use and to install. You can install a shower instead of or as well as a tub, or it can be incorporated with the tub. Shower stalls can be built in, or showers can be bought complete from a plumbing supplier. The controls should be near the entrance to the stall, so that the water pressure and temperature can be preset and controlled from outside. You can get a shower stall as small as 30 in (75 x 75 mm), which would be better

than nothing at all, but there are many more generous sizes than that. Try to find the largest shower pan possible, or the shower will feel cramped. A deep enough pan, fitted with an overflow, can be used to bathe small children. A seat is a good addition and the shower head should be adjustable so that it can be directed over the seat. A separate shower room should be completely waterproof and have a floor that slopes onto a central, unplugged outlet. The entrance must be protected by a waterproofed lintel or have steps leading down.

The Sink

Sinks can be made of traditional vitreous china or acrylic, reconstituted stone, stainless steel or Corian. A sink may be placed on a pedestal, set into the wall or hung on the wall. If the wall is not sound, use the pedestal type, but the best arrangement is to have a basin built into a vanity unit or counter that conceals the plumbing, makes splashes easy to wipe clean and gives a surface for bottles, jars and tubes. Choose a basin in a simple shape with recesses for soap, which will be easy to clean. Select a fixture that enables you to put the faucets where you want them (on the wall or in the basin). A wall-hung sink leaves the floor space free, making it invaluable in a tiny room.

The Toilet and Bidet

A toilet takes up more space than is often supposed. Toilets are usually only made in vitreous china, which comes in colors to match other bathroom fixtures. They vary in height, so make sure you choose one that is comfortable to sit on and not too low for men to use tidily. There are two types of flushing mechanisms: the syphonic, which is quiet and has a positive flush, or the wash-down, which is slimmer and cheaper. A narrow tank can be enclosed in to give a smoother look and this provides a storage shelf. Choose one with a push-lever. However, do make sure you can get at the tank easily.

Many bathrooms have no room for a bidet, which takes up the same sort of space as a toilet. Like toilets, bidets are made of vitreous china. Bidet plumbing is subject to strict regulations, and there must be separate hot and cold water supply pipes. Drainage must be directed into a vented soil-pipe.

Faucets

Don't be tempted by the first faucets you see. There are faucets to suit every style: from sleek, primary-colored modern faucets, to single-lever faucets and Victorian-style, cross-top faucets. They can vary enormously in price and well-designed chrome fixtures can look much better than over-ornate, gold ones. Some bathroom fixtures will have faucets designed to match them: hexagonal sinks can have hexagonal faucet handles, for example. However, before you commit yourself to a style, make sure that the faucets are easy

to operate. Cross-top taps are probably the easiest to grip, whereas lever faucets don't need gripping; they can just be pushed. Acrylic and stainless steel knobs are quite difficult to operate, particularly for people with weak hands. Don't be tempted to buy reconditioned antique faucets. These often look marvelous, but will not work satisfactorily for long. There is almost always something wrong with them. If the edge of the bathtub or sink is quite near to the wall, the taps can be set into it, which makes the fixture much easier to clean.

Floors and Walls

Bathroom surfaces should be waterproof and washable. Ceramic tiles are ideal, on both floors and walls. They are expensive so you can stop halfway up the wall and paint or wallpaper above that. White tiles always look good. Colored tiles can show up the mineral deposits in hard water areas (and this goes for colored tubs and sinks too). Mirror tiles

(above)
A small bathroom in which the toilet tank has been enclosed, creating a useful shelf.

also make good surfaces, provided you don't mind the sight of yourself in the nude; otherwise use them where they won't show the whole person. Plastic mirror tiling is less likely to steam up than glass. Washable paint can be used in a bathroom, and so can washable wallpaper, provided the room doesn't get too steamy.

Curtains and shower curtains can be made of specially treated fabric. They need no longer be made of that stiff plastic, which is so uncomfortable to the touch when you are taking a shower. Machine washable shower curtains are available, which look and feel just like ordinary fabric.

Heating and Ventilation

These considerations are especially important in the bathroom, which is always steamy and needs somewhere for the steam to escape. All electrical installations for the bathroom should be installed by a qualified electrician. An electrical outlet is generally placed near the sink. This outlet must be guarded by a ground-fault circuit interrupter (GFCI). The GFCI is a safety device that detects any break in the current and, in a fraction of a second, shuts off the electricity, thereby protecting you from being seriously hurt by contact between an appliance such as a hair dryer and water or by an appliance with faulty wiring.

To prevent condensation, you need constant warmth as well as good ventilation. A heated towel stand or radiator–towel rack can provide the warmth, either as part of a central heating system or heated separately by electricity. An open window or an exhaust fan can provide the necessary ventilation.

Safety in the Bathroom

- *Light switches should be of the pull type, or else they should be fitted outside the room.*
- *Every electrical outlet should be fitted with a ground-fault circuit interrupter (GFCI).*
- *Ideally, the room should be heated by a radiator on the central heating system or*

a specially designed, electrically heated towel rack-cum-radiator or you could fix a timed heater to the ceiling.

- All floor surfaces should be nonslip.
- The bathtub should be nonslip, and it is a good idea to have grab rails. Even if you don't need them now, somebody will find them useful one day.
- If elderly people use the bathroom, put grab rails at convenient places.
- Keep medicines out of reach of children, preferably in a lockable medicine cabinet.
- Clear the cabinet out from time to time and throw away any medicines which are out of date or have lost their labels.

Some Common Problems

CONDENSATION

This is all too often a problem, particularly in small bathrooms that have no windows. The only cure is to have constant low level heating, good ventilation and warm surfaces. Therefore, it would be better to have a bathroom carpet rather than ceramic or vinyl tiles, polystyrene-tiled walls covered with wallpaper as opposed to paint or tiles, and it is essential to be able to open a window or, better still, to have an effective fan installed. If you don't like the idea of carpet in the bathroom, use carpet tiles, or cork or linoleum (which could be wiped clean) instead.

LACK OF STORAGE SPACE

If the room is fairly tall, you can run a narrow shelf all round it, about three-fourths of the way up, to take innumerable bottles and jars that always seem to find their way into the bathroom. This is a particularly good idea if there are young children in the home, as it keeps dangerous medicines, cleaning materials and other substances out of reach. Most medicine cabinets are really too small to be very useful. The advantage of these cabinets is that they are lockable. It would be a far better solution, in most bathrooms, to have a bigger cabinet built in, and to have locks specially fitted.

The En Suite Bathroom

A luxurious en suite bathroom can be created in a very small space. Position a new shower stall on a wall so that it is as near to the bathroom as possible to minimize extra plumbing. Waterproofing the area is essential. Get an architect to check that the floor will take the weight of any new fixtures. If the ceiling is low, you may be able to sink the lower part of the shower into the floor.

Make the transition from bedroom to bathroom as discreet as possible. This doesn't mean installing pink, floral tiles in the bathroom to match pink, floral fabrics in the bedroom, because the bedroom decor may change. However, a Victorian bedroom could well lead into a Victorian bathroom, and a sleek Hollywood bedroom into a lavishly fitted, "hotel" style bathroom. In an old, landmark house, the introduction of an en suite bathroom is really out of context and creates an unwelcome "guest house" feel, at odds with the dignity and character of the house. Search for old-fashioned bathtubs and other fixtures at flea markets, antique shops, garage sales and auctions.

Washing Facilities in the Bedroom

If you are introducing a small sink into the bedroom, it should be given a special area in which there is a towel rack, a section of waterproof-tiled flooring, hooks for bathrobes, a wide shelf for toiletries and an attractive, movable screen to divide off the two areas. Build a special duct out from the wall to accommodate the plumbing, rather than opening up the wall for new pipes. This can be made into a far more attractive feature by installing it in a recess, then creating an alcove with a built-in cabinet positioned underneath, with a mirror at the back, a concealed lighting strip and elegant fixtures and hardware.

Decoration Ideas

In small rooms, use visual tricks to create an illusion of space. Light colors in cool shades will open out the room, while plain surfaces will confuse the eye far less than a mixture of patterns.

- *Plain tiles are generally more appealing than patterned ones.*
- *Add in a frieze or dado-height decoration, if you want a more interesting effect.*
- *A streamlined layout, with the plumbing enclosed, is easier to keep clean and gives the impression of a larger floor area.*
- *Pictures, shelves and pretty window curtains or blinds don't take up much space, but they all add immeasurably to the room's character.*
- *Painted tongue-and-groove paneling or wainscoting will add a cottagelike or colonial character.*
- *A circular, curtained shower enclosure round the bath is less claustrophobic than most other styles; the curtains can be tied back on each side of the bath, when it is not being used.*
- *If the window looks out onto a grim view, cover it with glass shelves and keep your toiletries there. The light will shine through the glass, and you will need fewer other shelves and cabinets, leaving room for pictures or mirrors.*
- *Glass mirrors are the most dramatic space enhancers, and a whole wall of mirror can visually double the size of a room.*
- *Hiding unsightly plumbing should be a priority, unless you are going to make them an intrinsic part of your decoration.*
- *There are wood, metal, plastic, plain and even decorated accessories, ranging from mirrors to towel racks, so shop around until you find what suits your own taste.*
- *Many plants thrive in bathrooms, where the steamy atmosphere makes tropical plants in particular feel at home.*

Bathroom Style

(above)
An ultra-modern bathroom, using white ceramic floor tiles, a white shower curtain, mirrors and a stainless steel sink, but the effect is softened by leaving the brick walls unplastered.

(opposite)
A pretty little frilly bathroom, showing charming use of a small space, in sea blues and greens.

Nineteenth-Century Style: Wealthy Victorians were among the first to introduce plumbing into their homes and they did so with enthusiasm and style. Little wonder that they have left a heritage of generously designed, ornate bathtubs, toilets and showers, which are still being manufactured today. The Victorian bathroom revels in bathing. The bathtubs have claw feet, the faucets are generously proportioned and comfortable to grip, the sinks have ornate brackets, and warm radiator-towel racks ensure dry towels, it has curtained windows and cork on the floor. It is redolent of leisure and comfort.

Hotel style: At the other extreme of the design are the tiny, enclosed, functional bathrooms provided in hotels. Hotel bedrooms often leave much to be desired, but many hotel bathrooms are models of compact efficiency. This is achieved by overall tiling on both walls and floors, and by incorporating plenty of shelf space and niches.

Budget Ideas

- An unattractive old table can make a perfectly satisfactory dressing table, if it is covered in a simple, cotton fabric with a skirt.
- Make a dressing table out of a couple of sawhorses and a board, and cover it with a skirt of pretty fabric.
- Wall-mounted wire storage designed for kitchens can make excellent bedroom storage for a young person's room and will house not just jewelery, scarves, belts, etc., but also compact discs, videos and other essential bedroom equipment.
- Indian bedspreads are a cheap and pretty solution and will fit into the style of many different types of bedroom.
- Sheeting by the yard is much cheaper than ready-made sheets and only needs hemming. You can make duvet covers with it, too.
- You can make a surround for the bath using MDF cut to size and then painted.
- Tile seconds are often available, either from the manufacturer or from tile shops or warehouses.
- Give your bathtub a new lease of life with a paint-on product (sold from do-it-yourself stores). This easy-to-use paint is sold in small bottles and is ideal for touching up small chips, or it can be used in larger quantities to paint the whole tub (and sink too).

Design Checklist: Bathroom

- Is the bathroom near the bedrooms? If not, can you move it? (Remember that putting in new plumbing is expensive, so it's best to make sure it is at least near the existing lines.)
- Does the plumbing make noises which can be heard in other rooms? If so, a wall of shelving or cabinets in the next room will help to baffle the sounds, though it would be better to solve the problem by installing a pressure regulator on the water supply. Get a plumber to check your plumbing system.
- In many countries there are regulations that require that bathrooms open onto a ventilated lobby and not into any cooking or eating rooms.
- Does the bathtub take up too much space? Look out for narrow bathtubs, short bathtubs, sit-in bathtubs and corner bathtubs, which can all save space.
- Does the toilet take up too much space? Perhaps you could move it to another room. It is difficult re-siting the toilet, especially in a small bathroom because it requires a soil pipe that is separate from the other waste pipes, and moving it may be expensive or even impossible.
- Is there room for a bidet? If you want one and there is no room, you may have to move the toilet to another room (see above).
- Is there enough room for a separate shower stall? Including a shower in the bath itself is second best to a separate shower. It is often difficult to find a shower curtain or door that will look good and not get in the way.
- If the sink unit takes up too much space, look for corner units or very small basins.
- Check that floor surfaces are nonslip.
- Make sure that the bathtub has a nonslip bottom and grab rails, if necessary.
- Include a shelf for house plants, which will enjoy the steamy atmosphere.
- Check that both heating and ventilation systems work efficiently.
- Build cabinets round the sink for extra storage and a coordinated look.
- Make sure there is a lockable medicine cabinet.

Workrooms

Any sort of work that is done at home requires some sort of defined area, even if it's only for filing papers and paying the bills. The efficient running of a home can include the storage and organization of any of the following: list of emergency telephone numbers, receipts from purchases, and home bookkeeping ledger, warranties and instruction manuals for home appliances, car documents, insurance policies, school records and reports, calendar, lists of useful shops and suppliers, recipes and menus, and more.

However, many people do more than just run their home: they earn their living from home as well, and nearly every home has a computer of some sort, which is used at least partially for work of some kind, so the workroom or work area should be seriously considered. An element of office work involving desks, files, computers, telephones, and office supplies is common to nearly all households. However, other specialized workrooms are important too, and these include music rooms, workshops and sewing rooms.

A good workroom or work area should be inviting, a pleasure to use, suitably lit, convenient and efficient, in a calm atmosphere conducive to work. That doesn't mean it has to lack any humanizing elements, such as color, soft textures or pictures on the wall. If there is space for such things, they will be an encouragement to work.

The Priorities

Most workrooms have very similar require-ments. The priorities include a fairly calm atmosphere away from other, more domestic tasks, children and visitors, the necessary equipment (for example, telephone, fax and an answer machine, or sewing machine and cutting table), suitable furniture and good storage. Some people need more work surfaces, others more storage, while everyone needs good clear working light, good background light, a comfortable environment and ergonom-ically sound seating.

You will have to decide which room to use as your workroom, then make a list of the equipment and furniture you will need, where to put it and how to arrange it; list your stor-age requirements and decide what you will need in the way of lighting.

Most work spaces are best sited away from any activity room, such as the kitchen or chil-dren's rooms, or it will be difficult to work in peace. In this respect, an attic, a garden room

or a basement would be ideal. Remember that an attic may not be designed to take a lot of weight. If you are thinking of introducing heavy equipment, such as a piano, get expert advice first. If you are thinking of building or converting a work space, you will have to comply with local building codes.

All too often, a garden workroom tends to be a minimum-cost shed, with no insulation, and it is not integrated visually with either the house or garden. Yet it is so easy to install a shed that is insulated (or to insulate it your-self), to add electrical outlets and lights, and to decorate it inside and conceal the outside with leafy plants or paint so that it becomes an integral part of the environment. Perfectly standard garden sheds are reasonably priced and can be fitted with shutters and locks to keep out the curious and the light-fingered. If it is well placed in a narrow urban garden, a sensitively treated shed can provide a satis-factory focal point. A skylight can provide good light distribution.

If you have no room at all for a shed in the garden and you can't extend your house, the spare room can be a satisfactory place to work in, so long as guests are willing to get up early if you need to work and don't stay long enough to take the room over completely. One end of quite a small bedroom can be turned into a satisfactory office, especially if you can provide a partition, such as a set of shelves which opens onto both bedroom and workroom. A large landing can be turned into a valuable work space, but only if you can eliminate drafts and the noises coming up from the rest of the house, and if it really is large enough to contain a sizable work surface and enough storage to be convenient.

Under the stairs can also provide space for work. It may be possible to remove the non-load-bearing wall from under the stairs and use the space there. It will depend on the siting of the stairs, how steep and how wide they are. Don't dismiss this potentially useful space, but get professional advice first.

A loft conversion is a good way of giving yourself separate space for work. This may be cheaper than renting an office outside the home, and there are many reliable companies who make loft conversions a speciality. They will advise you on whether your house is suitable for a conversion. You must make sure that any work you do conforms to local codes (many houses need expensive extra strengthening) and that insulation is good; otherwise a loft space can become very cold in winter and unbearably hot in summer.

The garage could be a useful work space, but it must have a window, and you may need a building permit to make it work-worthy. As garage interiors are extremely basic, it is more important than usual to make sure the space is softened with colors, textures, pictures and pleasant background lighting, as well as efficient task lighting. A sunroom can make a satisfactory workspace, but it will have to be insulated with double-glazing and blinds; otherwise, like an attic, it will be too

(above)
A well designed mobile computer cart can be the answer for office work in the home.

(above)
A neat desk used for domestic
organization, with a prettily
upholstered easy chair and an
armchair for relaxation, could
form part of a bedroom.

can be used effectively for both dining and all manner of office equipment.

If you live in a contemporary or high tech environment and your life is centered around computing, then computers and software can all go into the living room, where they will blend well with a sound system. However, computer design is rather uncompromising and most people prefer to find an alternative area for it.

The Plan

LIST OF EQUIPMENT

List the equipment you will need for work. This might include computer, and peripherals; telephone, fax machine, photocopier; projector and screen; slide library; drawing board and trolley; sewing or knitting machine; carpenter's bench or portable workbench with a full set of carpentry tools. Work out how much desk space you will need for all these things so that you can reach and use them easily. Does your computer have separate components that need space? Will they fit under the table, or can you get a low cart for them? Where will you put the printer?

Furniture

When you've listed the equipment, it will be easier to decide what sort of work surface you want and how it should be oriented. Before buying anything, remember to measure both the space and the furniture or storage. Check where electrical outlets and phone jacks are located, and if the furniture is going to cover them, get them moved first.

WORK TABLES

One of the cheapest and most convenient work surfaces for the home office can be part of the shelving system. If you use an upright-and-bracket system to create storage shelves for equipment and materials, use the longest available brackets to hold a deep shelf or a hollow-core door as your desk top. A cheap

cold in winter and too hot in summer. As the gateway to the garden, a sunroom can be a pleasant place to work, but only if it is dedicated to that. It's almost impossible to concentrate in a place which is also used for leisure activities.

If it is not necessary to "get away" to work; any small space in the home will do, even the kitchen table, as long as there is enough shelf space for storage, enough room for a telephone, telephone directories, a note pad and pens. For day-to-day bill-paying and organizing of the home, a table should be quite adequate. It is only when the work starts to involve computers or other equipment that you will need more work surfaces. A dining room can make a good work space since it is frequently unused for a lot of the time. If it is large enough, you can keep work-in-progress at one end of the table, while you eat at the other. An adjustable ceiling lamp will create versatile lighting over your work, although an office lamp would help too. Modular storage

work surface can also be made from a board or door supported on folding trestles with a taboret underneath to hold pens, scissors, paper clips, bias binding, elastic and other miscellaneous bits and pieces that need to be accessible.

Desks themselves are available in all sorts of styles, shapes, sizes and complexities, from a typist's desk to an executive desk sold by office equipment suppliers, to small desks incorporated into a modular office system, or arranged under children's bunk beds. If you work in the living room and don't want the writing desk to appear too "officey," choose a small bureau that closes up when not in use. They are often designed with small compartments and drawers which can be useful for stamps and personal documents. Or choose any small, attractive table with drawers.

Place the desk by a window, if possible, so that you can get the benefit of as much daylight as you can. If it looks onto an attractive view, this can be refreshing for the mind.

CHAIRS

For desk work, there's nothing much better than a typist's chair with an adjustable height mechanism — an adjustable back support would be an added advantage. The chair should be set at a height where the feet sit flat on the floor.

If you have the space, you can give the room a more relaxed, informal feeling by including a small, upholstered chair or sofa. If the room doubles as a spare bedroom, a sofa bed will make it seem less like a bedroom when you are working there. Alternatively, have a divan bed with a pretty cover and cushions as a back rest.

Storage

Spaces for work need more discipline than spaces for leisure. You can never have too many shelves, and a filing cabinet can be invaluable. Two filing cabinets, supporting a deep work surface, can provide the desk under the shelves. Divide the shelves into compart-

(above)
This triple-purpose room would suit an adult or an older child, with its comfortable seating, workmanlike office space, well-lit bunk and a wall of shelving.

Draw up your own list of ideas, based on what you have to find places for. One list might look something like this:

- Pegboard for scissors, reels of tape, paint brushes, etc.
- Bulletin board for clippings, telephone numbers and other reference material.
- Mugs or jugs for pens, scissors, letter openers, etc.
- Sets of tiny chests of drawers for paper clips, rubber bands, pushpins and postage stamps.
- A narrow shelf for computer disks, tape dispensers, small notepads and card index boxes so they won't get lost behind larger items and won't get in the way of things on the work surface.
- Box files: There are endless uses for these in categorized filing, from bills to letters, travel brochures and garden information.
- Separate cubby holes in the shelving system for drawing paper, notepaper (fax and letterheads are kept separately), envelopes of various sizes; spare folders, computer disks, compact discs, videos, correspondence and business cards.
- Drawers for string, wrapping paper, bubble wrap, notebooks, colored paper, etc.

Lighting

Task lighting (lighting to work by) should shine on the work without casting shadows over it and without glaring into your eyes. Strong uplights are excellent for lighting office space over a desk. These shine the light onto the ceiling, and it is then directed down over the desk without shadows or glare. Spots are also popular for task lighting and can be fitted to track. Track lighting is easy to install and will take several spots, which can be angled in different directions to give you light where you need it. Recessed ceiling lights can be good, when positioned correctly

(above)
This workmanlike office space is still attractive enough to fit in well in a domestic space. Inexpensive units have been chosen in coordinated colors to give a cheerful effect.

ments so that you can quite easily identify different papers, envelopes, cards, disks, cassettes, card index boxes and other essentials. You will also need small containers (miniature do-it-yourself chests of drawers are good for this purpose), to hold the ungainly, but tiny bits and pieces that are very necessary to office work, such as paper clips, drawing pins, staples and staplers, adhesive papers and elastic bands. List absolutely everything you will need, from storage for a shelf to the different kinds of directories placed next to the telephone.

For filing, there are many options to choose from. Box files are invaluable if you collect newspaper and magazine cuttings and information on categorized subjects. Card index files can be useful, if only to hold information waiting to be fed into your computer. Slim files, concertina files, open files for magazines and closed files for loose bits of paper, all have their uses. They must also have their place on your shelves.

and adjustable spots, recessed into the ceiling, can be angled rather like regular spots but are not quite so obtrusive. Position all lamps so you are not sitting in your own light. It can be useful to carry a portable lamp and try it in various places until you know exactly what lighting you want.

Fluorescent lights give excellent working light, which is two or three times as efficient as tungsten, but they look bleak unless they are screened by a baffle (a device attached to a light fitting that helps prevent glare) or a shade. Suspend them well above eye-level and choose colors that simulate daylight. Better still are the new generation of halogen lights, which are available in stylish designs and give a white light, which is good for working. You can also fit daylight bulbs, which emulate daylight, into desk lamps.

An adjustable desk lamp will give you a strong beam, which you can direct to exactly where you need it from a sitting position, which makes it very flexible. Look for desk lamps with miniature fluorescent bulbs; they give efficient, longer lasting and cheaper light.

SHARED USE

If the work space has to share the room with another function, decorate the space in keeping with the rest of the room and keep the decoration simple. Work usually involves bits and pieces of some kind or another, and it is unwise to add more confusion to the scene with patterned wallpapers and frilly cushions, for example. If the work area is going to be very different in feeling or mood from the rest of the room, it would be better to divide it off from the work area with a screen. This could be a simple folding screen, or it could be a substantial room divider acting as shelving on the office side and treated simply as another wall on the other. This is a good way of treating a bedroom in particular, where the relaxed mood required may not be in keeping with the concentrated intensity of the area.

Heating/Ventilation

Continuous warmth and air are important in an office space, where work is done sitting still. The lack of physical effort soon makes one feel cold, and lack of air makes for sleepiness. In general, a temperature of between 68 °f – 71 °f (20°c – 22°c) is considered satisfactory for a working environment and if you have no radiator, a 2–3 watt fan heater should provide adequate heating. If you are reluctant to have the central heating on full blast in the whole house, fit a thermostat onto the radiator in the work space, or add a booster fan heater to bring extra warmth where you need it.

If your workroom is in a basement, make sure it is free from moisture before you set up. The moisture will affect paper, machinery and electricity; it feels uncomfortable and is conducive to cold. If you have to do radical improvements, you must allow a drying out period of several months before you decorate. You can speed up this process with a dehumidifier, which is available from rental shops.

(above)
A budget workspace using cheap furniture can still be very efficient.

Specific Solutions

LAUNDRY/UTILITY ROOM

A utility room is every housekeeper's dream. It's a place for all the bulky items such as washing machines, dryers, ironing boards and even shoe cleaning equipment, and avoids the problem of the rest of the house being full of clothes waiting to be washed, ironed or folded. If you plan it carefully, you won't need a big room. It must have a cold and hot water supply, a waste outlet and a work surface for wet clothes. This is a good place to fit a tall closet for equipment such as brushes and vacuum cleaners, with cleaning products on a top shelf out of children's reach. Install shelves all round the room at a high level, with wire baskets to hold miscellaneous items and for bleaches and cleaners. Floors should be waterproof: ceramic, quarry or vinyl tiles, for example. Provide hanging storage for the ironing board and pegs for newly ironed clothes to rest on coat hangers while they air. Track lights or a halogen uplight will provide plenty of efficient illumination.

COMPUTER ROOM

There are many inexpensive modular office systems on the market designed to hold computers, printers, paper and stationery, which may include shelving systems, room dividers, desks, conduits for electric wires, filing cabinets and even matching chairs. Most systems will be just as practical for any work done sitting at a table. Make a list of what you want your system to do and check that you can fit it into the space. For example, if you are buying a small table for your printer, is it low enough to fit under your desk? Is it tall enough to hold paper as well as the printer, and has it got casters so you can pull it out easily from under the desk when you need to have it serviced? If the telephone, fax or answering machine take up too much desk space, fix them to the wall. To reach items you

need from a seated position, a cart on casters, designed to hold a variety of different pieces of equipment and tools, can be pulled with you when you change position or move from chair to chair.

Many people suffer from muscle strain through sitting at a computer for long periods. This can be prevented or diminished by sitting in a correct posture and taking frequent breaks. The correct height for the work table, if you are writing, is elbow height when you are sitting down, but it should be about 4 in (100 mm) lower if you are typing or word processing. The best answer is to have two work surfaces, one lower and one higher, placed at right angles, and a swivel chair so that you can move from one to another more quickly. The keyboard should be 25 1/2 to 30 3/4 in (640 to 780 mm) from the floor (depending on the user and the chair height).

For a dual-purpose room, get a compact computer desk with a lower portion for the keyboard, which pulls out when you want to

(above)
A professional office in the roof uses the slope of the roof for generous windows, giving good light, and bookshelves are fitted into the A shape.

(opposite)
This well equipped, simple workroom has a secondary use as a bedroom, with a coordinated bed and lighting.

work. If you are very short of storage space, you can run a shelf right round the room at the level of the top of the doors. Such a shelf is good for papers, files and magazines which you only want to refer to at infrequent intervals, but which you don't want to throw away. They are unobtrusive at this height, but the shelf will hold a surprising amount. Use open box files for magazines which will hold them upright and enable you to see both the titles and dates at a glance.

Adjustable shelving will enable you to organize the space so that you can store different-sized items more efficiently.

Lighting for Computers

- *Make sure there is some background lighting in the room. The contrast between a darkened room and the brightness of the screen is confusing.*
- *There should be no reflection of light from the computer screen. If necessary, angle your lights differently.*

- *Daylight is the best light to work by, but directly under a window is not the best place. Position your computer sideways to the window, which will allow light to fall onto the screen without reflection. Adjustable slatted blinds can help with glare, if you are facing a window.*

MUSIC ROOM

The traditional music room for acoustic instruments may take the form of the Victorian music room, where one person can practice or several people can get together to play and sing. If music is the prevailing interest, why shouldn't a good-looking piano dominate the room? Storage would be simple: shelves or space in a piano stool for sheet music and cabinets fitted with locks to store valuable musical instruments.

A sound studio for electronic music takes up more space and requires electrical outlets for numerous pieces of equipment, from electric guitars to microphones and speakers. One of the main problems is noise, not only for the rest of the house but for neighbors, too. The basement is probably the best place for this use, as much of the sound can be contained underground. If the room is to be used permanently as a practice studio, you will need to get professional advice. Soundproofing can be expensive, but there are more immediate ways of helping to muffle the sound, such as having well-fitting insulated doors and double-glazed windows in which the panes are the correct distance apart for insulating sound, which needs a wider gap than heat insulation. Soft wall and floor coverings will help contain the noise; also an insulated ceiling. Ensure against fire by having plenty of electrical outlets, a smoke alarm and, if possible, some alternative exit. Surfaces should be tough, no-nonsense and plain. Good ventilation is very important too.

CARPENTRY WORKSHOP

This sort of workshop is too noisy and dusty to be satisfactory in the main part of the house. It is best in a garage, shed or addition. Tool storage is a priority, not only for convenience, but also to keep expensive tools safe. Keep tools above or beside the work bench on pegboard fixed to the wall. Screw holes in a wood block to hold drill bits. You will need to have plenty of high shelves for paints, glues, varnishes and small bits and pieces, such as nails and screws, which should be kept in a toolbox or specially designed miniature chests of drawers. Large sheet materials should be leaned against a wall with a wood cleat nailed to the floor to hold them in place. Industrial shelving is perfectly adequate. You will need a big waste bin and fluorescent lights to give efficient, shadowless light over the workbench. Constant low level heat and good ventilation are necessary to avoid the tools getting rusty. Good ventilation is essential, in fact, particularly if you work with adhesives. The room need not be very warm, as you will

generate heat just by working in it. Choose vinyl sheet or tiles for the floor and eggshell paint for the walls. Safety is vitally important. Keep everything orderly and all sharp or dangerous tools stored out of reach of children; use electric tools from an outlet at work bench height – a continuous electrical track in the ceiling is a good idea; make sure there are no trailing cords. Keep a fully equipped first aid box within easy reach and don't let young children into the room.

SEWING ROOM

Although sewing can be done on practically any table that is large and strong enough to hold the machine, if you do any serious sewing at home, then a separate room where you can leave the work out, ready to take up when you next have time can be a real blessing. Failing that, an "up-and-over" shelf, which can swing the work out onto the table whenever you need it, will make it much easier to use. You will need a steady table and an ironing board.

(above)

Storage for a garage workshop can be quite basic, but it must be fit for the purpose. This kit furniture can be put together in any combination to house most workshop tools and equipment.

(above)
This unpretentious little desk and chair is in Shaker style and would fit in well in a dual-purpose room in a small home.

(above right)
A long, narrow storage-cum-filing unit can fit into a small space and can hold a surprising amount.

If your room serves a dual-purpose, get a board that you can hang on the wall. You will need a comfortable upright chair and a good working light. Most sewing machines have their own built-in light, but you will need a good overhead light, which doesn't cast a shadow on the work, for cutting, choosing colored threads, threading needles, and so on. A halogen uplight would provide all the light you need for general purposes and for work too, but you might like an extra adjustable desk lamp. A varied arrangement of storage will be best, which should include drawers and cubby holes, a bulletin board and hooks. You will need small drawers or cubby holes for all the notions that go with sewing, as well as for materials, patterns, cuttings, shelves for books, useful catalogues and magazines, and other drawers for fabrics.

A knitting room will have similar requirements, with a large table for the knitting machine, and storage for wools, etc.

Style

If the office area is part of some other room, then you should try to make sure the two are either completely screened off from each other, or that the two separate parts complement each other and don't present two quite different moods.

It's usually best to stick to a fairly simple style for working, something which won't distract you from your work and which will act as a pleasant backdrop to the paraphernalia of work without being too "busy." There are various options for the home office in terms of style. The following types of workroom should provide a basis for most tastes and pockets, though you will impose your own preferences and tastes, and probably mix and match from one to another in matters of detail.

THE OLD FASHIONED STUDY/LIBRARY

This look will appeal if your house is full of books and you have literary or academic tastes. You need a fairly large room for it to

look its best. Built-in bookcases covering the whole of one or two walls should be well built and imposing with architraving and fluted pilasters. The thicker the shelves, the better: 1/2 in (13 mm) is the minimum; 3/4 in (19mm) will look more solid. Large books should have a large space allocated for them near the floor. Unshelved walls should be painted a plain, matte color (one of the new ranges of traditional colors would look good), with a sporting print or two or three watercolors. If the room is well proportioned, you could use a paper with a Regency stripe. Doors should be paneled with brass or porcelain handles. A polished, round pedestal table will look right for studying, though a leather-topped desk will take up less space. This style is particularly suited to people who deal with words, so it would not be out of place to have a computer. Dark, mahogany would be a good material for the furniture, although any polished wood will do. The floor should be carpeted. An old-fashioned fireplace would

look great with real or simulated coals, an inglenook and a leather armchair.

MODERN/WORKMANLIKE

This style is suitable for writing, drawing, sewing and similar occupations. It is sensible, no-nonsense, highly practical and will appeal to people who like clean lines and no fuss. Choose domestic upright and bracket shelving, or buy the cheapest available second-hand office furniture and paint it yourself with automobile spray paint or some other tough and colorful finish to create a coordinated whole, with no unnecessary embellishments. Choose modern office chairs, which are brightly colored and adjustable. The floor should be vinyl or cork tiled, or sanded and sealed. Walls should be painted white. The work surface could be made of sawhorses or low filing cabinets, with glass or a door laid across them. Modern track lighting, with an extra adjustable desk lamp, will provide excellent working light. Doors should be unpaneled

(above)
Unlike many artists' studios, this large, clean open space makes a comfortable sitting room, with excellent light flooding in from two directions.

with modern, brightly colored lever handles.

RELAXED AND INFORMAL

This is a good solution for a room which is part of another room, or in which you want a relaxed and easy-going atmosphere. If you use a fitted or modular system, choose a simple, wood one, and if you use freestanding furniture, stick to pale woods, such as pine or beech. Soften the look with cotton print curtains and introduce a comfortable upholstered chair or a wicker settee, or a combined office and dining room would look good furnished in Scandinavian simplicity using a pale, wood table and chairs for both office and dining use, with fabrics in plain colors, or simple stripes or checks. Lighting would be kept at a low level, with desk lamps for working and simple table lamps giving pools of light in the rest of the room.

If the office space is part of another room, carry the furnishings through to avoid a jarring juxtaposition of style and mood. If the main area is carpeted, carry the carpet right through to the workspace; if the furniture in the room is wood, use a similar wood for the desk and storage system, and if it is metal and glass, or any other modern design, choose compatible work furniture. If the main room has fitted units, use similar units in your office space and stick to matching or coordinating fabrics.

The chair, too, although ideally it should be adjustable or at least at the correct height for desk work, should look right with the rest of the room. There are many designs to choose from: you can find brightly painted chairs for a young person's room or upholstered executive chairs for a more heavily furnished room.

On the other hand, you can use the lighting to differentiate the work space from the rest of the room. If you have all the task lighting operating from one switch, you can switch them off quickly and attract the eye to other parts of the room instead.

Budget Ideas

- Buy furniture that you assemble, rather than ready-built units.
- Second-hand office furniture is often much cheaper than new. You can frequently buy quite expensive pieces which are well designed and still in good condition.
- Sawhorses, with a board or an old door laid across them, can be a very inexpensive way to create your desk initially. There will be no drawers, of course, but it will give you time to save for the desk you want.
- Secondhand filing cabinets are much cheaper than new. They may look terrible when you first buy them but, with a spray of automobile paint, they can be brightened up very easily.
- Secondhand box files are a good buy, if you can find them. These are remarkably expensive when new. The most motley collection can look stylish if they are all painted in the same color.
- Open-topped box files are cheap and invaluable for the upright filing of magazines, brochures, clippings, instruction manuals, paper patterns, correspondence and much more.

Design Checklist

As with most checklists, this will be quite personal to you. List every item you are likely to use in the work you undertake and decide what sort of storage would be most suitable for it. Make sure you make room for things you use every day, in places where you can easily reach them, and store only the rarely used items where you need to stand on steps to get at them. Don't forget to list all the small items you need. Consider the following points:

- Do you need a work space that is separate from the rest of the home?
- If you are working in a dual-purpose room, can you keep away from annoying interruptions (e.g., children)?
- If you have chosen to work from a shed in the garden, can you run electricity to it and is it insulated?
- List all the equipment you will need and check that you allow for it all in your plan.
- Check that your desk or table space is the right height and that you have a comfortable and adjustable chair.
- Make sure there is room for plenty of filing cabinets or boxes, shelves, drawers and a bulletin board.
- Are there adequate background lights?
- Is there a good desk lamp that casts strong light and so avoids eye strain?
- Is the room warm/cool enough to encourage an efficient way of working?

One-Room Living

A multipurpose room is a real challenge when it comes to planning. The person living in it may have to sleep, cook, eat, wash and work there. In a large room you can divide off some of the main functions with a permanent screen or room divider, but in a small room it is best to try and make the best of the one space; otherwise the room will become very cramped. Find the simplest, best-looking furniture and equipment you can afford to give everything a coordinated and deliberately designed quality.

The more customized the room can be, the better. A student will need plenty of shelves for books, but won't need "formal" chairs, whereas an elderly person should have furniture with no sharp corners, places to put photographs and ornaments, and upright chairs. Whatever you do, don't see it as a place to deposit pieces of furniture you no longer use, simply because they are there. Such pieces are often impractical, cumbersome and the wrong proportions for an all-purpose room. Good-looking, carefully chosen pieces (which needn't be expensive and can be secondhand) are exactly what is required. Second-hand furniture can be painted or covered to give it a coordinated look.

The Priorities

There must be room for a bed and at least one comfortable chair and table, however small, for eating or working; clothes storage; shelves and cooking facilities (if you want to provide them); and a sink or even a shower (choose a room near existing plumbing). Ideally, it will also be near a toilet. The room should be insulated against sound, and you should decide whether to install separate meters for electricity and/or gas and a separate telephone or a small payphone. Modern designs can make them quite suitable for domestic purposes. It will also need a separate hookups for a television and a stove.

Fitting a whole life into one small room presents some serious planning problems. How do you combine working and relaxing, cooking and sleeping, and how can you entertain friends among all these different activities? In a room where so much is going on, there is a temptation to squeeze in too much furniture so there isn't enough room to open

doors, swivel round in a chair, open the oven door without knocking into something, or walk comfortably round a dining table.

A list of what you expect to do in the room will help in your planning. It may be rather a long one and could look something like this:

1. *Sleeping:* Room for a bed (double or small single?), a bedside table and lighting.
2. *Relaxing, reading, knitting, etc.:* You will need a comfortable chair and good lighting.
3. *Working/eating:* You will need a table, however small, at which you can sit comfortably upright.
4. *Cooking:* You will need something to cook in or on. This need not be a conventional stove; you might have a microwave oven. You will also need an exhaust fan and a small refrigerator. Equipment designed for use on boats is worth looking at because it is ingeniously designed and compact.
5. *Washing:* There should be a sink in the room, however small, especially if there are cooking facilities.

6. *Storage:* You will need to have storage for clothes and shoes, books, papers, kitchenware, toiletries, sound system, computer, television and special interests.

The list above will apply to most multipurpose rooms, whether they are used for working or not. If you have special requirements, add them to the list as necessary.

SLEEPING

The bed is the largest piece of furniture you will have, so consider it first. It shouldn't dominate the room. There's a wide choice of dual-purpose beds or beds you can conceal: for example, those which will fold up into cabinets on the wall, so that they look like part of the bookshelves, and sofa beds, which open out at night. However, although folding and dual-purpose furniture certainly has its place in small rooms, most people would like to be able to simply flop into bed when they are ready, rather than having to pull down or unfold it first.

It's usually more convenient to have a divan or daybed, with cushions at the back, for daytime seating. Alternatively, you could build deep cabinets at one end of the room, leaving an alcove for the bed, thus supplying a large amount of storage and keeping the bed separate, although you would need a fairly large room to make this practicable.

TIPS ON BUYING BEDS

- *If you do decide on a folding bed, then try to avoid buying one with a mattress which creases when folded.*
- *A drawer under the bed will hold a duvet, fitted sheet and pillowcases which are much easier for making the bed.*
- *A bed on casters is apt to slip away when you prop yourself up in the morning.*
- *Make sure the mattress is a good one, either spring or good-quality foam.*
- *It is important that a bed that is also used for sitting, has a firm mattress which won't sink at the edges.*

(above)
The loft-style bed frees room underneath to provide comfortable seating
for even a guest-futon, as well as a feeling of spaciousness.

WORKING/EATING

You will need at least one upright seat for working and eating. Folding chairs can be useful here, especially if you provide hooks on the wall so they can be hung out of the way. If you are working seriously at home and sitting at a desk for long periods, then you should get a small typist's chair that allows the height to be adjusted.

Every home needs a table, no matter how small. You may be able to use the same one for working and eating, but only if you have shelf space to put your work on while eating and vice versa. If you work very long hours in the room, it would be better to have a small work station where everything can remain undisturbed. This can be a large shelf at desk height as part of a built-in shelving system using uprights and brackets, or a small, computer desk with a pull-out table for the keyboard. Shelves below will hold a printer, paper and so on. Choose your table carefully. There are various designs and combinations on the market, and some will suit your purposes better than others.

A table for eating may seem a luxury when you can lounge in front of the television with a plate and fork on a tray, but sitting upright when eating is better for the digestion, and eating at a table gives the meal a dignity and sense of occasion, which can be welcome in a small space. There are good, small semi-circular tables, which are hinged and fold flat against the wall and can be useful not just for eating, but for food preparation too, especially if placed near the cooking area. A cart with leaves that fold out to provide a table can be useful too, and might also act as the bedside table. Very small, one-person dining tables are also available.

Often, small, secondhand kitchen or side tables are cheaply and readily obtainable, and these can easily be sanded and sealed (or polished) for a natural look or even painted, if you prefer.

(above)
A corner of a large warehouse room, where the eating area is next to the sitting area in a moody interior.

(opposite)
A neatly organized space, where the double bed is also the sofa and the cleverly appointed small kitchen is separated from the rest of the room by a column.

You might question the need to have a bed at all. Why not a futon, which you just roll up during the day, or a raised foam pad on a fitted carpet and a sleeping bag?

If you want to use the bed as seating, place it where it can fit comfortably among any other comfortable chairs you may have, facing the television and near a low table. A folding bed must have space to unfold without your having to move other things out of the way. It's worth sacrificing some other piece of furniture to make this possible.

RELAXING

Young people can forgo an easy chair and rely simply on the bed and floor for relaxing. However, it is a good idea to have one comfortable chair to give a cozy look to the room and also for the comfort of older visitors. Neat, upholstered chairs and some folding chairs are very comfortable. Cushions can make comfortable seats but you should be able to put them on the bed when not in use.

COOKING

Cooking facilities are generally among the most difficult to incorporate into a one-room home without introducing a hardness and hygienic quality, which disturbs the general comfort. If at all possible, the cooking area should be kept separate, either by a counter level dividing unit or by room-height shelves, which can open out onto both sides so no space is wasted. If you can't divide the area physically, then try to make the cooking area as attractive as possible, either with open shelves, like a small dresser with pretty china on it, or closed behind attractive cabinet doors. Failing this, a folding screen would be useful. A heavy screen should have casters fixed to the bottom of the panels if you want to move it around.

The first thing, when planning this area, is to acknowledge that space is restricted and to stick to the simplest cooking you can think of to suit your needs. Give up the idea of a conventional stove and get a microwave instead. It will take up less room and use less power. The larger ones incorporate a conventional oven and some have a conventional grill as well. Alternatively, invest in a versatile plug-in casserole/frying pan. This sort of cooking will eliminate the need for lots of pots and pans. If you must boil the occasional egg, use a small plug-in immersion heater or get a two-burner hot plate and a set of stacking saucepans.

A small sink with a drain board will be necessary. A few shelves will provide space for everything you need, if you are disciplined in your choices. Don't insist on having lots of bottles, cans and jars of food you don't need. Do make a list of essential items and provide the right depth of shelf for each. Things you can do without include a bread box, vegetable rack (buy vegetables as you need them and display them on a dish, as you would fruit), and elaborate kitchen appliances (a small hand-held mixer fixed on the wall will do all you need). Keep decorative tins for foods you

need to store, such as tea bags, sugar and rice. A plate rack on the wall above the drain board saves space when washing and shelf space thereafter. Add a mirror with a small shelf above the sink to allow you to make up and keep your toothbrush and shampoo near at hand. The most satisfactory waste bin is one fixed to the inside of a door under the sink, whose lid will open and close automatically when the cabinet door is opened and closed. Make sure any bin you use will take plastic bags, so you can tie them up securely before taking them outside.

WASHING AND HEATING

A wash basin incorporated into the room can be a blessing. If you do have a cooking area, the sink can double as a basin. The cooking/washing area should be surrounded by waterproof flooring and should have cleanable surfaces to ensure hygiene. If the basin has to be within the living, rather than the utility area, it can often be concealed in a range of

cabinets or built into a group of fittings, which will give it more of a coordinated look. If the room is tall enough and big enough, you could incorporate a shower.

Some shower stalls fold back to take up very little room when not in use. It's important to get a good quality one which won't leak and, if possible, to put it next to the kitchen area, creating a compact utility space. You will need a heated towel stand or clothes dryer to prevent the room from becoming damp.

Hot water can be achieved with any of a wide range of gas and electric sink water heaters that are plugged into the normal electrical outlet and are fed from the cold tap, or even permanently connected to the water supply.

Heating, in general, can often be problematical in a small space. The choice of radiator is important. Narrow radiators will obviously take up less space, but you can also get skirting radiators and tall, narrow radiators, which are often easier to incorporate. It's useful to

have one with rungs, which can be also used as a clothes dryer. These radiators are expensive, but worth it for their convenience. Electric storage radiators take up lots of space and are not always the best solution in a small room.

Good ventilation is particularly important because the room is used for both cooking and washing activities, so install an efficient exhaust fan to the outside wall to prevent smells and condensation.

STORAGE

Open shelves are a good option for a small room because they can be exactly as deep as you want them to be, and they don't bring the walls farther into the room as cabinet doors appear to. In the kitchen, make sure shelves are as narrow as possible, thus saving space and making everything easy to find and to use: 10 in (25 cm) is enough space for most dishes and utensils, 5 – 6 in (12 – 15 cm) for cans and boxes and 3 in (7 cm) for spices and

herbs. Adjustable shelves can allow for changes and new acquisitions. Make the most of wire baskets and wire shelves inside both kitchen and clothes cabinets.

Don't take bookshelves right up to the ceiling; they will seem less overbearing if you leave a space at the top large enough to hold a painting or a sculpture, or some other decorative object. Two sets of freestanding shelves at either end of a wall can leave an alcove space between for a small table, with a painting or mirror placed above it. You will need to allow wider shelves for books, television and sound system.

In a small space, things tend to get stored wherever room can be found for them, and that's often on high shelves. There is a temptation to climb dangerously onto chairs to get things down. Keep things you use often within easy reach and have a small set of sturdy steps for when you do want to reach up high. Aluminum steps are lightweight and fold up very small.

SOME QUICK STORAGE IDEAS

- *A pole mounted under a shelf and fitted with some butcher's hooks can relieve precious drawer space.*
- *Use the space above and around windows for shelving, and the space under the window sill for box seating and storage.*
- *Attach hooks everywhere, inside cabinet doors, under shelves and on the sides of bookcases; they are invaluable for a myriad of small objects, from keys to scissors and sticky tape.*

SPACE SAVERS

- *A hinged ironing board can be fitted onto the wall, with a bracket to hold the iron. Make sure you can open up the ironing board easily without it getting in the way of other activities.*
- *A hinged table fixed onto a wall. A semi-circular one is the most space saving.*
- *Folding chairs: Hang them onto the wall, if possible, to save space.*
- *A card table – an invaluable piece of furniture – can be used for meals, playing games or working. With a cloth placed over the top, it no longer looks like a card table.*

Some Common Problems

SOUND INSULATION

Good sound insulation is essential to happiness and well-being when living in a densely populated building. Noise transmission can be alleviated by thoughtful planning. Sound transmits in two ways:

1. *On impact:* The sound of heavy footsteps and things being dropped travels through the whole structure of the building. The only practical way to reduce this is to make sure there is resilient flooring, such as a soft carpet on thick underlayment. Underlayment is a good insulator and can be used on the walls as well.
2. *Airborne noise:* This travels through gaps, holes and other small apertures, so find ways to stop up all such gaps. Double-glazing, with a 4 in (10 cm) space between the glass, is recommended (although this is too wide a gap for ideal heat insulation!) Modern, hollow-core doors have poor insulation; heavier-quality, solid doors are better but, of course, more expensive. They must fit well, so seal the edges, if necessary. You can find heavy, well-made doors (sometimes with a metal layer sandwiched in the middle as a fire barrier), in architectural salvage yards, usually originating from hotels that are being refurbished. They are among the few things that are cheaper when purchased in such yards and are worth looking out for.

SECURITY

If the room is in the basement, it will be vulnerable to break-ins, so make it burglar-proof. If it has its own separate entrance, install a sensor light which will light up when anyone approaches. Fit bars to the windows and get the door fitted with double locks,

(above)
Part of the wardrobe, as featured opposite, opens out to provide the bed. This is a good-looking and very space-saving solution for the tidy and well-organized person.

(above)
The simplest of daybeds,
covered with pillows during the
day, may be a better solution to
seating-and-sleeping than a
more sophisticated sofa bed.

- Make sure radiators are out of reach or on thermostats, so they don't get hot enough to burn.
- All storage should be kept within easy reach to avoid having to stand awkwardly on steps or chairs.

CALCULATING SPACE

Remember that low objects are easier to negotiate than tall ones and also that they don't visually divide the space.

- Allow 26 in (650 mm) to give room to bend down and open an oven door.
- Allow at least 28 in (700 mm) for your chair, when sitting at a desk or table.
- Allow 20 in (500 mm) for standing in front of a closet. If the doors are wider than this, exchange them for narrower, hinged doors or fit mirrored sliding doors on tracks, which will give an illusion of space.
- Handles in small spaces can catch on sleeves and pockets, so choose smooth door handles that don't project or recessed finger holds. Choose recessed handles for the kitchen units.
- Plan for doors to open without bumping into each other. Leave shelves and storage units open, or conceal them with a fabric curtain or roller shade, rather than doors.
- As so many activities have to take place in one room, allow plenty of outlets on each wall, preferably at work surface height.
- Round tables are easier to negotiate.
- Furniture should have straight legs, not awkward ones, which could trip you up.
- Avoid deep wall cabinets or brackets at forehead height.

with bolts on the inside and safety chains. In an attic space, always get expert advice on fire escapes, fire extinguishers and fire-retarding measures.

VENTILATION

There should be a small amount of permanent ventilation at high level to prevent the build-up of stale air, which tends to be hot and therefore rises. An airbrick will be enough ventilation for most rooms. Condensation is likely to occur in rooms where cooking and showering are frequent and, if possible, smells, steam and grease-laden air should be removed at source by a range hood or exhaust fan.

EXTRA PRECAUTIONS FOR THE ELDERLY

- Nonslip, wall-to-wall carpet is best on the floor as it is warm and comfortable.
- Ensure that there are enough outlets so that electric wires don't trail about dangerously across surfaces.

DIVIDING THE AREAS

Run low storage units around three sides of a sofabed. Low units won't divide the room visually, but they will create a psychological division, and you could use such a unit as alternative seating for a dining table on the other side of the bed.

Use existing furniture in arrangements that isolate particular areas. Modular foam seating units can be put together in various combinations to suit the room. Several shelving systems, beds, low and high cabinets, storage boxes, and chests are all available in modular form in different styles.

A narrow table butting up to the back of a sofa or divan will give working space, a place to put library books and current magazines, and act as a psychological room divider. A small wardrobe, with its back to the foot of the bed, will provide a more private sleeping space. Alternatively, you could build the bed itself into a boxlike structure containing cabinets, so that it is in an alcove. Folding doors can be used to divide the whole room, if it is big enough, or they can divide off a small section for a kitchen-in-a-cabinet. Portable folding screens can be useful to conceal parts of the room. Heavy screens can be fitted with casters so that they are easily wheeled about. Narrow panels will be easier to store when the screen is folded. For a permanently positioned screen, you can fix shelves or hooks so that one side of the screen can be used for storage.

LIGHTING

Well-lit spaces seem larger than dimly lit ones, and lighting can greatly affect the comfort of a small room. It's much better to use several lights than to rely on one central hanging light fixture. Each space should have its own lighting so that you can create a range of moods for different purposes and times. Keep lights from cluttering up the floor and desk surfaces by mounting them onto the wall or ceiling instead. Uplights, which throw light back off the ceiling, adjustable spots recessed into the ceiling, or directional spots fixed to track in the ceiling can all be used. You will need a desk lamp, but use one with a clamp, which can be moved around and won't take up desk space. A similar lamp can be used as a bedside light. If you switch the

lights separately, they can also be very versatile, concealing parts of the room you don't want to emphasize, while highlighting better aspects. Tungsten halogen lamps, which have their own transformer, and dimmer switches give a pleasant, white light, and although the bulbs are expensive, they last for a long time.

DECORATION AND FURNITURE

Many people will only be living in a studio apartment for a year or two and won't want to spend unnecessary money on furnishings. Cheap solutions are the best. However, by its very nature, a multipurpose room suggests the occupant will be spending a lot of time in it, so it is important to decorate it in a way that will be easy to live with. It will inevitably be a concentration of many objects and items and different types of functions, so something simple, which will coordinate and unite all this variety, is called for.

Plain colors are easier to live with than patterns: small patterns will be too "busy"

(above)
A low platform can be enough to differentiate one part of a room from another. Here, work, sleep and seating are all incorporated in a well coordinated design.

and large ones can compete with furniture shapes in the room. If in doubt, paint the whole room white, or if you prefer, choose one of the many nearly white colors available. Color is easy to add with paintings, cushions, fabrics, china, books and rugs. You could accent alcoves with a deep paint color, but choose colors which relate to each other and with other colors already in the room, or you will have a fragmented and disturbing scheme.

The flooring should be carried right through the room to give cohesion. Carpet will be warm and comfortable underfoot, and to sit on. Bare boards and rugs can look good if the room is not too crowded. Choose a plain carpet. The confused mass of color often found in carpets will immediately make a busy room seem chaotic, whereas a plain color can unite the various elements. Contrary to what most people think, a dirty, patterned carpet looks just as bad as a dirty, plain one and modern carpet cleaners are really very effective. For a cooking or washing area, try to choose a waterproof floor of the same color as the main flooring. Where the two floors join, use a wood strip, which will be less obvious than a metal one.

One-room living often responds better to a modern treatment than an old-fashioned one. All-black furniture, with white or colored walls, can give elegance to a busy room.

As a general guide, closely related colors, with the occasional use of a strong contrast, give a satisfactory and sophisticated scheme. Clear, contrasting colors of a similar intensity on both bed and chairs, against a white wall, will give a lively scheme. Too heavy a contrast tends to emphasize each color, which, in a small space, could dominate the room at the expense of a coordinated whole. If you are using pale colors on the walls, do make sure there are spots of deeper color in the furniture or fabrics, or the room will lack character. Resist the temptation to use outdated furni-

ture from other parts of the house, unless it really is relevant to your plan. An unsuitable or out-of-scale piece can ruin the whole room.

From the textural point of view, natural cottons and linens will look fresh and add lightness to a room full of different activities and moods. Muslin, natural linen, simple Scandinavian cotton checks and stripes will all add a lighter touch and give freshness to the room, particularly if you are using second-hand furniture.

If you long for pattern, you could stencil cabinet doors or create a frieze around the top fourth of the wall. Curtains should be simple, but a roller, Venetian or Roman blinds would be a better choice because they take up less space and have an elegance which a busy room can well afford.

SOME SPACE SAVING IDEAS

- *Gate-leg or other folding tables: Use them in the normal position, half folded.*
- *Cart table: These often have a useful shelf underneath.*
- *Bentwood hat rack for hanging clothes: A semi-circular one takes up even less space. Modern hat racks may be made of metal, with attachments for holding shoes and other clothes. This is a good solution if you don't have many clothes, but check that it will not take up more space than it's worth.*
- *A lightweight storage unit, made of fabric fitted round a metal or wood frame, then mounted on casters, would probably use less space and be more flexible than a conventional closet. These units often include hangers, drawers and shoe pockets. Again, check that the function is as useful as the idea.*
- *An enclosed bed, using the end wall to hold shelves on both sides, will have additional storage on the "roof." Make sure the structure will support everything safely.*
- *Use wall brackets as hanging storage for folding chairs.*

BUDGET IDEAS

- You can buy freestanding shelving, which is quite simple to assemble and easy to remove afterward. You can often buy it in modules, so you don't need to buy a whole lot all at once.
- Make pillow covers out of old bedspreads or from remnants in fabric shops.
- Build your own bed with a simple frame and slats and buy a new mattress for it.
- Buy a futon mattress, which folds up as seating when not in use.
- Buy a carpet sweeper instead of a vacuum cleaner. They are very efficient for use in small spaces.
- Use rush or coir matting instead of carpet. This is usually made with a backing to stop it from wrinkling, which also makes it easier to clean.
- Throw a length of pretty fabric over ugly or worn chairs. Anything from an Indian bedspread to a length of tapestry or plain cotton weave can look good.
- Milk crates and orange boxes can be lined up or stacked against a wall. These make useful storage for all sorts of odd items, from socks and sweaters to knitting or magazines.
- Boards on bricks, a well-worn idea, are still one of the cheapest ways of creating a set of low shelves.

Design Checklist

- Is the bed comfortable as a sofa? Or should you invest in a sofa bed? Will there be enough room to open it out?
- Is there comfortable seating for a visitor or two?
- Is there somewhere to eat in comfort?
- Are the cooking facilities (a) safe, (b) convenient and (c) simple?
- Is there enough room for clothes storage?
- Do you have plenty of storage room for kitchen items, books and personal possessions?
- Are there any washing facilities and are their surroundings waterproof? Is there an electric towel stand or radiator?
- Is there an acceptable division between the cooking/washing and living/sleeping areas?
- Is there adequate lighting to read in bed, to work and to relax?
- Are there enough electrical outlets, a television hook-up and a telephone jack?
- Are you making the most of well-placed mirrors to make the space seem larger?
- Are you making the most of the height of the room, with shelves running round the wall or even above the door?

Attics, Warehouses & Basements

A space under the roof or in a basement can provide play space for children, a serious work area for adults or bring in income from a renter. Remodeling, insulating and interior finishing can be expensive, but will add to the usefulness and value of the house. Large commercial spaces, such as warehouses, lofts and barns, have become popular as complete homes, giving a living unit a great feeling of space and height and, with the addition of new windows, more light.

Any structural work, such as raising the roof or knocking down walls, putting in new windows, or extending the basement will be governed by local building codes. For example, the whole building may have to be reinforced to carry the extra weight and stress, and when putting in a staircase, you will be required to provide headroom of a certain height to conform to local specifications. If yours is a registered historic building, you will need to get extra permits. In fact, existing stairs can often be realigned by half landings, which will give the necessary headroom.

Several different types of permits may be necessary, so employ a professional architect or a specialist, who will be able to see the potential of the space and deal with all planning permits and the necessary paperwork. Make sure the company or individual you employ is a member of a reliable trade organization and that all work is guaranteed.

What Is the Purpose of the Room?

Before any work is done, decide what you want to use the room for. An attic might make a good room for a renter or a young person, but only if there is enough headroom and you can create easy access to it. Obviously, it would not be suitable for an elderly relative who might find it hard to cope with the stairs. Even if the ceiling is too low for standing upright, it could provide a permanent site for a train set for older children.

In attic conversions, the steeper the pitch of the roof, the better. Generally, anything with a pitch of more than 20 degrees will convert satisfactorily without the need to raise the roof. For habitable purposes, you will need a roof of at least 7 ft 6 in (2.25 m) over at least half of the clear floor space, depending on local codes. You may be able to lower the attic floor at one edge to give this headroom. Basement space can also be useful as a recreational room for teenagers. In most base-

ments there should be room for table tennis or even a pool table. Don't design a room so rigidly for play that it cannot be turned to another use when the children grow up.

Renovation of commercial property has become popular in most countries. Huge buildings, such as unused warehouses, factories, hospitals and schools are bought, gutted, made safe, reroofed, divided into living units and supplied with drains, water, electricity and telephone lines. Everything else is left to the new owner to provide. This is one unique way of buying spaciousness and, since large windows are a characteristic of such buildings, often good light as well. The areas with plumbing such as kitchen and bathroom are usually partitioned and the rest of the space is an open area with infinite possibilities. This sort of conversion is useful for painters and sculptors, but can be enjoyed by anyone who would like to try a different way of living.

Access

The way you get into the space may be crucial to its success. Ladders are really only good for reaching stored items and are not a long term solution. If you can put in an external or a separate internal staircase and make the place truly self-contained, it will have much greater potential as a usable area. Building codes are strict on the subject of staircases, specifying precise dimensions and positioning for handrails. Always get professional advice. A spiral staircase takes up less room than a standard one, but because the full weight of the stair is carried on a single point, some extra support such as a structural wall or beam may have to be installed underneath. There is a limit to the size of objects that can be carried up a spiral staircase: for example, you may not be able to get a large table or a double bed or a sofa up the stairs. Remember, too, that the stair opening will take up some of the floor space in the room.

Stairs to a basement are often very steep, uneven and without a handrail. It may be worth extending them into the space below to give greater length and make them less steep, with more generous treads. Again, make sure you comply with local codes and get any necessary permits.

Light: Attics and Lofts

The marvelous thing about a space at the top of a building is the way light can come flooding in directly from the sky. Windows should be an integral part of your planning. Well-designed, functional skylights are available, which can be set high in the roof for privacy (say, in a bathroom or bedroom), or set lower to give a view. Some makes of skylights are very practical and come with their own waterproof flashing. They are available in many shapes and sizes, can be pivoted or hung from the side and can fit neatly between rafters. Lanterns are glazed, framed structures in the

roof, often seen on domes, which can flood the room with light, but they have to be custom-designed and built.

You can bring more light into the room by inserting arched or circular windows into the gable end of a house, a wall that is usually wasted as far as windows are concerned.

Light: Basements

Bringing light into a dark basement is more difficult to achieve. Deep basements are rather like caves, and even if they open out onto an area or small garden, they may still not get much light, particularly if they are overlooked by trees or other buildings. You can then make the very most of the available natural light, particularly in terraced houses, by dividing the front rooms from the back rooms with an internal pocket of space devoted to areas that don't require natural light, such as the bathroom, storage and utility rooms. Or you can open up the space by removing unnecessary walls, painting the

(above)
The combination of parallel stairs and hallway in this New York loft gives a a splendid vista of its iron columns.

walls white, then illuminating them with fluorescent tubes or tungsten halogen lamps,
which give a bright, whitish light, which looks
more like daylight than conventional bulbs.
If the room is to be used as a kitchen or living
room leading out onto a garden, you can light
it as for any kitchen or living room, but use
more light sources and stronger wattages
than in other rooms.

If one wall opens out onto an open space or
alleyway, you can bring in extra light by using
glass bricks for the wall. This will bring in
opaque light, rather in the way of a Japanese
screen. If you are creating a flat-roofed
addition in the garden, bubble skylights of
safety glass will also help to bring in light
from above. You can also add light by cutting
the garden back far enough to create
a decent-sized terrace, with room for a
table and chairs, to let in the sun. Enlarging
an original window to allow sliding doors
will increase the light and the feeling of
space.

Insulation and Sealing

For an attic conversion, you will require good
insulation in the roof space or the room will
become like an oven in summer and a refrigerator in winter. A basement will probably
need to be protected from moisture by lining
it with a barrier such as a watertight cement
coat. If this is done, the cement coat must not
be damaged (for example, by screws or nails),
so you will need freestanding furniture and
special picture hooks, which will not damage
the surface.

Plumbing and Electric Wiring

Make sure, while the main work is being done,
that adequate plumbing and electric wiring is
installed for all possible future needs. If you
want to put in a sink or toilet, for example, get
the plumbing done now. This will make it
cheaper and easier to install the units when
you are ready. Fit the best insulation you can
afford between the rafters, with an appropriate air gap and vapor barrier. Don't block up

essential ventilation openings. Basements can often be cold because so little sunshine gets into them. Here, too, good insulation is vital. But get any moisture proofing done first. Always make sure you get advice when considering electrical, plumbing or insulation work and make sure it is inspected or carries a guarantee.

Some Common Problems

ATTICS: LACK OF HEIGHT

You can make good use of the very low side walls that are so typical of attic spaces by installing low storage-seating or built-in cabinets all round the walls. A taller, desk-height shelf can be fitted under a window along one wall, if the wall is tall enough. When sitting at it, you won't bump your head and you have the advantage of working in the natural light coming from the window.

Useful space in the attic is often confined because there is clear headroom only in the center under the ridge of the roof. Steep roofs may have plenty of space in the middle, but not much useful floor area. The most common answer is to install dormer windows, which sit vertically on a sloping roof, have their own roof and give you space to move inside. A row of small dormer windows can add a lot to the space. Or they can be merged into a dormer strip and, as such, will dramatically enlarge the space. If dormers are installed at the front and the back of the attic, a ceiling of uniform height can be placed across. This gives the impression of a "normal" room, rather than an atticlike appearance.

If the room gets very hot in summer, then the roof insulation is insufficient. It will probably also be difficult to heat up in winter. Polystyrene or cork tiles on the walls may help. If the tiles are made of polystyrene, cover them in wallpaper to prevent molten bits from dropping onto people or furniture in case of fire. If tiles are made of cork, they may be left as they are. Roller blinds fixed to sloping skylights may help to save valuable space.

BASEMENTS: LACK OF LIGHT

Install patio doors with laminated double-glazing. If you have a flat-roofed addition, install bubble skylights, which add greatly to the natural light. Use daylight bulbs and tungsten halogen lights to give the impression of more daylight.

If the space has been sealed against moisture, you will not be able to use normal hardware for hanging pictures, mirrors, etc. You can buy hooks with three or four short prongs to use instead. They are not as sturdy, so be wary how you use them.

BASEMENTS: MOISTURE

Moisture needs skilled treatment. Always get professional advice. You may need a plastic membrane in the wall to prevent moisture from rising, or you may need to cover the inside with a concrete coating or skin.

(above)
A cheerful treatment for an attic room, with yellow paint on both blinds and walls, a mattress on the floor and a set of shelves built into the A of the house frame.

Safety

An outbreak of fire is probably the most worrying aspect about having a room in the roof. It is very important that all wiring should be done by a professional and inspected for correct installation. Central heating is a better choice than electric or gas heaters (because there is less likelihood of fire or fumes); and certainly avoid using wood-burning stoves, particularly if there are likely to be flammable materials in the room. Make sure that there are enough electrical outlets in the room so that none of them is overloaded. Check appliances frequently for damaged and frayed cords and wires.

Fire that originates from another part of the house is, of course, just as dangerous since drafts will spread the fire straight up the stairs, and there is often no other means of escape. It is always wise to get the advice of the local fire department or other local authority when planning a renovation. An expert should be able to advise you best on how to approach the job.

If possible, when you first begin using your attic space, arrange with your neighbors downstairs or next door that you may use their window or balcony as an escape route, should the need arise. Provide a rope or chain ladder firmly mounted on the window sill on the side of the house farthest from the staircase. Get professional advice about a suitable fire extinguisher and keep it where it can be quickly grabbed. Make sure the people who are using the room know all the exit routes and how to operate the fire extinguisher. If possible, install smoke alarms not just in the attic or basement itself, but in the stairwell and kitchen too.

Other safety precautions are to make sure the stairs (or ladder) up to the attic are well lit and that the stairs themselves conform to all safety regulations.

Furniture and Decoration
ATTICS

If the floor is wood, make sure it is strong enough to support everything. If you want to house heavy equipment, you may want to add a plywood surface over the joists. This can be stained, painted or covered with rugs, matting or carpet. Run the carpet part the way up the wall to give a greater feeling of space; it will be easier to vacuum too. If the floor meets the ceiling, as in some A-frames, you can enclose the angle of both floor and roof to give a neat finish and to hide electric wiring.

Make the most of good-looking beams, even if they are old, by papering or painting between them. You can leave the finish fairly rough. If the beams are not particularly old or interesting, paint them white or black. Tongue-and-groove ceiling and walls will conceal insulation, pipes and water heaters and will look attractive, while helping to insulate the room at the same time. If you like the natural look of the wood, you can give it a

(above)
Unconventional spaces can use unconventional furniture. This TV was created specifically for a loft.

(opposite)
Lovely, simple and bright attic bedroom with long, draped curtains hung on a wrought-iron pole.

matte finish but it can also be painted. White, or one of the nearly white colors, or oatmeal would be most suitable for a "living" room or workroom, but bright, cheerful colors would be more fun for a children's play space.

Use the bright daylight of an attic space to best advantage by making the most of pale colors. Provide interest with deeper-colored cushions, paintings or rugs. Natural fabrics, light colors, small prints, simple curtains or blinds will all complement the informal shape of an attic room. Light-colored does not, of course, mean wishy washy. Be bold with white and contrasts of pale and dark colors. Attics will respond well to a modern look, with freestanding metal furniture, metal-framed tables and chairs, a black and white scheme punctuated by primary colors and simply-framed prints on the walls.

If you think you may have difficulty getting large pieces of furniture up the stairs, remember that stores that sell enormous sofas and other big pieces of furniture are adept at taking out windows to get the furniture in. Alternatively, choose modular units, which can be carried up separately and are easier to move around, in case you want to rearrange the room. If you want to install something really heavy, get expert advice.

Lofts, Barns and Studios

What characterizes most large buildings of this type is their generous space and height, their stylish architectural and decorative features, and their grand scale. Decoration and furniture must be positive in concept and large in size. All-white walls always make a background with which you can do anything. However, large spaces can also accommodate deep, bold colors, enormous paintings and contrasts of walls with door and window frames. If possible, talk to the developer before too much work is done and get him or her to put electrical outlets wherever you want them. If a mezzanine floor is being built, you might persuade the developer to do some detailing of your own choosing. Once the plumbing is installed, you can build a kitchen and bathroom to your own plan. Any wall you add can carry services such as pipes and electric wires. You may want to have one separate room for sleeping and dressing. Build a wood frame, attach it to the floor, fix plasterboard on each side and paint it, and there is your bedroom. You can create a less permanent private space by running big screens along track in the floor, or fix a pole from which you can hang a muslin or more dramatic style of curtain. Heavy screens can run on metal rollers. Freestanding screens need to be large and will probably need casters, if you want to move them around. Make sure they are stable and won't fall over. A framework of bookshelves, specially built or as part of a modular system, is another way of forming a separate room. Mezzanine floors, designed to make the most of the height in a tall room, can be used in many different ways. The floor will cover a huge area, so make the most of the existing flooring. Old floorboards look very good when sanded and sealed, then covered with rugs. If the floor is concrete, you could cover it with heavy, industrial canvas treated with a water-resistant coating and given a good underlayment. You can paint flooring to emulate a carpet or tiles. Wood strip flooring can be used to cover concrete and so can parquet.

Walls look best when painted in white or dramatic plain colors, although a decorative paint technique can give a rich quality without distracting from the spaces and furniture in the room. Metal furniture and a modern minimalist look go well with warehouses, but period furniture on a large enough scale, if it is robust and workmanlike, will look good too. Among the attractions of these large spaces are their uncompromising strength and structure, so try to preserve this.

Floors can be made of anything from

concrete to wide, wood floorboards and covered in all kinds of materials, from matting to linoleum or industrial vinyl flooring (of the kind often used in airports and other public spaces).

Furniture can be giant-sized and it can be used to create its own divisions. In such a big space, you can use one end as a workshop or workroom and even create large works there, while living comfortably at the other end without the two uses clashing. One part of the space can be divided from the other by storage units with built-in or freestanding screens, whereas a change in level (a low platform, for example, will often create an effective psychological division) or you can build a separating wall. Changes in floor level also allow for a change in floor covering, without that rather awkward joining that is necessary when both styles of covering are on the same level.

Basements

In partially excavated basements, where one side of the house opens out onto a garden and there are only a few steps leading down to the house on the other side, you can make the most of the available natural light by installing plenty of mirrors, making all the windows as large as possible and double-glazing the doors throughout.

Cheerful yellow and white colors will add to a feeling of sunshine, and light wicker or pale wood furniture, with fabrics in fresh gingham and checks, will also make for a brighter look.

In many deep basements, when most of the light has to be provided by electricity, it will be frustrating to try and make the room something it is not. It may be better to turn it into a comfortable tent or cave. Dark reds and other warm colors, woven woolen fabrics, kilims, cushions and fabrics on the walls will all help to make the room seem inviting, and good lighting can make it even cozier.

Design Checklist
- *What do you want to do in the room?*
- *Will there be enough room for the activity you have in mind when the room is complete?*
- *Can you organize satisfactory access?*
- *Is the room dry?*
- *Can you get the furniture you want into the room? Don't guess; do measure and check that the room can support the weight.*
- *Are there enough electrical outlets on all walls?*
- *Do you need special lighting?*
- *Are you making the most of the natural light?*
- *Do you need telephone jacks?*
- *Which items in the room will need storage space? List them and plan storage for each.*
- *Do you need a desk or work surface?*
- *Where does the work surface need to go to get the best use of the light?*
- *Will children use the room?*
- *What are the potential dangers?*
- *How will you overcome them?*
- *Do get professional advice.*

Outside Meets Inside

The entrance to your home is important from your own point of view and tells other people something about you. If the house is one of a group or row, you should consider it as an integral part of the street. It doesn't have to conform in every respect to the surrounding houses, but whether you want to add a porch, alter windows or doors, or extend upward, the result should be in proportion and in sympathy with the existing architecture.

Windows and doors have a very dramatic effect on the appearance of a house. Georgian houses are particularly admired because of the elegant proportions of the windows, mullions, fanlights and frames. Many houses have suffered from inappropriate replacement of both windows and doors over the years, but there are many professionals specializing in period homes who can double-glaze and repair windows in an appropriate way. Any addition should use the same materials as the original structure, and the proportions should be in keeping with the style.

The other important factor is color. In countries which get a lot of strong sunlight, bright, intense colors are often used, whereas in the grayer light of northern countries, these colors appear too bright, and it is better to choose something more subtle. Researching local color traditions is fascinating. Try to find something compatible with the neighboring houses.

What's Required?

There are so many ways for the outside of the house to meet the inside, from a small front door opening onto the street to a large conservatory leading into a garden. In this chapter we shall look at several transition points: the entrance hall, porch, or sunroom and doors leading onto a patio.

Entrance Hall

The entrance hall is the gateway to your home. First impressions are very important, and people should feel welcome from the moment they set foot inside. Spacious halls offer plenty of opportunity for furnishing and decorating, but even cramped, narrow entrances can provide a welcoming atmosphere and can be made to appear more spacious. The simple addition of mirrors and soft wall lights can make them seem less bleak.

If you can, remove part of one wall, opening up the space to the living room, but leave a small portion of the wall intact so that it

can be used as a lobby for hanging coats. However, always get professional advice before moving any wall. Halogen uplights, throwing light onto a white ceiling, will give a much friendlier impression than ceiling lights shining down.

Paneling the wall up to dado height and painting it a different color than the upper area will seem to lower the height. You need not even panel: you can simply paint the lower part of the wall in a different color than the upper area, and mark the change with a piece of simple beading. Choose bright, cheerful colors if the hall is dark. Alternatively, choose two different co-ordinating wallpapers with a border to replace the beading. A narrow console table, narrow chests of small drawers or open shelves will take up far less space than a wide chest or table, and they are invaluable for holding gloves and letters.

In a remodeled house, the original hall is often divided, leaving a space into which it would be impossible to fit any sort of chest

(previous page)
This pretty little first-floor addition fits in beautifully with the character of the architecture of the house.

(above)
Stone has been used here to create a really stunning entrance hall – the eye follows the pattern to the door.

or even a folding table. You could even install a wall-mounted coat rack, however, with hooks, a narrow shelf and a small integral mirror. These racks can sometimes be found in second-hand shops, or you might find a modern version in metal and bright paint. Try to avoid the ubiquitous, safe oatmeal and brown scheme for narrow hallways. These colors will add to the impression of second-class space. It's much better to go for light, sunny yellows and clear, cheerful colors. A row of small paintings or mirrors take up little space and will attract the eye away from the narrowness.

A larger hall can be made very attractive with the addition of a circular table and a couple of upright chairs. Gertrude Jekyll, the famous Victorian garden designer, used to receive visitors in her hall, which had benches designed so that she could sit with visitors and look at landscape plans.

The sort of lobby to be found in tall blocks of apartments, which are usually square boxes, can be treated simply and boldly. It is useful to have a large mirror with a painting or trompe l'oeil opposite for it to reflect. Lighting should be discreet, but bright enough to see clearly, with perhaps adjustable spots recessed into the ceiling or uplights mounted on the wall. A trompe l'oeil has to be painted by a first-rate artist; otherwise it will look ridiculous. It's better to use a panel or section of grisaille wallpaper in grays and black. Hallways attract dust, mud and leaves and a small doormat alone will not prevent this from encroaching into the rest of the house. It's best to buy door matting by the foot and use this to cover a large area of the hall floor. The hall should be efficiently heated — another welcoming feature. Make sure the front door is solid and fits into its frame when closed to prevent drafts. Weatherstripping is cheap and easy to install and makes a great difference to the insulation in a hall. A heavy curtain placed over the front door is a traditional form of extra insulation.

(above)
A shady veranda with a long, sociable bench is an attractive halfway house between home and garden.

Porch/Veranda

A porch is usually a small structure which acts as a transitional area between the outside and the home. It frames the front door and, in cold or windy areas, it can be completely enclosed, providing an effective capsule against the elements. In warmer areas, it can be just a roof over the heads of people waiting to come in. An enclosed porch gives invaluable extra space for boots, while a glassed in porch can become a miniature greenhouse, providing a warm showcase for geraniums. Just because a porch is small, this doesn't mean that you can afford to ignore the architectural character of the building. If you live in a tiny nineteenth-century Gothic cottage, a Gothic porch, with a sloping roof and carved wood uprights, will look quite at home, but on a sixties house, a flat-roofed porch supported by a slender pier would be far more in keeping, although you could certainly exchange the pier for a more substantial one.

Houses that get a lot of sun will be more likely to have a verandah than a porch. This should be furnished with comfortable reclining chairs and small tables for drinks. Wicker looks good; simple wood benches and canvas deck chairs are all in keeping. The floor can be slatted or made up of wood boards. Paint the woodwork white, unless you want to choose the acid pastels of traditional seaside towns.

Additions

The materials used for an addition should always be kept in sympathy with the rest of the house, and the structure should be similar in proportion too, so the finished result still looks like one house. There are many different types of additions available, from brick boxes to sunrooms and greenhouses, but anything too grand on a cottage or small terraced house will not be in keeping with the style and always sits uneasily next to the house.

An addition can be useful not only for creating a whole new room, but also for enlarging a room that already exists. It is usual to add onto the back of the house, where the addition can take in part of the garden, but sometimes a house can be extended sideways to create a new hallway or to increase the size of the original rooms.

A small, boxlike addition can sometimes have another room built above it, creating an extra bedroom or bathroom. The most skillful additions are those that you wouldn't know had been built on. You will probably need building permits, so always get professional advice before any work is started.

Sunroom/Conservatory

Conservatories were originally designed in Victorian England to provide a garden in winter when everything outside looked dead. They were called "winter gardens." Today's conservatories, called sunrooms or sunporches, are usually less grand and are available in a wide range of styles, to complement any house, from a Victorian mansion to a small house or country cottage. There are also some interesting examples of tiny conservatories jutting out from the first floor of a house or little Gothic edifices designed to complement the architecture of a house.

If you are building a new sunroom, make sure that it faces a direction where plenty of sun will get into the room. Try to ensure that the proportions of the windows and that mullions are in keeping with the style of the rest of the house. Choose a design which incorporates double-glazing with window frames suitable for standard double-glazing units; otherwise condensation may be a problem. Various glazing materials are available today, the most common being single-paned glass and double-glazing. The cheapest option of all is a double-walled translucent plastic, which adapts well to curves and provides some insulation, but which you

cannot see through (although most plants will thrive behind it). Tempered glass is a good glazing material and polycarbonate is unbreakable, but both of these are rather expensive options. Don't have too much glass. Some solid wall will help to prevent the place from becoming too hot, diminish temperature fluctuations and provide privacy. The windows should come far enough down so that you can see outside when seated. **(See Lights, Glass & Mirrors, page 280.)**

There are many different styles of furniture that work particularly well in sunrooms. Contemporary metal chairs are suitable, provided you have plenty of soft cushions. Wrought-iron and perforated metal can look good because they let the light through. Rattan and wicker give a light and easy feeling to the room, and folding canvas chairs can easily be taken outside if you want to move onto the terrace later on.

Decorating a Sunroom

Try to get a light, airy, garden feeling with plenty of plants, rattan and wicker chairs or canvas. Metal furniture, perforated cast-iron or curved wrought-iron, or tiny folding metal chairs with slatted seats, like French park furniture, can look charming, although you may need cushions if you want to sit on it for any length of time. If you enjoy an informal look, fill the room with a motley collection of secondhand furniture. You can paint everything one color to give it a coordinated look. White can look good, but if you use too much in a large sunroom that gets a lot of sun, the effect can be quite blinding. It might be more soothing to choose a dark green. Darker colors are very often used to paint the frame as well, for the same reason and because white paint deteriorates more quickly than other colors when exposed to sunlight. If the room is purely for leisure, fill it with sculptures and odd objets trouvés. Ceramic or quarry tiles will look best on the floor, although if it is a room

which is more part of the house than the garden, a wood floor would be perfectly in keeping. A vinyl floor in a pattern of bricks and tiles could look elegant too. However, beware: the most upscale vinyl is almost as expensive as the real thing.

You will certainly need blinds or some sort of shade for the windows; otherwise the sun will make the room too hot for both plants and people.

Glass Doors

Top floors of buildings have a lovely, bright, airy feeling, whereas (particularly in cities), the ground and lower floors may be quite dark. The darkness of a ground floor interior can fade into insignificance, however, if one wall can be glazed to provide a frame for a garden, however small, beyond. Even in cold weather, when you don't want to open the door, the garden becomes a viewable space, providing an always interesting view and allowing light inside.

One worry for many people is the vulnerability of so much glass. If you want elegant, old-fashioned French doors, then it may be necessary to have safety bars installed or metal folding shutters behind it, which you slide and lock whenever you leave the house. Alternatively, you might have the doors double-glazed with safety glass. An effective alternative would be a modern patio door. The most satisfactory doors from the security point of view are the commercial ones, which can take the place of a complete wall. They have a simple locking mechanism that cannot be tampered with from the outside. These doors are usually made from PVC-coated frames, which need no maintenance apart from the occasional wipe with a damp cloth, and are made of strengthened double-glazing, which makes it almost impossible for anyone to break in. Wood or metal frames, with large, square panes of such double-glazed glass, are very secure. You can have a small, similarly glazed, metal-framed door opening

(above)

A very large space with big arched windows can be enhanced by the added splendor of stained glass.

within it. Doors such as this, looking out onto even the smallest area or alleyway, can give a great feeling of space and provide somewhere to grow plants and a place to sit and relax.

Budget Ideas

- *You can often buy secondhand furniture, such as umbrella stands, hat stands and bedside tables, which are the right size for a small hall or sunroom. They will look as though they are matching pieces if they are painted, perhaps in white for a small sunroom or colors to suit the decor of your hall.*

- *Secondhand deckchairs or cane chairs can be given a completely new look if you paint and cover them with new fabric. Deckchair canvas is available in really good, bright plain colors or stripes and there's an enormous choice of upholstery fabrics.*

- *A very long, narrow shelf positioned above a hall radiator can provide space for letters, gloves, etc., which otherwise often end up* on the floor. Place a mirror above the shelf, and it will seem to double the width. You can give the mirror a frame by fitting beading all round the edge of it.

- *If you want tiles in your sunroom, it is worth looking for seconds in tile shops. Some manufacturers have these near the factory, and there are often warehouses in large cities. You may have to search through lots of tiles you don't like, but there are often good bargains to be had. Terracotta is the best choice because it absorbs moisture. You will need a humid environment if you want to grow plants.*

- *Matting is one of the cheapest forms of flooring and makes a good covering for a hall, provided it is properly laid and doesn't curl up at the edges. Modern matting usually has some sort of backing to prevent dust and dirt from slipping through to the floor below, which makes it easier to vacuum. It also comes in attractive colors.*

- *If you want to cheer up a dull floor, why not*

stencil a design onto it? Modern paints are available that will withstand the tread of feet. (Automobile spray paints are especially good for this.)

- Mirrors can add style to a room and also light and a feeling of spaciousness. Cheap mirror can be fixed onto the wall and surrounded with beading or a wider wood-frame. Paint the frame white or a color to match the wallcovering, or give it an ornate top and paint it gold.
- Paint the exterior walls white for extra light.
- Old-fashioned hat stands, incorporating hooks, a mirror, a narrow shelf and an umbrella rack, can often be found in junk shops and can be stripped or painted.
- A very large door mat will absorb plenty of outside mud and dust, and make cleaning the house easier.

Design Checklist

HALLWAY/PORCH

- Is there room to hang coats and hats, store boots, etc?
- Is there room for a small chair?
- Is there room for a vase of flowers?
- Does the decor lead into the rest of the home in a co-ordinated way?
- Is there adequate lighting? Is it pleasant? (Lighting is one of the things that can do most to transform an unwelcoming space.)
- Is it in keeping with the architecture of the house?
- Is it big enough to grow plants?
- Is it big enough to hold storage for boots and other things best kept out of the house?
- Is it secure? It could be that the porch itself is easy to enter and then provides screening for burglars. Make sure the inside door is fitted with secure bolts and locks.
- Is it glazed? This can be a very good opportunity to introduce a little stained glass into your home. A traditional home may well have stained glass in the top half of the door anyway, and some stained glass in the porch could complement it. More modern homes can also be given a cheerful appearance with stained glass in the porch.

SUNROOM/PATIO DOORS

- Is there good shelving for plants?
- Is there room to sit comfortably?
- Will the sunporch be too hot?
- Does it make the most of the view?
- Are the doors secure? Patio doors should be double-glazed and use safety glass. Get professional advice on the type of glass.
- Do they give a good view of the garden from inside? (The garden may be no bigger than the small area of a basement and may still be big enough to sit in and also to grow greenery.)
- Would curtains get in the way of the window/door? If so, consider using blinds instead. There are so many different styles of blind, from the simplest roller blind to adjustable Venetian blinds, and some of the gathered ones look very like curtains.

A Short Guide to Interior Styles

Over the centuries, styles have evolved, have then been absorbed by other styles, overlapped, faded out, reemerged and arrived in different parts of the world at different times and with slightly different characteristics. Many have survived as models for today's eclectic interiors. A great deal of research has been done on what materials, colors and techniques were used in the past, and many fabrics, wallpapers and other products are available that are made with historical accuracy.

This brief introduction to some of the most popular and longer-lasting styles is arranged in alphabetical order. For further reference, there is a chronological table at the back of this book. The dates are fairly arbitrary because many styles kept going for decades alongside others, while some were already in the making before they were recognized and given a name. The styles here have been categorized as "historic" (with dates) and "timeless" (regional or national).

Many interior styles have received their names or titles from the architecture they were designed to complement. However, interior furnishings had more scope for variation and change than their buildings and did not always coincide exactly with the dates of the houses that they furnished. This style directory is only the briefest introduction to a fascinatingly complex subject.

American Country

From 1620, the first settlers in New England and Pennsylvania lived simple, spartan lives relying on furniture, rather than decoration, to create their interiors. A multitude of woods was available to them, but sophisticated tools were lacking. Their houses were basically log cabins based, whenever possible, on the familiar architecture of their European homes. Everything had a rustic, handcrafted look. A chair known as the Boston Rocker, which resembled a high-back Windsor chair, was the first chair designed specifically for rocking.

Almost everything had to be home-made, so rag rugs and patchwork quilts were created out of precious scraps of old clothes and bits of burlap. Floors were mainly of sand or painted sailcloth and, up to 1775, rag carpets were placed onto them for warmth and a little comfort in a bleak world. Carpets were woven on hand looms strung with a linen warp and woven with scraps of used textiles of all sorts, cut into strips and sewn together. Pieces of rug, the width of the loom, were stitched together to make larger carpets. Rugs were also made of patchwork; knitted or crocheted wool and hooked rugs, in particular, were characteristic of the style.

Decoration on walls and furniture was provided by paint. Stenciling was a cheap and simple way of decorating, its repeat patterns producing a characteristic country look. The shape and function of early pieces of furniture were based on the European (largely Dutch and English) provincial furniture that the settlers had known at home, and some were decorated in recognizably Austrian and Swiss motifs. Furniture included settles, corner cupboards, ladder-back and rush-seated chairs, drop-leaf and refectory tables.

As people spread out across the country, the style adapted to suit the weather, materials and resources, and different areas evolved their own styles. In general, walls, ceilings, floors and many furnishings had natural finishes, such as undyed cotton, calico and

crash, cream whitewash, limewash, terra-cotta, earthenware, natural stone, slate and cedar wood. Vegetable dyes often produced rich, natural colors and all of these were enlivened with splashes of color in quilts, naive paintings and portraits, appliqué and other embroidery. The fireplace or stove was a focal point and might be in the form of a European-style ceramic stove. The simple windows usually had a deep recess, and roller blinds were popular, often with both internal and external shutters.

- *Curtains were usually short and simple in style to save on material and they were mainly used to retain heat; ceilings were wood clad.*
- *Doors were made of timber planks with metal hinges and latches.*
- *The bed would be well built and was often a four poster or half-canopy.*
- *Many copies of original designs of quilts, stencils and furniture are now available in coordinated collections.*

Art Deco (1925 – 1939)

This name was given to the fashions that dominated the decorative arts in the years between the First and Second World Wars. Also known as Jazz Modern, it originated in France and was imported en masse to Britain and the United States. Art Deco was influenced by the Bauhaus experiments in Germany (see Modernist), and by Cubism, Diaghilev's Ballet Russe and Egyptology. It is epitomized by Clarice Cliff pottery in England and the interiors for Radio City Music Hall in New York, by the architecture of Le Corbusier and the furniture of the Irish designer, Eileen Gray, who worked in Paris. The look was one of disciplined curves, large furniture, bold backgrounds, lacquered screens, Lalique glass, sculptural light fittings (for example, of a girl holding a glass globe), tasseled cushions, opulence and modernity. Pattern consisted of highly stylized flower clusters, flattened geometric faces, rich reds, blues, purples, pinks and chrome yellows. Art Deco was a very popular style for bathrooms, which were a great novelty in the 1920s.

Art Nouveau (1895 – 1939)

Art Nouveau succeeded, yet dovetailed with the Arts and Crafts movement. Its name came from a shop that opened in Paris in 1895. In Italy it was called *Stil Liberty* after the London store; in Germany and Scandinavia, *Jugendstil* (youth style). Its chief characteristics were curvilinear, elongated forms, often described as organic because shapes found in nature and vegetation were used. Colors were clear and bright, particularly a brilliant peacock blue. Bentwood furniture, manufactured by Thonet, was an innovation in mass production, introducing new possibilities for furniture in houses, public places and offices. Tiffany in New York produced Art Nouveau stained glass lamps, and the Glasgow architect, Charles Rennie Mackintosh, produced

(above left)
An Art Nouveau glass lampshade and an intricately carved, tall-back chair.

many Art Nouveau designs for buildings, furniture and textiles. His own home in 1900 was designed in typical, if exaggerated, Art Nouveau style with an all-white painted interior, thin voile curtains, huge white fireplaces, a pale gray carpet and embroidered cushions. The dining room walls were covered in gray-brown wrapping paper and the high backs of the chairs formed a decorative screen around the table. Furniture was inlaid with stylized motifs in purple, pink and green glass. Some of Mackintosh's furniture designs are being reproduced today, in Glasgow and in Milan. Liberty of London commissioned many pieces in the Art Nouveau style in silver, glass and fabrics.

Arts and Crafts (1888 – 1939)

One of the prime influences of this movement was William Morris, who felt that industrialization had debased ornament and design. The Arts and Crafts movement aimed to produce designs for furniture and other household arts inspired by "truth to materials" and "fitness for purpose." Great emphasis was put on simplification and honesty of decoration, and inspiration from the Middle Ages and the natural world in naturalistic but formal patterns and a return to high standards of craftsmanship. Designers used light, clear colors, and an airier style served as an antidote to Victorian clutter. Morris himself designed tapestries, stained glass, wallpapers and fabrics, and was very much influenced by medieval craft designs. The style was adopted in America at the same time, with a strong emphasis on handmade objects and furniture. The American architect, Frank Lloyd Wright, was also a promoter of the Arts and Crafts philosophy.

Throughout the nineteenth century, rooms were divided into compartments. Screens were popular and so were simple, wood standard and table lamps and centrally hung chandeliers. Ungathered lengths of fabric were often fixed to a wall instead of wallpaper, stopping at dado height in a similar fashion to eighteenth-century tapestries. Pale wood, often oak, was used for paneling, and hand crafted furniture was essential.

- *Curtains were hung simply from bold rings on a pole and were only lightly gathered to show off their pattern.*
- *Fireplaces were tiled with stylized floral motifs around a small iron grate with a simple wood border.*
- *Shelves were popular and were generally intended for display. It was common to have a narrow shelf at picture-molding height to show off plates and china.*
- *Stained and leaded glass in clear, jewel-like colors was used for decorative objects and in windows.*

The look was of pale woods, applied patterns and uncluttered interiors (although the prints on wallpapers, fabrics and tiles were very busy). Many of Morris's own wallpapers and fabrics are still produced today, and antique or machine-made tapestries are widely available.

Biedermeier (1815 – 1848)

Biedermeier has been described as a pot pourri taken from various aspects of the classical tradition. Its lines were graceful, but simple and sturdy – a reaction against the elaborate style of Rococo, but also an answer to the evident shortages of materials and money during the Napoleonic Wars. Straight lines and angular shapes were the main keynotes, with fluid, stocky-curved legs, rolled arms and generous upholstery. The simple lines of the furniture were embellished by lavish veneers, making it look very rich and precious. The Biedermeier bed, with its elegant lyre-shaped sides or swan necks, was known as the sleigh bed or *lit bateau*.

Sumptuous finishes were used, such as mahogany and other rich veneers and woods

(opposite)

A Biedermeier-style room showing the typically curved, yet solid lines, the exquisite golden veneer and the striped upholstery fabric.

that were stained to resemble ebony, inlaid in paler woods featuring classical motifs, such as scallops, stars, urns, sun rays and lyres. The decoration was rich, but kept to a strict minimum. Fabrics were utterly plain in color and texture. Strong, hardwearing natural fiber, ribbed silk, good quality worsteds or corduroy would be a good choice, with Persian rugs or hand-knotted rugs on the floors.

- Walls were kept as plain as possible; if wallpapers were used at all, they would be Regency or Gustavian stripes.
- Windows would either have lightly gathered or swagged curtains, draped muslin or voile across the top window, hanging at each side over projecting roundels or Austrian balloon shades, with or without frills. The style was embraced by Germany, Austria, Scandinavia and Central Europe.

By 1853 the style had become unfashionable, but at the end of the nineteenth century, it had made a comeback, with a major exhibition in Vienna. In the 1920s its simplicity was an influence on the Bauhaus movement and eventually spread to Holland, Italy, France, England, America and Russia.

Nowadays reproduction, antique or modern versions of the furniture are widely available.

Bohemian (1910 – 1930)

This was a highly colorful style, based on the artistic and literary lives of the Bloomsbury Group in London. Virginia Woolf, Duncan Grant and Vanessa Bell were all involved.

The style is epitomized by the work of the Omega Workshop, started by Roger Fry in 1913, where leading artists of the day—supported by the writers and artists who made up the Bloomsbury Group—were persuaded to produce painted walls, fabrics, cushions, lampshades, decorated furniture and ceramics. Fry believed that the pleasure he and his colleagues took in the production of these objects would be communicated to their users. Charleston Manor, home of Duncan Grant and Vanessa Bell from 1916, was decorated entirely in the style. No surface or object was left undecorated and the house was visited by many artists during the First World War and later. Its highly personal style requires confidence and panache and sees decoration as an art form, rather than just repeat patterns. The bedroom was intimate, with watercolors hung on the walls and very similar to Provençale interiors. Window recesses were painted and the whole room was in soft, slightly faded colors. China, plates, bowls and so on were seen as objects to decorate. Informality is the name of the game, but not naïveté. It is an unconventional artist's studio approach, with fabric paints and dyes, stylized almost abstract motifs, stencils with exaggerated enlarged motifs and trompe l'oeil. The Bohemian style of trompe l'oeil was not the meticulous depiction of ruined buildings and broken columns of Gothic interiors, but a sketchlike picture of, perhaps, a garden with clothes hanging out to dry on a line. The Omega workshops closed in 1919 but Charleston Manor has now been restored and is open to the public. Many modern pieces of pottery and some curtain fabrics have a similar painterly quality.

Chinoiserie

Chinese taste spread throughout European countries during the later seventeenth century to the early nineteenth century, and imports included fine porcelain and hand-painted wallpapers. Chinoiserie describes a style which reflected the fanciful notions that Western artisans held of China, which had been fashioned by travelers' tales since the Middle Ages and by a rather imperfect understanding of the designs of fashionable imported textiles, porcelain and objets d'art. Chinoiserie is a mixture of Chinese motifs with a Western interpretation: wallpapers were designed with oriental hunting scenes, but the hunters would all have European

faces, and the flora and fauna would have the meticulous accuracy of Chinese paintings.

Colonial

This style, sometimes known as Colonial Georgian, prevailed in America from the late seventeenth century to the Declaration of Independence in 1776. By this time there was an established merchant class on the eastern coast and the demand for comfort led to new designs. American architects and artisans developed the Classical and Palladian idiom into a distinct national style, retaining some of the simplicity of the Queen Anne style. They were influenced by English handbooks of architecture, interior design and furniture design. Interiors of large Palladian mansions were formally elegant and Italianate, less folksy and basic than American Country style, with gracious proportions, grander fireplaces, taller ceilings and more elegant furniture. However, many of the design elements were exactly the same: natural

(above)
This small chair is upholstered in the sort of floral chintz often used in American Colonial interiors.

fabrics, floral motifs, home-made rugs and quilts, and tongue-and-groove paneling. These new larger houses had a central hall, two parlors and a separate dining room. One parlor was for entertaining and was furnished formally with a sofa, chairs, mirror, several small tables and perhaps a desk. The other parlor was for the family's use, with a daybed, chairs, pine tables and perhaps a cradle for the baby. Furniture-making in the eighteenth century was one of the first trades in which American artisans could compete with Europeans and produce pieces with a true American flavor. Garlands and scrolls were introduced as decorative motifs, often in relief patterns. From mid-century, fashions changed as rapidly as they did in England, reflecting influences from Rococo, Gothic, Chinoiserie, Greek Taste and, in particular, from the Adams brothers' use of these styles. Australian Colonial has a Victorian eclecticism and a generosity of proportion. Wide balconies run all around the house to provide protection from the sun. Australian Colonial includes filigree cast-iron balconies on the first floor and shallow, sloping roofs made of corrugated iron. It is quite a Victorian Gothic look.

All the American countries occupied by the Spanish have a European look, but with a carefree informality and a celebration of vivid color, which is all their own.

- *Houses have wood balconies running all round, painted in sea blues and greens, mixed with midnight blues and complemented by bright reds, oranges and yellows.*
- *Furniture is made of wicker or simple, heavy wood pieces because the high humidity causes delicate furniture to warp and split.*
- *Cooking facilities are primitive and the furniture is kept to a minimum, except for chairs to lounge about in and a large table.*
- *Lighting is by converted oil lamps and kept at a low level, providing pools of light.*
- *Floors would be wood boards, covered with rush or woven mats.*

- *Textiles are handwoven, brightly colored and highly patterned.*
- *Curtains run on simple rods and windows have wood shutters. Bead curtains and muslin are used to keep out insects.*

Directoire (c. 1793 – 1804)

This was a transitional style in French taste somewhere between the Neo-Classicism of Louis XVI and Empire style. Like Empire style, it corresponds to English Regency style. The name derived from the Directorate, established in 1795 and overthrown when Napoleon formed the Consulate in 1804. This style was influenced by contemporary archaeological discoveries in ancient Egypt, Herculaneum and Greece. None of the interiors have survived to the present day, but the characteristics were the Greek chair or *klismos*, with a concave or rolled-over back, stools with X-shaped supports, bronze vessels resembling the ancient Roman model and beds with triangular pediments.

Edwardian or Nineties

This was an English style of the late nineteenth century, which blended Victorian taste with a touch of Arts and Crafts (although the look was much more conventional). It was much in evidence in the ordinary homes of the newly wealthy and incorporated many new-fangled ideas, such as gas and later, electric lighting, and furniture was chopped up and altered without any scruples to achieve what the owner considered to be smart. Families used to buy up portraits at auction houses and put them in the hall, to seem as though they were their own family ancestors. Polished mahogany furniture was popular.

The living room would be arranged in separate seating areas: a large sofa and comfortable chairs placed in front of the fire in winter, or turned toward the window in summer. This arrangement was for the family

and important visitors. Behind that were several small tables with chairs, where the vicar and other lesser visitors might sit.

Elizabethan Empire (1804 – 1814) (see Tudor)

A style that originated in France, whose name was derived from the First Empire. It first started in Paris after the French Revolution and then spread throughout the whole of Europe in a more or less desultory fashion until a form of Gothic revival occurred around 1830. Empire corresponds to the Regency style of design in England and was largely invented by the two architects, Charles Percier and Pierre François-Leonard Fontaine, who decorated the state apartments of the First Consul. Interiors that were devised by these architects still survive and can be seen at Fontainebleau, Compiegne and Malmaison. The style of Empire was basically in the Neo-Classical, but it was combined with an attempt to copy what was known of ancient furniture and decorative motifs, including ancient Egyptian styles. Its main claim to fame is the creation of the chaise-longue, the sleigh bed and the long looking glass.

English Country Style

This highly successful look has evolved over many centuries to become an important style that has inspired decor in every Western country. It covers all sorts of country homes, including farmhouses, country cottages and manor houses. English Country Style relies on a careful, but informal arrangement of good quality furniture and fabrics and has the same magic as the seemingly casual, but carefully tended English country garden. Indeed, it brings the garden right into the home in the form of floral wallcoverings and chintzes with florid cabbage roses or sprigs of rosebuds. The look requires upholstered sofas and chairs with loose covers, low, circular tables, ladder-back and Windsor chairs, mixed with the odd dark-oak Jacobean piece. Perhaps a

(above)

An Elizabethan interior with bare floorboards, linen paneling at the far end of the great hall, heavy, carved oak furniture and an enormous tapestry.

grandfather or wall-hung grandmother clock and collections of china, glass and other objects are mixed in. Glass-doored bookcases and showcases are used for holding special china and books, as they keep out the dust. Anything from the seventeenth century onward will fit in with this style, if it is carefully placed and of the right proportions and materials. The first known use of flowers on wallpaper was in the seventeenth century.

Bedrooms may be either pretty or grand in style and these are often more formal than the rest of the house, but the look for children's rooms or boudoirs is much lighter and simpler. A small table is placed by the arm of every upholstered chair, for placing a tea cup, for writing correspondence or for holding reading matter. Informal arrangements of different paintings decorate the walls; there are large, ceramic table lamps with fabric or parchment shades, built-in cupboards and several sets of library shelves.

The kitchen should have plenty of wood

surfaces, including a large kitchen table with drawers, perhaps a dresser and a fuel-burning stove, which is always warm for drying laundry and gives the kitchen an inviting atmosphere. Decorative paint techniques such as stippling and ragging can be used, all with a matte finish.

Country cottages have a similar look, but they are based much more on practicality because originally, the inhabitants were villagers and farm workers, with not much time for leisure. Walls were painted plaster or papered in small-scale patterns. Curtains consisted of simple, cotton checks or ginghams, or floral patterns. Materials were natural: wood, brass and iron.

The cottage would have farmhouse furniture, but a scaled down version: a small dresser, a two-seater sofa and Windsor chairs. There would be embroidered cushions, samplers and small pictures and perhaps photographs hung individually on the wall. There would be a small open stove in the kitchen and open shelves lined with pots of homemade jams with a wood plate rack above the sink. This sort of kitchen would have muted, natural colors, stained or painted wood, not stripped or pale.

French Provincial (Style Rustique)

A distinctive style which, like English Country, is based on country homes (particularly in the South of France), over many centuries and can be adapted to large or small houses. The key quality is elegance, with tall doors, tall French windows, cool colors and surfaces.

- *Filigree lace is often used around windows to keep the sun out. Nothing is hidden and there are exposed beams in the ceiling, with ceramic tiles or polished wood on the floors.*
- *The kitchen is unfitted and generously large with a big cast-iron stove.*

Everything is in the open, including open shelves, and arranged for maximum ease of use, rather than for neatness or prettiness, giving an overall feeling of elegance and utility.

Fabrics are cotton, often Provençale prints, which were originally block-printed by hand in Marseilles in imitation of the printed cottons, which came over by boat from India. They are now machine-printed in Tarascon en masse. Earthenware pottery, faience tiles and glazes in green, ocher, blue, white and terracotta all feature strongly. Armoires for linen, bedding and clothes are to be found in the bedrooms, with side buffets or sideboards for cutlery and table linen in the kitchen or dining room, and rush-seated wood or willow chairs and banquettes. Wardrobes and shelves are lined with fabric and edged with embroidered borders.

The bedroom is simple in style and kept uncluttered, with a circular side table covered with an embroidered cloth and tall, narrow windows are lace or cotton-curtained.

Georgian (1714 – 1830)

This was a general term for various styles in English architecture and interior design from the accession of George I to the death of George IV. "Early Georgian" denotes the historical period from circa 1714 through the 1730s; "Middle Georgian" covers the 1740s and 1750s, and "Late Georgian" means the 1760s to circa 1830. The movements during these periods included Adam style, Rococo, Greek Taste, Neo-Classicism, Gothic Revival, Etruscan Taste, Egyptian Taste and so on, and the design movements in furniture were Chippendale, Hepplewhite and Sheraton. The main characteristics that held these styles together were respect for good crafts-manship and a leaning toward a classical system of design and proportion, flexible enough to accommodate phases as different as chinoiserie and Pompeian. The style began with a revival of the Palladian arch and the introduction of the English Palladian country

(above)

This is a typical Georgian interior: its classical proportions are furnished with elegance and grace.

Interior Styles **195**

painting of crumbling, classical buildings in a wide landscape.

The Victorian Gothic revival in the eighteenth century was more earnest and tried harder to be historically accurate. The newly rich built themselves Gothic fairy tale castles; even workmen's cottages and lesser houses were built in the Gothic style. Two architects are particularly associated with the nineteenth century Gothic revival: Augustus Pugin and Giles Gilbert Scott. For Pugin, Gothic architecture and religion were as one and stood for truth: there would be no more blind windows or fake features just for the sake of symmetry. This was in keeping with the Arts and Crafts movement, which emerged at about the same time. Pugin was responsible for many of the interiors of the Houses of Parliament in London. He designed dozensof wallpapers and carpets for the buildingand his papers are still hand-printed fromthe original blocks for refurbishment of the building. Scott took Pugin's ideas a stage further, designing all manner of Gothic ornaments, such as gargoyles, buttresses and leaf moldings, which could be made in iron and then veneered with stone.

Gothic style relies on architectural effects. Windows are important and should be vaulted, then pointed with plain, ogee or trefoil arches. Square sash windows can be screened to form arches by attaching cut-out plywood arches to the tops of the window frames. Curved mullions can be added over glass to form arches. Leaded lights can also be added. Most Gothic cathedrals and churches had stone or tiled floors, and nineteenth-century England saw a sudden revival in tiles, including encaustic floor tiles that were both mass-produced and hand-made. You can still find tiles in these Gothic designs today. Other floor materials include wood floor boards and matting. Curtains can be a problem: if the window cannot be seen into, leave it uncurtained, and hang a tapestry portière over the doors instead. The nineteenth-century

house in a style introduced a century before by the architect Inigo Jones (1593 – 1652). Shelved recesses, framed with pilasters, were a distinctive feature of the style. In the middle of the century, the popularity of wallpaper or silk-decorated walls made wood paneling more or less obsolete.

Gothic

Gothic style takes its inspiration from the cathedrals and churches of the Middle Ages, with their painted arches, stained glass windows, wrought iron hinges, heavy oak furniture, elegant candelabras and heavy, woven fabrics, particularly tapestries. A Gothic revival first appeared in England in the eighteenth century, epitomized by Horace Walpole's conversion of his small farmhouse, Strawberry Hill just outside London between 1750 and 1770. He used the style with wit and humour, incorporating staircases from cathedrals, a chimneypiece design taken from an archbishop's tomb and a trompe l'oeil wall

Gothic look requires heavy furniture, and carved screens may be used to separate different areas of a room. A refectory table, for instance, would be ideal for a Gothic look. Hepplewhite and Chippendale made some furniture in the Gothic style, but antiques are almost impossible to come by.

Light and airy eighteenth-century Gothic style uses pastel colors and whites to allow delicate arches and tracery to dominate. Whitewash, wood and stone colors, with pale yellows would be acceptable.

- Floors should be tiled or wood.
- Lighting can be candlelight to supplement other lighting. Choose chandelier-style lamps and wall sconces, which reflect light back off metallic or mirrored backs.
- Modern designs of cast-iron furniture, candle holders, curtain poles and other fixtures and fittings, including radiators and washstands, are available.
- Plaster wall niches can be good for displaying ornaments. Use Gothic-style motifs when painting doors, dados or friezes.
- Fabrics would be rich velvets, brocades in deep reds, dark greens and golds.
- Walls can be covered by woven tapestries as they used to be in the great cathedrals, where they brought an element of warmth and comfort to cold, drafty interiors.

Gustavian (1770 – c. 1810)

This Swedish style, taking its name from King Gustav III and inspired by French Empire and Rococo, has a distinct character of its own with a slightly embellished Neo-Classical elegance. Gustavian was used mainly in country and seaside residences, but looks good anywhere. The paintings of Carl Larsson, who painted many pictures of his own country house during the 1890s, epitomize the look, which is simple, but highly decorative and similar in feeling to English and American Arts and Crafts style.

The basic color was white; others were soft blues and grays in narrow stripes or checks.

(above)
The simplicity and elegance of this painted furniture and the painted wooden panels behind give a Gustavian look.

A typical early sixties interior with inflatable furniture, blue and green woven rug.

Walls were painted in plain colors or textured, using limewash or dragging techniques. Woodwork was plain or similarly painted, often in white and always with a matte finish. Stenciled borders were used as frieze decorations. Rugs and carpets were laid on wood boards and simple, handwoven runners were turned over on themselves at right angles, if they were too long for the room. Upholstered furniture had delicate wooden frames, often painted and embellished with narrow, gold lines. Chairs had carved wood backs and padded seats, with bowed legs and curved or classically straight styles. They were always elegant. Mirrors had oval or round frames in brass or gilt, and brass was used for curtain fixtures, candle sconces and lamps. The emphasis was on harmony and elegance, achieved without the use of opulent materials and finishes, even in the grandest palaces.

High Tech (1960s –)

This is a style which uses industrial components to create a clean, uncluttered and frankly utilitarian environment. The aim is to provide an efficient living space with no fuss. Materials used are glass, steel, rubber and synthetics. Industrial metal stairs, straight or spiral; space heaters; metal-based tables with glass surfaces; office shelving, filing systems and furniture and ergonomically designed seats are all utilized.

Everything should be designed for function. Metal exhibition systems will divide up large spaces; floors are synthetic-studded rubber, painted hardboard panels and industrial vinyl. Colors are strong: black and white or primary. Light fittings are low-voltage, installed throughout, or metal factory shades over bulbs hanging in a row from the ceiling and adjustable office desk lamps. Other possible furniture would be mobile metal storage on enormous casters, stainless steel hospital equipment and metal shelving. Catering equipment, which is made to withstand hard wear, such as ovens, toasters and cookware is the required style. It is uncompromising and not cheap. Everything should be of the best quality and designed for strength and ease of use. It relates well with the Minimal and the Modern styles, but won't live easily with traditional styles of furniture or furnishings.

Indian (National)

This style is not the Colonial Indian, but based on artifacts made in India from local materials. Rattan and wicker furniture, caned wood tables, cotton woven dhurries, Indian block-printed fabrics and brass objects, such as candlesticks. These are simple furnishings that rely on color and craftsmanship.

Japanese (Ethnic Style)

The traditional Japanese house was simple, disciplined and rectangular. It was built on a grid system based on the size of the seagrass tatami mats, which made up the floor. Rooms were referred to as six- or eight-mat rooms. Interior walls were in the form of sliding screens, covered in paper to let some light through. Beds consisted of roll-up futon mattresses. In Western homes, they are usually given a slatted base and used as seating during the day. The Japanese sat on the tatami mats, and what little furniture there was would be low, very simple and angular, often in black. Traditional shoji screens are often available in futon shops and shoji paper can be bought by the roll from specialist suppliers.

Belongings were minimal. A house might have a built-in niche in the most important room, where a disciplined arrangement of flowers or twigs would be the only piece of decoration. The tokonoma was a recess for hanging scroll pictures, with a small storage cabinet below (nowadays this is often used to house the television and video). Alternatively, there might be a scroll painting hung on one wall. Lighting must be subtle.

Concealed tracks, low-voltage lights and dimmer switches are suitable, and small table lamps with paper shades are widely available. Tatamis often make good cushioned covers for window seats and other low seating and relaxing areas because they are both soft and comfortable.

Space-saving fitted cupboards with sliding doors covered in decorative Japanese papers would be suitable for storage use. Furniture is often covered with lacquer and consists of low tables and small boxes or chests. Textiles are brocades: brocade patchwork quilts; bold, hand-blocked prints and *kasuri* (folk weave), which is like small-scale ikat and usually in dark blues and black. Black, red and the natural seagrass tones of the tatami mats are the main colors.

(above)
An Indian-style room, mostly in dusky reds and yellows, with a canopied look, low carved furniture and a wood, carved horse.

(above)
Slabs of white wall, with a glass
and metal table, African wood
sculpture and an enormous
white room divider make a
minimalist interior.

Mediterranean (Regional Style)

This is a timeless look, exemplified by a simple fishing cottage by the sea. It must be practical and simple to look after. Windows are deliberately small to keep out the relentless sun. Thick, whitewashed walls, sparse furnishings and cool, cavernlike interiors contrast to the heat outside.

Floors are inevitably of rough, unglazed brick or large, square terracotta tiles, glazed or unglazed. Inside walls are rough finished. If you are re-creating this look, don't use too much plaster applied too thickly. Doors are simple, of vertical board construction or perhaps made from bead curtains hung in the doorway. Fabrics are rough wool or cotton weaves, peasant embroidery and Provençale prints. Whites, reds and blues all look good.

Shutters are considered an integral part of the window treatment, not simply added as decoration. Thick walls make deep window recesses, which can be tiled or left in the same finish as the wall. They make good spaces for pots of pelargoniums. Much of life is spent outside so furniture is sparse: basket chairs, rush-seated chairs, simple, wooden chairs and benches, which can be taken outdoors for meals, mostly made of dark or stained wood. Virtually no decoration is necessary. Most objects tend to have a purpose: they are for eating, drinking, sitting or sleeping. Kitchen facilities are basic and freestanding: nothing is fitted. Most kitchens would consist of a simple stove, a small table covered with a cloth, upright wood chairs possibly with rush seats, open shelves for pots and pans, china (nonmatching) and olive wood bowls. Fabrics should be kept to a minimum. If you do decide to use fabric, Provençale cotton prints would be the obvious choice, with their bright, uninhibited colors and tiny, floral motifs. For a Greek Mediterranean look, choose woven, unbleached wool fabrics.

Modernist/Minimalist (1920s –)

The 1920s saw the beginning of the Modern Movement, which introduced a change that was, in its way, just as important as the sixteenth-century Renaissance. The greatest influence was the Bauhaus School of Art and Design in Weimar, started by Walter Gropius, whose main aims were to bring handcrafted quality into industrially made objects. It was closed by Hitler in 1930 and most of its talent went to the United States. Standardization of storage units for mass production was first developed at the Bauhaus by Marcel Breuer in the 1920s, and this influence can still be seen in today's fitted kitchens.

Like Hi Tech, which was developed later, Modernist is an uncompromising style and won't mix-and-match with traditional styles. Load-bearing glass bricks could take the whole weight of a building and were used as exterior and partition walls, bringing in far more light, and the development of plate glass allowed large table tops to be made of glass. Shapes of furniture were strikingly simple and often blissfully comfortable in spite of the lack of upholstery. Stark, industrial shapes and materials were used to make tubular steel furniture, glass-topped tables and geometric forms. Window treatments were sparse and uncluttered, with neat Roman or slatted Venetian blinds. Lighting was indirect with concealed spotlighting, or adjustable spots, and dimmer switches creating reflected or diffused light, which didn't glare off so many shiny surfaces. Students at the Bauhaus created a range of brilliantly colorful and highly distinctive abstract patterns on ceramic tableware, vases and textiles.

Leather-covered sofas with boxy shapes gave softness and contrast. A large, single picture or print on the wall was preferred to groups of paintings. Attractive copies of many original Bauhaus designs are available today, as are objects that emulate the style.

Minimalist style was summed up by the architect Mies van der Rohe of the Bauhaus as "less is more," and is an extension of Modernist. Black and white are the predominant colors, with severe, rectilinear shapes. Large bay windows were designed to bring in as much light as possible and were left uncurtained, or fitted with the simplest blinds. Extraneous objects, such as the television, video, sound system, records and books are all hidden away. There should be only one picture at a time (or none at all) on the walls. Sources of heat and light are often hidden from view. Hard surfaces can often encourage the build-up of condensation, so minimalist interiors must always be kept well ventilated, heated and insulated.

1950s Style

The 1950s in Great Britain were still years of austerity after the Second World War. There was an extreme shortage of materials, and the design of furniture and the quantity allowed

to be manufactured was regulated by the government, so a spartan style dominated with severely utilitarian designs. Perhaps because people had been deprived of new things for so long, they were generally much more receptive to modern design. For the first time in many decades there was a genuinely positive attitude towards progressive design, which was christened the contemporary style when it first appeared at the Festival of Britain in 1951. A positive attitude toward modern design was reflected in much of the imagery used as a source for decoration. This decorative application of science was demonstrated most forcefully in the work of the Festival Pattern Group, which devised a range of abstract carpet and wallpaper patterns based on crystallography structures such as, for example, the chemical structure of insulin.

However, many ideas that dominated the 1950s were actually originated in the late 1940s and it was Scandinavia, Italy and the United States rather than Great Britain that were the true innovators of the style. In Scandinavia, designers and a group of enlightened manufacturers worked together to promote modern design and their use of pale woods, simple, but modern designs and careful craftsmanship, and bold, but disciplined colors were very seductive.

In America, furniture was developed using techniques invented for military purposes, such as bonding wood, marble, metal and glass, and the casting of aluminum, which prepared the way for many 1950s characteristics, such as plywood furniture and bent steel chair frames.

The main characteristics of the 1950s look were long, low lines; open-plan spaces; plain, unornamented walls; woodblock or hardwood floors, with Scandinavian tufted rugs. Regularity and coordination were out; three-piece suites or matching fabrics were not allowed, and everything that was old had to

go. Fireplaces were torn out and central heating installed. There were no picture moldings or wall moldings, and no paneling on doors. Curtain rods were out; track was in. It became fashionable to paint three walls white and one in orange or olive, or perhaps one wallpapered while the others were painted in a color picked up from the wallpaper.

- *Modular storage units were fixed to some of the walls and used as room dividers, often with black metal uprights and mahogany shelves.*
- *Printed furnishing fabrics often had motifs outlined in black and there was a stylized African influence, with jungle prints or bold animal prints, such as zebra or leopard. Or fabrics had a spiky, disjointed quality and were made up of small motifs without having any obvious connection to each other.*

Furniture, studio pottery and objects were irregular in shape: lampshades were pleated paper or glass bowls fitted against the ceiling. Colors were strong: yellow, slate blue, black and orange.

Neo-Classical

No other style in history has been as universally successful as the Neo-Classical, offering formality, grandeur, proportion and elegance. Around 1750, painters and sculptors in Rome were reverting to classical themes and styles, and by 1760, architects were establishing the style. By 1800 its influence had spread to all the major European countries. The classical components of ancient Greece and the Roman arch were adapted for contemporary needs, and in some cases, motifs were mixed by combining Greek with Etruscan, and Egyptian with Roman. Wealthy young men made the Grand Tour, visiting Europe and especially Italy to complete their classical education. On their return, they enthusiastically set about rebuilding and redecorating their homes, filling them with a formal style of furniture,

(above)
A splendid Neo-Classical interior with an ornate plaster ceiling.

objects and paintings according to the Neo-Classical ideal. The ideas were taken up all over Europe and in America, each country imbuing them with its own character. Fibrous plaster was molded into classical niches, arches, cornices and ceiling roses. The Neo-Classical window was tall and elegant, with large oblong panes and varied from a simple sash to Gothic-style arches with a fanlight on top. Most mullions were much narrower than their contemporary equivalents, and when you are refurbishing in classical style, it is very important to get the proportions right.

Colors in the early part of this period were surprisingly bright. The backgrounds of walls, ceilings and paneling were painted deep terracotta, sunflower yellow, orange, black, blue and green, often embellished with gold, and the moldings of walls, ceilings and paneling were white or ivory. The red and black painting on Greek vases was much admired. Wall and ceilings were plastered and painted,

then given decorative moldings or decorated with sophisticated paint effects. Later, the Adam brothers introduced a slightly faded, more pastel look. Light colors were often used for paneling, which might have had a black motif painted in the center. Walls and ceilings often incorporated painted murals, framed with beading or plasterwork.

Curtain poles carried draped side curtains and decorative headings. Heavy fabrics were used so that they would hang well—velvets, brocades and chintzes were all popular. Tie backs held curtains during the day.

- *Rich, textural contrasts were important: marble or stone, inlaid wood or sumptuous silks and brocades with Persian carpets.*
- *Trompe l'oeil painting was used to achieve a wood grain look or to create murals of classic mythology.*
- *Four-poster beds were canopied and draped with magnificent fabrics, and large mirrors were often used on walls.*
- *Tapestries were framed between panels.*

Robert Adam designed several tapestry rooms to show off sets of tapestries bought in Paris and a matching, finer weave on the upholstered chairs, which lined the room.

In important rooms, floors were made of marble, terrazzo or parquet, and furniture was carved with warriors, lions, griffins, sphinxes or owls. Upholstered chairs, all lined up against the walls, were usually straight-backed, wood-framed styles and not very comfortable—looks were much more important than comfort.

Nomadic (Regional)

Nomadic tribes, by definition, are travelers who live in tents and must be prepared to pack up and move on frequently. There are only a few tribes left who still live like this. Nevertheless, the nomadic way of life, with its necessary simplicity and limited but distinctive furnishings, has an attraction for many Westerners as an antidote to their more sophisticated lifestyles. The nomadic tent was furnished with kilims woven by the women of the tribe. Lengths of woven cloth were used for everything: as room dividers, to make up bags for carrying salt and other foodstuffs, as cradles for babies and as cushions and floor rugs. The floor was used for sitting on, so everything was low.

Handwoven fabrics, in wool or cotton (or a cotton and rayon mixture), become the keynote of this look. Kilims are woven in wool and have a characteristic pliability and softness. Dhurries are the Indian version of kilims and are woven in cotton, so they are heavier and less flexible. They are invaluable as floor rugs on polished boards and can be used as wall hangings. Lighting should be discreet. Use perforated metal candle holders, wall sconces and converted oil lamps. Kilims can be hung on walls, thrown over settees or spread on the floor. They are often used to upholster ottoman stools and large sofas, giving a long-lasting and attractive finish, and floor cushions are

always right. The rest of the furniture should be extremely basic. Colors are the traditional rich reds and browns, together with black and oatmeal.

Postmodern

This is a style which started in the late 1960s as a reaction to the less is more philosophy of the Bauhaus and began to reintroduce decoration for its own sake. Architects started to impose their own personal interpretation of classical Greek and Egyptian styles, using modern materials and technology. The whole style involves appropriation. The plainest wood furniture and surfaces are painted in trompe l'oeil finishes, and wood, glass-reinforced plaster or polystyrene moldings in several sizes can be attached to furniture legs to give a fluted look or to walls to create arches, columns and niches, and to give visual interest to bare surfaces. Special adhesives are available to fix these moldings. Decorative self-adhesive lead strips can turn a picture window into leaded panes. Lengths of plastic drainpipe are used to create small columns. When they are marbled over, nobody would know the difference.

Postmodern is an unabashed love of deco for its own sake. You have to be knowledgeable and very confident to achieve this look. Get an architect or designer to advise you.

Regency (1811 – 1820)

This is the name given to the latter part of Late Georgian style, which corresponds to the French Empire and Directoire styles. It was named after George, Prince of Wales, who was Regent for his father, George III. It began, however, with a revolution in taste during the last decades of the eighteenth century and continued into the 1830s. The style took much from current interest in Greek, Roman and Egyptian antiquity. Many features popular in houses today had their origins in Regency style: central heating, open-plan rooms and

linear curves evocative of shells or foliage for walls and furniture, all in a sophisticated, urban, luxurious wallow. Motifs were water gods and goddesses, garlands of flowers and foliage, dripping water effects, fish, seaweed, waves, eels, crabs, creeping plants, serpents, birds, monkeys and cartouches (armorial shield shapes). Walls were paneled in white or pale pastel colors, and wallpapers were block-printed or flocked. Windows were elaborately festooned in delicate fabrics. Furniture was bulbous, bow-fronted with cabriole legs and S-shaped curves, seen in the commodes and cabinets of the time and in the Middle Eastern ottomans, fauteuils, well-padded, round chairs and gilded, carved and inlaid cabinets. Finishing touches were carved and gilded wood and plaster, delicately painted porcelain, mirrors everywhere and gilded picture frames and candles.

Between 1740 and 1760, Rococo style was adopted with characteristically national modifications, by most European countries. Germany carried it to extremes with extraordinary cake-icing interiors, but in England the strict Palladian tradition of the 1730s and 1740s restricted its development. Fashionable cabinet makers, such as Chippendale, produced some furniture in The French Taste, but it never became very popular. A revolt against the extravagances of the style in the 1760s led to the triumph of the Neo-Classical style in France, England, Italy and America. From about 1820 onward, and with their usual extravagance, the Victorians took up Rococo again, although it was frowned upon by many, including the Oxford English Dictionary of 1909, which described it as "excessively or tastelessly florid or ornate."

Scandinavian (National Style)

Scandinavians have an eye for practical, good-looking simplicity and a talent for making the best use of natural materials and plain, primary colors offset by white. The area is rich

(above)
A modern version of a Shaker bedroom, with a wood, framed bed and furniture, and a patchwork quilt.

(opposite)
Modern Shaker furniture is neat and practical and will suit a small, modern interior.

large window areas. Houses were often built with semi-circular window bays, corresponding with an interior apse, which gave interest and elegance to the interior of a room.

Furnishings were simple and elegant, with little or no carving, and pieces were small and lightweight so they could be moved about, instead of being arranged stiffly around the walls. One Regency invention was the sofa table with end flap. From 1815, brass inlays became popular in rich, dark woods, such as mahogany and rosewood.

Rococo

This lighthearted and humorous style was originally developed during the first half of the eighteenth century, mainly appearing as wall surfaces, furniture, plate, porcelain and ornament. It was largely a protest against Classical principles inside the house and the bizarre etiquette of Louis XIV's reign, and turned more toward informality and freedom. It used Chinese motifs and grotesque, sinuous

in forests and wood is the material that Scandinavians appreciate. It is ideally suited to the beautifully made, elegantly designed furniture, which is their special forte. Carefully designed and produced china and glass, handwoven rugs and screen prints are all hallmarks of Scandinavian interiors.
See also Gustavian, pages 197–198.

Shaker

An American religious sect, consisting of mixed communities of men and women living in celibacy, was established near Albany on the Hudson River in 1784. Many of the men were woodworkers and they made furniture in a strong and simple style without ornament, which remained more or less unchanged until the 1860s. Characteristics of the style are rows of hooks along the wall, on which to hang chairs and other furniture including dual-purpose pieces, such as an armchair whose back folds down to become a tabletop. There has recently been a revival of interest in Shaker-style furniture and several companies are producing their own variations. Shaker's simplicity and practicability fits in with many modern lifestyles.

Tudor (Elizabethan) and Jacobean (Sixteenth and Early Seventeenth Centuries)

This is the style of furniture and decor used during the time of Elizabeth I. Most of life was centered around the great hall and the furniture was made of solid wood, often in oak. It was basic and chunky-looking, consisting mainly of refectory tables, huge dressers, chests and chairs, which were often carved. Woven tapestries hung over the walls to prevent drafts and provide color and warmth. The style goes well with **Gothic style — see pages 196–197.**

Victorian (Nineteenth Century)

The newly prosperous, middle-class English Victorians were proud of progress and happy to fill homes with proofs of their importance and wealth. Styles of furnishing were grandiose and varied, ranging from Gothic and Rococo, to Arts and Crafts and Elizabethan. Fabrics were heavy and ostentatious, making use of the jacquard loom for machine tapestries and of chemical dyes

to create strident colors. Velvets, Jacobean designs and chintzes were all popular. Curtains were heavily draped and would hang across interior doorways, as well as windows to keep out drafts. Portable folding screens were widely used for the same purpose and were often covered in cut-out scraps from magazines, or specially printed. Furniture was large and important-looking, with overstuffed upholstery. Floors were covered with large, Persian carpets in the main rooms; elsewhere there would be stained floorboards with Persian rugs. Walls were papered in florid florals or heavy flocks. Every other surface was covered in fabric, usually fringed. Embossed Lincrusta paper was used on ceilings to imitate plasterwork. Stained glass was popular in front doors and above interior doors. Bathrooms, when they did exist, were given pride of place. They had freestanding baths and sinks, rather ornate in style with lion or clawed feet, and the toilet would have a mahogany seat and often a highly decorative, ceramic bowl.

By the 1840s, some Victorian homes had gas lighting, but oil lamps were still widely used.

Brass bedsteads (a product of the industrial revolution) were popular, being sturdy, unpretentious and decorative. A fireplace with a cast-iron, carved wood or marble front was essential. Some were big and imposing, but others were tiny and designed to fit into a maid's room or upstairs bedroom (and also to save on costly fuel).

- *There was ornament everywhere. Pictures and photographs were hung together in groups, with family portraits on the stairs or in the dining room, or there were collections of delicate watercolors painted by spinster aunts, intricate engravings or hunting scenes.*
- *Intrepid explorers came back from abroad with amazing collections of colorful butterflies or birds' eggs, fine porcelain, miniature boxes and interesting artifacts gathered from all over the world, which were displayed in specially designed wood boxes placed on small tables around the living room.*
- *Vases and bowls of flowers were seen in abundance because the Victorians were passionate about plants.*

(above)
A late Victorian interior, unbelievably cluttered and full of collected items.

Wood

Wood is warm to the touch and a friendly and adaptable material. It has heat-insulating properties and can help to muffle sound. Once regarded as purely useful for the structural elements in the home, nowadays wood floors, ceilings and stairs are left uncovered so that their natural beauty may be appreciated. Wood has considerable uses in the home: from house construction to flooring, paneling, furniture and decorative carvings, as well as bowls and utensils. Apart from its visual and tactile qualities, it has the unique value of being the one basic resource that man can renew.

Different woods have very different characteristics. For example, teak has strong chemical properties that make it resistant to decay, so it is widely used for outdoor furniture; the resins of heartwood cedar make it nearly impervious to insects and decay, which is why it is used for roof claddings and window frames. Bird's-eye maple shows the decorative effect of small sprouts or shoots, which did not develop, and this is often used in veneer. African woods often have perfumelike smells; maple is a rich, golden color, often used for butcher's blocks; versatile oak (known for its durability and good looks) has often been used for centuries for structural purposes, furniture, paneling and carving. This chapter will look at the different kinds of wood and the ways in which they can be used, and also at materials that can be used like wood.

Sources

(previous page)
Wood has always been considered one of the most sympathetic materials, as can be seen in this most elegant of interiors. This example is in Wimpole Hall.

(right)
MDF is a versatile alternative to wood and can be intricately cut to make filigree patterns as in this radiator cover.

Commercial timber is extracted from three main types of forest: the coniferous forest, which is the source of the world's softwoods, extending across the arctic and subarctic zone of the northern hemisphere and also found in East Africa, south-eastern United States and Central America; temperate hardwoods, also found in the north (where they merge with the softwoods), as well as in Chile, New Zealand and Australia (where eucalyptus forests area major resource); and tropical hardwoods, most of which come from rain forests in South America, Africa and Southeast Asia. Second-hand wood, which once used to be floorboards or wall cladding, can often be found at architectural salvage stores; you may find anything from random-pitch pine boards to original Georgian oak.

Buying Timber

- *Many do-it-yourself shops, building supply and hardware stores sell wood panels, strips, blocks and sheets, precut and packaged with a guide showing how much of an area they will cover.*
- *Lumberyards sell wood already planed and cut to standard sizes and most will cut hardwood to a special size.*
- *Lumberyards may be cheaper than do-it-yourself stores, particularly when buying in larger quantities. It is much easier to check the quality and they will usually give good advice.*
- *Before buying, check boards for defects and try to avoid those that are bowed, twisted or heavily knotted or show the first signs of termites.*
- *Hardwoods are generally more durable and decorative, although more expensive than softwoods, but they vary in quality and may not be so easy to obtain.*
- *Many suppliers sell a range of accessories, such as moldings and trims.*

Other Compatible Materials
PLYWOOD

Plywood is available in a variety of thicknesses and can be used to make small pieces of furniture and shelves, then painted, stained and sealed. Alternatively, it can be cut into squares or purchased as tongue-and-groove paneling and laid as a floor like any other wood. When using plywood as flooring, it can be difficult to cut precisely around odd shapes and hard to attach with nails. Ask the supplier to cut to size. Lay plywood on boards or joists (if it is thick enough), or, using adhesive, on screeded concrete. Then seal and paint, or stain and seal.

MEDIUM-DENSITY FIBERBOARD (MDF)

This is a relatively new composite material that is made out of sawdust and adhesive. The advantage of this material is that it is very stable and won't crack, warp or shrink. It comes in a variety of sizes and thicknesses and, due to its smooth surface, it is a good material for use as kitchen cabinets and shelves. Because of its density, it lends itself to all sorts of design effects using a router to make grooves, etc. It can be cleanly cut into fairly intricate shapes and is used to make filigree radiator covers and items such as decorative headboards. MDF can be painted directly with a very good finish. Baseboards are now available in prepared MDF in very long lengths to minimize joins. MDF is sold in 8 x 4 ft (2.4 x 1.2 m) sheets, so it becomes more economical to make a number of items, rather than just one. Use standard 3/4 in (19 mm) MDF sheeting for extra rigidity.

HARDBOARD

A thin, fibrous sheet board made from soft-wood pulp, hardboard can provide a good, even surface on which to lay another floor. It can be used as an inexpensive floor in its own right, when sealed or painted, but should be graded for this purpose.

CHIPBOARD

This is made from urea formaldehyde resins and wood-chips bonded under pressure. It is available in tongue-and-groove form for floors or in sheets, and looks rather like cork when sealed. Chipboard is quite durable and acts as an efficient insulator, being warm and resilient. It is often used instead of wood floorboards in new homes. Don't use chip-board wherever water may be spilled because this can cause damage.

Melamine-faced chipboard is sold in shelf widths and lengths, usually finished in wood grain finish or white, although it is possible to get it in bright primary colors.

Some Popular Woods for Interior Use

Afzelia: Hardwood; distinctive rich, mahogany red color, with a rather coarse texture. *Straight grain*: Used for window frames, doors and floors.

Ash: Hardwood; creamy brown, wavy grain. Bonds well. Used as veneered sheets for wall paneling and for strip or block flooring; also staircases.

Beech: Hardwood; creamy brown, light grain, hard-wearing. Used as strip or block flooring. Available as veneered boards with a clear, lacquered surface.

Birch: Hardwood; fine textured, almost white, straight-grained. More often used for plywood than as solid timber, but also for wooden components and flooring.

Cedar: Softwood; similar to mahogany in color, but with a coarser texture. Attractive, stable, durable and pliable. Used for joinery, furniture, solid board paneling and all kinds of domestic use.

Cherry: Hardwood; medium wavy grain. Used for furniture and cabinet work. American cherry is easier to obtain than European cherry, and is used for veneered wall paneling, furniture and high class joinery.

Chestnut: Hardwood; pale brown color with

(above)
This Edwardian downstairs bathroom has wood paneling and a long, wood bench with a hole cut out for the toilet.

(opposite)
An unusual wood
bathroom with a refreshingly
unsophisticated feeling.

prominent growth rings, a little like oak to look at. Good for flooring and staircases.

Douglas Fir: Softwood; gold, reddish brown, pronounced wavy grain. Used as solid boards for wall paneling. There is a trend for leaving the surface rough and staining or painting directly onto the unfinished surface.

Elm: Hardwood; pale brown, sometimes with a reddish, coarse texture and irregular grain. Widely used in furniture for its decorativeness and as strip or block flooring; also staircases.

Iroko: Hardwood; yellow-brown to deep brown, a bit like teak, but coarser in texture. Used for the same innumerable purposes as teak, including parquet flooring.

Jarrah: Australian hardwood; coarse-textured, medium-reddish brown wood, sometimes with darker markings. Very durable, used for flooring and, in Australia, for high class exterior and interior joinery.

Knotty Cedar: Softwood; golden, reddish brown, wavy grain. Used as veneered sheets for wall paneling.

Knotty Pine: Lodgepole, Eastern or Western white): Softwood; pale yellow-cream with pronounced knots. Used for various types of wood paneling and staircases. Reclaimed pine is deeper and richer in color than new wood, and less prone to cracking and shrinkage.

Mahogany: Hardwood; reddish brown, very hardwearing. Used for high-class furniture (especially reproduction), fine joinery and veneered wall paneling, and strip or block flooring and staircases.

Maple (Sycamore): Hardwood; pale, normally straight-grained, with a fine, even texture, exceptionally hardwearing. Useful for kitchen units, kitchen counters, kitchen utensils and flooring. Engineered planks and strips (three or five layers of solid hardwood, cross-laminated under high pressure and bonded with waterproof glue) can be glued directly onto a variety of wood or concrete subfloors.

Oak: Hardwood; beige-brown, long, straight grain, very durable. Used as solid or veneered

sheets for wall paneling, and for strip and block flooring and furniture. Engineered planks, strips and parquet are also available.

Parana Pine: Softwood; straw-colored to pale brown with occasional bright red streaks. Used for indoor joinery, especially staircases, and for cabinet framing and moldings. Particularly good for do-it-yourselfers because it is easy to work.

Rosewood: Hardwood; dark brown in color, wavy black grain. Often used as veneered sheets for wall paneling.

Rubber-wood: This is available as tongue-and-groove flooring.

Sapele: Hardwood; reddish brown in color, straight, open grain. Used as veneered sheets for wall paneling, doors, window frames and staircases.

Spruce (Whitewood): Creamy white to light, golden yellow, sometimes with a pinkish tinge. Used for joinery and as solid board paneling.

Tasmanian Oak: Hardwood; cream, straight grain, fairly hard-wearing. Used as strip or block flooring.

Teak: Hardwood; reddish brown, attractive graining. Resists acid, fire and rot. Used for fine joinery and also as veneered sheets for wall paneling.

Tupelo: Hardwood; yellow to pale brown, occasionally has darker patches with a fine, even texture, but an irregular grain. Moderately lightweight. Used as plywood core veneer and very hardwearing plank flooring.

Walnut: Hardwood; gray-brown with almost black streaks and often variable in color. Outstandingly decorative wood used for cabinetwork. Also for veneered paneling.

Uses in the Home
WALLS

Wood paneling is one of the most attractive finishes for a wall and was used a great deal in traditional homes, partly to act as insulation and partly to show off the beauty of particular woods. At its simplest, it was made

up of plain squares or rectangles joined together to form a complete wallcovering, but in important homes it was often elaborately carved. Simple paneling was popular in the sixteenth and seventeenth centuries and is a good choice when aiming for a country manor look. It is still made using seventeenth-century techniques.

Manufacturing developments have brought wood paneling within the reach of most home budgets. Large areas, which would once have had to be paneled in lots of small elements, can now be covered with veneered plywood sheets. These thin plywood or hardboard sheets come with a variety of surfaces. The best quality sheets have a veneer of real wood. Many kinds of wood are cut into veneers, one of the most attractive being quartered walnut. This is an ideal way to cover up poor walls, where extensive plastering would be needed to make them presentable. Sheets are usually tall enough to cover a wall from floor to ceiling in one sheet without horizontal joins.

Alternatively, use tongue-and-groove boards, also known as matchboarding or vee-jointed. They are usually made of knotty pine. Tongue-and-groove is usually sold in the form of planks 4 to 6in (100 to 150 mm) wide and 1/2 – 3/4 in (12 – 19 mm) thick in lengths of 8 – 10 ft (2.4 – 3 m). One edge of each board has a tongue machined along it, while the other edge has a groove. These allow adjacent boards to interlock without a gap being visible between them. Plain boards look rather like narrow floorboards when butted together, but the addition of chamfering along each face edge emphasizes the joint line and gives a more attractive overall effect. You can also get tongue-and-groove boards with a concave outer face or with grooves in the surface to give reeded or piped effects.

When calculating the quantities needed, remember that because one board slides under another, they cover slightly less wall

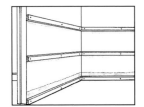

Furring strips screwed to the wall (2)

than their measurements suggest. Many types can be attached directly to walls, using adhesive recommended by the manufacturers but, since perfectly smooth walls are essential, a framework of furring strips will usually have to be fixed to the wall. There is no need to panel a whole room, or even a whole wall. You can panel up to dado rail height or inside an alcove or a section of a wall where a feature (such as a fireplace) has been removed.

Fixing Paneling and Tongue-and-Groove Boarding

You will need: A hammer and chisel for removing baseboards, dado rails and picture molding, a saw, adhesive or nails, insulation, if required, a nail punch and hammer, screws and wall plugs, a steel straightedge and plumb line, plus the correct amount of paneling or tongue-and-groove boarding.

1. Carefully pry away door architraves and picture molding. Take particular care if you intend to refit them.

2. Screw furring strips firmly to the wall horizontally at the top and bottom of where you intend to position the paneling and at 16in (40 cm) intervals between, then countersink all screws below the surface (i.e., make sure they don't stick out beyond the furring strips). Cut short strips to fit around light switches and power sockets. Use a steel straightedge (or spirit level and a plumb line) to ensure all furring strips are truly vertical or horizontal. (If insulation is to be incorporated, this should be placed between the strips before the boards are fixed in place.)

3. Disconnect the electricity to the room and take the face plates off switches and outlets and set them aside, ready for refitting over the new paneling. Fix a new, metal electrical box to surface.

4. Use a plumb line to find a true vertical for the outside edge of the first board and mark it with pencil or chalk.

5. When using boards, use a nail punch and

hammer to sink nail heads below the surface. This allows the groove of the next board to slide into position over the tongue. Fix them diagonally through the tongue. For paneling, use a recommended adhesive, according to the manufacturer's instructions. Leave a very small gap down the length of all boards, where the tongue has engaged a groove. If the boards lock too tightly and the wood expands, it will bulge.

6. Use quarter molding to give a good finish at the bottom.

Useful Tips

- *Store wood in the room for a couple of weeks before work begins. Wood expands and contracts, and this will give it time to adjust to the atmosphere.*
- *Prime the furring strips with primer paint before using, in case there is moisture in the outside walls and it reaches the wood from the back.*
- *When putting up paneling, cut the boards to*

the required size and shape before applying the adhesive to the battens.
- *When putting up paneling, attach furring strips as for tongue-and-groove boarding or follow the manufacturer's instructions. Follow the same procedure as for tongue-and-groove boarding, starting in a corner.*

Floors

Wood has been used for centuries to create attractive floors: from simple timber floor-boards to interlocking parquet strips and intricate mosaics. Parquet flooring, usually consisting of oak rectangles fitted together in a herringbone pattern, would be too expensive for most home owners today, but sanded and sealed floorboards are attractive, particularly when decorated with rugs—and bearing in mind the fact that the sanding can be done over a weekend. Modern sealers can be used on their own if you want a matte finish, while there are varnishes available on the market that will give a satin or gloss finish. Alternatively, you can apply wax polish over the boards instead. A liming wax will give a white-grained effect. Wood block or wood strip floors are also attractive, available in various woods and very easy to lay.

Sanding Floorboards

You will need: large and small electric sander and disks or bands of coarse and medium grade sandpaper (available from rental outlets), hammer, vacuum cleaner, protective clothing (i.e., overalls, protective mask), wood stain (if you wish to color the floor), varnish, matte seal or wax. Remember that floors darken naturally over time, so as a rule of thumb, choose a lighter wood stain rather than a darker one.

1. Carefully hammer in any protruding nails, which will damage the sander, if left exposed. Check all round the floor.

2. Tip the sander to raise it off the floor before switching on the machine. Lower gently, while

(above left)
A rich, red wood has been cleverly used here to lead the eye forward.

(above)
Wood block flooring is the modern home's answer to parquet. It comes in several different woods, including this rich oak, and is not at all difficult to lay.

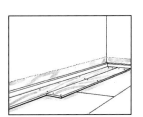

Laying wood strip flooring (3)

moving slowly forward, so you don't gouge too much wood out of the floor. Draw the sander backward and forward over the whole floor. If the floor is badly damaged or very dirty, take the sander across the boards diagonally at first. Then follow the line of the boards until the floor is smooth and pale. Start with coarse sandpaper and finish with medium or fine-textured paper.

3. Go all around the edges of the room with the small sander. Get into the corners by sanding by hand with a small piece of sand-paper wrapped around a piece of wood.

4. Vacuum thoroughly.

5. Apply any wood stain according to the manufacturer's instructions and allow to dry before varnishing or sealing.

Wood Strip Flooring

A narrow version of conventional floorboards, with the width varying from 5in (130 mm) to 6 1/2 in (165 mm), in lengths of between 5 ft (1.5 m) and 7 ft 8 in (2.4 m). The strips are made by laminating two layers of softwood with a surface layer of decorative hardwood, such as oak, beech or elm. The flooring is stable, of consistent quality and usually cheaper than solid wood boards. Wider strips are available which look very like solid boards. Laying wood strip is not difficult as the pieces are of tongue-and-groove construction and fit together well. Strips 1/3 in (8 mm), 3/8 in (9 mm) or 1/2 in (12 mm) thick can be laid over an existing wood floor or onto plywood or hardboard: it is particularly important to have a level base.

Laying Wood Strip

You will need: tape measure, graph paper, the correct amount of wood strip for your floor (the package will give the area it will cover), hard-board (for wood floors) or leveling compound (for concrete floors which are not level), hammer, saw, tacks, long strip of softwood 3/8 in (10 mm) wide; nails, PVA adhesive, enough cork to run a strip 3/8 in (10 mm) wide round the walls of the room under the baseboard.

1. Measure the room and make a scale plan on graph paper. Calculate how much wood-strip you will need. (The package will give the area covered by its contents.)

2. If the existing floor is timber, tack hard-board over it. If it is a concrete floor, use a leveling compound to ensure a completely level surface. Leave access for any wiring or plumbing work.

3. Remove baseboards and doors. Nail a temporary 3/8 in (10 mm) batten to the longest wall and start laying the flooring using this as a guide. The gap formed when the batten is removed will prevent the strip from bulging upward if it expands for any reason (for example, in wet weather).

4. Continue placing the wood strips across the room, staggering the end joints, leaving 3/8 in (10 mm) at the ends of each row. Use a length of softwood and a hammer to pack the pieces tightly together.

5. Use nails (ideally stainless steel or corrosion will cause them to stain the floor), hammered at an angle through the tongue of the strip, when attaching sections to joists or an existing wood floor. The groove of the neighboring strip will conceal the nail. You can use adhesive to fix wood strip to a concrete floor, by running a line of adhesive into the groove. Some makers supply clips to hold the strips together.

6. Fill the 3/8 in (10 mm) extension gap with a cork strip and replace the baseboards and doors.

Wood Block Flooring

This is also called wood mosaic and is the poor man's parquet, but it is made of solid wood, always looks good and is easy to lay. Each panel or tile is made up of rectangular hardwood strips arranged in a basketweave pattern to a 18 in (45 cm) square bitumen-felt backing sheet. They are laid like tiles with a suitable PVA adhesive and are available in various woods, sealed or unsealed. If you buy them unsealed, you will have to seal them after they've been laid, but that may be the cheaper option.

Laying a Wood Block Floor

You will need: string, tape measure, the correct amount of wood block for your floor (the package should tell you the area it will cover), hardboard or cork (for a wood floor), leveling compound (for a concrete floor), hammer, fine saw, suitable adhesive.

1. Prepare and level the floor as for wood strip flooring (see opposite). One type of panel has tongue-and-groove edges and these should be laid loosely on an underlayment of cork. Other kinds of paneling butt up to one another and should be fixed with adhesive.

2. Start laying tiles from the center of the room, which makes it easier to cope with the inevitable irregularities at the edges: lay a tight string from the middle of one wall to the middle of the opposite; repeat with the other two walls.

3. Lay some tiles loosely along one string from wall to wall, starting where the strings cross and butt the tiles up closely. Aim to have a nearly full-size tile at both edges. Shift the tiles along the string and remove one, if necessary, to achieve this. Repeat along the other string.

4. When you are satisfied with the layout, begin sticking the tiles down, carefully following the manufacturer's instructions and using the recommended adhesive.

5. Cut tiles to fit along all the edges; for complicated shapes, make a template out of cardboard or use a proprietary shape, which can mold itself to the contours of the wall or obstruction.

6. Leave a 3/8 in (10 mm) gap around all the edges to allow for any wood expansion. This can be filled with caulk.

Cleaning Up an Old Floor

You can give an old floor new life with vinegar and steel wool (grade 00 or 0), which will remove old wax, dust and dirt, and leave the surface ready to be repolished. Alternatively, you can buy specially formulated products to use instead.

Baseboards, Dado Rails and Picture Molding
MOLDINGS

Wood moldings are both decorative and practical, and can make a big difference to the character and look of a room. It's often worth replacing original baseboards, architraves and other woodwork, or even adding in features where there were none before. Most lumber yards carry a wide choice of moldings in a range of sizes and profiles, and in soft or hardwoods. Softwood moldings are usually primed and painted, or stained and varnished; hardwood moldings are normally just varnished. It is easier to sand the moldings so that they are ready for decorating before cutting and fixing.

ARCHITRAVES

These are decorative surrounds to a door or window frames, usually 3 to 4 in (75 to 100 mm) wide, although wider moldings were quite common in the nineteenth century. Profiles on architraves are much the same as those found on baseboards. They may be plain or have a decorative shape along the top edge. Architraves are set slightly away from the edge of the door or window frame, and neatly cover the join with the surrounding wall finish. They are usually fixed to the frame of the door or window with oval nails.

BASEBOARDS

Generally between 3 and 4 in (75 and 100 mm) high and 3/4 – 1 in (19 – 25 mm) thick. They can be plain or have a decorative shape along the top edge. You can get taller ones, which look better in generously sized rooms with tall ceilings. In older houses, the plaster often finishes at baseboard level and the boards are nailed onto short, wood battens of the same thickness as the plaster, then nailed to the masonry at about 3 ft 3 in (1 meter) intervals. In more modern houses, the plaster usually goes down to the floor and the boards are nailed through into masonry behind. On hollow walls, boards are fixed with nails driven into the timber studs.

DADO RAILS

These carry a decorative molding on both edges with a flat section in between. They measure between 1 1/2 and 2 1/2 in high (38 mm and 62 mm) and project by 1 in (25 mm).

PICTURE MOLDING

These have a deep groove running along the top edge in which picture hooks can be fixed. Most are about 1 1/2 in (38 mm) high and project by about 1 in (25 mm). Dado rails and picture molding are usually fixed on top of plaster. In older houses, however, they may have been

positioned before the walls were plastered, so the plaster overlaps the edges. If you are moving them to renovate, you may have to do some extensive plasterwork.

In the past, carpenters made many different shapes and patterns for use as baseboards, moldings, dados and picture moldings. Many of these are available today in stores and specialist wood suppliers. However, it is possible to make them with plain strips of wood and a power router. This is a tool which rotates at high speed and can produce a smooth shape in the wood, which will require no sanding. Hundreds of different shapes of cutter are available, but only a few should be needed to produce a simple baseboard or picture molding or dado rails from strips of wood. A router should be used with a special router table and both can be rented from rental agencies. Follow safety instructions carefully because these are powerful tools. Wear eye protection, overalls and a dust mask as the machine creates a very fine dust. One of the most useful shapes is a simple rounding-over bit with a bearing on the tip, and this, together with a straight, fluted cutter, will produce the classic ovolo pattern often used as a molding for the top of the wall, where it meets the ceiling, and on many baseboards.

Another cutter, which produces attractive results on softwood, is a Roman ogee, which will give an attractive, rounded shape at the top. The smooth section of wood in the center can be cut with a flute bit to form a uniform round recess along the wood. This style of decoration is also seen on fireplace fronts. An experienced carpenter should be able to produce these patterns and others for you, if you don't feel up to doing it yourself. The size of wood for both picture molding and dados may be 4 x 1 1/4 in (75 x 25 mm), but a small, rented router should not be used for anything larger. For picture moldings, you will need a small groove at the back of the top section to allow traditional picture hooks to be hung over it.

Doors

The style and quality of the doors in your home will affect the overall look. The most widely known types of door are described below:

- *Eight-paneled solid mahogany doors (with two small panels at the top and bottom, and four wide rectangles in the middle) were popular in the first half of the eighteenth century.*
- *Six-panel doors (two small panels at the top and four equal-sized, longer ones below) became the most popular from the late seventeenth century onward, especially for front doors.*
- *Four-panel doors (two long panels above, two smaller ones below) were very popular in the nineteenth century and remained standard in Great Britain and the United States throughout the century.*

Pine doors are often stripped of layers of paint and then left bare. This can be a pleasant and cheap alternative to modern, hollow-core, unpaneled doors, particularly in a country-style room, although in the seventeenth and eighteenth centuries, pine doors would never have been left unpainted.

Wood in the Kitchen

You can make a very simple and visually attractive wall of hanging storage for smaller items, such as scissors, baskets, a knife rack, and the odd bits and pieces that so often get lost in drawers, by attaching upright battens to the wall and nailing 2/3 x 1 1/4 in (15 by 30 mm) slats horizontally across them, leaving a gap of 3/8 in (10mm) between them.

Buy 'S' hooks to hang over the slats or make your own from a wire clothes hanger. This slatted storage can take up as much or as little space as you wish, and the wood can be painted, stained or varnished to match the kitchen. This is an ideal feature in which to incorporate concealed lighting.

Dressers are available in many sizes and various levels of decoration. The cheapest and smallest kind can be made out of a small pine cupboard, with a set of pine shelves standing on it or fixed to the wall above. This can be effective in a small house, where there might not be space for a larger piece. Cheap pine furniture is available in many furniture shops and superstores. Wood work surfaces are more pleasant and less hard on knives than standard melamine surfaces. Maple, oak, mahogany or other hardwood is best. Pine is more likely to soften if it is left continually wet. Oil the wood occasionally with teak oil or linseed oil, applied several times.

Inexpensive wood stair rods and rails were often painted during the 1950s and 1960s, but it is not difficult to bring them back to their original state by using a paint stripper and then polishing, staining or varnishing the natural wood.

(above)
The wood on this panel door and the dado paneling have been left in their original rich golden wood.

Plaster, Brick & Stone

Both plaster and decorative moldings have existed for almost as long as the bare walls they embellish, and decorative plasterwork is a good indication of the age and importance of a house. Intricate wood moldings were popular in Tudor times, and plaster, which takes so well to classical motifs, was used by the Adam brothers in the eighteenth century. Georgian plasterwork was molded on site: gradually diminishing in grandeur and size, from the public rooms at the front of the house to the bedrooms and servants' quarters. The Victorians turned the craft into a mass-production industry, making thousands of moldings, which could be ordered from books.

During the 1960s in Great Britain, many moldings were ripped out or hidden behind partition walls and suspended ceilings, but the current popularity of classically proportioned walls means there are now plenty of choices for replacing moldings, ranging from traditional designs to modern ones. Today, the craft is coming into its own again, and you can now get plaster architraves, capitals, corbels, cornices, covings, ceiling roses, friezes, plaques and more. You can even buy an arch to create an elegant room divider. Fake wood carvings, made with plaster casts, then finished in wood imitation paint effects, are also available. There are a number of plaster specialists who can make virtually anything to order, or you can buy standard pieces in large building-supply outlets.

Uses for Plaster

(previous page)
Plaster moldings are available in a wide variety of shapes and styles. This is a cornucopia with grapes spilling over the top.

(above)
The rough draft, stone walls in this house in Normandy give a particularly exotic effect in direct contrast to the elegant handmade green tiles.

In most homes, the majority of rooms will have plastered walls and ceilings. Plaster is a wonderfully flexible material, and whether it covers stone, brick, wood or cinder block, the plaster covering makes it both dust and draft-proof, and gives a smooth, flat surface for paint or other wallcoverings. The color of pink plaster is beautifully subtle and can be left unpainted, then polished with beeswax to finish, once all the moisture has dried out. This surface can then take stenciled borders or blocked patterns, or be polished and left undecorated when it looks rather like kid or pale suede. You can create an illusion of grandeur for fun, or as a convincing introduction to a classic interior by using decorative elements cast in plaster.

Plaster was already used in the fifteenth century to insulate and give a smooth finish to interior walls between beams and over thin wood laths. Some fifteenth- to seventeenth-century houses still have their original lime plaster, which is made from sand and slaked lime and glue, with horse hair often added to increase the strength and improve setting. Most modern plaster walls consist of pieces of prefabricated plasterboard with a finishing top coat.

Tips on Plain Plaster Walls

- *New plaster should be left to settle for several months and up to a year in wet climates, before being painted or papered. If you don't want to wait that long before decorating, you will find the paint gets covered in an efflorescence from time to time. Rub this off with a dry cloth. Don't apply gloss paint over plaster within a year of plastering because this will prevent the drying out process, whereas flat latex will allow the plaster to "breathe."*
- *Small plastered areas can be painted with latex after three or four weeks.*
- *Prime new plaster with diluted latex paint before painting, or use a sizing solution or*

diluted wallpaper paste, before putting on any wallcovering.

- Plaster containing lime should be treated with an alkaline primer.
- Check old plaster for cracks, moisture damage and loose areas that may need replastering. Tap the wall firmly with your knuckles. If it changes from a dead noise with no resonance to a hollow noise, that indicates the plaster is coming away from the wall.
- Cover uneven plaster with lining paper, hung horizontally, to provide a smooth surface for paint or paper.
- Plasterboard must be sealed and primed, or treated with a combined primer/sealer before it is painted or papered.
- Previously painted or papered plaster should be stripped first using a chemical or steam stripper, then washed down with water and detergent, with a drop of ammonia added to the solution. If the surface is glossy, wash it with soap. Then rinse and allow to dry. By the time you have finished the room, it should be quite dry and ready for painting.
- If the paint is old and flaky, strip or burn it off. Take all safety precautions; wear goggles and gloves. Stripper is caustic so don't let it near any floor coverings or furniture. A blow torch can be very dangerous and should only be used by someone with experience: it can damage the wood and cause a fire.
- Unless you replaster the whole wall, it may be difficult to reconcile large areas of old plaster with large areas of new, because the level of the surfaces may vary. If you want a good paint finish, paper first with a heavy covering material to conceal any unsatisfactory joins.

Decorative Plasterwork

Exceptionally versatile, fibrous plaster can be molded into quite intricately detailed designs, and it is a durable, inexpensive and environmentally friendly, molding material. Plaster moldings are generally fixed to the wall using tile adhesive, screws and pins. They can be gilded, made to appear textured with paint effects, or simply whitewashed or painted with latex. Fine detailing on old plasterwork often becomes blurred due to years of numerous applications of paint. Restoration can be painstaking and should always be undertaken by experts. A combination of resin and polystyrene is a cheap, light, easy to paint and quick to fix modern material, which can be used for moldings. Its use is best limited to ceiling roses and cornices.

The versatility of plaster is best seen in the infinite variety of ornaments that it was used to make, the most universal being the cornice. The practical function of a cornice is to hide the junction of wall and ceiling, but the idea and general forms used for cornicing first came from Classical architecture. The most common form of cornice is the plain, continuous molding seen in various forms right through from the seventeenth to the mid-twentieth century. In the eighteenth century, cornices followed Classical examples fairly closely. The plain, molded Tuscan cornice (or simplified versions) were often used, or richer Doric, Corinthian or Ionic cornice patterns could be taken.

In fact, decorative plasterwork is a good indication of the age and importance of a house, as well as being a beautiful form of embellishment. The eighteenth-century plasterwork used for large houses was carefully mixed and molded by hand on site. In the main public rooms, it would be used large and heavily embellished, gradually diminishing in size and flamboyance in the lesser rooms and bedrooms. In the 1760s, Robert Adam started a fashion for lighter, more elegant plaster decoration. He used small-scale ornament on walls and ceilings. From the mid-eighteenth century, plaster models were taken directly

The revival of decorative plasterwork means that there is an ever-increasing range of motifs to choose from.

from the publications of people such as the Adam brothers in England. These were still Classical in style, but took different forms such as ox-skulls, vases, mythical beasts, leaves and stylized honeysuckle (anthemion). Chinese and Gothic decorations were also included, and all these motifs could be put together to make a fantastic ornamental concoction. Such motifs were usually cast in small pieces, then fitted together, as required. Ornate rosettes and other details could be cast and then fixed into a classical cornice. The plastering itself was often carried out by specialists from Italy. This was much quicker and cheaper than carving wooden decorations by hand and cast ornaments soon began to appear in even the humblest of homes. They were commonly made into friezes along the top of the wall under the cornice, as well as being used for wall panels, arches, spandrels and overdoors, and to decorate ceilings.

During the first decades of the nineteenth century, houses were built in a variety of architectural styles including Greek, Gothic, Italian, Swiss and Tudor, before becoming mainly Gothic. Reinforced plaster was introduced, enabling plaster moldings to be mass-produced, with thousands of ceiling roses, covings and corbels designed in a suitable Gothic style (for example, Tudor roses and Gothic pinnacles), and also to imitate wood and stone. One nineteenth-century introduction was the ceiling rose, or "flower," which gave an elegance to the gas pipes used for the new gas lighting. This new plaster was tough enough to be transported by steam or carriage to newly built houses, then fixed on site, and the various motifs could be ordered direct from pattern books.

In more modest homes, plastering did not become popularly used until about 1740. Before that, wood panelling was more commonly used. But plastering was widely used until well into the first half of the twen-

tieth century, although designs became much sparer. The wall panel moldings and delicate shell or floral patterned corbels of the eighteenth and nineteenth centuries disappeared in favor of lengths of plain, concave cornicing, although a baseboard, dado and dado rail remained in use for a while, providing a balance to the cornice above, as well as protecting the wall finish from the bumps and scrapes of the furniture, which was lined up against it.

During this period, there was stiff competition from the makers of papier mâché, which was cheap, lightweight and suitable for very elaborate and delicate ornament, which was difficult to cast in plaster. There may still be houses with decorative moldings of papier mâché masquerading as plaster today.

Prefabrication, standardization and the fact that plasterwork was used in the most humblest of homes lowered the status of the craft in the eyes of the supporters of the Arts and Crafts movement, who greatly despised it and who had a strong influence on the taste of the time. They insisted that, if it was used at all, plasterwork should be seen as a craft, and they introduced much more basic Tudor and Jacobean styles, with naturalistic flower and animal motifs.

After the First World War, plaster decoration went into a slow decline. Cornices were painted over many times and so lost their definition, modillions (ornamental brackets under the cornice) became shapeless lumps and enrichments turned into strings of quite featureless blobs.

Today you can obtain new plaster, which is molded to match or replace existing damaged moldings. Some companies will take casts of existing plasterwork to match it exactly. This is expensive but can be the answer for registered historic buildings (for which you will need permission and may be able to get a grant), or for large, modern buildings, which require some embellishment.

You can also buy copies of old moldings, niches, corbels and even fireplaces in many large home and do-it-yourself stores, which are often made to a smaller scale to suit the size of many small houses or house remodels. Ceiling coving nowadays is often made of expanded polystyrene and can be used to hide cracks between the wall and ceiling, or to give a gentler, attractively curved appearance to the angle between them. Once painted, these covings are perfectly acceptable in appearance and conform with the general style.

Maintaining and Repairing Decorative Plaster

MAINTENANCE OF MOLDINGS

- *Decorative moldings and cornices should only be vacuumed once a year.*
- *Fit the vacuum cleaner with the flexible hose and crevice attachment, and protect the plasterwork from knocks by binding a piece of foam plastic round the attachment.*
- *Brush out finely carved moldings with a paintbrush.*
- *Never use liquid on plasterwork, as it can be affected by water.*

REPAIR OF MOLDINGS

It is perfectly possible to strip off old paint and reveal the original plaster molding, but care and time are required.

Decorative plasterwork lends a true flavor to period rooms, and in spite of its delicate appearance, it is quite able to withstand careful stripping and repair work. Some minor repairs can be undertaken by anyone who is good at do-it-yourself projects, but a professional plasterer should be called in to run a plain cornice or cast new lengths to match existing cornicing. "Running" means forming a molding by scraping a metal template across wet plaster to give the required shape. It gives a crisper effect than cast work.

Small ornaments, individual modillions and parts of large patterns can be made by casting plaster of Paris in a vinyl mold made from an existing example. The vinyl compound necessary to make such a mold is quite widely available. It is important to clean the original molding carefully in order to get a clean cast. Set the cast in place with more plaster of Paris. Large pieces, designed for repair work, can be purchased ready-made. Several companies produce different sizes and styles. Joints can be repaired with plaster of Paris. There are various plastic imitations available, which can look fine when used in a new interior, but it is probably best to use fibrous plaster when matching up with old plaster. Large areas of plasterwork should always be dealt with by a professional and if you live in a registered building, you should get advice before attempting any repairs yourself.

REPAIRING CRACKS

If there are cracks or small holes in the coving, clean away the dirt with a sponge and warm water. Fill, where necessary, with plaster repair filler, forcing the mixture into the gaps by dragging the filler knife across the damaged areas. Use the same technique to repair any shrinkage of cracks.

Tips on Do-it-yourself Repair of Plasterwork

- *Before doing any work, strip off all the old paint. Strip a small area first and then, if in doubt, call in a professional.*
- *Follow the safety instructions when using a stripper and always wear goggles and rubber gloves. If you are using a blow torch or electric stripper to strip oil-based paints, wear a mask over your nose and mouth as the fumes are toxic.*
- *Have plenty of clean water at hand to wash stripper from both plaster and tools.*
- *If a cornice or moldings are discolored, check whether moisture is the problem and seek professional advice.*

- *If the ceilings are high, either buy or rent a lightweight aluminum tower scaffold fitted with wheels so you can move it around.*
- *If you want to knock down a wall in an older house, you will need to match any cornices. Since this is costly, consider creating a large arch instead of knocking down the wall entirely.*

Painting Decorative Plasterwork

In an ordinary eighteenth-century house, the ceilings and cornices were usually painted white or gray, or a similarly plain color. Gilding might be introduced. Robert Adam used delicate colors to pick out his decorations, but plain colors were the general rule in the early nineteenth century. The cornice was usually painted in the same color as the ceiling. In low rooms, it might be painted the same color as the wall so as to emphasize the height. Plain-colored moldings might have their shape defined by being painted in lighter and darker shades of the same color, and the dominating color in a wallpaper was often continued in the cornice. It was fairly common to make the cornice seem wider by painting lines on the ceiling side. The ceiling roses were normally painted a plain color, too, probably because in gas-lit rooms they had to be painted to disguise any fume stains.

Exterior Rendering

In its most durable forms, such as stucco or cement, plaster is good for external work. In the early nineteenth century, stucco was often used to look like stone in order to hide indifferent and not very weatherproof brick-work. Sometimes it was tinted with stone dust. Originally this was an Italian skill and, in the eighteenth and nineteenth centuries, the Italian plasterers were so skilled that it can be difficult to differentiate between stucco and painted stonework.

Pargetting is a medieval English form of exterior decorative plastering usually seen in the form of simple patterns, which are made by pricking or scratching the wet surface of the plaster, or as symmetrically arranged patterns, which are made by pressing molds into plaster before it sets.

Repair and Maintenance of Exterior Rendering

Although original stucco is now often found to be damaged and cracked, it is well worth preserving. Once it has become damaged, rainwater can permeate the outer rendering and attack the masonry behind it. Moisture gets trapped and expands in frosty weather, forcing patches of the rendering off the wall. Small amounts of damage can be mended with simple do-it-yourself techniques, but large amounts of damage should always be dealt with by a professional. If it is left for too long, cracked and flaking stucco will deteriorate rapidly. You can fill cracked stucco with a mortar made up of 1 part Portland cement; 1 part hydrated lime; 6 parts sand and a little proprietary bonding agent to help it stick. Soak the cracked rendering then, using a pointing trowel, fill each crack flush with the wall. Mixes are available and more economical if you are only dealing with small areas.

Brick

In certain settings brick can be left without plaster or plasterboard, allowing the bricks to be part of the visual and textural design of the place. Large spaces, such as warehouses or lofts, can look very good with the bare brick exposed; it can give a warm, attractive look to a country-style room and provide a strong, textural contrast to smooth, shiny surfaces, such as glass-topped tables or metal furniture. Coat the bricks with a clear sealer to prevent crumbling or spreading dust.

If the wall was previously plastered and is now left exposed, the bricks may not be in good enough condition to remain as they are and, in this case, they may be painted white or off-white. White-painted brick can bring light into a dark interior and can co-ordinate with the rest of a white-painted room. White-painted brick looks good in most modern settings. Use an alkali-resistant primer first because the mortar used would otherwise affect the paint. An oil primer sealer will bind friable brickwork and seal porous surfaces.

Brickwork can be treated with a light coat of waterproof plaster, so that the bricks still show through, and then painted white. This treatment can be very effective in curved basement and cellar ceilings. If the brick is in poor condition, repaint or fill in the worst gaps with a proprietary filler and then paint thickly.

Tips on Brick

- *Always check carefully for moisture before painting bricks.*
- *Check whether the mortar needs repointing. Repointing makes an enormous difference to the look and weatherproof quality of brick. Get professional advice on this.*

Stone

Don't rush to plaster natural stone walls. Stone can make a very attractive finish in a suitable setting, such as an old stone farmhouse or a vacation cottage, and can look particularly good in hot climates, where its rough coldness is often quite a welcome relief from the heat.

Marble and stone are often used for fire-place surrounds, sometimes with plasterwork overmantels, and these were traditionally given a smooth finish. Nowadays molded reconstituted stone is often used instead. It looks very much like the real thing, but is less expensive. Bath or Portland stone are commonly used in this way and can be used for open hearths, wood-burning stoves, or gas or electric stoves. Artificial stone first became available in 1760. Decorative moldings made from a mixture of clay and sand, then fired in a

kiln to produce a hard ceramic, were produced. They made all sorts of decorations for the exterior of the house, from small blocks for door surrounds to large, ornate relief panels and sets of keystones. These were obtainable through a catalogue, and since they were not nearly as expensive as stone, they became popular and were exported to Poland, Russia and the United States.

Avoid washing stone fire surrounds or anything else made of stone with an acid-based product or bleach. Stone is porous, and such substances can discolor it. You can use hydrogen peroxide and a stiff brush, but layers of dirt on historic pieces should be removed by a sculpture conservator. If in doubt, get expert advice. A protective coating can be applied after cleaning stone to help restore the polished finish and prevent dirt adhering in future. Be wary of these protective coatings as they can give the stone an unpleasant, varnished look. Test it on a small sample of stone first or, better still, get expert advice.

(above)
The lovely varied colors on the stone floor lift this kitchen out of the ordinary.

Paint

Paint is one of the easiest, cheapest and most satisfying ways of adding color to a room, in addition to being one of the most reliable of decorating materials. What's more, you can paint over it, if you don't like the initial result. There is practically no limit to the colors available and what you can't find on color charts can be specially mixed up for you by computerized machines. Many paint stores now have such machines, so it is not difficult to achieve any color you want.

The effect of a particular color is altered, of course, by whether the paint is matte or gloss, what colors are placed next to it, and it is greatly changed by the size of the wall area and where the light comes in. Plain paint, whether pure white or bright colors, can be used very effectively, but many people prefer to give the color a little depth by painting some sort of contrasting wash over the base coat, so that the base color shows through. There are many decorative techniques, such as sponging, ragging, stippling and so on, which use two or more paints in this way. Most are not difficult to do at home and they can be very effective. More sophisticated finishes, such as marbling, require practice or a professional to get the right effect. There are many short courses that can teach you the basic techniques and which paints and equipment to use, if you want to set about it in earnest. This chapter will give some basic information on color washes and glazes.

Paint Types

(previous page)
A basic little chest of drawers is charmingly handpainted, ad hoc fashion, in different colors.

(above)
A freestanding bathtub, pleasant furniture and a fitted carpet make this a good addition to the rooms in this home.

The most commonly available paints are two types: oil-based (solvent-based) and water-based. Oil-based paints are always soluble in mineral spirits, whereas water-based paints, are thinned with water.

Most oil-based paints smell strong while drying and can cause headaches, running eyes and sickness, and they will taint food if it comes in contact with freshly painted surfaces. Try to take frequent breaks when working with oil-based paints and work with the windows open. One old trick is to drink a lot of milk while you work, which seems to neutralize the toxic effect. French painters leave a cut onion upturned on a plate in a newly painted room to absorb the smell.

Water-based paints are now recommended as the most suitable choice for interior use on large surface areas, such as ceilings and walls, and you can buy water-based gloss and satin finishes for woodwork. Special water-based paints are available for kitchens and bathrooms, and there are also water-based natural wood finishes. These are long-lasting and as easy to clean as oil paints, but they don't smell as strong and are less polluting to the atmosphere. By the year 2000, solvent-based paints for domestic interiors should have been more or less phased out.

The following paint types, described by their level of gloss, may be given different names by various manufacturers, but they constitute the most popular range of modern paints for everyday use:

Eggshell: Soft, sheen finish. Needs two or more coats. Use this on walls, woodwork or metal. Washable. No undercoat needed, use two coats for good coverage. Prime bare wood first. Coverage per pint/liter: 172 sq ft (16 sq m).

Satin: Silky, low-sheen finish. Good for kitchen and bathroom walls. Ideal for highlighting relief patterns in wood or plaster. No undercoat needed. Coverage per pint/liter: 140 – 150 sq ft (13 – 14 sq m).

Matte Emulsion: A soft matte finish.

Normally used for walls and ceilings. Can be used on wood. No undercoat needed. Coverage per pint/liter: 150 – 162 sq ft (14 – 15 sq m).
Roller Paint: Available in matte or satin. Comes ready packaged in a paint tray. Won't drip or run. Use on walls and ceilings.
High Gloss: Very shiny finish. Mainly for wood and metal. Needs primer and undercoat. Coverage per pint/liter: 183 sq ft (17 sq m).
Non-drip Gloss: High shine finish, gel-like texture, will not drip or run. Mainly for wood or metal. Good for plastic surfaces, such as gutters and drainpipes. Prime bare wood; no undercoat is needed. Coverage per pint/liter: 130 – 162 sq ft (12 – 15 sq m).
Self-undercoating Gloss: Thick consistency, dries to a high shine. Covers most colors with one coat. Use on wood, metal or plastic. Coverage per pint/liter:108 sq ft (10 sq m).
Textured Paints: Use for hiding cracks and irregularities in walls and ceilings. They are thick and leave a rough finish.
Polyurethane Paints: Use these tough, hard-wearing paints for radiators, pipes and metal windows. They resist moisture and chipping.

Traditional Paints

In recent years, a lot of research has been done to identify what traditional paints were made of and what their true colors would have been, and there are a number of companies producing ranges that recapture the chalky, dense quality of old paints, as well as the earthy colors. The following paint finishes are now available:
Whitewash: This was the kind of paint that was slapped onto all walls, unless they were going to be given some more sophisticated finish. It is powdery, non-washable and often left white. If it was colored, the colors were based on earth pigments and were mainly browns, greens and yellows. The vibrancy and density of the colors makes them a good choice for matte decorative paint techniques, such as distressing and ragging.

Latex: The modern equivalent of whitewash is washable and can be painted over, but it doesn't have the same attractive, powdery texture.
Casein Paints: Made with milk. Very similar to whitewash, with a similar flat matte finish. Not quite so powdery.
Limewash: This used to be applied to furniture, paneling and floorboards, and gives a characteristic pale look to the grain.
Tempera: Pigment bound in egg yolk. It was used for murals, which crudely copied tapestry subjects. Fresco colors are now available in water-based emulsions.
Flat Oil Paints: Similar to whitewash, but harder wearing and suitable for use out of doors.

Some Useful Specialized Paints

Swimming-Pool Paints: Waterproof and very durable. Good for floors or in bathrooms.
Spray Paints: There are spray paints for many different purposes. Automobile spray paints are excellent for stenciled floors or other places, where you want a durable finish.
Blackboard Paints: Good for children's rooms. Paint straight onto a wall or onto a board.
Metallic Paints: Decorative paints used for metal window frames, window bars or radiators. Will inhibit rust.
Flame-Retardant Paints: These are particularly suitable for plastic tiles, which are highly flammable if left uncovered.

Some Hints on Choosing and Using Paint

- *Hold the color chart in an upright position to give a better impression of what the colors will look like on a wall. When held vertically, colors appear darker than if viewed horizontally.*
- *A strong color in a color chart will look darker and stronger when applied to a large area. Use paint samples first to try out colors before committing yourself to large quantities of paint.*

- *Make sure the surface is sound, clean and dry before painting.*
- *Use a plaster sealer on new or bare plaster.*
- *Seal powdery masonry surfaces, including surfaces that are finished with a texturing compound, with a plaster sealer.*
- *Don't use textured coatings in a kitchen: they harbor grease and dirt.*

Hints on Period Painting

Some hints on the use of color and putting together harmonious schemes can be found in Chapter 2, page 32. However, if you want to achieve a period look, here are some indications of what was used when. The question of color is the subject of much argument between experts on historic buildings. Hardly any ordinary homes have perfectly preserved color schemes, so don't be afraid to experiment. Here are some hints on what is thought to have been used in different periods.

PRE–EIGHTEENTH CENTURY

Most plastered walls in country homes were whitewashed and often had stenciled patterns imitating the fabrics that were hung in great houses. A popular stencil pattern was a pineapple. In grander homes, paint techniques were used to imitate special materials, such as tortoiseshell or lapis lazuli.

EIGHTEENTH CENTURY

Eggshell finish comes close in effect to eighteenth century oil paint, rather than full gloss, and could be used to color a white base. Within the limited range of colors available, most eighteenth-century home owners treated room colors as a matter of taste and there are no strict rules for the colors of different rooms. However, pine woodwork should never be left stripped. Window frames and moldings would probably have been painted white and doors were often in dark browns.

Elaborately executed marbling and graining was usually carried out by professional

A selection of paint color swatches from the V&A range by Fired Earth.

painter–decorators, who specialized in glazed effects on walls, achieved by applying thin washes of transparent color over a white ground. Graining was not necessarily intended to look like real wood, but to give an interesting finish. This is easy to do, but marbling needs a little more practice. The idea intended was not to mimic real wood and marble, but to create a pleasing effect.

NINETEENTH CENTURY

Matte oil paint was mainly used on wood, often in black with Indian red and a bluish green. The Edwardians used to experiment with newly formulated high-gloss enamels on walls and woodwork. The main areas would be in pastel shades, with ornamenting and details picked out in the brightest colors.

1920s AND 1930s

Cream, buff, white and yellow were the generally preferred colors. Generally matte or only slightly glossy paints were used. However, if you were a Bohemian, you might use smoky shades of gray, yellow, brown and red in haphazard, angular patterns on the walls.

1950s TO 1970s

Color schemes included cream and white, dove gray, duck egg blue, lemon, mushroom and shades of pale to mid-green, in eggshell finish. Often one or two walls were papered and the others were painted in a color that was picked up from the pattern. Sometimes one wall was painted in a strong color (i.e., orange) and the rest were painted white.

During the 1960s, colors became much more dominant. Purple and red, orange and a vibrant apple green were popular as background colors, usually in large, swirling patterns or with primitive, stylized flower heads in reds, yellows and greens, the general idea being the more color, the better. Such powerful colors dominated the room, making it hard for the other elements to compete.

The 1970s saw a sharp reaction to this chaos, and brown became the background color most favored and it was often used with oatmeal-colored contrasts.

1980s AND 1990s

Gray was the background color during the 1980s, often used with pastel pinks, peaches and candied almond colors. This led on to natural colors, with white as the basic ingredient. There are hundreds of different white paint colors to choose from: whites with a hint of, say, peach or primrose. The warmer whites soften walls in a dark basement, while still reflecting the light to make the most of what natural light is present.

Always remember that although looking for authentic paints in the context of restoration work is the right approach, when restoring your own period home, there is no need to be too restrictive. If the paint technology of past centuries had allowed people to be as adventurous with paint as they were with textiles and wallpapers, they would no doubt have jumped at the chance to use them. Modern drapes and textiles may not look their best against some of the flat, unstable, but "correct" paints now available to us. On the other hand, these paints can look marvelous in modern settings. You have to look at them in the context of your own home.

General Painting Tips

PAINTING WITH A BRUSH
- *Make sure the bristles are dry and clean.*
- *Dip up to one-third of the bristles into the paint to load the brush.*
- *When applying paint, hold the brush like a pen. Work with random, directional strokes to ensure even coverage.*
- *When applying gloss, paint with vertical strokes, then spread the paint sideways to even out the coverage. Finish with light, vertical strokes.*
- *When painting on wood, follow the grain of the wood.*

(above)
A simple, modern bathroom painted in a distressed pink shade – an easy, yet effective technique.

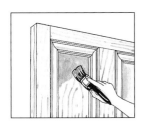

Painting a panel

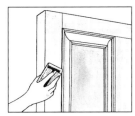

Rub down with finishing paper

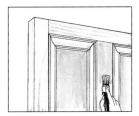

Painting a stile

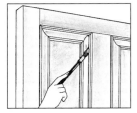

Using a fitch

PAINTING WITH A ROLLER

- *Use a brush to paint all the edges and corners before painting the main area with the roller.*
- *To load the roller, roll it backward and forward in the paint tray, pushing it up to the top of the slope to remove excess paint.*
- *Apply the paint with criss-cross strokes to the wall, ensuring a smooth start and finish to each stroke.*
- *Blend the edges of the next application while the paint is still wet.*
- *When applying eggshell, you will get a good finish by using a small roller on a long handle. (These are really designed to get at the back of radiators.) It is epecially useful as the preparation coat for a special finish, such as marbling when no brush marks should be visible.*
- *There are different kinds of rollers: always choose the one recommended by the manufacturer as being most suitable for your particular purpose.*

Painting a Kitchen

You can transform an old kitchen without replacing the cabinets by painting them in a different color. This particular method will suit melamine, varnished wood and previously painted units.

1. Remove drawers and door fronts, and unscrew handles and knobs.

2. Scrub the surfaces with hot detergent solution to remove all traces of grease.

3. Rub the surfaces all over with fine grade, abrasive paper such as wet and dry, to provide a key for the paint, then rinse and leave to dry. Wipe down with denatured spirits (this is better than mineral spirits). Apply with a soft cloth. Outline the area to be painted with masking tape.

4. Paint with water-based gloss or eggshell. Leave to dry, then smooth with fine grade abrasive paper and remove all traces of dust before applying the next coat. (Use the brush head of the vacuum cleaner.)

5. Repeat as above, applying as many thin coats as you need to cover the original color and give an even finish.

6. When the paint is completely dry, reposition handles and knobs, and refit doors and drawer fronts.

If you are painting over oil-based paint or laminate, prepare the surface like this: Clean and rub down the units as before, then prime with an acrylic wood primer. Leave to dry before painting as before. When the top coat is dry, finish with clear, matte` varnish for a hardwearing, water-resistant finish. Ask for a non-yellowing varnish or, in time, the color will be altered.

Painting a Paneled Door

You will need: a 2 in (5 cm) paintbrush, round fitch (a type of round brush used to paint moldings), finishing paper, rag, paint.

1. Start with the panels: Dip the brush halfway into the paint can and wipe one side on the edge of the can. Begin painting from the center top of the panel, just below the molding, working down and out toward the bottom and sides. Finish off at the top of the panel, when there is less paint on the brush to create runs.

2. Paint the moldings in the same color: Use the same brush, but on its side, or use a smaller brush. If any paint spills over onto the horizontal pieces of the door (rails) or the outside verticals (stiles) or the central vertical pieces, wipe it off as you go along, using a damp sponge for water-based paint or mineral spirits on a cloth for oil based.

3. Paint the rails, stiles and central vertical pieces, following the grain of the wood and the joints in the woodwork. Paint the top and bottom rails again, then the stiles.

4. Paint the outside edge of the door: leave to dry, then paint two coats of top coat, rubbing down between each coat with finishing paper. Remove any dust with a soft brush and a clean rag. The nozzle or brush of the vacuum

cleaner is the best way to ensure that no traces of dust are left behind.

5. If you want to paint the moldings in a different color, choose a contrasting or darker or lighter tone of the basic color.

6. Use a round fitch, which will hold the shape of the molding and doesn't have any odd bristles sticking out. Hold the brush at the end of the handle to give you greater control. If you smudge paint over the edge, wipe with a damp sponge for water-based paint or mineral spirits for oil-based paint. It is important to use good quality paintbrushes, which don't lose their bristles with every stroke. They cost more, but they last much longer.

Basic Information on Glazes and Washes

Matte water-based paint, when diluted to a watery consistency and applied very thinly over a base coat, is known as a wash. A glossy, transparent, tinted oil- or water-based finish, applied very thinly over a base coat is called a glaze. These finishes allow the base paint to show through, giving, in its most simplest form, a slightly three-dimensional effect with the color of the base coat slightly hidden and altered by the transparent coat.

A colorwash gives a charming and unobtrusive matte, old finish to a wall. You can see this sort of finish in weathered European cafés, and it is one of the most attractive finishes for a country-style or any other simply furnished interior — kitchens, living rooms, and hallways. It is a very simple technique if you are a complete beginner; in addition to being a lot of fun, you can experiment away to your heart's content. Colorwashing can help to disguise flaws, whereas ordinary paintwork tends to show up every imperfection. Water-based paints leave a powdery, fresh-looking finish, which many people find appealing. Latex paint is fine to use, but because of the plastic content of modern paints, you won't

(above)
A selection of ideas for painted cabinet doors for kitchen units.

get that particular powdery quality, which makes washes so effective.

With a glaze, you have to work quickly and the result will be glossy rather than matte, giving a more sophisticated finish, which is suitable for the best rooms in the house, for paint effects on paneling, and for halls and passageway in period homes or in grand interiors of any age. Both glazes and washes can be patterned with rags, sponges, brushes or rollers to create complex textures and colors.

Preparing a Colorwash

Mix the wash in a white plastic paint bucket. To get the right color, put a dollop of gouache (try burnt sienna, or a little black or gray or the color of your base coat) in the paint bucket with a tablespoonful of white latex paint to give it body. Add water gradually, mixing thoroughly as you go. Half a bucket of water to one tablespoon of paint should be about the right consistency. This will actually resemble puddlelike water, rather than anything else, but that small amount of paint is enough to bind the mixture and hold it onto the wall. Experiment with the base paint and the wash in small patches on the wall until you get a result you really like.

Applying a Colorwash

You will need: base paint (flat is satisfactory, though a satin finish base coat helps prevent the colorwash from being absorbed too quickly), brushes (a roller gives a slightly stippled effect, which is not really suited to this technique), a bucket of prepared colorwash, wallpaper pasting brush, soft-bristled brush (such as a painter's dust brush) and plenty of paint rags.

Clean and prepare the walls first, as you would for any painting job.

1. Apply a coat of your chosen base paint and allow this to dry following the instructions.
2. Use a wallpaper pasting brush to apply the wash color and a second, soft-bristled brush

Applying a colorwash

for picking up drips and to soften streaks and brush marks that are too noticeable. Move fast, using the brush lightly. If the wash seems too thin and just runs off the wall, add a level tablespoon of a commercial bonding agent per 1 pint (half litre) of paint.

You can add a second coat of wash, if you want to emphasize the effect. If you do this, apply a coat of matte varnish between the two coats following the manufacturer's instructions. Use a separate brush for applying a matte varnish. You can varnish over the final wash coat, but then you lose the powdery quality which is half the charm. Varnish is liable to yellow with time, but there are matte acrylic varnishes that are reputed not to yellow, and it might be sensible to use one of these in places where the wall might get damaged, such as on staircases. Remember:

- *Start in the top left-hand corner and move across the wall in broad, arched sweeps that are not too symmetrical.*
- *Don't stop until you have finished a complete wall, or you will get some very obvious edges.*

Glazes

Today ready-made colorless glazes that are formulated specially for decorative painting over walls are produced by specialized paint firms and come in various consistencies. However, they all have added substances to make them dry faster and give a long-lasting finish, which does not require any varnishing, although you can varnish over glazed walls, if you wish to do so. For complete beginners, the commercial glazes are the most foolproof. The oil-based glazes should be mixed with mineral spirits and artists' oils or commercial stains. A useful and easy recipe uses equal amounts of commercial oil glaze and mineral spirits, plus the tinting color. If you wish, you can also add a tablespoon of white oil-based paint per 1 pint (half litre) to give a slightly softer look to the glaze.

Mixing a Glaze

1 pint (half a litre) should be enough glaze to paint a small living room. Pour the glaze into a paint bucket and add the white base now if you are using it. Add mineral spirits gradually and stir well (as though you were making mayonnaise). Mix up the tinting colors separately in a white bowl and transfer this to the bucket, then mix it up well. Test the result on the wall or on paper. You cannot be exact about the amount of pigment or stain, but use very little. You can always add more. Start with a toothpaste-sized squeeze of the main color, with smaller amounts of any other colors. If you have never done this before, it is useful to follow a specific recipe until you feel more confident. Keep lots of rags handy for wiping – old cotton sheets are good for this. Practice glazing on paper or on a white-painted board first.

Glaze Colors

Experimenting with paint is the greatest fun, but here are some suggestions for colors.

- *A pale color over a white base allows the reflectiveness of the white to glow through the glaze.*
- *Try a pastel color as the base coat, with a slightly darker tone of the same color as the glaze coat.*
- *If you are adventurous, try a bright color such as orange or deep red, or midnight blue, with a contrasting or paler glaze over the top. Dark brown over bright red, orange over yellow, dark brown over sea green, sea green over raspberry, and verdigris over terracotta can all produce exciting results.*
- *If you have a very steady hand, you can make stripes to emphasize the contrasting textures and tones, using a radiator roller or a paintbrush, well loaded to minimize any track or brush marks.*
- *Experiment with color ways on paper: it will help acclimate your eye and give you ideas.*

(above)
A small bedroom has been given a fresh look with white curtains and yellow-green walls.

- *Paler glazes over darker base coats can create attractive, milky effects and these can be used to tone down the color, if the wall turns out to be too bright.*
- *Remember that glazes are flammable, so do not store saturated rags, which may self-ignite. They should be washed out as soon as possible or destroyed. Never use them near open flames, and don't smoke in the same room where glazes have recently been applied. Always make sure there is good ventilation in the room.*

Decorative Techniques

Washes and glazes are attractive finishes in their own right. They can also be used to create a number of rather more sophisticated finishes. Some of these are quite easy for a beginner, while others require rather more skill. Change hands from time to time when painting; otherwise there is a tendency to reproduce the same gesture, which will repeat similar markings over and over again, on a piece of work that is supposed to be random in appearance. Popular techniques include:

Ragging: Pressing soft, scrunched-up rags into wet glaze in a changing direction to make a flowing, abstract pattern. It can be used subtly with a darker tone on a lighter shade or, more dramatically, with a completely different color over the base.

Rag-rolling: Similar to ragging, but the cloth is rolled up into a sausage shape and then rolled up the wet paint, from bottom to top.

Dragging: Leaves brushmarks on the dried paint. Use a paper-hanger's brush or a varnish brush to get fairly regular stripes, or a very old, worn brush for a rougher effect.

Stippling: Brush on the wet glaze, one strip at a time and then dab it with the tip of a soft, bristled brush to break up the color into tiny dots. Work quickly.

Marbling: This can be done on any surface, provided it is in good repair and has been given two coats of eggshell finish paint first. This is really a technique for experienced painters.

Spattering: Spatter two or three colors onto a plain, flat base. It is probably best to keep to two or three tones of one color. A variation of this can be achieved on a glaze finish by loading a clean, medium-sized paintbrush with a little mineral spirits and flicking the brush hairs with your index finger, so the mineral spirits lands on the still-wet glaze. The spirits will open up little pools in the glaze, revealing the base coat to look like small craters. Use very little spirits and don't go over the same area twice. Practice on a piece of cardboard. This technique achieves an amazing effect very cheaply.

Sponging: Use any sort of sponge, although a true sea sponge will give the most interesting effects. You can use the squareness of a plastic sponge to create a grid pattern, if you wish. Wring out the sponge in the chosen paint and squeeze it gently onto the wall in a fairly even pattern. If using an oil-based glaze, soften

Sponging

Rag-rolling

Splattering

brush with short, thick bristles, or use spray paint. Automobile paints give a lovely effect. These are especially good for use on floors or other surfaces that get a lot of wear.

Caring for Paintwork

- *Always rinse off all detergents and cleaners directly after use.*
- *Avoid using too strong a cleaner or you will damage the surface of the paint.*
- *Protect windowsills (and other gloss-painted areas that get heavy wear) with a little furniture polish.*
- *Clean latex paint with a mild detergent solution or an all-purpose cream cleaner.*
- *Remove pen marks with methylated spirits.*
- *Rub out crayon and felt-tip pen colors with an all-purpose cleaner.*

Exterior Painting

Water-based exterior paint provides a durable finish and contains fungicide to prevent the growth of molds. It gives a matt finish, which repels water and dirt, but it looks best on unblemished walls because it is impossible to cover cracks well.

To cover hairline cracks, use textured exterior paint, which is reinforced with fillers. This is weatherproof, but it will need repainting more often than nontextural exterior paint will. Solvent-based masonry paint is the hardest-wearing of all exterior paints. This has a smooth, eggshell finish that repels dirt. It can be used to cover walls that have been treated with a silicone sealant. This paint is more expensive than water-based and is usually obtainable only from building-supply outlets. Use a weatherproof, textured coating for very poor walls, which will cover extensive cracking.

Check that the surface underneath is sound and not flaking, damp, porous or stained. Weatherboarding, plastic gutters and also UPVC frames require no maintenance or other covering.

the sponge with mineral spirits first. If using latex, dampen the sponge with water.

Stenciling: Charming even at its simplest, although when used with subtlety, stenciling can be a sophisticated method of merging ornament with architecture. It can be a good way of creating a horizontal division in the wall at dado height, or to make a frieze or to decorate the area above doors, or on furniture, or even on floors (where it is essential to protect the effect with tough varnish).

There are a great many stencil ranges, which vary from simple, stylized floral motifs to classical acanthus, jungle animals, Paisley motifs, and so on. You can even make your own stencils. There are many books describing how to do this and illustrating the way you can create the grandest effects by using this basically primitive device to repeat patterns.

Artists' acrylics are good paints for use in stenciling because they dry so fast and won't smudge. You can either apply the color with a sponge, with a stencil brush or any other

(opposite)
A glazed decorative painting technique gives an opulent look to a small bedroom.

(above left)
A small chest has been handpainted in green with red detailing for definition.

Wallcoverings

Wallpaper and paint are the cheapest and easiest forms of wallcovering, and wallpaper has the added advantage of being suitable for covering rough walls, cracks and damaged areas. It is also available in an enormous variety of both type and pattern, and can add grandeur, color, style and interest to any sort of room. Large building-supply outlets carry a vast quantity of different types of mass-produced wallpapers, with quite a wide range of designs, usually at very good prices. Some papers need pasting, while some are prepasted and just need wetting, and others can be hung straight from the roll onto the wall. They are usually well displayed, with helpful information on what wallpaper is suitable for different purposes, what is washable, what is easy to hang, and so on.

However, big stores do not tell the whole story, and it is worth looking in specialty stores if you want something in a particular style or with a certain quality. Here you will find imported papers, hand-printed papers, reproduction papers, "document" papers and modern papers of a quality not usually found in the large stores. You will also get much more knowledgeable advice from staff. Faux-painted effects of every kind are available on paper, including marbling, dragging, sponging, ragging and stippling, architectural, stone and stucco trompe l'oeil finishes, woodgrain and colorwashes.

Wallpaper Types

(previous page)
A charming example of
hand-painted paper in an
stately English home.

MACHINE-PRINTED WALLPAPERS

Many of the most common wallpapers are roller-printed onto a white ground, although some are coated with a ground color first. Cheaper papers are usually thinner and harder to hang, since they often stretch slightly when wet. They are best used in bedrooms and other rooms where they won't get rough treatment. Thicker paper will help to hide blemishes. Some papers are pre-pasted, which makes them easier to hang. Some may be washable, while others are not. (Vinyl papers are usually machine-printed.)

VINYL WALLCOVERINGS

Tough and waterproof, this type of wallcovering can be washed and gently scrubbed, if necessary. It is made from PVC, with a paper or cloth backing. The surface may be textured. It is available in many designs and colors, although always with a characteristic sheen. Vinyl wallcoverings are a popular choice for bathrooms, kitchens and children's rooms. They need a special fungus-resistant adhesive because any moisture trapped by the protective surface coating between the plaster and the paper, can promote mildew in the underlying paste.

HAND-PRINTED PAPERS

Hand-printing is done with blocks, screens or stencils. The result is sharper, and the color is applied more thickly than most other papers and leaves a slight texture. It is more expensive than machine-printed papers, but many people prefer the tailor-made quality. Hand-printed papers are now made by a number of companies. Some are able to use the original blocks from old wallpapers. William Morris papers are still being printed, for example, by Sanderson in Great Britain, and the enormous Gothic papers that were designed by Pugin for the Houses of Parliament in London are still being printed in London. French scenic block-printed papers, first introduced at the end of the eighteenth century and representing panoramic views of places and exotic scenery, were intended to run round a whole room without a repeat (although they were often cut up and used in panels). There were also antique frescoes, baroque trompe l'oeils of drapes and tassels, and antique statuary in grisaille (gray tones). These are still produced in France by companies such as Zuber & Cie (one of the original manufacturers). They are very expensive, but fantastic decoration for large spaces.

HAND-PAINTED PAPERS

Hand-painted Chinese papers can sometimes be found at auctions and in specialist shops. They were used in stately English homes throughout the eighteenth and nineteenth centuries, and were painted in China specifically for the European market.

EMBOSSED PAPERS

This is a type of paper with a raised and patterned surface. It is available in anything from geometric textures to imitation leather and woodgrain. Embossed paper will cover up a multitude of cracks and imperfections in a wall. Use it over lining paper and apply with a thick paste. Don't press too hard or you will flatten the surface. Anaglypta and Lincrusta Walton are all trade names for a type of embossed paper made with cotton fiber.

INGRAIN PAPERS (Woodchip or Donkey Paper)

This paper has small wood chips and sawdust added to it to give a knobbly finish. It is widely used to cover uneven walls, but the effect is not beautiful.

FLOCKED WALLPAPER

A paper with a velvety pattern created by tiny fibers glued onto the paper. Patterns usually imitate traditional eighteenth-century fabrics.

LINING PAPER

Thin underpaper that helps to give a good finish. It is available in various weights. Hang horizontally, if you are papering and vertically, if painting.

Alternative Soft Wallcoverings

WOVEN FABRIC

This can be anything from plain canvas or burlap to silk, cotton or wool. Such coverings effectively conceal defective surfaces. They can be stapled over an underlayer directly onto the wall with a staple gun or stapled over boards and then attached to battens on the wall, or if it is tough enough, the fabric can be fixed directly onto battens. Don't use delicate, pale-colored fabrics in rooms where they will get hard wear. Maintain by lightly vacuuming or gently sponging, or cleaning with an uphol-stery shampoo. Fabric wallcoverings do absorb smells, particularly tobacco and cooking smells, so they need regular maintenance. This is particularly the case with the area above radiators, where the heat will "fix" in any dirt in the atmosphere into the fabric, which is then very difficult to remove. Vacuum these areas often.

FELT

Felt is warm and colorful, and can be tacked onto boards, which are then attached onto battens. Some felt is paper-backed and can be hung like wallpaper, but it is difficult to clean.

IMITATION SUEDE

Alcantara is a synthetic imitation of suede, which is available in gorgeous colors and in generous widths. It is washable and, although expensive, is very resilient and long lasting.

CORK

Available as tiles or sheets in natural dark or light brown or dyed bright colors. It is good insulation material. Some cork has a protec-tive vinyl coat, otherwise it should be sealed by applying a clear, matte seal with a brush.

(above)
A pretty floral paper. Its roses are reflected in the vase of fresh flowers on the dressing table.

(above)
A William Morris wallpaper has
been charmingly used in this
room, where the small Victorian
fireplace and the woodwork
frame it in a vivid yellow.

POLYSTYRENE

This is usually available in tiles or rolls. It is an insulation material and should not be left uncovered. Polystyrene should be secured with a nonflammable adhesive and covered with some other wallcovering, because in the event of a fire, it will become molten and drip off the wall or ceiling, and it can cause bad burns.

Using Wallcoverings Imaginatively

- *Many of today's wallpaper collections are designed to coordinate through several different patterns with borders, friezes and fabrics. The unifying feature is the color and type of design.*
- *Borders and friezes can be used to adjust the dimensions of a room and to emphasize different areas. There's no reason why they shouldn't be run down a wall, as well as along it, or used to frame a chimney, an alcove or a doorway. They can be used without the main paper, to give emphasis.*

- *Vinyl wallcoverings can be practical for kitchens and bathrooms, since they are impervious to water and are also washable. The surface has a curious, dulling effect on colors, which not everyone finds attractive.*
- *You can use conventional wallpaper in kitchens and bathrooms, with a matte glaze for sealing and to give it longer life. The glaze will have a yellowing effect which, if you are using matching fabric for curtains and blinds, will be really noticeable. Otherwise, the yellowing can give a period feel reminiscent of the old Victorian "sanitary" wallpapers, which nearly all had a yellowish tinge to them because they were varnished during manufacture.*
- *Wallpaper can be used to cover an old screen to match the rest of the room.*
- *Use wallpaper to make a focal point of an alcove. Large, shallow alcoves respond particularly well to this sort of treatment.*
- *Pretty wallpaper can be used very effectively when cut to fit into door panels.*

- *A set of individual shelves fitted in a child's room can be backed with wallpaper and used as a decorative detail on a plain wall.*
- *Hang wallpaper on the top portion of a wall and paint the dado in a plain color, picking out one color from the paper. Divide the two with a dado rail or stenciling.*
- *Cover a blank wall in a very large room (say a warehouse), with a scenic paper – this is one of the few spaces that is large enough to use these papers to best effect.*
- *Use a flocked paper in a nineteenth-century period dining room.*
- *A flat door can be given panels by cutting strips of wood molding and then sticking them to the door. Kits of wood-molding strips to make panels for one door are widely available.*
- *Use a formal paper to cover the panels of a portable screen. Make small cuts at the corners and around curves, so the paper folds flat and use a staple gun to fix it. Cover the raw edges with braid or ribbon.*
- *Cheap wallpaper may be a false economy. It is usually flimsy, tears and stains easily; it may also stretch when wet and won't wear well.*
- *Use Regency stripes only in Regency or very formal interiors. If you want stripes in a pretty bedroom, choose a wallpaper which combines stripes and floral decoration.*

Period Wallpapers

Wallpaper has an interesting history. The first known use of decorative papers on the wall was in China. In Europe, papers are known to have been used on walls from the fifteenth century onward, but they were simple papers in small, single sheets used for lining boxes, coffers and also cupboards. Wallpapers were sometimes used on ceilings and might be block-printed to imitate wood grain or elaborate woodcuts with coats of arms. Patterns were often taken from the tapestries that hung on the walls of grand mansions, and, in fact, for several centuries the inspiration for wallpaper designs came mostly from textiles.

SEVENTEENTH CENTURY

Decorated papers were produced by stationers using single sheets of paper printed in black. Colors were added by hand with colored inks. Rolls were made by pasting individual sheets together. The patterns were often based on embroideries, printed fabrics and lace, and, occasionally, plasterwork and woodwork. The Victoria & Albert Museum in London has examples of such papers.

EIGHTEENTH CENTURY

Chinese papers were often imported in great numbers by the East India Company and sold to most of the great castles and houses all over Europe, where they were hung in the dining rooms and best bedrooms. They were also exported to America, but after the revolution the Americans bought papers from China direct.

Truly magnificent flocked papers imitating formal damask or devorée velvet were the first styles to give wallpaper a good name among the rich and were used in the Queen's Drawing Rooms in Hampton Court Palace, as well as in several town and country homes. In France, where fine quality Rococo patterns were popular, Madame de Pompadour is said to have set the style by having some hung in her bathroom in Paris. Small-patterned flocks were used in smaller homes and remained popular right through the nineteenth century.

Textiles were still the main source of inspiration for patterns and motifs. Floral and small-scale prints using a combination of printing with stenciling colored over, were popular throughout the century. (Paper stainers achieved good imitations of Chinese painted papers in this way.) Small-scale diaper patterns and stylized floral designs, such as those that were used for lining boxes, reappeared once more as wallpapers.

Gothic papers combined fanciful medieval architecture with Rococo scenes and other decorations.

French papers were the most exquisite of all the papers during the eighteenth century. The best known manufacturer was Reveillon, which paid the finest artists, particularly those who designed especially for the tapestry weaving industry, to produce his designs. Papers were exported to America from Great Britain and France, although home production increased quickly after the revolution in 1784. These patterns were similar to European designs, but with a patriotic flavor.

NINETEENTH CENTURY

Floral papers depicted large antique vases filled with brilliantly colored garden flowers: there were also imitations of damask and free-flowing, floral patterns with colorful and complex borders, patterns imitating drapery, lace and even buttoned upholstery. Classical motifs were used a good deal. French scenic papers became immensely popular in France and were exported in great numbers to America. Some were enormous — one measured 52 ft (16 m) long by 10 ft (3 m) high. Several hundred blocks were needed for a design and, in some cases, over two hundred colors were used. Each layer had to dry before the next color could be added, and a complete set sometimes took two years to be completed.

The introduction of machine printing in Great Britain, with the range of new dyes and inks, produced richly elaborate papers filled with garden flowers designed in intricate detail, with plenty of brash color. With the discovery of "endless sheet" printing, the sales of wallpaper increased enormously. Another innovation that became popular was the "sanitary" or washable, paper, which was glazed to make it washable. These papers were often in geometric motifs and usually in yellow brown colors.

The designs of William Morris deliberately renounced mass production and returned to simpler, medieval designs and techniques, natural dyes and fewer colors.

In the late 1880s and 1890s, people used to divide the wall up horizontally into three highly patterned sections: a frieze, a dado and a middle section. This is still a most attractive way to deal with a room which has high ceilings.

TWENTIETH CENTURY

The wall between the dado and the frieze was now plain, rather than patterned, but a deep frieze of molded or patterned paper was considered an integral part of the decoration of a house. Friezes included landscapes, exotic flowers and foliage, in strong colors. Rich, dark friezes were thought to emphasize the intimacy and comfort of dining rooms without being too distracting; billiard rooms attracted friezes with sporting motifs, and nurseries offered endless opportunities for seaside and nursery rhyme scenes.

In the late 1960s, Sanderson produced the first Palladio range with large, strong and very modern designs, which influenced the wallpaper designs for some years. By now, fabrics were no longer the sole inspiration for wallpapers, and all sorts of motifs were introduced, from abstract painterly designs to kitchen motifs and bathroom fishes in washable papers, stylized sixties flower heads and illustrations from children's story books.

The 1980s and 1990s saw the introduction of many ranges of matching wallpapers and fabrics. Initially, these ranges consisted of a fairly limited selection of designs and color, but the choice has become very much wider and more versatile, with many plain colors matching and complementing the patterns. The patterns themselves were available in a range of different sizes and designs: the emphasis is placed very much on a good variety of choice.

During the 1980s, many old wallpapers were discovered in historic houses, which were being refurbished. Languishing under layers of paint and paper, they retained their original color and this has encouraged research into old papers. Reproductions of traditional papers are now being made by several manufacturers, sometimes using the original blocks and colors, sometimes adapting the scale and colors to give a traditional look to suit modern homes.

Tips on Buying Wallpaper

- *Check that the batch and shade numbers on rolls of wallpaper match. Colors and patterns tend to vary from batch to batch.*
- *Buy one roll more than you think you need, especially if the pattern is a large one.*
- *Always follow the manufacturer's instructions carefully.*
- *Hand-printed papers will probably need trimming and are best trimmed and hung by a professional.*

- *Choose easy-strip wallcoverings if you think you will want to change the covering at a later date.*

Assessing Quantities

A standard roll of wallpaper measures up to 32 ft 8 in (10.05 m) long by 20 in (520 mm) wide. Lining paper rolls are usually slightly wider. Measure the floor-to-ceiling height of the room (not counting the skirtings and friezes), and add 4 in (10 cm) to the total to allow for trimming after hanging. Find out the distance between the repeats in the pattern you have chosen – this will affect the quantity you need. Add 10 per cent for waste when choosing a large pattern.

- *When working out exactly how many rolls you need, aim to take into account the pattern repeat, if there is one. The larger the pattern repeat, the more paper you will need to guarantee matching it.*
- *Ignore door and window openings when taking measurements.*

(above)
Embossed wallpapers can add a particular quality to a room without adding extra color. This Anaglypta has been subtly used in a bedroom.

fine sandpaper to provide a surface for the wall covering to adhere.

- Fill all the cracks and holes with filler, then smooth down with sandpaper.
- Gently scrape powdery or flaky painted surfaces to remove loose paint, then wash and apply a stabilizing primer. Leave to dry for two days. Hang lining paper horizontally first before hanging your chosen paper.
- Strip back covered surfaces to the original wall. Old coverings may be pulled away by new ones. You might need to rent a steam stripper to remove stubborn papers.
- If you are papering both the wall and the ceiling, paper the ceiling first so that the paste will not drop down onto the newly papered walls.
- Beginners should start with a firm, good quality paper with a small pattern. Very thin papers tear easily and may become stained by the paste.

Hints on Preparation for Hanging

- *Always do whatever painting is necessary to doors, baseboards, window frames and ceilings before you hang any paper.*
- *If the ceiling is to be painted, continue the paint color 1 in (25 mm) down the wall to conceal any unintentional gaps that may occur between wallcovering and ceiling.*
- *New plaster must be left to dry before you hang any paper. Brush off any efflorescence, sand with medium sandpaper, then brush on a watered-down application of the wallpaper paste. This provides greater adhesion for the paste and allows the paper to slide into position more easily.*
- *If the wall is in bad condition, prepare the wall surface by applying one layer of lining paper going horizontally around the room. Flatten the joins down well to avoid them showing through the main wallpaper.*
- *For latex-painted walls, wash them first with detergent, then sand with medium or*

Simple Step-By-Step Paperhanging

You will need: Sponge and rags, folding utility table, wallpaper scissors, plumb line (or a very long spirit level, if you have one — which has the advantage of acting as a ruler as well), bucket for mixing the paste, utility knife, soft pencil, seam roller, wallpaper and recommended wallpaper paste, brush for applying paste, paperhanger's brush, long steel rule and folding rule.

Remove the heaters from the walls if you can. You should be able to cap the pipes or electrical lines. If this is not possible, see opposite for instructions on papering behind a radiator or other heater.

Start at a corner near the main window or the center of the chimney, so you can get a good match where people will notice it most. Work from here in both directions until you reach the door or the darkest corner of the room, where joins will not be so noticeable. Don't hang a full width of paper around a corner. Hang it in two parts, allowing the edge to overlap slightly onto the next wall, then trim off the excess about 1 or 2 in (25 or 50 mm) around the corner. A large overlap of paper will crease and pucker.

1. Accurately measure the height of the wall. Decide where you want the pattern to start and measure the height on the paper from this point. Allow 2 in (50 mm) above this and at the bottom of the length. Draw a starting line using the plumb line or spirit level.

2. Cut all the lengths you need, making sure the pattern matches between each one. Mark and number the top of each one to get them in the right order. Also mark the top of any end-of-roll, which you might be able to use in a recess or above a door. You can sometimes use small, left-over pieces upside down in inconspicuous areas, particularly if it is a small print or striped paper. Put all the lengths in sequence, face down on the table, with number one on top. Pull the first one toward you so the paste does not get on the table. (If it gets onto the backs of the other pieces it doesn't matter because they have to be pasted anyway.)

3. Follow the manufacturer's instructions for mixing and pasting. Some wallpapers are prepasted and only need to be dampened. You might find it easier to wet the paper evenly if you use the bathtub, rather than the tray suggested by the manufacturers.

4. Paste from top to bottom down the middle and outward to the edges. After pasting half to two-thirds of the paper, turn the top over on itself, finish pasting and make a smaller fold back on itself at the bottom. Leave to soak or hang immediately, according to the type of instructions on the package.

5. Unfold the top and position the paper so that it aligns with the starting line and there is a 2 in (50mm) overlap onto the ceiling. Brush across the top and into the join, then brush down and outward to remove any obvious air bubbles.

6. Unfold the bottom of the paper and work down with the brush to make a crease at the baseboard. Lightly pencil in the top and bottom line. Pull the paper gently from the wall at top and bottom and cut off the trim line with scissors, then brush the paper back into place. Use a seam roller to stick the joins down well.

Papering Behind Radiators

Radiators are awkward objects to paper behind. Turn the radiator off and mark the approximate position of the fixing brackets with masking tape on the face of the panel. Hang the paper in the normal way, but let it rest over the radiator. Use the tape as a guide and cut out sections of paper, where necessary, so that it can be maneuvered around the brackets. Use a radiator paint-roller or brush to smooth it down the back. Trim at the baseboard as usual.

Hints on Hanging

- *Use the plumb line on each length of paper and trim the paper wherever the wall is not quite straight.*
- *Try to get rid of bubbles at this stage, using a folded rag or the smoothing brush. Usually they will disappear through the drying process.*
- *Trim the paper to fit round corners so that it laps 1 – 2 in (25 – 50 mm) around the corner. Then re-plumb and hang the off-cut so that the pattern matches as accurately as possible.*
- *Cut around door and window architraves (cut away most of the waste before pasting).*
- *To paper around light switches, turn off the electricity first, then cut a hole in the paper slightly smaller than the face plate. Unscrew the face plate, tuck the paper smoothly through, then tighten it again. Some invisible plates that are suitable for use on very expensive wallpapers do not require any cutting, except to allow the switch through.*

Matching patterns

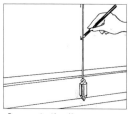
Draw a starting line

Folding and carrying

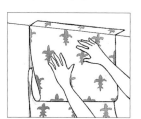
First length

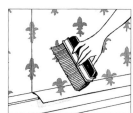
Work down with a brush

Textiles

From earliest times, woven and printed textiles have been used to soften, warm and enliven the home. Medieval cathedrals and castles were lined with woven wool tapestries, eighteenth-century mansions were dressed in woven silks to create a feeling of luxury and wealth, and pretty floral prints and toiles de Jouy have been used to brighten bedrooms and smaller homes.

Today natural and manmade fibers and computerized weaving techniques produce an almost endless variety of fabrics and color ways. There has never been a greater choice: from new types of fabric and modern designs to exact reproductions of historic fabrics. If you cannot afford to use expensive fabrics, a smaller piece of exquisite fabric can still add presence. Occasionally, fabrics originally intended for use as clothes can also be used for furnishing, but you must make allowances for different widths and check that the fabric will actually hold up with wear. Many people search for historical accuracy when restoring or replacing furnishings.

Fabrics may be made of natural or manmade fibers, or a mixture of both. Cotton is one of the most versatile fabrics and is often mixed with linen. Wool has a marvelous texture and good insulating qualities and takes colors particularly well. Horsehair, once used for stuffing upholstery, is woven into a very hardwearing and good-looking plain fabric. Silk is the most luxurious of fabrics and it takes colors well. Of all the manmade fibers, rayon is often used in soft furnishings because it drapes well, and nylon and polyester are often combined with natural fibers for extra reinforcement and to lengthen their lives without sacrificing looks or texture.

Some Popular and Versatile Fabrics
BASIC WEAVES

(previous page)
Here is just a selection of
seductive trimmings out of the
many hundreds available for
you to choose from.

(above)
A simple, fresh-looking
check design, with a slightly
raised pattern, has been used
to upholster this pretty,
two-seater sofa.

Canvas or duck (sailcloth): Heavy and stiff unbleached cloth made of cotton or linen. Can be used to upholster chairs, as awnings, stretched over a wood frame to make a screen or over a four-poster bed as a canopy. It can also be painted and stenciled, and used as floor rugs. Canvas is not usually preshrunk, so it should be washed before being made up. It can be dyed or painted. Buckram and drill are similar fabrics.

Calico: Unbleached cotton fabric similar to canvas, but lighter and softer with dots of cottonseed still left in the yarn. It can be used for curtains (calico looks good combined with tie backs and tassels), cushions, loose covers and tailored slip-over covers for dining chairs. Calico is not usually preshrunk, so this fabric should always be washed before sewing. Use in generous quantities as curtains: it can be draped or pleated.

Cambric: Plain, fine weave in bleached cotton. Best used for curtains and drapes as it tears easily. Not preshrunk.

Ticking: Originally used as a covering for mattresses, ticking has fine blue or black stripes woven into it and is widely used as curtains, upholstery and loose covers, or as a subtle lining for a more dramatic fabric.

All the above fabrics were traditionally used for linings, mattress covers or for covering furniture while the household was away, but have become part of today's furnishing scene in their own right.

Rep: A heavy-ridged, uneven cotton in a good range of plain colors, invaluable for use as loose covers, upholstery and cushions.

Twill: Strong weave in heavy cotton, produces durable material suitable for upholstery and loose covers. Brocaded twill has an extra surface pattern woven onto it.

Herringbone, ladder stripe, or any simple, small, allover pattern (diaper): Basic weaves that are all available in a great variety, usually in cotton or cotton and linen mixtures and they can all make good upholstery covers in many interior schemes.

RICH TEXTURAL WEAVES

Damask: Traditionally, this silk material was woven in France and Italy during the late fifteenth century. Many of today's most sumptuous modern damasks are based on the Renaissance designs, with luxuriant, large scale, floral scrolls including the acanthus motif, pineapples and pomegranates. Today damasks are also made in cotton and linen.

Brocade: A damasklike fabric, which has additional colors applied to the woven surface. Brocatelle has a raised pattern.

- *Damasks and brocades are too stiff to drape well and are more suited to formal curtains with swags and full length, sweeping curtains. They look their best with old furniture and in a period interior. Remember that this is a heavy fabric and even heavier when lined, so make sure the pole or track is fixed securely and that the wall or window frames can take the load.*

Plain woven silk: Mass production has made it easier to produce iridescent silk, nubby silk and moiré, rather than intricate patterns. Silk can be used for bed curtains, where the light is less likely to fade the magnificent color than directly by a window. Plain silks of various colors can be mixed together for a particularly splendid effect. Silk damasks were often used in grand mansions for covering the walls. If silk is used at windows, it should be lined and interlined to prevent the light fading the fabric. The simpler silk weaves drape into good folds and pleats. When used above the window, silk needs no lining and can be draped and looped to create great effects.

Checks and stripes: These have many uses in the home and can be either formal or informal in style. There is a wide choice available, from Madras cotton (now often woven with rayon or other synthetic fibers), which can be used where accent is wanted in bedrooms and living or dining rooms, to cotton gingham – a a fairly thin, cotton fabric, usually in blue, red or green, and white. Gingham is both informal and pretty, and useful for small, unlined curtains, for kitchens, bedrooms and Scandinavian-style interiors.

Tartan: A wool twilltype fabric originally designed as a clothing textile. Although tartan is a checked fabric, it deserves a mention on its own. It has become very popular as upholstery because of its strength and its bright, yet disciplined colors. Nowadays tartan is available in wool, cotton or silk. It is versatile: in silk, it drapes wonderfully for curtains; in wool, it is strong enough for upholstery; and in cotton, it makes cushions, bed drapes and tablecloths. In style, tartan can be serious or lighthearted. In Europe, checks are used only in rustic settings, whereas in Scandinavia it is only seen in more formal interiors (for example, Gustavian interiors). Today, it can be comfortably used in both rustic and town houses.

Tapestry: A woven fabric (and not the same as embroidered tapestry). Enormous pictorial tapestries were woven during the Middle Ages, to give the huge stone cathedrals and castles some semblance of comfort. These tapestries covered the vast stone walls, providing draft-proofing, color, room dividers and even depicting stories. They showed hunting and battle scenes, everyday scenes such as wine making and lovers' meetings. Gradually, they became more and more sophisticated, incorporating classical motifs, huge borders and woven frames that resembled carved wood. During the eighteenth century, coordinating tapestries and chair covers were being woven for tapestry rooms. (Several of these rooms were designed by Robert Adam and can still be seen in English stately homes.) Antique tapestries can still be found, some in good condition. Fragments of old tapestry can make charming cushions or wall decorations. Reproductions of old tapestries are still produced in Aubusson, one of the original tapestry-making towns in France. Modern tapestries are made in workshops in

Scotland and Australia, and individual designer-weavers produce contemporary designs, both large and small. Machine-made reproductions of old tapestries are usually woven in slightly smaller sizes to fit into today's smaller spaces. Tapestry is a heavy, stiff material, not much use for curtains, but good for giving focus and color to a room. Machine-made tapestry is a wonderfully tough upholstery material, giving a subtle and textural quality to the furniture.

Pile weaves: These are velvets and velours, corduroys, moquettes, chenilles and cut pile fabrics. There are various types of velvet and velour, and the stiffer fabrics are best kept to upholstery as they will not hang well as curtains. Otherwise, pile fabrics hang well: the colors will glow in the light and they are excellent for curtains and have good insulating properties.

Tribal weaves: These are African weaves, often woven into narrow strips and sewn together into larger pieces, ikat, some Indian cottons and Navaho blankets. They can be used as bedcovers, tablecloths, wall decorations and curtains, depending on the style of the room and the quality of the cloth. These weaves also include kilims and dhurries, which are useful as wallhangings. Kilims are sometimes used as upholstery covers for armchairs, sofas and stools. Their strength makes them long-lasting and their colors fit in with many schemes.

Sheer fabrics: These have an open weave, usually in a lightweight yarn that lets light through the cloth. They include muslin, lace, organdy and net. (Tutu netting is very inexpensive and pre-stiffened so that it doesn't crease too much.) Available either patterned or plain, modern sheers provide a fascinating solution for letting light in, while concealing the room from outside. They can be used with more formal curtains or on their own. Sheer fabrics need not be strung along a plastic-covered wire, but can be tied, looped or held back to create an interesting effect in their own right. They can be used in a similar way to mosquito nets hung over an ordinary bed or draped over a four-poster. Small ball bearings sewn into the bottom hem will help lightweight curtains to hang well. Indian fabric stores can be a marvelous source of diaphanous silk, which should be left unlined to let the light play through it. Indian fabric stores are also a good source for braids and ribbons.

Printed fabrics: These are usually comparatively lightweight and are not always suitable for upholstery. The range is vast: from floral sprigs to abstract and pictorial prints, classical motifs, chintzes, paisleys, block-printed Indian prints and Indonesian batik.

Tassels, Borders and Trimmings

Braids and trimmings are widely used for interior furnishings. Their popularity stems back to the eighteenth century, when they were highly fashionable in Great Britain and France. When added to curtains, cornices and upholstery, they can add extra definition.

Tassels can be larger for curtains or tiny, for use on cushions. They are available in wools, cottons, linens, velvety or plain and in an endless range of colors. The same goes for braids, cords and other trimmings.

You can buy separate tapestry borders to give definition to wall paneling and window fabric finishes, such as valances, tie backs, etc. Such borders are in a very fine weave with meticulous color shading. On the whole, horizontal and vertical patterns are easier to use than spiraling ones.

Tie backs and hold backs for curtains can be purchased in a matching or coordinating fabric, or you can make your own at home. By catching the fabric in attractive folds, they can define a window and add enormously to the decorative quality of the curtains, Almost any piece of fabric – including dressing gown

cords, belts, scarves and rope – can be used to tie curtains back, provided it fits in with the general style of the room.

Rods, Tracks and Hold Backs

Curtains usually look their best when full and generous, especially those used for large windows, so the pole or track should always extend well beyond the sides of the windows. This allows the curtains to be drawn right back, letting in as much light as possible.

Curtain Rods

Rods are a great way to hang curtains if you want to make a feature of the curtain fabric and give a window a positive, finished look. You can drape fabric round them, tie it up in loops, or hang one set of curtains in front of others, which makes rods very versatile. They are available in wood, brass, wrought iron and bamboo (imitation or real), and in a wide variety of designs and finishes to match many different styles of interior.

Simple wood rods, fitted with wood rings, look particularly good in Victorian and Edwardian interiors, but can be right in any country or eclectic setting. Stout brass rods and rings are designed for more dressy interiors and need smart fabrics and furnishings or else they will look cheap. Gothic metal rods with fleur-de-lys motifs or curly, wrought finials, sometimes asymmetrical or with antiqued verdigris finishes, look good in today's sparse settings and go well with metal furniture, candlesticks and heavy, rich curtain material. If you use rods, rather than track, the curtain will hang a little way out from the wall, so this is a better method of covering windows that protrude. Standard lengths are available from home-decorating stores and do-it-yourself stores, or you can have custom orders cut to size. The rod should extend several inches (or centimeters) on either side of the window to balance its proportions and also allow for the fabric to be pulled back. Calculate the position of the track or rod

(above)
Curtain rods are available in a wide range of styles, ranging from traditional to modern.

Textiles **257**

since they do not need to be touched by the human hand). There is also track which will open or close the curtains by electronic remote control or on a timer.

Hold-Backs

These are wood or metal knobs or hooks fixed to the wall, which the curtain can be draped or looped over. Hold-backs fixed above the window frame can hold fabric temporarily while you decide what sort of curtain you want, and farther down the frame, they can be used instead of cord tie backs. They will work best with a flexible, easily draped lightweight, such as the sheers or fine velvet.

Tie-Backs

These are pieces of fabric used to tie-back the curtains during the day. They lend a gracious quality to curtains and allow you to loop the fabric as much or as little as you wish. You can tie back curtains with ready-made tie-backs or tasseled rope, or make your own from the curtain material (or any other suitable material such as burlap, canvas or ticking). This can then be secured with a bow or a loop to the curtain pole.

Types of Curtain

CURTAINS HUNG FROM RODS

These curtains are often gathered from a heading tape fitted with hooks, which hook into curtain rings running along the rod. However, they may be hung from matching fabric tabs threaded over the rod. This method is suitable for large- or medium-sized curtains, which cover or frame the window and they do not usually have a valance.

CURTAINS HUNG FROM TRACK

Pleated and gathered curtains, when hung from track, consist of panels of fabric with standard gathered heading tape threaded with cord, which is then stitched into the heading. When pulled, the cord gathers the

before you attach it to the wall. If the top of the curtain is going to hang somewhat below the rod, make sure the rod is high enough so that the window frame is concealed. You can get clip-on curtain rings to go with rods, so no stitching or heading tape is required. These are particularly good on tapestry-type fabrics, which are difficult to sew and are better if not too gathered.

Curtain Track

Aluminum or nylon tracks are designed for traditional gathered curtains and are fitted with sliding runners, into which curtain hooks can be slotted. They are discreet and not intended to be a feature in themselves. You can purchase lightweight track for small, lightweight curtains; heavy-duty track for triple-lined and heavy curtains; flexible track, which will run round a bow window or even around the arch at the top of a window; and track with pull cords (this is good for curtains made from luxurious and expensive fabric,

fabric into the required width. Different tape headings produce various types of gather or pleat, some using more fabric width than others: take this into account when deciding how much fabric you want. Different tapes available include pencil pleat, pinch pleat and triple pinch pleat.

LOOPED CURTAINS

Swathed or looped curtains are inexpensive alternative to hung curtains. These are simply lengths of fabric looped in various ways over a curtain rod or pole. The fabric should be very pliable, easily draped and not too heavy. Muslin or any sheer can look very effective. You may have to sew lengths of fabric together to form one long piece. To calculate the amount needed, add the width of the rod to twice the height of the rod from the floor. Add another rod-and-a-half to allow for folds and swags. Start from the center of the fabric and loop it over the center of the rod as a starting point. You can experiment with different ways of draping it until you get the effect you want. You may have to tack very slippery fabrics into place.

SMALL CURTAINS

With the many alternatives available today, there is really no need to have dingy net curtains at a window. A lightweight, sheer or loose woven fabric can be threaded onto a pole or plastic-coated wire in place of a net curtain. The wire doesn't have to be placed at the top of the window. Halfway up can be enough. Café curtains are effective in a lightweight cotton, such as gingham and can be given a short, gathered valance of the same fabric.

Brass eyelets can be a good way of hanging curtains that are set inside the reveal of a window. They are easy to fix and can be strung straight across a wire or you can make loops from string or fabric to loop over a narrow pole. Most small curtains do not require any lining, unless you want to give

them an opulent feeling or keep out drafts. Lightweight fabrics will always hang much better if you starch them to give extra body.

Making Your Own Curtains

Ready-made curtains are available in a wide variety of patterns and sizes and, of course, curtains can be custom-made in any fabric you choose. However, they are not difficult, and are much cheaper to make at home. For the complete beginner, inexpensive, no-sew curtain kits are available, with iron-on headings and hemming tapes, hooks, cord, and so on. You have a choice of pleats or gathered headings, or ready-to-hang curtains with tabs secured with Velcro strips, which you loop round a pole. These look very effective on large windows, particularly in lofts, where they have a strong, medieval look.

Measuring

Measurements will depend on the style of window and type of treatment you have

(above)
Long curtains at a narrow window make an elegant statement and coordinate with the small settee in front.

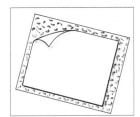

Lining versus curtain size

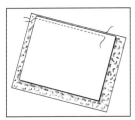

Stitching the widths together

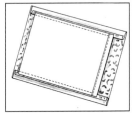

Lining up the two edges

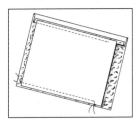

Machine stitching

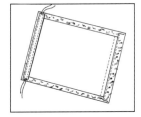

Finish by pressing lightly

chosen. Decide whether you want the curtains to hang above the window, on a batten, or on the molding itself. If there's space above the window and you want to have a valance, hang the track as high as you can, so you will lose as little of the window as possible. If you want the curtains to draw back in a bow window, you will need a pliable track designed to fit round the curve.

How you measure for the curtains depends on the type of heading you have chosen. Follow the manufacturer's instructions for your track. Be generous with fabric: it is better to use cheaper fabric and more of it, than to decide on an expensive one, and not have quite enough fabric.

Short curtains can fit neatly on the sill or end a little way below it (for example, at radiator height), or they can be floor length. Silks and luxurious fabrics can fall with a length or so of extra fabric to lie in folds on the floor, although this would be quite unsuitable for a home with small children or dirty floors. The width of the fabric you need depends on how full you want the curtains to be. Standard heading tapes require between one-and-a half and two-and-a-half times the curtain width. The following calculations are for a pair of plain or randomly patterned curtains.

1. Measure the width of the track or pole – not the window. (When using cross-over track, measure each side as far as it goes, then add the two measurements together.)

- *For heavy fabrics, add half as much again to the measurement of the track or pole.*
- *For cottons and rayon, add three-fourths to the measurement of the track or pole.*
- *For sheer fabrics, add up to twice the measurement of the track or pole.*
- *For pinch pleats, add an extra allowance of 4 in (10 cm) per curtain length.*

Now divide the total by the width of your chosen fabric. (Most household fabric is 54 in wide/137 cm.)

2. Round this up to the next whole figure. This gives you the number of widths of fabric you will need to make two curtains.

3. Measure the drop from the pole or track to the level you want the curtain to hang. Add 12 in (30 cm) to allow for hems and headings, and multiply this by the number of fabric widths to find the total length of fabric you need to buy.

Making a Simple Curtain

To make a nongathered, lightweight curtain to cover the window inside the reveal, you will need: muslin or voile or any other lightweight or sheer fabric, fabric adhesive or hemming tape, eyelet kit, two sturdy brass hooks, heavy picture wire or plastic-covered curtain wire, trimmings of your choice.

1. Cut enough fabric to cover the window, allowing about 5 cm (2 in) extra for sides, top and hem. Use fabric adhesive or iron-on hemming tape to secure hems.

2. Attach the eyelets on top of the fabric at roughly 6 in (15 cm) intervals. Follow the instructions on the eyelet pack. Attach a large, brass hook at each side of the window top. Thread wire through the eyelets and attach each end to one of the hooks.

Lining

Many of the simpler curtain effects and smaller curtains do not require any lining at all. Formal curtains and heavy fabrics look better if they are lined, and linings can certainly help with insulation and will prevent the main fabric used from fading in sunlight. If you choose expensive fabric, you can use less fabric by making the curtains less full, and using a heavy lining and interlining to give body and make them appear opulent. In any case, this is a good way of dealing with patterned fabrics as the pattern will be more conspicuous with fewer folds. Cotton-sateen lining fabric is available in many different colors and, of course, other fabrics can be used for lining too, to provide contrasts in color and pattern. If you are choosing another fabric, check that it is compatible with the main fabric for washing, etc.

Loose linings: Some curtain hooks have an extra loop at the bottom on which to hang a second, lighter-weight curtain that is quite separate from the main curtain. This is easy to make and to remove for washing separately, or for use in summer when heavy curtains are not needed, or just to change the lining with another, from time to time. A colored lining can look effective behind a lace curtain, or you can tie back the main curtain, leaving the lining to act as a screen.

Making Curtains with Attached Linings

The lining fabric should be 9 in (23 cm) shorter and 5 in (13 cm) narrower than the main curtain, so that the curtain edges fold around the lining slightly at the back, and the lining finishes 2 in (5 cm) above the lower edge of the curtain.

1. Stitch the curtain fabric widths together to the required size and press the seams open. Follow the same method for the lining widths. Lay the lining fabric on top of the main fabric, right sides together and with the top of the lining fabric 3 in (8 cm) below the top of the main fabric.

2. Line up one pair of curtains and lining edges and pin them together down the length of the lining fabric. Then line up the opposite edges in the same way. You will need to pull the lining across because of the extra width.

3. Machine stitch the edges, starting at the top and stopping 2 in (5 cm) above the lower edge of the lining. Turn up the lining in a 1 in (2.5 cm) double hem to the wrong side.

4. Press the side seams open and turn the curtain right side out. Lay it flat so the lining panel is centered with equal margins of curtain down either side. Press the side folds. Turn down the top edge of the curtain so that

it encloses the raw lining edge and attach the curtain heading. Then turn up the bottom of the curtain in a 2 in (5cm) double hem and press lightly.

Valances

Simple or shaped valances can add formality or grandeur to large windows. On small windows, they can even be used on their own instead of curtains. This treatment is particularly suitable in kitchens, where you don't want to disturb items on the window sill. A narrow, wood batten can be covered with the same fabric as the curtains, or with a contrasting plain fabric.

A special valance, known as a lambrequin, can be used to frame the top and two sides of a window. It is made with multilayers of fabric formed into sculptural shapes then stiffened, and can be any shape or size. With this sort of frame, you will lose a certain amount of light so it is best when used for windows that are overlooking a bleak view.

(above)
These tall windows are prettily curtained in a floral fabric, lined to give a feeling of weight, which makes them hang well and also acts as insulation at night.

complement shutters. They can be a good alternative to curtains, particularly where there is not much room to draw curtains back, or where they would get in the way of, say, a windowsill, and they are excellent for displaying fabric. Curtaining windows, which get a lot of sun (for example, in apartments in high rises) can be expensive as the sun often ruins fabrics, and blinds can be a sensible alternative. There are various types of blinds, some as stylish and exotic as curtains.

Roller blinds: These good old favorites are probably the most versatile types of blinds. Stiffened roller blinds are available in numerous colors and in standard sizes in many stores. They are also easy and cheap to make because they use so little fabric. Roller blind kits are sold in standard sizes, but the rod can be cut to fit your own window and the fabric can be of your choice. You may need to stiffen it. Roller blinds should be fitted inside the window recess.

Roman blinds: Very elegant blinds and, again, economical in fabric. In this case, the fabric is pulled up in deep folds created by threading cords through loops at regular intervals down the length of the blinds. To make them effective against light, you can interline with a special lining designed to obstruct light.

Austrian blinds (gathered blinds): Fuller, fussier and dressier, with lots of fullness and gathers when the blind is pulled up. The fullness is created by a series of tapes running vertically through the blinds so that the fabric gathers into gathers when pulled up. They are easy to sew by hand with a special kit and may be lined or unlined.

Baloon Shades: Even dressier than Austrian blinds, they work on the same principle, but use more fabric and look flouncy.

Venetian blinds: Not fabric, but a useful alternative to fabric blinds. They are made of wood (stained or natural), or metal strips set in horizontal rows, which can be angled to let in light or to keep out the sun. Venetian blinds

Alternatively, gather a narrow length of fabric and fix it to the batten with Velcro strips. More elaborate valances can be made with MDF and elaborately draped.

Measuring for Valances

Box Valance: You will need a length of about 4 in (10 cm) longer than the rod, and about 2 in (5 cm) deeper than the box.

French-pleated Valance: Double the width of the rod to determine the width and then multiply by the depth allowing for hems.

Valance Frills: Measure the valance rod including the two returns. Add half the width to the measurement for fullness and multiply by 6 in (15 cm) for the depth.

Box-pleated Valance: Allow two-and-a-half times the rod length multiplied by 6 in (15 cm) for a plain valance of (8 in) 20 cm with folds.

Blinds

Blinds were originally designed in the eighteenth century as a decorative feature to can look elegant in a modern room, or in a study or workroom.

Problem Windows

- *Tilting windows: You cannot screen these windows easily when open, so always make sure that any curtain or blind can be drawn well away to the side or above the window frame, or it will constantly be catching in the frame whenever the window is opened or closed.*

- *Picture windows: These became popular during the 1960s and 1970s, often running from wall to wall, leaving no space to draw the curtains back. One solution is to have blinds instead, but if you like to have curtains, sheer fabric, which folds back into a very small space, may be the answer.*

- *Windows overlooking a boring or ugly view: Hang lace, muslin or other sheer fabric, which will not restrict the light too much, from the top or middle window frame. You can add visual interest round the window by draping a bolder fabric from a separate curtain pole fixed above the frame.*

- *A small window, set into a deep recess, can be fitted with a dormer rod, which is hinged at one end, so that instead of drawing the curtain back, you swivel the whole rod to lie inside the recess. The curtains should have double fabric in this case, because you will see both the back and the front at different times of the day.*

- *If a corner window leaves no room to draw the curtain back against the wall, you could hang a single curtain and simply tie it back during the day.*

- *Sloping windows: Blinds are probably best for these windows. Attach them to hooks at the bottom of the window frame to avoid any dangling.*

Fabrics for Beds

DRAPERY AROUND BEDS

It is possible to have draping all around a bed without resorting to a four poster. A simple bed can be totally transformed by draping interesting or luxurious fabric around it. Muslin is a cheap and enchanting fabric for draping a bed, and because it is so light and pliant, it can be tied at the corners so all you need are some simple supports, which can be fixed to the wall. All sorts of draped headings are easily made from a length of fabric, draped onto the wall behind the bed, to hang down on either side. You can do this with three drape hooks, one a few feet (meters) above the bed, and the others fitted on either side. Pull the center of the fabric through the center drape hook to create a rosette, then pull the fabric through the lower hooks, creating two more rosettes, allowing enough fabric for a slightly looser form of draping. This simple bed curtain can be very effective and the fabric can be lined or unlined.

MAKING A CORONA

A Regency-style corona and drapes is a popular and easy way of draping a simple bed. All you need is a shelf fixed onto a metal bracket above the bed to support the decorative valance and a pair of curtains. Choose a fabric that will drape well, such as chintz, muslin, a length of batik or a hand-printed Indian bedspread.

To make a corona for a double bed, you will need: a piece of MDF measuring about 24 by 5 in (600 x 130 mm – this is your valance shelf), shelf-edging trim, gold paint, latex paint, paintbrush, gimlet, metal screw eyes, two L-shaped brackets, wood adhesive, length of plastic-coated curtain wire and fixings, fabric, lining fabric, matching thread, Velcro strips, contact cement, curtain heading tape and curtain hooks. To measure the amount of fabric you need, hold the shelf at the height you want it above the bed and mark the position. Measure from the shelf to the floor and add about 2 in (5 cm) for heading

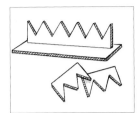

Constructing a corona

Fixing the brackets

Painting

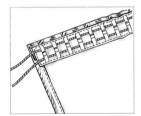

Adding heading tape

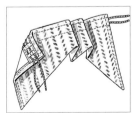

Valance

and hems. Cut the curtain lining to the same dimensions and measure for the back lining as you did for the curtain.

1. With the wood adhesive, glue the shelf edging to the edge of the shelf. When dry, paint the shelf with latex paint and let dry.

2. Use the gimlet to attach the screw eyes to the underside of the shelf, about 3/4 in (1 cm) from the edge of the shelf and at equal intervals round the sides and front, with one screw eye at each front corner. Attach two brackets to the underside of the shelf about 2 in (5 cm) from each end. Attach the shelf to the wall.

3. Carefully paint the edging trim with gold paint. Cut out two curtains. One width of fabric should be enough for each. Cut the lining fabric to the same size.

4. Sew the lining to the curtain, right side together, leaving the bottom unstitched. Turn the curtain to the right side and press. Pin and stitch the heading tape in position. Knot the threads, gather up the tape, insert the curtain hooks and hook them over the screw eyes under the shelf.

5. To make the valance, cut a piece of fabric one and a quarter times the length of the front three edges of the shelf plus a 1 1/4 in (3 cm) seam allowance all round and twice the depth you want it. Fold the fabric in half lengthwise, right sides together. Cut a gentle curve out of the bottom edges. Stitch along one narrow side, then slip stitch the other side edge. Stitch the heading tape along the top, tie the ends and gather up to fit the shelf. Glue a Velcro strip to the front edge of the board and to the top of the heading tape of the valance. Press.

6. To make the back lining (where you will not need your main fabric), use two widths of fabric, each the length of the drop from the underside of the shelf to the floor, adding 1 1/4 in (3 cm) for the seam. Join the two lengths by one long edge and press the seam open. Hem both sides and the bottom of the curtain. At the top edge, turn a narrow double hem to form a casing along the top of the curtain. Cut the curtain wire to fit along the back edge of the shelf and thread through the curtain. Fit a wire net hook to each end and gather onto the shelf.

Some Budget Ideas

- *Polar fleece is the softest, cuddliest fabric imaginable and available in a range of bright and cheerful colors. Make your own throw for an armchair by buying two contrasting lengths of fleece and blanket-stitching them together. However, this is not just a pretty chair covering: it also serves as a cosy cozy blanket for chilly evenings.*

- *Muslin can be simply draped over poles or held in place with special clips.*

- *You can cover an old chest or box with fabric to turn it into a useful and attractive piece of furniture. Any upholstery fabric will do. You won't need much, so you could probably splurge on something a bit special, but any good-looking fabric will do.*

You will need: Tape measure, tailor's chalk, impact or contact cement (some adhesives can turn a nasty yellow with age, which may show through the fabric so don't use them on fine fabrics), scissors, tacks and a hammer or staple gun, braid (optional), wood furniture feet (optional).

1. Measure each side and the top of the box, then add a few inches (centimetres) for over-laps. Mark and cut out the fabric for each of the surfaces.

2. You can glue the pieces, folding and pleating them carefully to fit. Follow the adhesive manufacturer's instructions for gluing. Tack or staple along the top for extra strength. Pull the fabric tight, and smooth out creases as you go. You can upholster the top with a piece of foam, if you wish to give a more finished look and a comfortable extra seat. Braid and round wood feet can be added if you like, to give a stylish finish.

Using Fabrics as Upholstery

UPHOLSTERY

Upholstery fabrics should resist abrasion and withstand dirt. They are often too stiff to hang well, so they won't work as curtains and some may even have an acrylic backing to make them firmer. Many manufacturers make matching or coordinating fabrics for upholstery and curtains, so that you can match the patterns and colors if you choose. If you have a variety of chair styles in one room, they can be unified by covering them all in one fabric.

The scale and size of the patterns are very important in upholstery. For example, a large sofa will fit better into a crowded room if it is covered in fabric that breaks its surface into smaller areas. Delicate chairs should be covered in finely woven fabric, and robust ones can take something more chunky, such as tweed.

Upholstery will affect the period style of a piece of furniture and its size and importance. Very basic shapes will take a wide variety of designs, but chairs with wood frames and fine detailing will probably look best with relatively plain fabric and in compatible colors. Pale wood such as natural beech or ash usually looks best in paler fabric, whereas strong oak or mahogany can take much deeper colors.

A common fault that is often found in cheaper, modern upholstery fabrics is their bland texture. They are all too often indistinguishable from one another and fail to provide that textural variation, which gives interest and pleasure. Try to include (even if only in cushions), either velvety, rough tweedy, shiny or ribbed textures to counteract this. Jacquard tapestry weaves provide gentle texture and an immense subtlety of colors and shading. Doublecloth can provide some interesting textures, often with a reverse side that can be made into a feature. Damask patterns have a sleek, sophisticated quality in patterns ranging from Italian Renaissance designs to those produced in Vienna at the turn of the century, to brightly colored, bold and modern abstract weaves.

Dark and light stripes can focus attention on a fine, small chair and wide bands of color can diminish the apparent size of a very large sofa. Simple two-tone stripes and colorful checks are particularly suitable for Scandinavian styles.

Fabric on Walls

Even the dullest of interior walls can be enlivened by fabrics and, they are especially useful in modern homes, where walls tend to lack architectural detailing. They are very effective in absorbing sound and, of course, in concealing uneven walls. Most furnishing fabrics measure 40 – 54 in (102 – 137 cm) wide, but some fabrics especially woven for paneling can be as wide as 72 in (183 cm).

You can drape ceilings and walls with soft, lightweight fabric to give a tentlike effect. This treatment would be particularly suitable for a room in a basement with few windows, or for a circular room. The fabric can be attached to a track at the top of the wall by a choice of techniques, as follows:

- *Stretching fabric over battens, previously attached to the wall, then tacking or stapling it into place.*
- *Wrapping fabric over padded, precut panels.*
- *Pasting the fabric into place. You do this by rolling the paste onto the wall and then pressing the fabric against it. The fabric is slightly dampened by the paste and can be stretched or contracted to fit. This method needs a fairly robust fabric and one which you are prepared to discard later because the paste will stiffen and damage the fabric over a period of time.*

Floor Coverings

The choice of floor covering in a home is a big decision. It is also a big financial outlay, since you expect the flooring to last for several years. The flooring fundamentally affects the look and feeling of the home. Practicalities are important, too: there's no point in buying long pile carpet for a room where children will play with building blocks, but they will need a soft, comfortable floor because they will spend a lot of time playing on it. Carpet is the most popular form of floor covering, but if anyone in your home suffers from asthma or chronic allergies, you should avoid any form of carpeting as the dust and fibers can be irritating.

In the kitchen you will need a floor that withstands dirt and is easily cleaned, while being pleasant to walk on, whereas in the living room, a luxury floor redolent of comfort and ease is more suitable. Hallways will need a really durable floor covering, which can be easily cleaned and will withstand the traffic of heavy boots and shoes. Study the options carefully.

It's a good idea to have a coordinated look throughout the home, particularly where you can see from one room into another, so that you keep a sense of continuity. The smaller the apartment or house, the more you should try to keep to one floor finish throughout to create a sense of space. Where a different form of floor is needed, try to make the transition as subtle as possible, unless, of course, you are using the contrasts as a feature of your design.

Hard Floors

(previous page)
The floor of a stately hall has been finished in limestone with slate insets, which certainly do justice to its fine proportions.

(above)
Best quality vinyl can imitate hard floors very realistically. This one looks good in a rather grand hall.

For centuries, most floors were made of beaten earth, patched with clay. During the seventeenth and early eighteenth centuries, prosperous houses were finished with brick tiles, shaped like bricks, but only about 1 1/2 in (4 cm) thick or square quarry tiles, measuring about 9 x 9 in (23 x 23 cm). Huge stone flags were also popular from the seventeenth century onward in modest homes or in servants' quarters. From 1900, all sorts of stone, slate and ceramic tiles were used indoors to complement the tiled paths that led in from outside. Hard floors made of natural materials are extremely durable, gorgeous to look at and easy to maintain, so although they are not cheap, it is hardly surprising that they are still popular and widely used today.

Hard floors are cold underfoot, so use them with rugs or mats. They look good with Persian rugs, kilims, tufted and hand-made rugs. Make sure any rugs or mats you use have a nonslip backing.

Popular Hard Floor Coverings

Stone: Nowadays this is not often used for domestic interior flooring, although older houses may have stone floors in the kitchen, basement or hall. Try to preserve old stone floors, if you possibly can. The randomly sized flags of natural stone have a unique mellow color and individual surface markings (fossilization) that cannot be copied. Stone is hard underfoot, but it is very hard-wearing, and most types are impervious to water. It is very heavy and needs a strong sub-floor. (See Preparing the Floor, page 270.) How you care for the stone will depend on how permeable it is: some stone may be left untreated, whereas other types need a resin-based sealant.

Bricks and Brick Pavers (pammets): These were popular in the late nineteenth-century, and engineering bricks, which are high fired, nonporous and have a matte shine, can look good in modern utility areas today. Original brick floors are usually prone to moisture, but are worth preserving. Adding a moisture barrier may be the only answer (see Preparing the Floor, page 270). Worn bricks can be turned over to present a fresh face, or salvage yards may hold matching replacements.

Slate: A natural material, which is available in various shades of deep gray. It is very hard-wearing, although cold underfoot, but it can be softened, like all stone, with rugs or matting and can look very attractive in a hall, kitchen or sunroom. Slate is usually sold as square or rectangular paving slabs. It is very heavy and needs a firm subfloor (see Preparing the Floor, page 270). Always get it professionally laid.

Seal slate with a special sealer, or use a water-based polish. For a traditional finish, dress with a mix of one part linseed oil to four parts mineral spirits, rubbed on sparingly.

Marble: This is one of the most elegant floorings available, and it is impervious to water and stains. Marble is available in square blocks or tile shapes, in a variety of thicknesses, and it is also available in strip or shaped form. It is suitable for small kitchens and bathroom areas, but would be very expensive for larger areas. Marble is very heavy and needs a strong subfloor, so it should always be laid by a professional. Most marble is pre-polished before laying, so a little care in handling is needed.

Bricks: These are porous, but may be sealed, which will enhance their looks and protect the surface from grease and dirt. After that, you need only wipe them with a damp mop.

Tiles

Tiles are available, not only in squares, but also in octagons, hexagons, triangles and oblongs, in sizes ranging from about 6 x 6 in (150 x 150 mm) to 1 3/4 in (300 mm) wide. They are hardwearing, hygienic and easy to maintain, and they are among the most popular hard floor coverings. Tiles will complement a wide range of styles and are available in hundreds of variations, and their looks will improve with age and wear.

Handmade Tiles: These have some variation in size and thickness, and attractive color variations, even minor chips, blemishes and imperfections, but it is these features that give handmade tiles their unique and rich quality. They are characteristic of the product and not the result of faulty workmanship.

Machine-made Tiles: Uniform in size and color, machine-made tiles are usually much cheaper than handmade.

Quarry Tiles: Quarry tiles are made of clay, which is baked at a very high temperature to force out air, forming a semi-vitreous material. They are hard, cool to the touch, but very durable. Quarry tiles are good for halls, kitchens, utility rooms, country bathrooms or other rustic uses.

Terracotta Tiles: Terracotta comes from the Latin meaning "fired earth." These tiles are fired at a lower temperature, and some air

pockets remain trapped in the clay, which act as insulation, taking up some of the room heat and making them feel warm. They have a warm, variegated color which is very pleasant. Terracotta tiles are good in sunrooms, kitchens, bathrooms, utility rooms and halls.

Ceramic Tiles: Thinner than quarry or terracotta tiles. The exactness and regularity of this particular type of tile may not lend itself to a very old house. Authentic, unglazed, encaustic tiles go well in Victorian homes. They are suitable for halls, bathrooms, kitchens and utility rooms. Choose nonslip tiles for use in kitchens and bathrooms.

Mosaic Floors: These are the most visually dramatic of all floorings and were often used in the nineteenth century to enliven the hall, porch or bathroom. Mosaics are traditionally made of glass, sometimes of marble or even ceramics, which is either glazed or porous (terracotta type), and tend to be fairly harsh underfoot, but very hardwearing. Mosaics will have to be laid onto a level, moisture-proof sub-floor, with a base of either concrete or specially treated latex. Individual mosaics are usually about 1 in (25 mm) square and slightly irregular in shape. Mosaic design possibilities are endless because of the wide range of colors and textures.

Some mosaics have a paper or mesh backing, but these do not allow nearly as much scope for interesting designs. There are a few specialty companies that create and restore mosaics, often doing the initial design work, precasting the mosaics into sections and installing them on site. Today's machine-made tiles are thinner than traditional ones and can be laid using an adhesive rather than mortar, which makes it easier to lay them.

Terrazzo: A material made from marble chippings and dust, which is set in cement, colored and ground smooth. This is a heavy-duty, hardwearing material, but rather hard on the feet. Terrazzo, made from marble aggregate that is set in a polyester resin, is

(right)
A mosaic floor is set among
small, square tiles that are
laid on the diagonal.

slightly more flexible and softer underfoot. Tiles can be useful in bathrooms. The material must be both professionally laid and polished after laying.

Preparing the Floor

In old houses, the original stone, slate and marble flags, which were laid on ash or bare earth, often suffer from moisture. The answer is to have a moisture barrier laid. You may be able to apply to a local agency for funds for this work, which involves removing the floor slabs while a new base is made of hard core, a moisture-proof membrane, concrete and a sand and cement screed, on which the slabs are re-laid. This is a very skilled job, so don't try it for yourself. Most salvage yards will be able to put you in touch with an experienced contractor.

- *If you have a suspended timber floor, it will need to be strengthened with 1/2 in (12 mm) exterior grade plywood screwed down at regular intervals.*
- *Treat depressions in solid floors with self-leveling compound: only quarry tiles and stone won't need this, as the mortar will fill any slight hollows in the floor.*

Laying a Tiled Floor

You will need: tape measure, string, chalk, two wood battens, tile adhesive, notched trowel, wood spacers, heavy-duty tile cutter or electric tile saw (you can rent these from a rental agency).

Measuring for Tiles

Measure the length and width of the floor, then multiply the two measurements to give you the complete area in square feet (meters). Add any recesses, such as the bay of a window, and subtract protrusions, such as the fireplace. Decide how wide you want the grouting gap to be and add this to the width and length of each tile, and multiply the two to get the area taken up by one tile. Divide the

There is a wide range of natural
floor tiles, whose size, shape
and color can be chosen to
suit all styles of room.

floor area by the area of one tile and you will arrive at the number of tiles needed.

Laying the Tiles

1. Find the middle of the room and use chalk lines to mark the center lines across and along the length of the floor.

2. Using the lines as a guide, lay the tiles on the dry surface to see where the edges will be in relation to the walls. Adjust your lines to make equal sections of cut tiles around the room. Also, make adjustments to avoid thin sections of tile as these break easily when cut.

3. Temporarily tack two battens at right angles, meeting at the selected starting point for tiling. Spread about a square foot (or square meter) of adhesive between the battens with a notched trowel.

4. Lay the tiles on the adhesive, using the spacers to form a grouting gap between them. Quarry and larger terracotta tiles need about a 1/4 in (6 mm) gap, whereas ceramic tiles need less space.

5. Continue laying tiles across the floor until all the tiles have been laid. Leave to set for 24 hours. Then cut and add the off-cuts round the edge of the room. Practice cutting a few broken tiles before you start on the good ones.

Some Guidelines for Tiles

- *Use border tiles to frame a door, edge a room or connect patterned sections of tiling.*
- *In bathrooms, put down coving to seal the joint between the floor and walls.*
- *You can lay tiles diagonally, if you want to give a feeling of space.*
- *A complete wall of plain tiles often looks better than if it is interrupted by randomly patterned tiles. You can introduce pattern with a row of tiles positioned at dado or shoulder height.*
- *Large areas of plain, square tiles can be brightened up with insets (groups of four tiles that form a pattern), or larger-framed areas of patterned or contrasting styles of tile.*
- *For a hall or sunroom, try the geometric or encaustic tile designs, which were so very popular with the Victorians and Edwardians. These tiles are hardwearing and enhance nineteenth-century rooms.*

Soft Floor Coverings

CARPETS

Know your carpet types in detail before you make any decision on flooring. A cheap carpet may cost you more in the long run if it wears out quickly, but there's no point in buying an expensive carpet if a cheap one will look just as good and do the required job. Carpets are graded for different uses, so always refer to the label on the back of the sample when making decisions. In general, the hallway and stairs need extra-heavy grade carpet, living rooms require quality heavy grade, while bathrooms and kitchens can have carpet tiles or a carpet with a water-resistant pile. Bedrooms require only light duty carpet. If you

eat in the living room, you will probably want the same carpet throughout, so choose one without too deep a pile, which you can clean easily after meals. Carpets are categorized as follows:

1. Light domestic use: for example, bedrooms.
2. Medium domestic use: bathrooms.
3. General domestic use: dining and living rooms.
4. Heavy duty: halls and stairs.
5. Luxury: not intended for areas of heavy wear.

Most carpets should be professionally installed because they must fit very precisely over a gripper fitted all round the room and may require stretching, although a foam-backed carpet is quite easy for a competent do-it-yourself enthusiast to lay in a small, square bedroom. Carpet tiles, however, are quite easy for almost anybody to lay.

Include underlayment in your budget and make sure you buy the right type for the carpet. Ask the advice of the carpet retailer. This padding prolongs the life of the carpet,

(above)
If you are going to have a really strongly colored and patterned carpet, make sure you don't have too much competition from the furnishings.

Velour or velvet has a very smooth pile and is very hardwearing, but tends to show footprints. Cut-loop combinations have some loops cut and others not, thus creating sculptural textures.

Carpet quality depends on the type of fiber being used. Wool is the most robust and has great resilience, and bounces back after being crushed. It is fire-retardant and does not suffer from static. It can absorb 30 per cent of its weight in moisture without feeling damp. Contrary to what is generally supposed, it is easy to clean. Wool takes dyes very well, and for this reason, it is available in a wide range of colors.

Nylon is the most widely used man-made fiber in carpet construction. It wears well, although it is less resilient than wool and gets dirty very easily. However, it can be treated with antistain finishes. Acrylic carpets are hardwearing and look very like wool blends, whereas wool and nylon blends usually consist of 80 percent wool and 20 percent nylon, combining the resilience of nylon with the good looks of wool. Polypropylene is a cheap and hardwearing manmade fiber. It is very resistant to stains, but crushes easily. This fiber is often combined with wool. Polyester is a bulky fiber, often used in bedroom and bathroom carpets. A spinning system has been developed to create a durable carpet with clearly defined tufts, less shedding and no fiber pilling.

improves heat and noise insulation, reduces drafts and prevents dust from rising. The better the quality of the underlayment, the longer the carpet will last. Ripple padding allows air in underneath and gives a soft, spongy feeling to the carpet. If you choose a carpet with integral foam backing, it should be fitted as recommended by the manufacturer or it won't meet the conditions of the guarantee.

MATERIALS

Pile height and density (the number of tufts per square inch/centimeter) affects the look and life span of a carpet. Shorter pile wears better than long and is best for heavy traffic areas, while longer pile is more luxurious. There are three basic texture choices: loop pile (loops of yarn of equal length – one of the most expensive options) or cut pile, which will show imprints of furniture rather noticeably. Single tufts can create a smooth or textured surface, depending on the length of the tufts.

Carpet Types

There are two main methods of carpet construction: woven and tufted. Woven is the longest wearing and the most luxurious.

WOVEN CARPET

There are two types of woven carpet: Wilton and Axminster. In both of these cases, the pile yarn and the backing are integrated during weaving to provide stable, wrinkle-free carpets. There are technical differences in their construction, but visually the main

difference is the pattern. The manufacturing technique of Axminster lends itself to intricate designs, whereas Wilton is usually plain or in very simple, all-over designs. Brussels weave is a variation on Wilton and very expensive. Woven carpets tend to be expensive and use higher quality materials.

TUFTED CARPET

These carpets are made by stitching the yarn into a ready-made backing, which is then secured with latex and strengthened with jute, polypropylene or foam. It is available in all qualities and prices. Tufted carpets are often plain, but patterns can be made during tufting or by printing.

FUSION-BONDED

Fusion-bonded carpets are made of fibers that are bonded to a prewoven backing. They are cheaper than woven ones, but more expensive than tufted. They are not very flexible, so should not be used on stairs.

FIBER-BONDED

Fiber-bonded carpets are made of loose, synthetic fibers felted onto a synthetic backing. They are hardwearing and inexpensive, but rough underfoot and difficult to maintain. This kind of carpet is used mainly for carpet tiles. Backings for carpet tiles vary: the toughest ones are usually guaranteed for several years.

LAYING CARPET TILES

Generally speaking, tiles can be laid on most floors except carpet, underlayment or vinyl. When measuring for tiles, remember that you buy them in boxes, so buy a box extra rather than a box too few. One of the advantages of tiles is that you can lift any damaged or stained ones and replace them, so keeping a few extra in case they are needed is a good idea. Generally speaking, carpet tiles should be laid loose. However, in some cases, it may be necessary to glue one or two tiles down

(above)
Carpets don't have to be wall-to-wall. A section of carpet with a border fits well into this room.

(above)
An intricate, colorful design like this will look good on the floor of a restrained interior.

first, particularly on an uneven floor, and for this, you can use double-sided tape especially manufactured for carpet tiles or use a spray adhesive.

You will need: tiles, a sharp knife such as a utility knife, template (optional), spray adhesive or double-sided carpet tile tape.

1. Prepare the floor and make sure it is clean and dry, with no nails sticking up.

2. Follow the instructions for cutting the tiles. Some manufacturers will tell you to cut from the back, whereas others recommend you cut from the front, so always read the instructions very carefully.

3. Check if the tiles have an arrow on the back. With plain tiles, if you lay all the arrows in the same direction, you will get a broadloom effect. If you lay every second arrow in a sideways direction, you will get a checkerboard effect because of the way the light falls on the fibers. Start where the tiles will be most obvious, in the middle of the floor. If the floor surface is not very even, use spray adhesive or double-sided tape

to secure every third tile or so as you go along.

4. When you get to the edges, cut the tiles using a template if you wish, or holding the tiles against the wall, mark where they are to be cut and then cut them.

BINDING THE EDGES OF CARPET OR MATTING

If you are using part of a cheap carpet or piece of matting as a rug, it is best to bind the edges to prevent fraying and to give a finished look. These instructions are for using carpet binding tape glued over the edges of the carpet. Tapestry borders can make good edges for matting and can be glued onto the top part of the matting only. Measure all around the piece of carpet or matting to establish the length of tape needed, plus a little extra for overlapping at the corners.

You will need: binding tape (this is not the same as carpet laying tape and it has no adhesive), scissors, impact adhesive and a hammer.

1. Lay one edge of carpet on a table and lay the binding over it. Spread half the width of the tape with adhesive. Spread the carpet edge to the same width.

2. When the adhesive is nearly dry, turn the tape over and align the two adhesive-covered edges together. This will bond immediately. Tap the two edges with a hammer.

3. Turn both the carpet and tape over, and spread the edges with adhesive. When nearly dry, align them together, exactly as before, allowing the two edges to touch. Hammer these edges gently to ensure a good bond. Pleat the tape at the corners to give a good fit.

Carpet Hints

- *Always get carpets fitted by a professional, and if creases appear, or you have to take the carpet up for any reason, get a professional to reinstall it.*

- *Carry carpeting right up to built-in cabinets – it looks more finished.*

carpet, or to make an extra mat to put in front of the fire.

- Keep any carpet joins away from doorways or main traffic areas. It's always better to have two joins, rather than one, in the middle of the room.

Natural Fibers

Natural fiber floor coverings include jute, seagrass, coir and sisal. They are made in batches and are subject to color variations depending on the growing season. Natural fibers may also have knots and minor imperfections, which many people consider part of their charm, and this will not really affect their wearing qualities. Colors range from bleached oatmeal to warm brown, and many different weaving patterns are available. The main types of natural fiber coverings are:

Coir: A coconut by-product, available in up to 12 ft (4 m) widths or as rugs. It may be woven with sisal.

Jute: This is an Indian plant, widely used as backing for carpets. It is soft and suitable for bedrooms. Jute is often dyed in pastel colors.

Sisal: This is made from the leaves of the *Agave sisalana* plant. Sisal floor covering is hardwearing, but much smoother than coir. Wool and sisal mixes are available.

Seagrass: A tough, "flat" fiber that is very resilient to stains and dirt, and good for halls and sunrooms. It should be watered with a spray from time to time to keep it supple.

All these natural floor coverings can look good if they are given a tapestry border. They also take well to stenciling or painting. Natural fibers are suitable for use as floor coverings in most rooms, but not the kitchen or bathroom, since nearly all of them are adversely affected by water. They are particularly well suited to bedrooms and play rooms, where their comparatively flat surface is quite comfortable, warm and practical. These floor coverings can look equally good whether they are used in a cottage or a barn.

- Plain carpet is often easier to live with than patterned. It is not really true that patterned carpets don't show the dirt – they do. Modern carpet cleaners make it much easier to clean up spills and stains anyway. Patterned carpet can make a small home seem too busy.
- Regular maintenance and instant mopping of spillages should keep a carpet in good condition for years.
- Protective sprays are supposed to increase resistance to staining, but these are not recommended for use on wool carpets.
- All carpets should be thoroughly cleaned occasionally. This can be done by a professional cleaning company or you can do it yourself using dry foam or a dry residue shampoo. Test a small scrap or an unseen piece of carpet that is hidden behind furniture first, to make sure that the colors don't run. Always follow the manufacturer's instructions carefully.
- Keep scraps to repair damaged or stained

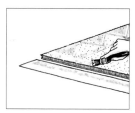

Applying adhesive

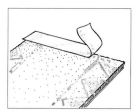

Taped carpet

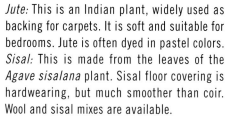

Finished carpet

(above left)
Natural floorings are available in many weaves and colors. This one is used to make a warm and welcoming entrance hall.

Rugs and Runners

Rugs and runners can brighten up a room or corridor and soften a floor surface. In the eighteenth century, carpets and rugs were a luxury. Floorboards were usually scattered with sand to absorb all the dirt and then rubbed with dry herbs to freshen them up. Rugs were cheaper than large carpets, but people who could not afford these would use printed or painted floor cloths.

The bold geometric design of this woven kilim would suit both a traditional and a modern setting.

Cottage rag rugs, once in the dispiriting grays and blacks of used-up old stockings and aprons, are now available in bright and cheerful colors. The middle Eastern flat-woven (or tapestry-woven) woolen kilims, woven for centuries for tribes' own use, are popular now and so are Indian cotton dhurries, using the same weaving techniques. Textile designer, Shyam Ahuja has revitalized the weaving of dhurries. He introduced pastel shades, then went on to dhurries inspired by kilims and Persian carpet traditions, then seventeenth-century floral tapestry designs and marble inlays from Mogul palaces. Rug designers all over the world have been inspired. There are rugs and runners in every conceivable weave, color and pattern, from hand-tufted rugs in bright colors to miniature machine-woven carpets and rugs woven from natural fibers.

- *There is a move to combine innovative contemporary design with traditional craft methods. Western artists are commissioned to design rugs, which are then woven in the weavers' own homes in the Caucasus, using the best Kurdish handspun chrome and vegetable-dyed wools that retain their rich color. Expert local weavers will undertake small commissions and make up your own design. There can be a real pleasure to gain from something which has taken time and skill to produce.*
- *Important: All rugs should have antislip strips fitted onto the back, when used on polished floors.*

Cork

Natural cork is pressed into tiles or "planks" and may already have a clear, nonporous backing; otherwise it will need to be sealed or varnished. These tiles are lightweight, good for insulation, quiet, warm and comfortable. There are some superb quality cork tiles on the market, which do not bear any resemblance to the cheap, eminently sensible, but boring tiles of the past. The best quality cork tiles are perfectly durable, if laid correctly. They are easy to lay, but do need a very smooth base. Use the recommended adhesive and butt the tiles very closely together to prevent water seeping between them. They are good for kitchens, bathrooms and children's rooms.

Vinyl

Vinyl is a manmade product. Sheet vinyl may be solid or a sandwich of vinyl and glass fiber. Cushioned vinyl has a spongy layer, which makes the flooring more comfortable to walk on. Vinyl tiles are generally solid vinyl. Vinyl is hard-wearing, particularly the more expensive ranges. Sheet vinyl can be loose-laid, but must be left in a warm room for 24 hours before laying. Various widths are available in a wide range of colors and patterns, including designs which imitate wood, tiles, brick and marble. It is generally used in kitchens, bathrooms and halls.

Hints on Laying Vinyl

- *Laying vinyl is similar to laying carpet tiles, except that vinyl tiles must be stuck down with a special adhesive.*
- *Preparation of the floor is important. Floorboards need to be covered in hardboard. If they are uneven, they should be planed or sanded; otherwise the vinyl on the raised areas will wear out noticeably more quickly than the rest. Tiles can be laid directly onto concrete in good condition; otherwise the concrete must be prepped.*

- Sheet vinyl should be unrolled and left to warm up at room temperature for 24 hours before being laid.
- Sheet vinyl should be fixed all round the edges with special double-sided tape. It is better to fix it in the middle too, to stop it from moving or tearing.
- With sheet vinyl, it is better to have no joins. Buy a wider sheet, if possible. Cutting must be exact (which can be a problem), and in an awkward room with a lot of projections and corners, it's probably best if this is carried out by a professional installer unless you are very confident of your ability.

Linoleum

Good old Victorian linoleum is making a comeback. This material is made from linseed oil, resin, wood, flour, chalk and cork pressed onto a burlap backing. It is warm, resilient and durable, and gets tougher as it grows older. Linoleum is resistant to stains and chemicals, and is available as tiles or sheeting in an attractive range of colors. This flooring is good for kitchens, utility rooms, bathrooms, halls and children's rooms. It is also being used to create some imaginative floors, which could almost be marble, with central motifs, borders, color contrasts, and so on. Linoleum needs a very smooth base, and professional installation is recommended for this particular type of flooring.

Rubber Flooring

This is one of the toughest floorings available on the market, being designed especially for use in airports, hospitals, and so on. Rubber floors are shock-resistant, extremely durable, resilient and waterproof, and they come in a range of wonderfully clear, deep colors. This particular flooring is also expensive and because it is basically a "contract" material, you will have to order it through a professional architect or interior designer.

Style Hints for Floor Coverings

- Carpets in traditional nineteenth-century homes were often covered in bouquets or vases of flowers, golden scrollwork and other extravagant decorations.
- For a busy environment, choose a plain carpet in a middle tone or one with an unobtrusive, allover pattern.
- Pale colors will help to make a dark room seem much lighter in appearance.
- Patterned carpets will make a large room seem smaller and friendlier.
- Some manufacturers offer a custom-dye service, matching the carpet color to a sample of material.
- Angular, abstract shapes and autumnal colors will give an authentic thirties look to your floor.
- Many manufacturers now produce border edges, which can be sewn together to form stair carpets or to define a room edge. This often works better than plain, fitted carpet in older houses. Borders are available in many designs and colors.
- Carpets are available in checks and stripes, florals, and ethnic and many other patterns.
- Floral and geometric designs are a direct development of early carpets and look especially good in larger rooms.
- Lay patterns diagonally across the floor to give an impression of space.
- Patterned carpet should look symmetrical, from the entrance to the room. The pile should run away from the main window, ideally toward a door. This helps to prevent the shading that is especially noticeable on plain carpets when they are walked upon.
- For a Swedish interior, use runners and rugs as a foil for pale, wood floors. These might be handwoven from rag strips or in rich, opulent French styles of rug. Many of the paintings of the famous Swedish artist Carl Larsson show runners folded over to fit into a particular space.

Lights, Glass & Mirrors

Lighting is probably the most neglected aspect of designing the home, but it is also one of the most important considerations. Not only do you need to see clearly for safety's sake and for practical tasks, but lighting can also transform the dullest interior into a friendly, interesting space.

Both glass and mirrors enhance natural and artificial light in many ways. Natural lighting, flooding in from windows, glass doors and skylights, is the first priority, so make the most of it. Glass bricks built into a wall, skylights in a sloping roof, reinforced bubble lights in a flat roof and glass doors can all help to bring in light. All homes need artificial light too: for rooms without natural light, for special tasks during the day, and to provide attractive and practical light at night.

Glass can also be used to add decoration to your home. Stained glass can brighten up front doors and windows, but it can also be used on interior windows. Many glass manufacturers produce decorative glass in different forms, or you may prefer to get something custom made for you by an independent craftsperson.

Natural Light

WINDOW GLASS

Windows had no glass at all until Tudor times, when it became possible to cut small pieces into diamond shapes, held together by strips of lead. The first vertically sliding or sash windows with larger panes appeared in the eighteenth century. These windows let in much more light and created both airy and lit internal spaces. During the nineteenth century, both double- and single-paned sashes became popular and the existing small-paned windows were often rehung with much larger panes. Nineteenth-century window shapes were quite exuberant with Gothic arched and semi-circular shapes. Sashes were grouped together to let in more light, often in a bow-front design, creating a much wider window. Old glass has a pleasant, slightly undulating surface, which is different from modern glass.

Modern window types come in all shapes and sizes. They allow for a larger area of glass to be fitted and consequently improve the light. Today's windows are more likely to be horizontal than vertical and often consist of one large sheet of glass with no mullions at all. If they are hinged at the top or sides or pivoted, they will get in the way of curtains and blinds.

Fanlights fitted above front doors (with lead or wood bars) were introduced in the mid-eighteenth century and these gradually became more delicate and varied in design.

Types of Plain Glass

Float glass: This is the product used in today's windows, which is formed by floating the glass on molten metal to give a flawless surface on both sides. It does lack character for restoration work, however.

Crown glass: Produced by artisans by blowing a bubble of glass and flattening the molten shape to create a large square that can be cut into panes. It has a gently bowed appearance from the outside. Until 1830, crown glass was used in all windows, and is still produced by some specialized companies for replacement glazing in eighteenth-century windows.

Cylinder glass: A development of the crown-glass process, cylinder glass is handmade from a solid mass of glass. It is ideal for restoration use.

Plate glass: Large sheets of glass produced by casting methods dating back to the 1850s. The surface requires extensive polishing.

Drawn sheet glass: Large sheets of molten glass, which are cooled to form a more optically correct product than plate glass.

Glass for Safety and Security

Glass can be manufactured and treated to make it safer and more secure. Treated glass should be used in downstairs windows, French windows and patio doors, and any other vulnerable part of the house or sunroom. There are two main types of safety glass. Check that the glass you choose conforms to national safety standards.

Laminated glass: Made of several layers of glass with interlayers of transparent plastic or resin bonded together. It is practically indistinguishable from any ordinary glass. Laminated glass is very difficult to break and, if it is broken, fragments stay bonded to the interlayer so that it can still keep out burglars and won't cause serious injuries. It can be used in double-glazed windows, patio doors and sunrooms.

Toughened glass: Has been thermally treated to give strength and resistance to heat. If it breaks, it shatters into relatively harmless, small granules. It can be used for partitions and overhead windows, glazed doors, bath and shower screens and furniture.

Heat-strengthened glass: Is produced in the same way as toughened glass, but it is cooled at a different rate and is not a safety glass.

Low-emissivity glass: Is given an invisible metallic coating that lets the short-wave heat rays from the sun pass through into the house to be absorbed by furnishings, but prevents long-wave heat from the inside from escaping. It can be incorporated into a double-glazing unit and this is sometimes included as a standard.

Film Coatings for Glass

There are various types of plastic in many different formats that can be applied easily to existing windows, glass doors and partitions. You can get safety film to prevent the glass from breaking or to keep fragments in place. Some film will filter out ultra-violet and infra-red rays and most have scratch-resistant surfaces. Always get professional advice.

Double-glazing

Large expanses of glass in modern homes are usually double-glazed when they are installed. If not, it is worth getting them done. The benefits of double-glazing and exactly what it does are as follows:

- *It lessens heat loss through a window or door. Low-emissivity glass or triple-glazing makes it even more efficient.*
- *Double-glazing increases comfort: it can help to keep a room warmer in winter and cooler in summer, and eliminates cool areas by a window in a room.*
- *It cuts condensation: with good ventilation, it can lessen even severe condensation.*
- *Double-glazing can help to reduce noise levels. Efficient window construction and installation can also lessen noise pollution. The thicker the glass used, the better the glazing will be.*

Types of Double-glazing

Insulating glass–sealed unit: Insulation glass consists of two sheets of glass, spaced apart and hermetically sealed in the factory. It looks similar to single-pane glass. The windows open and close normally. Specialized companies can double-glaze sash windows in this way.

(right)
Stained glass windows, such as these, can look wonderful. These windows were custom-designed, but you do not need to have enormous windows to commission special glass.

Secondary sash: A second pane of glass fitted in its own frame of metal, wood or plastic is secured to the existing frame, or to the inner or outer sill. You must be able to separate the panes for cleaning and to store them, if necessary, during the summer.

Coupled windows: Consist of two frames hinged together, which can be separated for cleaning. They are only suitable for new homes or where entire frames are being replaced during conversion.

Wood, aluminium or UPVC: These can all be used as frames. Wood and UPVC have lower heat loss. Metals can form a cold bridge, causing condensation, but new designs can be made with a thermal barrier that reduces heat loss.

Glass in Sunrooms and Greenhouses

You can get more or less any style of sunroom or greenhouse window built to your specific requirements, but there is a wide range of standard designs supplied by many manufacturers. Always aim to match up the frame and style of the window to the materials and style of the house. For instance, a house with aluminum frames will not look its best with a red-cedar sunroom jutting out of it.

Victorian: The Victorians generally favored Gothic designs with sloping glass roofs and decorative cast-iron embellishments, now usually made using modern techniques and materials.

Georgian: Semi-circular, often built with a solid, rather than a transparent roof.

Lean-to: These can be all-glass or they may have solid brick or wood sections making up the lower portion. They can be designed to fit many different spaces, such as awkward corners.

If you want to use the room all year round, it is essential to have double-glazing and low-emissivity glass, which will help enormously in retaining heat.

Frames

There are three main materials used in sunroom and greenhouse construction: wood, aluminum and UPVC.

- *UPVC is available in white or wood-type finishes and requires practically no maintenance.*
- *Aluminum is a low-maintenance material. It is very strong, so needs fewer support pieces and these can be narrow, to let in more light. Aluminum is available in a variety of colors, created using an enameling technique.*
- *Wood is the traditional material used for sunrooms and greenhouses, but it does need regular maintenance and repainting. Traditional hardwoods are very expensive so softwoods are normally used instead.*

Decorative Glass

Some nineteenth-century suburban houses often had bay windows, with large panes of glass fitted at the bottom; the upper part of the window was fitted with smaller panes, often of stained glass, and in deliberate contrast to those below. In fact, the Victorians loved stained glass and put it in porches, front windows, front doors and lamp shades. Designs were often influenced by Art Nouveau style.

Decorative colored glass was increasingly used in halls and stairway windows from the 1840s onward and sometimes appeared in bathroom windows. Some windows had colored glass on the edges, the favorite colours being amber, blue and ruby. Painted glass was used too. In better-off homes, acid-etched and cut-glass decoration might be used. By the 1860s, many front doors were decorated with glass panels. Surprisingly, old glass often survives in the windows of old buildings and it is worth salvaging. It can be cut from frames and used to good effect.

Types of Textured Glass

Acid-etched (frosted) glass: The surface is acid-etched to give a white, opaque finish. Victorians used many standard floral and geometric motifs to decorate their skylights, windows and hall doors. Today, the glass is often produced by sandblasting; there are many modern designs to choose from and some of the more common Victorian designs are still available. Use this type of glass to obscure an ugly view or for privacy.

Patterned glass: Embossed with patterns at the molten stage, it is very much associated with Edwardian interiors, but Victorians used it too. It is still available.

Colored Glass

Stained glass: The most labor-intensive and expensive glass. It includes leaded and painted glass. Repair should always be left to experts. There are stained glass artists who will create a window especially designed for your home, in traditional or modern designs.

Repairing a Leaded Window

Some windows are made from plain, patterned or colored glass held together by lead. Stained glass is a general term, which includes painted glass. You can tackle an isolated broken pane, but extensive work should be done by a professional.

You will need: masking tape, tracing paper, pencil, cardboard, glass cutter, scissors, pliers, craft knife, small piece of rounded wood (i.e., the top of a broom handle), all-purpose putty, black grate polish and a stiff-bristled brush. Always wear protective goggles and gloves for this work and, of course, care should always be taken when handling any glass.

1. Remove the leaded panels from the window frame and release the broken pane. Put together the old glass sections and secure with masking tape.

2. Make a tracing of the broken piece, adding on the area hidden beneath the lead. Make a cardboard template of the pane.

3. Score the surface with a glass cutter and gently tap out the bits of glass. Scrape out the remaining pieces and remove any putty or dirt from the channels left in the lead.

4. Gently bend one side of the lead flange all round the damaged area with a pair of pliers. Use a craft knife to cut into the corner solder joints if the lead won't bend out easily over the corners.

5. Take your template to a professional glazier and get him or her to cut an actual-size piece from matching glass. Fit the new piece into the leadwork.

6. Close the lead channel all round the glass with the help of the rounded piece of wood.

7. Weatherproof the repair by pushing a mixture of all-purpose putty and black grate polish into the gap between lead and glass. Brush with a stiff-bristled brush.

• *Lay used matchsticks along the base of the lead channel before inserting new glass to*

A broken pane of glass

Tracing off the shape

Cutting glass

Finishing off

(right)
Mirrors and lights complement
one another beautifully and,
when well planned, they can
have quite a magical
effect on a room.

bring it to the correct height for re-puttying.
- *If the leaded window seems fragile or sagging, it may need extra support, but always get this work done by a professional glazier.*

Artificial Lighting

Planning a lighting scheme is not difficult, but it is very rewarding. It need not be very expensive to install and certainly not to run: lighting makes up only about nine percent of an average electricity bill. If you do want to leave certain lights switched on more or less permanently, you could make substantial savings by switching to compact fluorescent bulbs, which are now available with screw or bayonet fittings and can be used like ordinary light bulbs.

When deciding where to position lights, do experiment. Invest in a clip-on lamp or a spot lamp on a long lead, so that you can move around the house, shining it in different places, and at various heights and angles to get an idea of the final result.

You don't necessarily have to have a great quantity of light to create a harmonious and efficient lighting system. It's the quality of the light, the choice of fitting and the way it works that counts. You only need a basic understanding of what sort of light is needed where, to be able to go out and buy exactly what you need. Redecorating offers a good opportunity to make changes in the lighting. This is the time to move a central ceiling spot to a different position, or to remove it altogether and install wall fittings instead.

Lighting Functions

You can divide home lighting into four different functions: general lighting, task lighting (lighting for work), decorative and feature lighting and lighting for safety. Some of these functions will overlap: for example, overhead spots can provide sufficient general lighting for a room and can act as task lighting as

well, while good general lighting will normally provide enough illumination for safety.

GENERAL LIGHTING

This is the lighting that enables you to see as you move about in your home and should be a soft spread of light over the whole room or particular area. If you are always losing things, it is probably because the lighting level is not high enough. General lighting in most homes is often provided by a single electric light fixture suspended from the ceiling, but there are much more pleasant ways of providing it. A wall-mounted or floor-standing lamp, which throws the light onto the ceiling to be reflected back into the room, is more attractive and just as efficient. Spotlights or recessed ceiling fixtures can provide adequate general lighting and give a much more attractive illumination than one suspended light.

TASK LIGHTING

This is lighting that is angled in a particular direction to enable you to see clearly when you are doing a specific task, such as reading or writing, doing homework, preparing and cooking food, sewing, and so on. Adjustable desk lamps are excellent for this purpose. Spotlights, if angled correctly, can be good too. In many workrooms and studios, fluorescent strips are used, but the light source should be concealed or the light becomes tiring.

DECORATIVE AND FEATURE LIGHTING

This is lighting that is purely there to create a very pleasing atmosphere, or to highlight particular objects or certain architectural features. It is lighting for effect and fun. You can highlight paintings with custom-designed lights mounted on the wall. Accent plants by placing unassuming lights (such as a small spot or a fixture with an opaque shade), behind them; you can highlight arches and plasterwork with spots and you can also create pools of gentle light, with individual lamps placed in different parts of the room.

LIGHTING FOR SAFETY

Good general lighting is also good safety lighting, but there are specific things to watch out for. Safe lighting should cast no shadows. Stairs, steps, sharp corners and edges of furniture, and appliances should all be adequately lit so not to cause accidents, especially in homes where elderly or very young people are living. Lighting should always be brighter for the elderly, whose eyesight is not as good as it once was. Older people are also more susceptible to glare than the young, so try to provide lighting that gives overall good illumination, not just bright spots in places. Tungsten-halogen uplights or fluorescent lights can be the answer. Lighting on staircases and along the corridors may have to be left on all of the time. (Remember that a compact fluorescent bulb will last eight times longer than a standard incandescent bulb and gives up to five times more light per watt.)

PREVENTING GLARE

Glare is when the eye is subjected to excessive brightness in a dimly lit room. A spotlight shining straight into your eyes will cause glare, and downlights should be angled so that the eye does not have to look directly at the bulb. The room should be adequately lit when you watch television or gaze at a computer monitor. Your eyes may get used to the situation, but you will become tired and irritated without realizing why. A room with uniform general lighting, which is virtually glare-free, sounds ideal but would, in fact, be quite boring. For visual interest, you do need some pools of light and some highlighted features, as well as extra, directed light for doing visual jobs but these should be moderate, not sharp contrasts.

Various Types of Light Fittings

Central Pendant: Pendant is the generic term for any light fitting that hangs from the ceiling, from a bare light bulb to a chandelier. It's the most common form of room lighting and is usually boring, being either too bright or not bright enough. A central pendant needs to be augmented by other forms of lighting in the room, or even removed and replaced with something else, such as an uplight or an adjustable ceiling fixture, which can be raised to give overall light, or lowered to give a more intimate light for dining. This doesn't have to be in the center of the room. Pendants can be satisfactory in a small hall or passageway, but they will give more light with one of the ubiquitous but efficient Chinese paper lampshades, than with a shade that does not cover the bulb or one which is too dark or opaque and doesn't allow the light out.

Downlights: These are lights that direct the

This highly individual lamp is a source of light as well as an interesting piece of art.

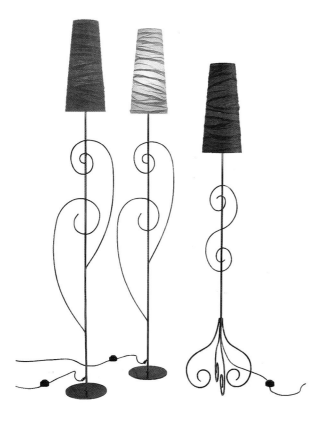

(above)
These delicate floor lamps seem to be a cross between Art Nouveau and fifties styles but could be used in all sorts of homes.

light downward, producing an attractive and a much more versatile light than ceiling pendants. They will not light up the ceiling or vertical room surfaces, so they should be used with other forms of lighting. Spotlights, semi-recessed lamps and recessed lamps are all downlights. Individual spotlights, track or cluster lights can be mounted on the ceiling. They can be used as task lighting (for example, shining down onto kitchen work surfaces), or as general lighting, if there are enough of them and they illuminate the whole room.

Uplights: The light is directed upward to be reflected off the ceiling and upper walls, and it produces a gentler, but equally efficient and shadowless light over the whole room. Uplights can either be wall mounted or floor-standing. Tungsten-halogen lamps are efficient uplights, available as floor standing or wall-mounted fixtures.

Wall Washers: These have a wide beam, which shines down from the ceiling or up from the floor to wash the whole wall with gentle light.

They can be used as general lighting for people moving about the room or watching television, or as feature lighting for curtains or plants. Wall washers have a separate, rather large, curved reflector. A spotlamp that is angled at the opposite wall is not a wall washer because the beam is too narrow and it won't give the necessary area of light.

Wall Bracket Fixtures: These either reflect light off the wall and may be enough to provide most of the general lighting, or they may be little pools of decorative light glowing through lampshades, augmented by some other form of general lighting. These fixtures are often used on either side of a fireplace, or in halls and passageways.

Cove or Cornice Lighting: You can give a room a soft and gentle light that is reflected from the ceiling and upper walls, by installing a whole run of custom-designed cornice light fittings. This probably won't be enough to constitute good general lighting, but it will need only a little backup from other sources of lighting.

Portable Lighting: This includes table lamps, desk lamps, standard lamps, decorative and sculptural floor lamps. Make sure you have enough outlets installed in convenient places round the room so that you don't create dangerous trails of cord if you move the lamps. And make sure that you untangle any twisted cords immediately. They can provide good working light, decorative or feature lights.

Dimming Controls

It's useful to be able to control the brightness of lights in living rooms, bedrooms and children's rooms, where various lighting levels may be preferred for different moods and activities. They are not expensive to buy or to have fitted. You can get a dimmer for an individual lamp or circuit, or sophisticated ones to control a number of lamps in a room. Some can be programmed to dim some lamps and brighten others. A dimmer must be used only with the type of lamp for which it was originally designed. Always read the instructions for installation and use.

Types of Light Bulb

Incandescent Bulb (also known as Tungsten or Filament): The most common light bulb, used in pendant fittings, wall and ceiling fixtures, standard and table lamps. Available in mushroom and globe shapes (these are better for positions where the bulb is exposed), or as internally silvered bulbs to use in task lights, downlights, wall washers and soft, accent lights. Available in clear, pearl, white or daylight and in various colors, with a screw or bayonet base. Pearl bulbs throw out softer shadows and generally provide a more pleasant light than clear ones, but give slightly less illumination. Architectural filament tubes are also available, which are really good for lighting at the back of display cabinets, or under wall-hung cupboards over a worktop in the kitchen. Filament bulbs should last for about 1000 hours.

Spotlights or Internally Silvered Bulbs: These are incandescent bulbs, which have a silver coating on the inside to create a specific beam. You can get them with a narrow beam (spot) or a wide beam (flood). They are used as task lights, downlights, wall washers and soft, accent lights. Available with screw or bayonet fittings.

Tubular Fluorescent: These give a bright, white light and are often used in kitchens and workrooms. The most useful sizes for domestic use are 18 watt (24 in long/600 mm) and 36 watt (48 in/1,200 mm) long. Choose a warm white shade. For lighting under kitchen cabinets, use a F8/29 8w miniature tube, 8 3/4 in (290 mm) long by 2/3 in (15 mm) diameter. Circular shapes are useful for pendant fixtures.

COMPACT FLUORESCENT (CFL)

These useful bulbs are really miniature fluorescent tubes, which can be used instead of conventional bulbs. They are economical on electricity, last for around 5,000 hours and are particularly good for replacing incandescent bulbs in light fixtures, which are on most of the time (in halls, passageways and living rooms), but it is not worth putting them in places where they are only occasionally used, since they take time to warm up and are not suitable for frequent switching on and off (for example, in bathrooms). Bayonet or screw bases are available in two versions: SL and PL. SL types will burn for 8,000 hours and can be used just like an ordinary light bulb, if they are adequately supported. PL types have a separate control gear, which has to be wired into the light fixture. When you buy one of these, the fixture and the tube are all one item. If you have to change the tube (after some years), take it back to your lighting supplier and get a replacement.

(above)
This lighting showroom demonstrates coving, lighting, downlights, recessed lights and a tungsten-halogen floor lamp on the far right.

(above)
The color of a lamp shade can radically alter the effect of light in a room.

A suitable growing lamp for plants is a 75-watt reflector with a special internal coating, which reflects infrared as well as visible light.

A PAR bulb is similar to a mushroom bulb, but is housed in a robust, glass envelope with a screw cap. PAR 38 is the most common type and 80-watt PAR 38 bulbs can be used as spike lamps for decorative garden lighting.

LOW-VOLTAGE TUNGSTEN-HALOGEN (LVTH)

This is an attractive way to provide spotlighting and feature lighting in your home. The tiny light bulbs, fitted with built-in reflectors, are more efficient than ordinary incandescent bulbs and have a life expectancy of 2,000 hours. LVTH capsule bulbs are used in some modern downlights and spotlight fittings, and in some desk lamps. Make sure any desk fitting which uses an LVTH bulb is fitted with an ultra-violet filter, as continuous exposure of the skin to such a light could be dangerous.

The 12v supply of LVTH lamps has to have a transformer. Some fittings have a transformer built in, but if you are getting this sort of lighting installed as part of your lighting system, always have it installed by a professional electrician.

Ideas for Choosing Lights and Light Fittings

- *In general, allow for more light sources, rather than fewer. They give greater flexibility and look more pleasant. You can have the system wired so that several work off one switch, if you wish.*
- *When you go shopping for individual fittings, take some color samples from your home with you to help you choose.*
- *When choosing small table lamps, remember that CFL bulbs are bigger than standard light bulbs and may poke out of the top.*
- *Table lamps with opaque shades can be decorative in their own right and can add a pleasant glow to a room. Pools of light at*

TUNGSTEN-HALOGEN BULBS

These are incandescent bulbs that are filled with halogen gas, which give a more efficient, whiter light than standard bulbs and have a life expectancy of 3,000 hours. They are used in uplights and wall washers. Bulb powers of 200 and 300 watts are used indoors. Don't touch the quartz envelope of a tungsten halogen bulb with your bare hand or it will fail early. The bulb gets very hot and stays hot for a long time, so make sure the lamp can't be knocked over. They can be used in suitable wall fixtures that are now available.

REFLECTOR BULBS AND PAR BULBS

A mushroom reflector is a large incandescent bulb, which has been internally silvered to direct the beam in a particular way. Three sizes and several colors are available. Make sure you pick the correct diameter for your fitting. Too large a bulb may restrict the air and cause it to overheat.

a low level can make your room seem very friendly and comfortable.

- If your home has low ceilings, choose an uplight that will have one or two compact fluorescent bulbs, rather than a very bright tungsten-halogen one, which may produce an uncomfortably bright spot of light on a low ceiling.
- If you are buying additional spots to fit into existing track, take all the details of track with you because these components are not always interchangeable.
- Fit architectural strip lights at the back of shelves to highlight collections of glass.
- Reflections from glass or oil paintings can be lessened according to the angle of the beam. Try putting a spotlight on a long cord and test the angles before actually fitting the lamp. Or try hanging the picture with its top slightly tilted away from the wall.
- Downlights, whether mounted on the ceiling or recessed or semi-recessed, look best in plain or modern ceilings. They can look incongruous in a period ceiling with plaster moldings. Avoid using fittings with very large apertures in a low ceiling: they can look enormous when too close to the eye.
- Don't place downlights so close to the wall that they produce arcs of light across the wall surface. Avoid placing them immediately above a chair or sofa. Instead, place them slightly in front or behind. Add a task light near the seating to ensure comfortable reading.
- Use uplighting if you have an interesting ceiling. Uplights are available in designs that go well with period styles. The most classical and simplest modern designs can fit in well with traditional furnishings, with the actual fitting almost disappearing into the background.
- Uplights using tungsten-halogen bulbs are the most efficient versions. One will be enough for the average room. They have built-in dimmer switches, so that the light intensity can be varied.
- Uplights using standard bulbs or spot bulbs will achieve soft effects, but you may need back-up lighting to give a good overall illumination.

Ideas for Landings, Halls and Staircases

- In a narrow hall, install ceiling-recessed downlights instead of one pendant light. Place mirrors underneath them to give a feeling of space.
- Concealed fluorescent lights positioned behind the cornice will give a much gentler, but efficient light.
- To avoid shadows on stairs, install a light in the ceiling at the top of the flight. Make sure the light source does not shine into people's eyes as they walk up.
- The top of the stairs is a good place to use a compact-fluorescent bulb (CFL).
- Wall lamps can provide pleasant and efficient lighting for a hall. There are many period lamps available. Uplight bowls usually provide more light, since it is reflected back off the wall and ceiling.

Ideas for Dining Rooms

- You won't need a high level of background lighting in the dining room unless the room doubles up as a work room, or is part of the kitchen or living room.
- Concentrate most of the light on the table. A rise-and-fall light can illuminate a wide area or be pulled down for a more intimate effect. Use a dimmer switch to give even more flexibility.
- Use tungsten or tungsten-halogen lights in the dining room because they make food look more appetizing than fluorescents.

Lighting for Kitchens

- The kitchen needs more than one source of light. Make sure you have satisfactory

This unusual pendant light would make a bold display in a modern setting.

general lighting and task lighting to work by. General lighting can be provided by downlights and, if placed conveniently, these can also provide the task lighting. Make sure you will not be in your own shadow when working.

- Don't use portable fittings in the kitchen. They could overload sockets and will use up valuable working space.
- Fluorescent lighting can be good to work by if the light source is concealed and you use one of the warm colors. For general lighting, use fluorescent tubes concealed on top of a wall-mounted cupboard, and attached at the back and against the wall, so they send the light upward. This creates an effective glow, rather than harsh light.
- Fit a strip light (fluorescent or architectural strip) under cabinets above the work surface – this can spread the light evenly onto the working surface and gives a pleasant glow.

Bedrooms and Children's Rooms

- High-level general light is needed, but supplement it with task lighting, which will be needed for reading in bed and also for dressing.
- You should have a light that illuminates anybody looking in the mirror, but not so that it is reflected in the mirror glass.
- Clothes in the closet should be well-lit, either by a spotlight directed inside or by an interior light, which comes on automatically when the door is opened.
- Make sure there's a good directional lamp for a child's work and hobbies.
- For children, choose light fixtures that are robust and can be mounted on the wall out of their reach.
- Night lights are good for scared children, or install a dimmer switch.

Lighting for Bathrooms

- Use custom-designed bathroom lights and make sure the switches are outside the door or that they are pull switches.
- Follow the required safety standards for your area and always keep water and electricity separate.
- Recess fittings into the wall or ceiling.
- Try to angle a light to shine into a shower stall so that you don't have to fit a light inside it.
- If you must have a shower light, ask your supplier for advice.
- Bare bulbs surrounding a mirror provide an efficient, clear light for shaving and applying make-up.

Outdoor Lighting

- Avoid dazzle and glare by keeping light sources hidden.
- Use light to provide safe walking areas along paths and up and down steps.
- Light trees and tall plants from below.
- One or two tungsten-halogen floodlights shining onto a garden wall will silhouette the branches of tall trees.
- Use mushroom-shaped fittings that you can spike into the earth to illuminate flower beds. You can then change their position from time to time.
- Accent fountains or pools with wide or narrow-beam spots.
- Choose fixtures designed for outdoors.

Safety Hints

- A floor-standing lamp should have a heavy base so that it cannot be easily tipped over.
- A tilt switch can be fitted to a standard lamp to isolate it from the electricity supply, if the lamp is tilted beyond a safe angle. This is particularly important with tungsten-halogen lamps, especially in homes where there are children. However, it might be better to install wall uplighters

while the children are young.

- *When shopping, look for the symbol of quality and safety, the UL label. This means that the product has passed the stringent requirements for approval by Underwriters' Laboratories, Inc.*
- *Metallic light fittings, for example, desk lamps and directional spotlights, should be marked double insulated or should have a ground connection and a three-prong plug.*

Lighting Indoor Plants

Most plants need between 12 and 16 hours of light a day. Foliage plants, such as ferns, dwarf-palms and aspidistras, usually need less light than do succulents, cacti and flowering plants. Feature or accent lighting can show up the plant and give it some of the light it needs. Any type of bulb can be used, but the ideal light has a mix of red, infra-red and blue rays. You can provide these by placing two 40- watt fluorescent tubes, one in cool white, the other in warm white, side by side, or use a grow light. Small plants and flower arrangements placed on a table are best lit from downlights, such as narrow beam spots from the ceiling. Tungsten-halogen lamps produce more heat than fluorescents, so don't put the light source too close to the plant.

Mirrors

Mirrors can completely alter the look of a room, open up dark corners, provide an extra "window" onto a garden, bring in more light and, if ornately framed, add grandeur and style as objects in their own right. A mirror can create the illusion of another room and provide visual surprises and delights, as well as bringing in extra light.

A large mirror, or three panels of mirror glass fitted on the interior wall of a garden room, will reflect the garden so that the room appears to open out at both ends. You can run a wood frame around it (use decorative molding), and paint it in old gold. Corridors and corridor rooms can be doubled in their apparent size, if you use large

mirrors on the walls, particularly if they reflect an interesting object, such as a real or trompe l'oeil window or some paintings. If you are mounting large mirror panels on a wall, make sure the wall is straight or you will get a distorted image. If necessary, attach wood supports and screw the mirror to them. Heavy mirrors should be attached with heavy-duty expansion bolts and screws.

Ideas for Mirrors

- *A mirror over a mantelpiece is an excellent focal point.*
- *Don't put mirrors where somebody cannot avoid looking at themselves, for example, on a wall in a dining room, where diners could be distracted by their own reflection.*
- *Avoid standing a dressing table in front of a window, where the mirror gets in the way of the light, rather than enhancing it.*
- *Mirror the panels on window shutters in a north facing room. White paint, which is more reflective than colored paint, will add to the impression of brightness, and shutters can be angled to make the most of the available light.*
- *Old wardrobes and dressing tables are a good source of decorative mirrors, which can be removed and put in a bathroom, bedroom or hall.*
- *Use an old decorative mirror to make a dressing tabletop with a collection of precious objects reflected in it. Decorate it with gilding or stenciling, or paint it in a bright color.*
- *Sometimes a mirror can emphasize a style or period interior. A mirror with a curvy frame and sinuous leaf design will go well in an Art Nouveau interior, while an angled frame and beveled glass will complement a thirties setting, and a large, mahogany- framed mirror would go well above a Victorian fireplace. Mirrors in jazzy, colourful frames will suit many modern settings.*
- *An over-the-mantel mirror can be used for a strong, visual image.*

Decorative mirrors can be a centrepiece in a room - sleek and simple or highly ornate.

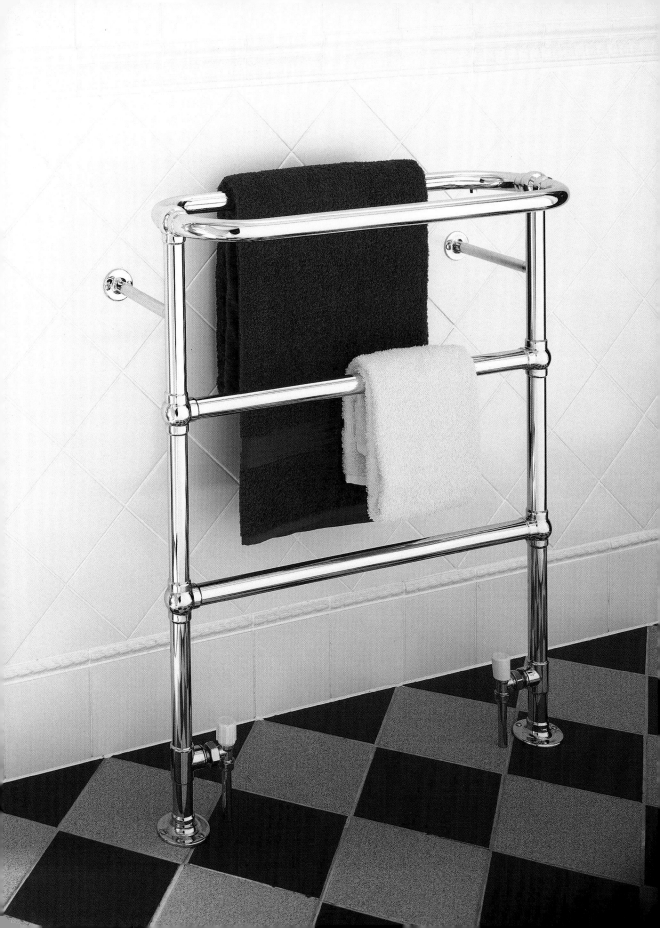

Heating

Central heating is found in most homes in temperate parts of the world. The Romans developed a system for using underfloor heating and hot water, but this technology was lost with the decline of the Roman empire and did not re-emerge until the seventeenth century. By 1898, nearly all of the larger homes had central heating of some kind, fired by wood-burning stoves. Floor and base-board grilles and radiators were often concealed behind lattice-fronted screens or window seats. Radiators were bulbous and bulky, and most houses relied on open fires to provide their main heating until the 1950s. In the 1950s and 1960s fireplaces were considered to be old-fashioned and dirty, and were ruthlessly ripped out and boarded up. Nowadays many people choose to have fireplaces, which are often gas-fired, in addition to a central heating system.

Modern central heating systems are efficient, but the design of radiators often leaves much to be desired and most people have to be content with the most basic panel radiators, painted white, because they do not realize that interesting sculptural and different-shaped radiators exist, which can be used as decorative objects in their own right or to occupy an unobtrusive space, that would otherwise be wasted. Experimental designs include elegant, cactus-shaped radiators, which can be used on any central heating system, but specially designed radiators are widely available already, so do shop around.

Types of Central Heating

(previous page)
An Edwardian-style bathroom heated towel stand is the perfect answer to heating a large bathroom.

(above)
These classic Victorian-style radiators come in a gorgeous range of metallic colors.

There are two main categories of central heating: hot water and forced air. In the former, the water is heated in a fuel-burning or electrically heated furnace and circulated through pipes to radiators. A more sophisticated underfloor system carries hot water through a network of pipes and emits heat through the floor. Forced air systems rely on air being drawn through a heater and passed through ducts into the room. The choice of a heating system is often a compromise between efficiency, economic viability and what will blend into the style of the house. If you are putting in a new system, consult a professional heating engineer who will calculate furnace size, output and potential risks to the building fabric. In an old house, new central heating can upset the moisture equilibrium of the building: air becomes dry, and walls and timbers split and crack. Humidifiers can help to replenish moist air. Central heating pipes can look wrong in an old house, puncturing floorboards and cornices, and damaging the period decor. So you should plan any installation very carefully, conceal as much ductwork as possible, and choose radiators and vents that are relatively unobtrusive.

Microbore pipes, measuring 1/3 to 3/8 in (8 to 10 mm) in diameter, are flexible and can be easily bent to go round corners. They are of special value in period homes because they can meander discreetly through the most tortuous routes and are very unobtrusive. Such pipes can be joined to conventional small bore circuits and cause minimum disruption when they are installed. A wet system is probably the most efficient kind of central heating, but it can be disruptive and expensive to install, with long pipe runs requiring major alterations to the structure.

Radiators

There are imaginative radiators, which are slim, colorful and often combine two functions (heated towel stands, for example, and room

of other places for them. Look at as many brochures as you can and you will begin to see the possibilities for using radiators as decorative features. They can even be used as room dividers. Remember that curtains that drape over a radiator will deflect heat and reduce efficiency. Radiator grilles are often used to conceal radiators and do so with elegance, but they will reduce the heat output by as much as one-fourth.

Types of Radiators Available

- *White Panel Radiators:* The cheapest solution, but not the most beautiful, although you can conceal them behind grilles.
- *Aluminum Radiators:* Slim, sectional, high output radiators available in many colors. Darker shades can blend discreetly within an older style interior; clear, bright colors can add glamor to modern interiors.
- *Tubular Radiators:* These are available in almost any shape or size, as tall and slim "ladder" types or undulating, sculptural shapes in bright and cheerful colors. They are particularly suitable for modern interiors, although a slim ladder radiator in white would not look amiss in a period interior. Slim, vertical radiators are a good solution where there is a shortage of space.
- *Chrome-plated Radiator–Towel Stand:* These were used in bathrooms around 1900; they need a large bathroom to look their best.
- *Victorian Traditional Cast-iron Column Radiators:* These are manufactured in sectional columns, so you can choose a model of the right height and depth for a particular position and then let your heating engineer calculate the number of sections needed.
- *Cast-iron Art Nouveau Models:* These have intricate decorative detailing.
- *Classic Nickel-Plated Fin Type Radiators:* Good for solid Edwardian or later homes.
- *Baseboard Radiators:* Long and narrowly discreet along the wall at baseboard level.

dividing radiators), and they can look good in any environment, particularly in modern, sleek or minimal settings, but also in period styles, if they are carefully chosen and placed. A slim, rail radiator can look very exciting in a modern interior, and Victorian column radiators, although bulky, can look attractive in a Victorian home.

For a truly authentic look, period radiators can be bought from antique dealers and salvage yards. These originals are inclined to crack if mishandled, but reproductions are available in a wide range of styles and colours. Special radiators can be used in any standard system. They are expensive, but installing just one in a bathroom, or where you want a special shape, can make all the difference to the look and efficiency of a room.

Radiators are usually placed under the window, where the hot air counteracts the down draft from the window and where they are unlikely to be so near to furniture as to cause any damage. However, there are plenty

(above left)
A large, ladder-style radiator can be used in many places in the home where ordinary radiators would not fit into the design.

Heater Ideas

- Install a radiator with an integral circular mirror fitted above.
- Modern towel–stand radiators in plain, bright colors can cheer up a plain, white bathroom. Some operate with low water content, so they heat quickly as soon as the heating comes on and the furnace works less hard. A converter can be added, so the towel stand can be used separately.
- If you have young children or elderly people in the house, you can get a low surface temperature unit, whose maximum panel temperature is 109°f (43°c).
- Electric heaters may be the best option in a downstairs cloakroom or small bathroom. Choose one that warms and dries towels at the same time.

Concealing Heaters

- The easiest and cheapest way to hide an ugly, white paneled radiator is to paint it to blend in with the surrounding decor. Always check that the paint you choose is suitable for heated surfaces.
- Several companies market radiator covers in wood or MDF in many styles and sizes to cover all sizes of radiator.
- Make your own radiator cover in MDF. There is a wide selection of grille panels available. Remember to leave plenty of room for the air to circulate and cut an access hole so the on/off valve is easy to reach. It's a good idea to cover the back of the wall, where the radiator is outfitted with foam-backed aluminum foil, to force the heat to be reflected out. This will help to make up for the loss in efficiency of radiators when they are encased.
- Don't forget that a central heating system should be serviced once a year.

Types of Energy

Gas is the most popular form of central heating. There are no fuel storage problems and it is clean and controllable and can be automatically regulated. It also offers the largest and most varied range of heaters, which include room heaters and floor-standing or wall-hung units. Where gas is unavailable, you can use liquefied petroleum gas (LPG), although this is more expensive and requires a large tank situated near the house, where delivery trucks can reach it. LPG is controllable, but not as clean as gas.

Solid fuel furnaces are efficient and less bulky than earlier ones, and can burn coal, wood or smokeless fuel. They have a slower response than gas or oil, and have to be stoked and cleaned. You will need storage space for the fuel. Many traditional-style kitchens have traditional-style stoves with a back boiler, which can be used to supply central heating (many of these can be fueled by gas, oil or electricity).

Electricity is the cleanest and simplest of all heating fuels, but only viable when used at off-peak rates. Night storage heaters store cheap rate heating and emit it during the day. You may need to boost this with some other form of heating in the early evening, when they have used up all the heat, but not started to store it again.

Fireplaces

The open fire is the epitome of comfort in the home in cold, winter weather. Stone and marble fireplaces can look gracious in a Classical setting, and a large fireplace with tiles is a very Victorian object. Many period fireplaces can look good in modern settings too. Don't install too grand a fireplace in a small interior, where it will put its environment to shame and be uncomfortably out of context. If you want a purely decorative addition to central heating, which will provide some warmth, cast-iron fireplaces are good for a modest Victorian look. There are gas or electric "real" fires, which are often more efficient than the traditional open fire and very realistic to look at.

If you want a fireplace but don't have a chimney, you can install a decorative gas unit, with a vent to expel fumes through the outside wall. Gas fires flicker very realistically and provide heat as well. Always have such fires installed by a reliable company, and make sure there is additional ventilation in the room, through wall or floor vents.

Wood-Burning Stoves

Stoves have been used for centuries for heating the home. Because they are enclosed, the fire burns much more slowly than in an open fireplace, and can often be regulated to stay burning all night. Heat radiates from the stove, but don't rely on it to add extra warmth by radiating from the stovepipe as well. Many modern stovepipes are so well insulated with double or triple walls that little heat escapes from them. Some stove models incorporate a system that forces clean air over the front glass panes and reduces the amount of soot.

Sheet-iron stoves are comparatively cheap to buy and will heat up quickly. Cast-iron models take longer to warm up, but will retain the heat for longer. A large stove can often provide heat for several radiators or for hot water.

There are many designs, from small, tubby black stoves, which look great in a cottage, to elegant modern ones finished in white, which look good in almost any setting. European tiled stoves, or *kacheloven*, are available and make a good centerpiece for a very large room, such as a warehouse. They are expensive, but very efficient and retain their heat for a long time. If placed in the corner of a room or built into a dividing wall, these stoves are capable of heating two or three rooms. Some stoves can be used for cooking as well as heating.

The heat from a stove is measured in kilowatts. A 4 kilowatt stove will heat a 15 ft (4.5 m) room efficiently, but a 10 kilowatt stove will be needed for larger rooms. It is useful to have a multi-fuel stove.

Controls

Whatever system you choose, adequate controls should be designed into the system right from the start. Room thermostats sense changes in room temperature and automatically turn the heat on and off. Thermostats for individual units can be useful in young children's rooms or workrooms. Get professional advice on the most efficient controls to have for your situation.

Safety Checklist

- *Gas heaters must be regularly serviced or they may cause fires.*
- *If you have a gas heater in a room, make sure there is good ventilation.*
- *Check that healers do not become so hot that they can burn people.*

Furniture

Few people have the opportunity to start from scratch and buy all the furniture they need for their home. There are nearly always some acquired pieces, that have become part of the family. If they are practical, comfortable and well designed, they should fit into your decor perfectly well. You can successfully mix different styles of furniture, provided they are similar in size, proportion and feeling. Reupholstering a chair or sofa in a fabric that matches the curtains or other upholstery, will give it new relevance. If upholstery is too expensive, have a new loose cover made for it, or make one yourself. It's not difficult for an experienced sewer to do; the main problem is managing the bulk of so much material. There are many excellent books on the market which tell you how to make covers, cushions and so on.

Remember, the more furniture you have, the less flexibility there will be. Sofas and tables can be as big as you like, but only if you leave plenty of space to comfortably walk round them, and to open and close doors, so if you've set your heart on a large piece, be willing to sacrifice other furniture to make room for it. A three-piece set takes up nearly all the available space in an average-sized living room, where a group of nonmatching, but compatible chairs might be just as comfortable and allow you more flexibility.

Guidelines to Quality

- *Check that any wood graining matches across doors and drawers.*
- *Ensure that the finish is evenly applied.*
- *Check that no adhesive can be seen around the joints (a sign of bad workmanship).*
- *Make sure that the drawers open smoothly and easily, and don't tip downward when halfway open.*
- *Check that handles, locks and hinges are of good quality and firmly attached.*
- *Ensure that any joins are firmly attached.*
- *Upholstered furniture should be comfortable and covered with closely woven fabric. Check that the fabric pattern matches all the way around and that the seams are straight. Fabric and fillings should conform to standards of durability and flame retardance. There should be a label to indicate this.*
- *The foam used in a lot of modern upholstery will give off a poisonous black smoke if it catches fire, which can kill within minutes.*

- *Check that any foam furniture you buy has a fire retardant label.*
- *If you are buying furniture that needs assembly, make sure all the pieces and the instructions are included.*

Antique and Reproduction Furniture

An antique is something valued for its age, workmanship, beauty or rarity and generally applies only to objects over 100 years old. However, objects that are less old can become collector's items, which can put their price up as though they were antiques.

Anything from a Tudor oak chest to a 1930s Art Deco piece is extremely expensive nowadays. If you want such a piece, check that it is well made and in a good state of repair and do a bit of bargaining for it. Later pieces from the 1950s and 1960s are beginning to be of interest to collectors.

A reproduction is an honest re-creation of an earlier object (as opposed to a dishonest forgery). It is made using the same techniques and materials as the original, and is often "distressed" by special techniques to make it seem honorably old. Reproduction furniture is almost as expensive as antique.

Making the Most of Secondhand Furniture

Some secondhand furniture is charming in its own right and simply needs cleaning or painting. You can still sometimes find dining and kitchen furniture of the 1950s and 1960s quite cheaply in junk shops, and these pieces be painted to fit in a modern interior. In fact, mass-produced pieces can often be altered, adjusted, repaired and repainted to become useful pieces in modern or period interiors. Choose with care: cheapness may indicate that a piece has one leg shorter than the others, or concealed insect damage. Don't buy obviously damaged furniture unless you are experienced at repairs. Professional repairs are very expensive. There are some things that are easy to fix, however, such as loose or missing hinges (as long as the doors or the frame is not warped). You may have to glue a new section of wood to take the screws or plug the old holes with a dowel.

- *New handles, locks and hinges will improve many pieces of old furniture.*
- *Secondhand veneered furniture may have cracks in the veneer showing that the base wood has buckled or shrunk. Avoid buying furniture that is warped. Warped wood is usually beyond repair.*
- *Test the leaves of tables to see that the hinges are securely fixed.*
- *Don't buy chairs that need recaning unless you are prepared to spend time learning how to do this, or can afford to get them expensively recaned by an expert.*
- *Avoiding buying upholstery if it needs repairing. Springs should be unbroken and attached to the webbing where two pieces cross. If an upholstered chair seems sound, apart from the covering fabric, you could have a new loose cover made. If the piece has torn webbing or lumpy springs or a sagging front edge, don't buy it.*
- *A tear in a leather cover can be patched with leather, and torn vinyl can be mended with a suitable adhesive.*
- *Dirty vinyl covers can be cleaned with car upholstery cleaner, leather with a damp cloth and leather cleaner.*
- *If the piece has uneven legs, cut a piece of pencil eraser or cork to the right thickness and glue it to the bottom of the leg.*
- *Create a coffee table from an old kitchen or side table by cutting a length off the legs and painting it. Crackle glaze or stenciling would both work well.*
- *When buying secondhand, check carefully for signs of woodworm and don't buy furniture that shows these small, tell-tale round holes, especially if there is fresh sawdust coming out of them. Woodworm thrives*

particularly on plywood, soft woods and wicker. Look for wormholes in drawers, and rough, unvarnished timber.

- *Treat small outbreaks of woodworm with a dose of proprietary woodworm product. After treatment, fill holes with wood filler to strengthen the wood.*
- *Scratches can be treated with a proprietary remover or by rubbing them with the cut end of a Brazil nut. Some scratches and marks are acceptable in old furniture and add to their character. Deep ones need filler.*

Filling Scratches and Dents

You will need: a proprietary wood stripper, fine steel wool or sandpaper, beeswax.

1. Strip off all old paint or varnish with a wood stripper, carefully following all the manufacturer's instructions.
2. Rub the wood by hand with steel wool or sandpaper, working in the direction of the grain. Remove all traces of sawdust.
3. Paint or wax the wood.

(above)
This beautifully made solid oak reproduction Tudor chair would go well in a Gothic interior.

Furniture Styles

MEDIEVAL, TUDOR, ELIZABETHAN, JACOBEAN (1500s – 1660)

Very little medieval furniture has survived, but from contemporary paintings and illuminations it can be seen that it was generally crudely constructed of thick timbers, usually oak boards, placed on trestles or wedged into place with pegs. The carved patterns usually imitated stone carvings. Later, these evolved into refectory tables, which had four or six heavily turned legs joined by stretchers to rest the feet on (away from the ubiquitous rats). Heavy Elizabethan pieces were made with joints and paneled frames, with elaborate carvings of strapwork, fluting, leaves and figures. Jacobean furniture was similar in style, but more diverse with folding tables, cupboards and chests of drawers; stools were given low backs and were called backstools. Designs were plainer, lighter, highly polished and with more slender supports and fancy spindles. All these styles are suitable for farmhouses, old country houses and Gothic interiors, and will also go with Victorian pieces because of their solidity.

RESTORATION AND QUEEN ANNE (1660 – 1720)

Oak gave way to walnut and other decorative woods, and was inlaid and gilded. Barley sugar carved legs were popular, and cabriole legs were typical of a new, elegant shapeliness. Japanning was used to imitate Oriental lacquerwork. Some Queen Anne furniture is suited to a seventeenth-century interior.

EIGHTEENTH CENTURY

Walnut became scarce, so mahogany was imported and became very popular. Chinese and Classical styles were popular and made in great variety, with bow-fronted commodes, curved and elegantly carved rococo chairs, ball and claw feet, secretaries, library furniture and steps. Chippendale and Hepplewhite came into their own.

Several new categories of furniture have appeared, including the dining room table (usually made up of two D-shaped ends with a gate-leg middle section), the sideboard and the roll-top desks. Mahogany revolutionized table design as it is very strong, doesn't warp or bend, is impervious to worms and can be highly polished, so there were round, oval and rectangular tables, drop-leaf and gate leg tables in great variety. Much of this furniture is too elaborate and grand for small homes, but smaller pieces in the style can fit well into most period interiors, from the early eighteenth century right through to Victorian and Edwardian rooms. Furniture was used with great restraint and contemporary watercolors show rooms that look rather empty to twentieth-century eyes, with most of the furniture ranged against the walls.

REGENCY (1800 – 1810)

Elegant, classically inspired designs in dark or patterned woods; especially rosewood and, of course, mahogany were the hallmarks of this period. Regency furniture is unpretentious and easy to live with. Finishes were often ebonized, gilded or painted. The style harked back to ancient Greece and Rome, and to Egypt and the Far East for decorative motifs. There were Grecian-style couches, tables with claw feet, chairs with saber legs and brass inlays in the seats.

VICTORIAN (1830 – 1850)

We tend to think of Victorian furniture as rather heavy, but in the early part of the nineteenth century, the look was quite spare and elegant. Later furniture was well made in the Classical, Rococo and Gothic styles. Mahogany was popular. Chairs and sofas had scrolled and carved cabriole legs, and buttoned upholstery, upholstered ottomans and Chesterfield sofas. Tables became more and more imaginative: there were ingenious extending tables; pedestal tables were more

heavily built and often carved with flamboyant marquetry borders, and boldly carved bases. These were often covered with velvet or chenille cloths. Mirrors were sometimes hung at opposite ends of a large room, extending the space and giving interesting reflections. There were plenty of pictures on all the walls, all heavily framed in gilt frames.

In 1840, Michael Thonet patented a unique process of bending wood, making it possible to mass-produce furniture on a huge scale. Thonet's bentwood and cane dining chairs sold in millions and are still produced today. These chairs work in almost any interior, having a grace and strength, which can complement almost any style.

Papier mâché, an ancient Chinese art, was introduced to England in 1847. It was used to make trays, and molded into furniture and architectural ornamentation, such as wall brackets and ceiling roses. It was lighter and cheaper than plaster.

ARTS AND CRAFTS AND ART NOUVEAU (1870 – 1914)

A new, sparer style was introduced, which ran alongside the florid Victorian furniture. It was intended as a reaction to mass-production and the loss of integrity it produced, and looked to medieval designs for inspiration. Hardwoods such as oak, ash, elm, yew and fruit woods were used for sturdy, simple furniture, where the joinery was simple and visible. Colored leaded glass roundels decorated sideboards and cupboards. Metalwork was an important feature, in the form of hinges and mounts of wrought iron or hammered copper. Chairs were in the country tradition of ladderbacks and rush seats, and high-backed wooden settees with loose cushions.

BETWEEN-THE-WARS

Simplicity and comfort sum up the furniture of the 1920s and 1930s. Spare experimental furniture and Art Deco dominated the period.

Marcel Breuer, a teacher at the Bauhaus in Germany, produced chairs made of steel tube, inspired by the bicycle, and Alvar Aalto, in Finland, produced bent plywood of great grace and simplicity. These designs and others are still manufactured today. Art Deco furniture was angular and geometric. Look for bentwoods, veneers, chrome legs, frames and supports, leather (white, black or yellowy brown), faceted mirrors, fake lacquer, gilding, hide or mock leopardskin upholstery.

1940s TO 1970s

A range of "Utility" furniture was designed for wartime use, and for a time it was the only furniture that was allowed to be manufactured in Great Britain. Utility furniture was well-made, of solid oak in no-nonsense designs. Probably the best known design was a square table with two leaves, which pulled out to form a large dining table. Utility furniture was much despised at the time, partly because it was obligatory, but the designs are beginning to creep back into modern furniture because they were good-looking, sturdy and practical. This was a time of experiment. A cardboard chair requiring assembly was never quite cheap enough and vanished, but plastic became popular because it was moldable and cheap, and metal was widely used for frames. The sack chair, filled with polystyrene granules, found its way into almost every interior and furniture kits became popular. Folding chairs too really came into their own. Designs that have become classics included the Charles Eames' black leather chair with its own footstool and the Magistretti chair, a sophisticated version of an Italian peasant chair in stained beechwood with a rush seat.

FURNITURE TODAY

There is practically no design that cannot be acquired today, whether antique, reproduction or modern. Reproductions of antique furniture and of some more modern classics — such as Charles Rennie Mackintosh Art Nouveau chairs, some Art Deco pieces, the Charles Eames chair and the exquisite bentwood chairs designed in Scandinavia by Alvar Aalto — are still available, although expensive. Look-alikes of many original chairs, such as the Windsor chair, the Magistretti chair and Thonet bentwood chairs, are most attractive and widely available, perhaps not always in quite the same materials and proportions as the originals. Country furniture inspired by cottage and Mediterranean pieces is very attractive, but by no means always as cheap as the originals.

The newest designs include many metal-framed chairs, and designer furniture is made in eccentric Gothic or asymmetrical space-age styles which are well suited to modern environments. The most practical aspects of much experimental and designer furniture are often incorporated into mass-produced ranges.

Folding furniture ranges from deckchairs and picnic chairs to copies of Edwardian and Victorian folding chairs and rockers. Modern folding stools, which can be hung on the wall, and the simplest folding tables are worth investigating for the smaller home.

Furniture wrought from thin metal rods, or hammered and welded into curious shapes, has become popular for twentieth-century Gothic homes, and some of the more restrained pieces are suitable for a wider range of modern styles.

Painted Furniture

The origins of painted furniture are quite diverse, ranging from commonplace Swiss and Bavarian peasant pieces to the more restrained Swedish Gustavian style in the seventeenth century and the ornate, floral Victorian pieces. Naive folk art styles, which originated in Pennsylvania (introduced by German settlers), are much copied and produced by today's artists and so are the

(opposite)
The original classic 3107 chair, designed by Arne Jacobsen, finished in white lacquer. Today it is available in many styles and colors.

many decorative techniques from the seventeenth and eighteenth centuries, such as dragging, ragging, stenciling and decoupage.

Many furniture stores play safe and show only the blandest designs, with little personality in shape or color. Don't be impressed with the first designs you see. Investigate small, modern furniture shops, individual artisans and workshops, furniture warehouses, second-hand shops and markets. Even in the most humdrum of shops, you may discover a piece that will look good if painted or given a different cover.

Alternative Furniture Ideas

- *If you can't find a sofa-bed you like, try a divan or daybed, which doubles as a bed. This takes up much less space than a sofa, and can look right in a modern or traditional style.*
- *If you can move your furniture around frequently, buy chairs, sofas and cabinets (even waste baskets) on casters. Casters themselves are cheap to buy and easy to fix onto most furniture.*
- *Look for country-style furniture: for example, Swedish or Shaker, with a solid, well-built quality, but restrained design, which can complement many different styles and is suitable for town or country.*
- *White or green cast aluminum garden furniture can double up for kitchen or sunroom dining.*

Hints on Hanging Pictures

Pictures and paintings are the finishing touches to your home, and how you display them will be crucial to the success of your whole scheme.

Placing Pictures

You don't have to cover every wall with pictures. A bare expanse of wall can be very attractive and can provide a background for an original flower arrangement or a lively piece of sculpture.

When you have decided to hang a picture, be purposeful about it. Either give one picture pride of place or group paintings together, rather than having one or two pictures dotted here and there with no relationship to one another. Get someone to hold a picture up, so you can see what exactly what it is going to look like and where it will be best placed.

Multiple paintings can be arranged on the floor beforehand, so you get a good balance before hanging them.

Some Hints on Hanging

- *Pictures in a group should be close together. They should relate in shape, size, color, frame or subject. If you include portraits, they should be facing inward.*
- *Photographs often look stronger and have more presence when framed or grouped.*
- *Symmetrically arranged groups of paintings should be the same size and have identical frames and a shared theme.*
- *Nonsymmetrical groups should always be balanced: distribute dark frames among pale ones, and balance one large picture with a number of smaller ones.*
- *Framing small pictures is not difficult. There are various kinds of framing kits available, offering a choice of assembly, fit and colour. Use monofilament or 3-ply picture wire knotted into D-rings (shaped rings specifically used when hanging pictures), screw eyes or back hooks.*
- *Pictures should be professionally framed if the sides are longer than 3 ft 3 in (1 m) because a frame as big as this is difficult for beginners to handle.*

Displays, Collections and Objects

- *Collections are often best grouped together, where their qualities can be compared and they reinforce each other.*
- *Bowls and baskets can be good contain-*

ers for tropical seeds, fossils and other asymmetrically shaped objects.

- Small "occasional" tables can look charming with a display of glass or china, or silver-framed photographs. This would be especially suitable for a busy nineteenth-century interior.
- Glass-fronted display cases are excellent for precious objects and china, especially if they are internally lit. Lighting from the front will merely reflect against the glass.
- Colored glass should be displayed with the light behind it; either on glass shelves in front of a window or in a well-lit case.

Small Wood Projects

WOOD FILLING

This technique should be used only on unfinished surfaces, as you have to sand the surface to complete the repair. For finished surfaces, there are wax sticks for filling and special crayons for retouching. If a repaired area is to be drilled or otherwise worked like wood, use wood filling for the repair.

Ready-to-use cellulose-based wood filling compounds contain wood dust and earth pigments to simulate woods such as Georgian mahogany, light and dark oak, golden and antique pine, and neutral tones. You can adjust the color by adding pigments or cellulose dyes.

1. Thoroughly clean off the wax and dirt from the area to be filled. A cotton swab dipped into vinegar makes a good cleaner.
2. Pack and spread the filler into the cavity with a painter's knife or similar tool. Allow to dry from 10 minutes to several hours depending on the size and depth of repair, the humidity and the room temperature.
3. Smooth with sand paper.

- When working on large areas, work in stages.
- When using wax sticks or crayons, allow the cleaned surface to dry overnight before applying them.

Liming Furniture

Any ordinary piece of furniture can be given an attractive limed finish.

You will need: liming wax, neutral wax, a bronze brush, tack cloths (resin-coated cloths that attract dust), a wood dye if you choose to color the piece and cotton rags, extra fine steel wool and a bronze brush. Coloring greatly enhances the contrast between the liming wax and the wood.

1. Open the grain of hardwoods, such as oak, with a bronze brush. You don't need to do this with softwoods, such as pine.
2. Wipe with a tack cloth.
3. Apply the dye with a cloth and wipe off all the excess left on the surface. Allow to dry.
4. Apply a coat of liming wax, working it well into the grain with extra fine steel wool.
5. Immediately remove most of the excess with a clean cotton rag, wiping new surfaces as the cloth becomes filled with wax.
6. Polish with a neutral wax to remove the white haze and to give the final finish.
7. Allow a few hours for the waxes to dry, then buff to a soft sheen.

Applying a Crackle Glaze

This finish is suitable for wood, metal or plastic surfaces. It can turn the most boring piece of junk furniture into something interesting.

You will need: two colors of water-based paint (for example, latex), medium-grade sandpaper; dusting brush; paintbrushes, crackle glaze and oil-based, matte varnish.

1. Sand the piece. Dust with the brush and apply a coat of paint. Allow to dry.
2. Apply a coat of crackle glaze. Change the direction of the brush strokes as you work.
3. Apply a coat of your second color paint, again using haphazard brush strokes. Work quickly and don't cover the same area twice. Leave to dry.
4. Apply a thick coat of matte varnish.

Applying dye

Working the wax into the grain

Polishing with neutral wax

Facts & Figures

FINDING THE EXPERTS

If you are considering alterations to your home, seek expert advice to help with planning and preparation for the work. Restrictions on what you are allowed to do are there to ensure the structural integrity of a building, but these vary from place to place. Placing additional loads on a building or altering support methods will probably require approval. Exterior alterations will usually need approval by planning or zoning departments to make sure they are in keeping with the character of the community and that additional rooms do not exceed density limits. Check whether there are any title restrictions. There are laws concerning the size and height of rooms, staircase treatments, amount of ventilation/light, etc. Fire regulations stipulate how internal layouts should be arranged and whether you need extra escape routes. Buildings that are of historic or architectural interest or located in historic districts may be subject to stringent conditions. Make time for preliminary planning and outline design, a feasibility study of options, drawing draft proposals and budgets, working drawings and a schedule of work, obtaining estimates and permits, and compiling a financial plan. You can go to your local planning department to get advice, but architects and interior designers are well versed in local building codes. They will also be able to advise you on reliable local contractors and deal with all the applications and paperwork. Always get in two or three quotes first before instructing suppliers.

INSPECTOR

Surveyors are trained in assessing the structure, surfaces and finishes of a building. They will advise on what needs to be done in the way of repairs and give an estimate of costs. A mortgage company's inspection may reveal basic faults, but this is intended to establish the value of the property, not the condition. It is wise to get a separate, full structural inspection. Make sure your inspector is a member of an accepted trade organization and is insured for failing to notify you of any faults.

ARCHITECT

Architects are trained to see the potential of space in a home and, if you are considering much structural work, it would be worth employing one to design the space for you and to deal with all local permits and paperwork. The local branch of the architects' professional association should give several names of local practitioners. There is usually no fee for an initial consultation.

INTERIOR DESIGNER/INTERIOR ARCHITECT

Some will simply provide designs for paints, wallpapers, carpets, upholstery and so on, while others may be able to organize the interior space in a more architectural way as well. Choose someone whose work you have seen and like. Otherwise go through a reputable organization. Always get everything in writing before going ahead.

BUILDER/CONTRACTOR

Once you have agreed on terms, establish when the builder or contractor will start the work and how long the job will take. Make sure "making good" is included in the contract. Once the work is agreed, do not ask the builder to take on extra small jobs, as this can be costly. Give a written specification of the work and the standard you expect, bringing in an architect, if necessary. Subsequent changes should be confirmed in writing.

LEGAL MATTERS

If you employ an architect to manage a project, he or she will deal with all the necessary paperwork. An experienced builder can do this, too. Otherwise, you should employ a lawyer to handle all the necessary consents.

CHRONOLOGICAL GUIDE TO POPULAR STYLES
(These dates are flexible and many styles overlap.)

Historic Styles

Gothic (roots medieval)	
Revivals in eighteenth, nineteenth and twentieth centuries	
Tudor and Jacobean (Elizabethan)	
	Sixteenth and seventeenth centuries
English Country	*Seventeenth century onward*
French Country	*Seventeenth century onward*
American Country	*1620 onward*
Rococo	*c.1690–1740*
Georgian	*1714–1830*
Neo-Classical	*c.1730–c.1800*
Colonial	*Early eighteenth century to mid–nineteenth century*
Gustavian	*1770–1810*
Regency	*c.1780–1820*
Shaker	*1784–1860s*
Directoire	*1793–1804*
Empire	*1804–1814*
Victorian	*1815–1900*
Biedermeier	*1815–1848*
Arts and Crafts/Edwardian/Nineties	*c.1860s–1900*
Art Nouveau	*c.1890–1910*
Bohemian	*1910–1930*
Art Deco	*c.1918–1929*
Modernist/Minimalist	*c.1920–1933*
1950s	*c.1945–c.1960*
High–Tech	*c.1960s–*
Postmodern	*1960s–*

Timeless Styles (Regional/National)

Mediterranean
Scandinavian
Japanese
Nomadic
Indian

GLOSSARY

Adjustable lamp *A lamp on an angled stand, which can be adjusted to wherever the light is required.*
Adjustable spots *Semi-recessed lights in the ceiling, which can be adjusted to shine in limited directions.*
A-frame houses *Houses built with wood frames in the shape of an A. Easy to build, popular in Scandinavia.*
Ambience *Environment, atmosphere.*
Architrave *A decorated wood strip that runs around a door, window or panel.*
Backsplash *Non-porous, easily cleaned surface fitted behind a sink. Prevents water from penetrating the wall.*
Baffle *A device attached to a light fixture, or in front of it, that helps to prevent glare.*
Balloon shade *A gathered blind developed in Austria, which falls into rows of folds.*
Baseboard *A wood strip running along the bottom of a wall, where it meets the floor.*
Bay window *Any window forming a recess.*
Bi-folding door *A door made of two narrow vertical pieces, hinged in the middle, which takes up less room when opened than a standard door.*
Bow window *A window projecting in a curve.*
Boxed storage *Boxes, either on casters or piled up to form a bank of storage.*
Bubble lights *Domed windows set into a flat roof, made of glass reinforced with mesh.*
Cabriole legs *Curved furniture legs, often like an animal's paw.*
Café curtains *Two pairs of curtains, one pair on top of another, with the lower pair hanging from a pole across the middle of the window.*
Cames *Strip of metal used to hold leaded light glass.*
Canopy *A covering or its support or both, fitted over a bed. (A half canopy is the same, but fitted over the top end of the bed only.)*
Ceramic *Made of glazed pottery or china.*
Chinoiserie *Furniture, fabric or wallpaper inspired by Chinese design.*
Chintz *Floral cotton fabric with a glazed finish.*
Combing *A paint technique in which a comb is drawn evenly through a layer of wet paint to create narrow, vertical stripes.*
Console table *A narrow table designed to stand against a wall. Useful in a narrow hallway.*
Corian *Very tough, good-looking, man-made material used for counters.*
Cork *Soft, warm material made from the bark of a tree. Good for floors (if sealed); also used on walls. Provides good insulation.*
Cornice *Decorative molding strip, usually made of wood or plaster, that runs round the wall of a room, just below the ceiling.*
Cross-top faucets *Faucets whose handles are in the shape of an X.*

Dado rail *A wood rail fixed horizontally onto the wall, usually about two-thirds of the way down. The area below is usually paneled or given a different paint treatment to the area above.*
Day lighting *A term used for artificial lighting that gives a white light for working by.*
Dhurrie *Indian flat-woven rug, usually made of cotton.*
Dimmer switch *A light switch which can dim the light, as well as turning it on and off.*
Dormer windows *Vertical windows that stick out from a sloping roof. They can often provide the necessary height to turn an attic into a habitable room.*
Downlights *Light fixtures direct the light downward.*
Dragging *A paint technique made by dragging a dry brush over wet paint.*
Dusting brush *A brush with soft, medium-length bristles in a wood handle.*
Eclectic *A mingling of different styles and inspirations.*
Eggshell *Mid-sheen or satin paint.*
Elevation *A diagram of a room as seen from the side.*
Ergonomic *Something designed for economical body movement. Used particularly in kitchen and bathroom planning, and the design of chairs.*
Exhaust fan *A fan which extracts stale air from a room.*
Fanlight *A window over a door, often semi-circular with radiating glazing bars.*
Fitch *Rounded, long-handled brush with flexible, but firm bristles.*
Flag *Stone slab used for flooring.*
Flock wallpaper *Wallpaper with a raised pattern created by tiny particles of fiber on the surface, often in designs similar to luxurious woven silks.*
Floor plan *A diagram of a room as seen from above.*
Fluorescent light *A tube with a gas fitted inside, which lights up when it is heated. Gives a brighter, whiter light than incandescent lighting and without shadow, so it is often used to work by.*
Foambacked *A foam backing for carpets and other flooring materials, which requires no underlayment.*
Focal point *An object or arrangement that attracts the attention and becomes the main feature of an area.*
French window *Glass-paneled, hinged door opening out onto a patio or garden.*
Futon *Japanese-style mattress made of layers of cotton wadding in a cotton casing. Laid directly onto the floor or on a slatted base.*
Gilding *The application of gold leaf or gold paint or cream to a piece of furniture or a frame.*
Gilt cream/gilt wax *Metallic powders suspended in a turpentine base for touching up old gilding or adding metallic highlights.*
Glass bricks *Thick, square bricks of glass that can be used to make a structural wall or part of a wall to let light into a basement or other dark space.*
Gloss *Shiny surface produced by particular paints, varnishes, ceramic tiles, etc. (As opposed to matte.)*

Graining *Paint technique used to imitate wood grain.*

Grisaille *Figures or trompe l'oeil painting in black and grays on white.*

Grout *The mortar used to fill gaps between ceramic tiles.*

Habitable room *A bedroom, kitchen or living room. Non-habitable rooms should be used just for storage.*

Haircord *Rough, durable fiber made from animal hair and used for carpets, matting and occasionally, upholstery.*

Incandescent *Light produced by heating a small filament within the bulb (the common light bulb is an incandescent lamp).*

Industrial *Describes shelving or other furnishings or structural systems designed primarily for factory or warehouse use.*

Jacquard fabric *Intricately woven pattern and designs named after a loom introduced in eighteenth–century France. These fabrics are now woven by computerized looms to emulate hand-woven tapestries of the past, but any design can now be woven.*

Japanning (See Lacquer.)

Joists *Beams supporting a floor or roof.*

Jute *A fiber that is used for sacking, doormats and tough floor matting.*

Kilim *Flat-woven (i.e., non-tufted) rug, usually originating from the Caucasus or the Middle East.*

Lacquer (Also known as Japanning.) *Hard varnish applied in many layers and polished to a high gloss.*

Laminate *Layers of various substances that are pressed and glued to create a tough surface material. Used for kitchen work surfaces.*

Lazy Susan *Shelving which fits into a corner cupboard and can be rotated for easy access.*

Limewash *Finish used on wood with a definite grain, such as oak and ash, in which limewash is diluted and applied to furniture, paneling or floorboards.*

Lincrusta *Make of embossed wallpaper.*

Lining brush *Brush designed specifically for creating straight lines for furniture decoration.*

Linoleum *Form of flooring made of cork and linseed oil; similar to vinyl but warmer to the touch.*

Linseed oil *Natural oil obtained from the seeds of the flax plant. Used as a finish for certain woods.*

Load-bearing walls *Walls that are necessary for holding up the building.*

Louvered doors *Doors made of slats set at an angle into a frame. These let a little light in (and air too). They usually come in narrow widths, so are useful for closets where two doors can be hinged together to take up less space than a normal door.*

Marbling *A paint technique imitating the veined and streaked look of marble.*

Matte *Flat finish with no shine or luster.*

Medium-density fiberboard (MDF) *Smooth, composite material made out of sawdust and adhesive, used for shelves, furniture, radiator covers, etc.*

Melamine *Type of tough plastic used for picnic ware and sprayed onto chipboard to provide a low cost material for shelving.*

Mezzanine floor *An extra floor halfway between two floors. Often used in just a portion of a room to create a balcony.*

Mineral spirits *Paint thinner for oil-based paints.*

Mixing faucet *A faucet with a single spout and hot and cold handles so you can adjust the heat of the water.*

Modular furniture *Furniture built to a module or particular measurement, which can be added to or used in different arrangements.*

Moisture barrier *A layer of impervious material laid in a wall to stop rising damp.*

Moldings *Decorative plaster or woodwork on cornices, arches, ceilings and so on.*

Niche *A recess in a wall. You can buy plaster niches to fix onto a wall.*

Ottoman *A low, stuffed seat without a back.*

Painter's tape *Low-tack tape used to mask off areas when applying a finish to selected areas only; for creating straight lines on decorative work and for sticking things temporarily onto surfaces.*

Palladian *Style of architecture introduced by the Italian architect Andrea Palladio in the sixteenth century, based on Greek architecture. Introduced to England by Inigo Jones in the seventeenth century.*

Panoramic wallpapers *Block-printed, non-repeat papers with a picture designed to run all the way round a room.*

Papier mâché *A modeling material made from shredded paper and water-based glues, such as wallpaper adhesive. Dries hard and can be decorated with paint, gilding and other finishes. Used for table tops, trays, bowls and, at one time, for decorative ceiling moldings.*

Partition wall *A wall erected to separate two areas of a home, but which is not part of the structure of the house.*

Patio door *Sliding glass door, usually in a metal or UPVC frame and double-glazed, leading onto a patio or garden.*

Pavers *Thin bricks used for flooring and paving.*

Pegboard *Hardboard perforated with holes. It can be used with small hooks for tool or kitchen storage.*

Pigment *The basic color source used for dyes and paints.*

Plumb line *Pointed weight on the end of a cord suspended to determine a true vertical.*

Polystyrene *Soft, man-made insulating material in the form of rolls or tiles. Should always be covered with wallpaper or placed behind paneling or plasterboard.*

Polyurethane *Plastic resin used in paints and varnishes.*

PVC (Polyvinyl chloride) *A flexible plastic used in some simulated fabrics and on table cloths to give a shiny, washable surface.*

Quarry tiles *Unglazed hard clay tiles, traditionally used in country kitchen floors. Available in various sizes.*

Ragging *Paint technique producing a three-dimensional effect when a crushed rag is pressed over wet paint.*

Rag rug *A rug woven with multi-colored strips of material, originally made of worn-out clothes. Used in cottage homes and by the early settlers in America.*

Range hood *A hood over the top of a stove, which incorporates an exhaust fan to remove cooking smells.*

Regency stripes *Formal, vertically striped wallpaper and fabric.*

Registered building *A building that has been officially recognized as being of particular historic interest. Permission is required for alterations or repairs and you may even be eligible for a grant to carry out the necessary work.*

Roman blind *Simple, elegant blind that folds into pleats when raised.*

Sconce *Lamp fixed onto the wall with a mirror or reflector placed behind, which reflects the light toward the room. Originally for candles; now used for electric lighting too.*

Scumbling *Similar to stippling; an opaque contrasting coat is added to a bright, shiny paint color with a dry brush. Generally used on furniture.*

Seal *A protective finish for floors or furniture.*

Semi-detached *Describes a type of house, characteristically joined to the next door house on one side, with an alley on the other and have gabled roofs and bow-fronted windows facing the street.*

Silicon carbide paper (See wet and dry paper.)

Spattering *Spraying paints in different colors onto wet paint to create a multi-colored look.*

Spirit level *Glass tube in a metal or wood case partly filled with spirit. The position of the bubble indicates if a surface is truly horizontal.*

Sponging *Paint technique achieved by applying layers of paint with a sponge to create a three-dimensional effect.*

Stenciling *Paint technique in which paint is applied through the holes in a template to create a frieze or other repeat pattern. Used on walls, floors or furniture.*

Stippling *Paint technique producing a grainy texture when using dry brushes or a dry roller on wet paint.*

Stovetop *The top of a stove, where the gas or electric burners are positioned.*

Stucco *Plaster used for coating outside walls.*

Suspended ceilings *False ceilings that can lower the height of a room and also conceal light fittings and wiring.*

Swag *Elaborate draping of fabric.*

Tanking *Method of lining a room or basement with a non-porous skin to prevent moisture.*

Tapestry *Hand-woven (or jacquard woven) wall hanging.*

Task lighting *Lighting for a particular purpose, such as reading, drawing, kitchen preparation and office work.*

Teak oil *Similar to linseed oil.*

Terraced house *One of several houses joined together in a row.*

Tiffany *Famous New York manufacturer of Art Nouveau glass lampshades.*

Toile de Jouy *Cotton fabric printed with pictorial scenes, usually in a single color on an off-white ground. Named after Jouy-en-Josas in France, where it was produced from 1770, but today "toile" indicates any fabric of this particular type.*

Tongue-and-groove *Wood boarding, which fits together to make an economical form of paneling. Often used below dado level in a room.*

Track lighting *Spotlights attached to a metal track fixed onto the ceiling.*

Trim (See Architrave)

Trompe l'oeil *A painted scene intended to deceive the eye. For example, a painted window looking out onto a painted garden.*

Tungsten halogen *Lighting in which a filament and gas heat up inside the bulb to create light.*

Tungsten light *Lighting in which a filament inside the bulb heats up to create light.*

UPVC *Plastic material for window and patio door frames.*

Valance *The fabric frill concealing the base of a bed.*

Venetian blinds *Blinds made of horizontal slats, which can be adjusted to let in more or less light, as you wish.*

Vinyl *Tough, but flexible plastic material used for practical and waterproof floor coverings and tiles, particularly in kitchens and bathrooms.*

Vista *A view through a long opening or passage. For example, from one room into another.*

Wet and dry paper *Also known as silicon carbide paper. Fine sandpaper that is particularly good for sanding down existing paintwork to create a key for subsequent coats to grip onto. Can be dipped in water first to prevent it from clogging up with fine particles.*

Whitewash *Non-washable, chalky paint that was originally used on plaster walls as a cheap finish.*

Windsor chair *Early English chair with bent back and turned rungs.*

Wood filler *Plastic used to repair wood. Looks like wood when dry.*

Work triangle *The arrangement and relationship of the three main kitchen operations: food storage, food preparation and cooking.*

ADDRESSES

Large department store and local shops often have a good selection of basic home furnishings and these can be very helpful. Design and architectural associations should be able to give members' names and addresses.

AMERICAN ORGANIZATIONS

American Institute of Architects, 1735 New York Avenue NW, Washington, DC 20006

American Society of Interior Designers, 730 Fifth Avenue, New York, NY 10019

International Association of Lighting Designers, 18 E. 16th Street, New York, NY 10003

National Association of the Remodeling Industry, 4900 Seminary Road, Suite 320, Alexandria, VA 22311

SHOPS AND SUPPLIERS

ABC Carpet & Home, 888 Broadway, New York, NY 10003 (Flooring)

Aga Cookers, Inc., 17 Town Farm Lane, Stowe, VT 05672 (Kitchen range cookers)

Anderson Windows, 100 Fourth Avenue, Baysport, MN 55003

Ann Sacks Tile & Stone, Inc., 8120 NE 33rd Drive, Portland, OR 97211 (Tile and stone flooring)

Arthur Sanderson & Sons, Ltd., 3 Patriot Center, 285 Grand Avenue, Eaglewood, NJ 07631 (Fabrics and wallcoverings)

Brunschwig & Fils, 779 Third Avenue, Suite 1222–1234, New York, NY 10022 (Fabrics and furniture)

Cole & Son (Wallpapers), Ltd., through Clarence House, 211 East 58th Street, New York, NY 10022

Colefax & Fowler, through Cowtan and Tout, 979 Third Avenue, New York, NY 10022 (Fabrics and wallpapers)

Crate and Barrell Catalog, PO Box 3057, Northbrook, IL 60065 (Home and kitchen accessories)

Crown City Hardware, 1047 N. Allen Avenue, Pasadena, CA 91104 (Moldings and ornamentations)

Crown Decorative Products, through Bentley Brothers, 2709 South Park Road, Louisville, KY 40219 (Paint and wallcoverings)

H & R Johnson USA, Inc., 190 Highway 18, East Brunswick, NJ 08816 (Ceramic tiles)

Hamilton Weston Wallpapers, Ltd., through Classic Revivals, Inc., 1 Design Center Place, Boston, MA 02210 (Historic wallpapers)

Hold Everything Catalog, PO Box 7807, San Francisco, CA 94120 (Home organization tools)

The Home Depot, 2455 Paces Ferry Road, Atlanta, GA 30339 (Fixtures)

IKEA, 17621 E. Gale Avenue, City of Industry, CA 91748 (Furniture and lighting)

Jenn-Air, 3035 Shadeland, Indianapolis, IN 46226 (Kitchen ranges and stoves)

Laura Ashley, 6 St. James Avenue, 10th Floor, Boston, MA 02116

Paint Magic, 2426 Fillmore Street, San Francisco, CA 94115 (Equipment, paint, videos, and books for decorative paint techniques)

Pergo, Persorp Flooring, Inc., 524 New Hope Road, Raleigh, NC 27604 (Laminate flooring)

Philips Lighting, 200 Franklin Square Drive, Somerset, NJ 08873

Pottery Barn Catalog, PO Box 7044, San Francisco, CA 94120 (Furniture and home accessories)

Pozzi Wood Windows and Doors, PO Box 5249, Bend, OR 97708

Renovator's Supply Catalog, PO Box 2515, Conway, NH 03818

Restoration Hardware, 6100 Topanga Canyon Blvd., Woodland Hills, CA 91367 (Moldings and ornamentations)

The Stulb Company, PO Box 1030, Fort Washington, PA 19034 (Williamsburg Buttermilk Paints)

Thomasville Furniture, PO Box 339, Thomasville, NC 27361

:use, 20 North Avenue, Larchmont, NY 10538 (Home accessories and fixtures)

Windsor and Newton, Inc., 555 Windsor Drive, Secaucus, NJ 07094 (Gouache and powders for coloring paint, stencil cards, paper)

Zuber et Cie, D & D Building, 979 Third Avenue, New York, NY 10022 (Panoramic wallpapers)

CANADIAN ORGANIZATIONS

Royal Architectural Institute of Canada, 55 Murray Street, Suite 330, Ottawa KIN 5MT

SHOPS AND SUPPLIERS

Arthur Sanderson & Sons, Ltd., 1595 16th Avenue, Suite 302, Richmond Hill, Ontario 14B 3N9 (Fabrics and wallcoverings)

W.H. Bilbrough & Company, Ltd., Design Walk, 326 Davenport Road, Toronto, Ontario M5R 1K6 (Fabrics)

Hamilton Weston Wallpapers, Ltd., through Charles Rupert Design, 2004 Oak Bay Avenue, Victoria, British Columbia V8R 1E4 (Historic wallpapers)

Paint Magic, 1019 17th Avenue SW, Calgary, Alberta T2T OA7 (Equipment, paint, videos, and books for decorative paint techniques)

BIBLIOGRAPHY

ARTLEY, ALEXANDER Putting Back the Style, *Swallow Publishing for Evans Bros., 1982*

ASHLEY, LAURA Complete Guide to Home Decorating, *Weidenfeld and Nicholson, 1989*

ATKINS, CAROLINE Decorating Your First Home, *Cassell, 1994*

BARNARD, NICHOLAS Complete Home Decorating Book,

Dorling Kindersley, 1994
BEIGEL, RENATE and LYONS, STANLEY
Lighting Your Home, Quiller Press, 1994
CHING, FRANCIS DK Interior Design Illustrated,
van Nostrand Reinhold, 1987
CHURCHILL, JANE and CHARLTON, ANNE
Decorating Ideas, Harper Collins, 1994
CLIFTON MOGG, CAROLINE and PAINE, MELANIE
The Curtain Book, Mitchell Beazley, 1988
CONRAN, TERENCE The Soft Furnishings Book,
Conran Octopus, 1986
COOK, CLARENCE The House Beautiful, Constable, 1966
(reprinted from 1870s)
DRAYTON, LOUISE and THOMSON, JANE The Stencil Book
Dorling Kindersley, 1994
GIBBERD, VERNON and PHILLIPS, BARTY Kitchens,
Winward, 1986
GILLIATT, MARY Period Decorating, Conran Octopus, 1994
GORE, ALAN and ANNE The History of English Interiors,
Phaidon Press, 1991
GUILD, TRICIA Design and Detail, Conran Octopus, 1988
HACKMAN, HILARY Edwardian House Style,
David and Charles, 1994
HALL, DINAH Ethnic By Design, Mitchell Beazley, 1992
HOGAN, ELIZABETH L. (ed) Ideas for Great Bathrooms,
Sunset, 1991
HOGAN, ELIZABETH (ed) Ideas for Great Kitchens,
Sunset, 1992
HOGG, MINN and HARROP, WENDY The World of Interiors,
Conran Octopus, 1988
INNES, JOCASTA Paintability,
Weidenfeld and Nicolson and Channel 4 TV, 1986
INNES, JOCASTA The New Decorator's Handbook,
Boxtree, 1995
JACKSON, ALBERT and DAY, DAVID How to Store Just
About Anything, Harper Collins, 1992
JONES, CHESTER Colefax & Fowler,
Barrie and Jenkins, 1989
LE GRICE, LYN Art of Stencilling, Viking, 1986
LE GRICE, LYN The Stencilled House,
Dorling Kindersley, 1988
MACK, LORRIE Making the Most of Workspaces,
Conran Octopus, 1995
MILLER, JUDITH Period Fireplaces, Mitchell Beazley, 1995
MILLER JUDITH Period Kitchens, Mitchell Beazley, 1995
MILLER, JUDITH and MARTIN Period Details,
Mitchell Beazley, 1987
MILLER, JUDITH and MARTIN Period Finishes and Effects,
Mitchell Beazley, 1995
PAINE, MELANIE Textile Classics, Mitchell Beazley, 1990
PARISSIEN, STEVEN The Georgian House,
Aurum Press, 1995
PHILLIPS, BARTY Guide to Decorative Lighting,
Webb and Bower, 1987
PHILLIPS, BARTY The Country House Book,
Ebury Press, 1988

PHILLIPS, BARTY Doing Up Small Spaces,
Merehurst, 1995
PRIZEMAN, JOHN Your House: The Outside View,
Hutchinson, 1975
SEPPINGS, KATHERINE Fireplaces for a Beautiful Home,
Merehurst, 1993
SLOAN, ANNIE and GWYNN, KATE Traditional Paints
and Finishes, Collins and Brown, 1993
SLOAN, ANNIE The Practical Guide to Decorative Antique
Effects, Collins and Brown, 1995
SPENCER-CHURCHILL, HENRIETTA Classic English
Interiors, Collins and Brown, 1990
WALKER, ADRIAN (ed) The Encyclopaedia of Wood,
Quarto, 1989
WALKER, MAUREEN Before and After Interiors,
Ebury Press, 1985
WILSON, ALTHEA Paint Works, Century Hutchinson, 1987
YAGI, KAGI A Japanese Touch for Your Home,
Kodausha International, 1982

PICTURE ACKNOWLEDGEMENTS

p.8, **Viaduct Furniture**, 1–10 Summerís St, London EC1R
5BD; 10, 12, **Perstorp Flooring**, PO Box 391, Crawley
RH10 2GE, UK (tel: 0800 374 471 for free brochure); 13,
Michael Marriott trolley at Contemporary Applied Arts,
2 Percy Street, London W1P 9FA; 14, **Neville Johnson
Offices**, Broadoak Business Pk, Manchester M17 1RW,
UK; 15, **Ed Honside, Elizabeth Whiting & Associate**;
16, **Charles Rutherfoord**, designer, 51 The Chase, London
SW4 0NP (photo: Judy Goldhill); 17, **EWA**; 18, **Andrew
Macintosh Furniture Ltd**, 462–464 Chiswick High Rd,
London W4 5JJ; 19, **Graham Henderson, EWA**; 20,
Greenwich Wood Works, 1 Friendly Place, London SE13
7QS; 22, **Tintawn Weaving Ltd** (carpets), 11 High St,
Dorking RH4 1AR, UK; 23, **EWA**; 24, **Gordon Russell
Detail Furniture**, D2 Metropolitan Wharf, Wapping Wall,
London E1 9SS; 27, **Bruce Hardwood Floors (UK) Ltd**,
185 Milton Park, Abingdon OX14 4SR, UK; 29, **Kahrs (UK)
Ltd**, Unit 1, Timberlaine Estate, Chichester PO19 2FJ; UK;
30, **Crown Decorative Products**, PO Box 37, Hollins Rd,
Darwen BB3 0BG, UK; 32, **Eric Crichton, EWA**; 33 **Andrew
Macintosh** (see p.18); 34, **Crown** (see p.30); 36, **Bentley
& Spens**, furnishing fabrics, Studio 25, 90 Lots Rd,
London SW10 0QD; 37, **Crown** (see p.30); 38,
A. Sanderson & Sons, 112–120 Brompton Rd, London
SW3 1JJ; 39, **Crown** (see p.30); 40, **Michael Nicholson,
EWA**; 41, **Totem Design**, 14 Arundel Gdns, London W11
2LA; 42, **Sarah Tisdall**, artist, 130 Bermondsey Wall East,
London SE16 4TT; 43, **National Trust**; 44, **Romo Ltd**,
Lowmoor Rd, Kirkby-in-Ashfield NG17 7DE, UK; 47,
Perstorp (see p.10); 48, **Paul Harmer Photography**,
5 Chester Ct, 84 Salusbury Road, London NW6 6PA; 49,
National Trust; 50, **Vermont Castings**, Ospreys Ct,
Hawkfield Business Pk, Bristol BS14 0BS, UK; 52,
Charles Rutherfoord (see p.16); 53, **Habitat**, 196
Tottenham Ct Rd, London W1P 9LD and branches; 54,
The Velux Co. Ltd, Woodside Way, Glenrothes, East Fife,
Scotland KY7 4ND; 56, **Sanderson** (see p.38); 57, **Keddy-
Poujoulat (UK) Ltd.**, Silverlands, Holloway Hill, Surrey
KT16 0AE, UK; 58, **John Cullen Lighting Design**, 585
Kings Road, London SW6 2EH; 59, **Tom Leighton, EWA**;
60, **Vermont Castings** (see p.50); 61, **Sanderson** (see
p.38); 62, **Lizzie Orme**, Unit 10, Waterside, 44–48 Wharf
Rd, London N1 7UX; 63, **John Wilman Fabrics and
Wallpapers**, Culshaw St, Burnley BB10 4PQ, UK; 64,
Sanderson (see p.38); 65, **Christopher Farr** (handmade
rugs), 115 Regents Pk Rd, London NW1 8UR; 66, **IKEA**,

255 North Circular Rd, London NW10 0JQ and branches;
67, **Bentley & Spens** (see p.36); 68, **Perstorp** (see p.10);
70, **Fourneaux de France**, Worton Rd Industrial Estate,
Isleworth TW7 6EU, UK; 71, **Rhode Design**, 65 Cross St,
London N1 2BB; 72, **Newcastle Furniture Co**, 128
Walham Green Ct, London SW6 4DG; 73, **Mark Wilkinson
Furniture**, Overton House, Bromham SN15 2HA, UK; 74,
John Tchalenko (tiles), 30 Therapia Rd, London SE22 0SE;
75, **Habitat** (see p.53); 76, **Rhode Design** (see p.71); 77,
H&R Johnson, Highgate Tile Works, Stoke on Trent ST6
4JX, UK; 78, **Perstorp** (see p.19); 80, **Aga-Rayburn**, PO
Box 30, Ketley, Telford TF1 4DD, UK; 81, **Totem Design**
(see p.41); 82, **IKEA** (see p.66); 83, **Divertimenti: London
shop**, 45-47 Wigmore St, London W1H 9LE, mail order, PO
Box 6611, London SW6 6XU; 84, **Fired Earth plc**, Twyford
Mill, Oxford Rd, Adderbury OX17 3HP, UK; 85, **Stonell
Corp.**, Unit 1, Bockingfold, Goudhurst, Kent TN17 1NY,
UK; 86, **Andrew Macintosh Furniture** (see p.18); 87,
Totem Design (see p.41); 88, 89, **Sanderson** (see p.38);
90, **Greenwich Wood Works** (see p.20); 91, **Clearview
Stoves**, Bishops Castle, Shropshire SY9 5HH, UK; 92,
Aga-Rayburn (see p.80); 93, **Totem Design** (see p.41);
94, **Perstorp** (see p.10); 95, **Nick Carter, EWA**; 96,
Andrew Macintosh (see p.18); 97, **The Holding Co.**,
243–245 Kings Rd, London SW3 5EL; 98, The Velux Co.
(see p.54); 100, **Mothercare**, Cherry Tree Rd, Watford
WD2 5SH, UK; 101, **The Carpet Council**, 1 Chelsea Manor
Gdns, London SW3 5PN (design: Ben Findlay); 102,
The Carpet Council (see p.101); 103, Thistle Joinery,
77 Ilderton Rd, Bermondsey, London SE16 3J2; 104,
Enzo Mininno, EWA; 105, **Perstorp** (see p.10); 106, **Crown**
(see p.30); 107, **Charles Rutherfoord** (see p.16); 108,
Junckers, Wheaton Ct. Commercial Centre, Witham CM8
3UJ, UK; 109, 111, **The Holding Co.** (see p.97); 112,
Georgie Day, 19 Ermine St, Huntingdon PE18 6EX, UK;
113, **CAA** (see p.13); 114, **Habitat** (see p.53); 116,
The Futon Co., Tottenham Court Road, London W1P 9LH
and branches; 117, **Simon Horn Furniture**, 117–121
Wandsworth Bridge Rd, London SW7; 118, **Peter
Woloszynski, EWA**; 119, **Simon Horn Furniture** (see
p.117); 120, **Deptich Designs**, 7 College Field, Prince
George's Rd, London SW19 2PT; 121, **Michael Dunne,
EWA**; 122, **Deptich Designs** (see p.120); 123, **Lizzie
Orme** (see p.62); 124, **Enzo Mininno, EWA**; 126, **Crown**
(see p.30); 127, 128, 129, **C.P. Hart**, Newnham Terrace,
Hercules Rd, London SE1 1DR; 130, **Tintawn Weaving Ltd**
(see p.22); 132, **Paul Harmer** (see p.48);

133, **The Carpet Council** (see p.101); 134, **Perstorp** (see p.10); 136, **IKEA** (see p.66); 137, **Matthews Office Furniture plc**, PO Box 70, Reginald Rd, St. Helens WA9 4JE, UK; 138, **John Wilman** (see p.63); 139, **IKEA** (see p.66); 140, **EWA**; 141, **Cubestore**, 58 Pembroke Rd, London W4; 142, **IKEA** (see p.66); 143, **Graham Henderson, EWA**; 144, **The Carpet Council** (see p.101), 145, **Cubestore** (see p.141); 146, **Shaker Ltd.**, 322 Kings Rd, London SW3 5UH and **Aero Wholesale Ltd.**, 96 Westbourne Grove, London W2 5RT; 147, **Charles Rutherfoord** (see p.16); 148, **Matthews Office Furniture** (see p.137); 149, **Tim Street Porter, EWA**; 150, **Perstorp** (see p.10); 152 **Michael Dunne, EWA**; 153, **The Futon Co.** (see p.116); 154, **The Manhattan Loft Corp.**, 12 Queen Anne St, London W1M OAU; 155, 156, **Karl Dietrich-Buhler, Graham Henderson, EWA**; 157, **Crown** (see p. 30); 158, 159, **Gordon Russell Detail Furniture** (see p.24); 160, **Kelly Hoppen Interiors**, 13 Roland Gdns, London SW7 3PE; 161, **Michael Dunne, EWA**; 163, **The Futon Co.** (see p.116); 164, **Manhattan Loft Corp.** (see p.154); 166, **Neil Lorimer, EWA**; 167, 168, **Manhattan Loft Corp.** (see p.164); 169, **Crown** (see p.30); 170, **Habitat** (see p.53); 171, **Paul Badham**, 2–4 Southgate Rd, London N1 3JJ; 174, **Crown** (see p.30); 176, **Bruce Hardwood Floors** (UK) Ltd (see p.27); 177, **Andreas von Einsiedel, EWA**; 179, **Oak Leaf Conservatories**, Kettlestring Lane, Clifton Comon, York Y03 8XF; 180, 181,182,183, **Spike Powell, Michael Dunne, Neil Lorimer, Anne Kelley, EWA**; 184, **National Trust**; 186, © **Tria Giovan, Colonial Homes Magazine**; 187, 188, 190, **Spike Powell, Andrew Kolesnikow, Tom Leighton, EWA**; 191, **Bentley & Spens** (see p.36); 193, 194, **Michael Dunne, Andreas von Einsiedel, EWA**; 195, 196, **National Trust**; 197, Sasha Waddell, 4 Delaford St, London SW6 7LT; 198, **Tim Street Porter, EWA**; 199, **The Nursery Window**, 83 Walton St, London SW3 2HP; 200, **Bisque Radiators**, 244 Belsize Rd, London NW6 4BT; 202, **Tim Street Porter, EWA**; 203, 204, **National Trust**; 206 Oatlands Studio; 207, **Shaker Ltd** (see p.146); 208, **Dulux Advice Centre**, UK, Tel: +44 (0) 01753 550555; 209, **EWA**; 210, **National Trust**; 212, **Perkins Radiator Covers**, 105 Ack Lane East, Bramhall SK7 2AB, UK; 213, **Crucial Trading**, The Market Hall, Craven Arms, Shropshire SY7 9ZZ, UK; 215, **Habitat** (see p.53); 217, **Perstorp** (see p.10); 218, **Kahrs (UK) Ltd** (see p.29); 221, **Winther Browne & Co Ltd**, Nobel Rd, Eley Estate, London N18 3DX; 222, **Asprey Newton**, 16 The Terrace, Barnes, London SW13 ONP; 224, **Fired Earth** (see p.84); 228, assortment of ceiling roses from **Asprey Newton** (see p.222); 229, **Stonell** (see p.85); 230, hand painted by **Rare Creations** for **The Holding Co.** (see p. 97); 232, **Crown** (see p.30); 235, **Imperial Bathroom Company**, Imperial Bldgs, Northgate Way, Walsall WS9 8SR, UK; 237, **Rhode Design** (see p.71); 239, **Lizzie Orme** (see p.62); 240, **Dulux Advice Centre**, UK (see p.208); 241, **The Holding Co.** (see p. 97); 242, **Crucial Trading** (see p.213); 245, 246, **Sanderson** (see p.38); 247, **Crown** (see p.30); 250, **Brunschwig & Fils**, 10 The Chambers, Chelsea Harbour Drive, London SW10; 252, **Sanderson** (see p.38); 254, Kingcombe Sofas, 302–304 Fulham Rd, London SW10 9EP; 257, **Cope & Timmins**, Angel Rd Wks, Edmonton, London N18 3AY; 258, **Muriel Short Designs**, Hewitts Estate, Cranleigh GU6 8LW, UK; 259, **John Wilman** (see p.63); 261, **Romo Ltd** (see p.44); 262, **Sanderson** (see p.38); 266, **Fired Earth** (see p.84); 268, **The Amtico Co.**, Kingfield Rd, Coventry CV6 5PL, UK; 270, **The Metropolitan Tile Co.**, Lower Audley Centre, Blackburn BB1 1DE, UK, tiles by **Elon Ltd**, 12 Silver Rd, London W12; 271, **The Carpet Council** (see p.101); 272, **Fired Earth** (see p.84); 273, **Hugh Mackay Carpets**, PO Box 1, Durham City, DHI 2PX, UK; 274, Tamara Salman rug from **Christopher Farr** (see p.65); 275, **The Carpet Council** (see p.101); 276, **Fired Earth** (see p.84); 278, **John Cullen Lighting** (see p.58); 280, **Harrison Drape**, Bradford St, Birmingham B12 OPE, UK; 282, **Jack Wimperis**, Piccadilly Mill, Stroud GL5 2HT, UK; 284, **John Cullen** (see p.58); 285, **Shiu-Kay Kan**, 34 Lexington St, London W1; 286, **Mr. Light**, 275 Fulham Rd, London SW10 9PZ; 287, **John Cullen Lighting** (see p.58); 288, 289, **Shiu-Kay Kan** (see p.285); 291, **Jack Wimperis** (see p.282); 292, **Radiating Style**, 194 New Kings Rd, London SW6 4NF; 294, 295, **Bisque Radiators** (see p.200); 296, **Aga-Rayburn** (see p.80); 298, **Viaduct Furniture** (see p.8); 300, **Mark Gabbertas**, 3 Normand Mews, London W14 9RB; 301, **Deacon & Sandys**, Hillcrest Farm Oast, Cranbrook, Kent TN17 3QD, UK; 304, **Aram Designs Ltd**, 3 Kean St, Covent Gdn, London WC2B 4AT.

INDEX

A
additions 103, 178
  down 18
  out 18
  up 17
afzelia 213
Aga 296
alcove 118, 121, 131, 246
  kitchens *see* kitchen, alcove
Anagiypta 249
  antique furniture *see*
    furniture, antique
antislip strips 276
arches 59
architectural styles *see*
  style, architectural
architrave 220
areas
  activity 54, 55
  dividing 160
Art Deco 32, 187
Art Nouveau 87, 303
artificial stone *see*
  stone, artificial
arts and crafts 189, 303
ash 213
attic 17, 20, IG3, 136, 165
  access 167
  bedrooms 118
  escape routes 171
  flat 14
  plumbing 168
  remodels 166
  safety 171
  spaces 100
  wiring 168
Aubusson 256

B
baby's room 100
barn 64
baseboards 57, 59, 219, 220
  radiators 295
basement 20, 103, 136, 141, 165
  access 167
  plumbing 168
  wiring 168
bathtub 127
  corner 127
  double 127
  exotic 127
  materials 127
  sit-in 20, 21
  stone 229
  sunken 127
bathrooms 115, 126
  built-in 126
  en suite 131
  decoration ideas 132
  fixtures 129
  safety 130
  through kitchen 79
bay window *see* window, bay
bedroom
  second 119
  washing facilities 131
bedrooms 115, 116
beds 116
  bunk 109

drapery 263
  one-room living 153
bedside table 116
beech 213
bidet 129
Biedermeier 124, 189
birch 213
blackboard 106, III
blinds 46, 262
  Austrian 262
  balloon 45, 262
  roller 46
  roman 46
  slatted 46
  Venetian 262
Bloomsbury group 190
bohemian 190
boudoirs 61
braid 256
brick 223, 228
  bare 228
  flooring *see* flooring, brick
  paving 85
brocade 255
budget ideas
  bathroom 133
  children's rooms 112
  dining room 96
  hall 182
  kitchen 92
  living roams 153
  one-room living 163
  sunroom 182
  textiles 264
  workrooms 149
budgeting 29
building permits 26, 77
bunk beds *see* beds, bunk
butcher's block 82

C
cabinet guidelines 26
cabinet 25
  medicine 127
calico 254
cambric 54
canvas 254
carpentry workshop 145
carpet 85, 107, 271
  binding 274
  fiber-bonded 273
  fusion-bonded 273
  materials 272
  runners 276
  tiles, laying 273
  tufted 273
  types 272
  woven 272
cedar 213
ceilings
  low 57
  suspended 17
central heating 294
  fuels 296
  furnaces 296
Charleston 190
checklists, rooms 12, 13, 14, 15
checks 255
cherry wood 213
chestnut 213
childproofing 91

children's flooring 102, 107
  furniture 100, 109, 110
  rooms 99
  rooms, safety 104
  rooms, shared 103
  windows 102
  work space 103
Chinoiserie 191
chipboard 213
coir 275
collections 306
color 34
  adding 37
  as camouflage 36
  rules 35
  wheel 34, 35
colorwash 237
  applying 238
  preparing 238
common problems
  attics 169
  basements 169
  bathroom 131
  bedrooms 118
  one-room living 159
  computer room *see*
    room, computer
condensation 131, 160
range hoods 87
cooking 71
Corian 86, 91, 92
cork
  flooring *see* flooring, cork
  wallcovering see
    wallcovering, cork
cornice 57, 59, 225
  lighting *see* lighting, cornice
corona 263
corridors 20
cot 109, 111, 112
cottages 64
coving 227
crackle glaze *see*
  glaze, crackle
cradle 109
curtain
  rods 257
  styles 45
  tracks 257, 258
curtains 257
  attached lining 261
  bead 42
  guidelines 46
  hold backs 257, 258
  hung from poles 258
  lining 260
  looped 259
  making 259
  measuring 260
  pleated and gathered 258
  ready made 259
  small 259
  tie-backs 256

D
dados 219, 220
damask 255
decoration
  attics 171
  barns 172
  basements 173
  bathroom 132

bedrooms 122
  children's room 106
  lofts 172
  one-room living 161
  studios 172
  sunroom 180
design checklist
  attics 173
  basement 173
  bathroom 133
  bedrooms 125
  children's room 113
  dining room 97
  hall 183
  kitchen 97
  living rooms 67
  porch 183
  sunroom 83
  workrooms 149
  one-room living 163
desks 138
dimmer switch 108
dimming controls 286
dining rooms 69, 94
  heating 95
  lighting 95, 96
Directoire 192
displays 306
distressing 233
documenting, importance of 26
door
  handles 42
  knockers 42
doors 23, 41
  bi-folding 23
  double 76
  Dutch 23
  exterior 23
  French 22
  glass 24
  interior 42
  jibbing 23
  kitchen 76
  paneled 221
  patio 22, 24, 183
  sliding 23
  wood 221
dormer rod 263
double glazing 95, 119, 281
  sealed unit 281
Douglas fir 214
downlights 285
dragging 240
duckboarding 126

E
Edwardian Style *see* style,
  Edwardian
eggshell paint *see* paint, eggshell
elderly, precautions for 160
electrical outlets 102, 104, 117
electricity, in the bathroom 130
elevation drawing 28
elm 214
Empire style *see* style, Empire
entrance hall 19, 176
Erno Goldfinger 43
exhaust fan 75, 87
  hood 74
exterior rendering
  maintenance 228
  repair 228

Index **317**

F
fabric 265
  on walls 265
fabrics
  printed 256
  sheer 256
family room *see* room, family
fanlight 43
faucets 129
farmhouse look 91
filing cabinet 138
fireplaces 21, 220, 229, 297
flagstones 85
flock 244
floor coverings 267
  soft 271
  style hints 277
floor cushions 55
floor boards 217
  sanding 217
flooring
  brick 268
  cork 276
  marble 268
  natural fibers 275
  rubber 277
  slate 268
  stone 268
  tiles 268
  vinyl 85, 276
  wood 85, 218, 219
floors
  hard 268
  mosaic 269
  wood 217
flush 129
focal points 59
food
  preparation 71
  storage 71
formal dining 95
friezes 106
furniture 299
  alternative 306
  antique 300
  attics 171
  barns 172
  children's room 100
  Jacobean 302
  liming 307
  lofts 172
  Medieval 302
  one-room living 161
  painted 305
  quality 300
  Queen Anne 302
  Regency 303
  repairing 300, 301
  reproduction 300
  Restoration 302
  second-hand 300
  studios 172
  styles 302
  Tudor 302
  twentieth-century 303, 304
  Victorian 303
futon 153

G
garage, changing use of 15
glare 285
glass 279

bricks 87, 168
  doors 181
  colored 283
  crown 280
  cylinder 281
  decorative 282
  drawn sheet 281
  film coatings 281
  float 280
  frosted 283
  heat strengthened 281
  laminated 281
  low emissivity 281
  patterned 283
  plain 280
  plate 281
  safety 281
  stained 181, 283
  sunroom 282
  textured 283
  window 280
glaze 237, 238
  colors 239
  crackle 307
  mixing 239
  gloss
  flame-retardant 233
  non-drip 233
  liquid 233
  paint 233
  self-undercoating 233
Gothic 196

H
hardboard 213
hardwood 86
harmony, creating 32
hat stand 118
heating 293
  bathroom 130
  children's room 108
  dining rooms 95
  kitchen 86
  one-room living 157
  safety 297
  workrooms 141
height 59
  use of 19
herringbone 254
highrises 32
hints
  carpet 274
  hanging pictures 306
  laying vinyl 276
  paint 233
  paperhanging 250, 251
  period paint 234
homes
  ninetheenth century 32
  modern 32
  thirties 32
  traditional 32
  twenties 32
house numbers 42
houseplants 132

I
inspiration, sources of 33
insulation
  attics and basements 168
  sound 28, 159
interior styles, history of 185

see also style
interiors
  formal 47
  informal 47
iroko 214
irreguiar walls, in the kitchen 79

J
jarrah 214
jute 275

K
kilims 256
Kingston Lacey 186
kitchen 69
  alcove 74
  appliances 72, 73, 75, 76, 79
  basement 18
  base units 75
  budget 92
  cabinet doors 76
  cabinet 81
  childproof 91
  columns 79
  common problems 76
  cook's 87
  cottage 92
  drawers 82
  electrical outlets 72, 79
  family 91
  flooring 84
  heating 86
  high tech 88
  island 74
  layout 72
  lighting 80, 86
  L-shaped 73
  one wall 72
  other uses 96
  painting 236
  peninsula 74
  planning
    for comfort and
    efficiency 75
    the work flow 70
  plumbing 76
  radiators 87
  safety 79
  shelves 81
  single galley 72
  small 88
  storage 81, 83
  U-shaped 73
  ventilation 76
  wall hung cabinets 76
  windows 77
  work sequence 70, 71, 76
  work stations 73
kitchen-dining 96
kitchens
  for the disabled 80
  for the elderly 80
knotty cedar 214
knotty pine 214

L
lambrequin 261
laminates 86
lamps
  recessed 286
  semi-recessed 286
landings 20

pantry 82, 92
  shelves 82
laundry hamper 126
laundry room *see* room, laundry
leaded lights *see* lights, leaded
library 59, 146
light
  bulbs, types of 287
  fittings 285, 288
  natural 280
lighting
  artificial 284
  attics 167
  basements 167
  bathrooms 290
  bedrooms 290
  children's rooms 08, 290
  for computers 144
  cornice 286
  cove 286
  dining room 95, 96
  feature 285
  functions 284
  general 284
  halls 289
  kitchens 289
  landings 289
  lofts 167
  one-room living 161
  outdoor 290
  plants 291
  portable 286
  safety 285, 290
  staircases 289
  task 284
  workrooms 140
lights 279
  leaded 283
  skylights 54
limewash 233
lining paper 245
linoleum 85, 277
registered buildings 26
living rooms 51
  children in 55
  common problems 57
  decorating 60
  decorating tips 62
  design checklist 67
  formal 52
  informal 52
  inspiration 62
  location 52
  requirements 52
  storage 56
loft 64
  remodel 137
lumber
  buying 212
  sources 212

M
mahogany 214
mailboxes 42
maple 214
marble 229
  flooring *see* floating, marble
marbling 240
matchboarding 216
matting 85, 107
MDF 212
measuring, importance of 26

medicine cabinet *see*
    cabinet, medicine
Medium-Density Fiberboard *see*
    MDF
metallic paint *see* paint, metallic
mirrors 36, 117, 279, 291
    bedroom 122
moisture 141
moisture-proofing 141
mosaic floors *see* floors, mosaic
moldings
    maintenance 227
    repair 227
murals 106, III, 112

N
Neo-Classical 32, 203
noise 119

O
office
    chairs 138
    making space for 137
    space 96
one-room living 151
    cooking 156
    eating 154
    washing 157
    working 154
Osterley Park 204
outdoor lighting *see*
    lighting, outdoor

P
paint 36, 38, 231, 243
    blackboard 233
    brush 235
    casein 233
    decorative techniques 240
    eggshell 232
    eighteenth century 234
    latex 232, 233
    exterior 241
    metallic 233
    nineteenth century 234
    oil-based 232
    polyurethane 233
    pre-eighteenth century 234
    roller 233, 266
    swimming pool 233
    textured 233
    twentieth century 234, 235
    types 232
    water-based 232
paintwork, caring for 241
paneled door, painting 236
paneling 57
    fixing 216
pantry 82
paperhanging, step-by-step 250
papering, behind radiators 251
papier mâché 226
parana pine 214
pattern 38
    adding 38
    coordinating 39
    diaper 254
    juxtaposing 39
pegboard 107
picture
    molding 219, 220
    windows 45, 263

pictures 306
pile weaves 256
plan, drawing 28
planning
    bathrooms 126
    importance of 27, 28
    kitchen 70
    work 28
    workrooms 138
plants 59, 132
    lighting 59, 291
plaster 223
    maintaining 227
    moldings 224
    repairing 227
    uses 224
plasterwork
    decorative 225
    painting 228
plumbing
    attics and basements 168
    kitchen 76
plywood 212
porch 178
power router 220

Q
quarry tiles *see* tiles, quarry
Queen Anne style *see*
    style, Queen Anne

R
radiators 28, 294
    aluminum 295
    Art Nouveau 295
    chrome plated 295
    concealing 296
    fin type 295
    ladder style 295
    tubular 295
    Victorian 295
    white panel 295
ragging 233, 240
rag-rolling 240
range hoods 87
ranges 297
registered buildings 26
remodels 96, 121
rendering 228
repp 254
rewiring 102
Robert Adam 204
Rococo 206
roller paint 233, 236
Roman Ogee 220
room
    baby's 100
    computer 143
    family 63
    garden 136
    laundry 96, 143
    music 144
    older child's 103
    sewing 145
    sun 178
    teenager's 103
    utility 92, 143
    young child's 99
    young girl's 250
rooms
    awkwardly shaped 121
    changing use of 15

cold 36
    dividing 17, 54
    large 121
    L-shaped 55
    multipurpose 63, 141, 143, 151
    narrow 121
    north facing 36
    square 57
    tall 55, 121
rosewood 214
rubber
    flooring *see* flooring, rubber
    wood 214
rugs 276
runners, carpet 276

S
safety
    attics 171
    in the bathroom I30
    catches 104
    children's rooms 104
    gate 104
    glass 281
    heating 297
    in the kitchen 79
    lighting 285, 290
Sapele 214
scale drawing 27, 126
Scandinavian style *see*
    style, Scandinavian
screens 21, 56
seagrass 275
seating 53, 54, 55
secondary sash 282
security 159
shaver outlet 130
shell buying 166
shelves 24
    fixing 25
    library 59
    pantry 82
shelving guidelines 25
shower 116, 128
    cabinet 128
    curtains 130
    head 128
    room 128
shutters 45, 46
Shyam Ahuja 276
silk, woven 255
sink 28
    pedestal 128
    wall hung 129
    wash 116
sisal 275
slate 86
    flooring *see* flooring, slate
socket guards 102, 104
sound insulation *see*
    insulation, sound
sound-proofing 103
space
    altering 17
    calculating 160
    clothing 31
    creating 11
    extending 17
    pockets of 19
    savers, one-room living 159
    saving 21, 162
    uses of 12, 18

spaces, large 55
spattering 240
sponging 240
spotlights 286
door *see* doors
stained glass *see* glass, stained
stainless steel 86
stairs 21
    spiral 21
    under 20
Starck, Philippe 127
stenciling 241
stencils 106
stippling 240
stone 223, 229
    cleaning 229
    artificial 229
    flooring *see* flooring, stone
    Portland 229
storage 24
    bathroom 131
    bedrooms 117, 118
    built-in 57
    children's rooms 101, 103, 109
    food and drink 82
    kitchen 81, 83
    one-room living 158
    workrooms 138
stoves 297
straight grain 213
stripes 255
    horizontal 36
    vertical 36
structural alterations 12
studio apartment 103
    kitchens 73, 74
studios 172
    artist's 147
    sound 144
style
    1950s 202
    American Colonial 123, 191
    American Country 186
    architectural 32
    bathroom 132
    colonial 191
    cottage 123
    Edwardian 192
    Egyptian 42
    eighteenth century 302
    Elizabethan 193
    Empire 192
    English Country 193
    English country house 122
    evolving 48
    farmhouse 123
    French country 123
    French Provincial 195
    Georgian 195
    Gustavain 197
    High-tech 198
    hotel 132
    Indian national 199
    Jacobean 208
    Japanese 125
    Japanese ethnic 199
    Mediterranean 124, 199
    Mexican 77
    modern 48
    modernist/minimalist 201
    Neo-Classical 124
    New England 124

Nineties 192
Nomadic 205
Postmodern 205
Queen Anne 191
Regency 205
rustic 48
Scandinavian 61, 64
Scandinavian national 206
Shaker 81, 91, 206
Swedish 197
town house 124
Tudor 208
Victorian 125, 132, 208
for workrooms 147, 148
style hints, floor coverings 277
see also flooring
Style Rustique 195
sunroom 95, 178, 282
blinds 95
frames 282
Sutton House 49
Sycamore 214

T
tapestry 255
borders 256
tartan 255
Tasmanian oak 214
tassels 256
teak 214
tempera 233   tenting
121
tetracotta tiles *see* tiles, terracotta
terrazzo 269
textiles 253
texture 40
balance 41
delicate 40
dense 40
matte 40
shiny 40
textured paints *see* paints, textured
thermostats 297
ticking 254
tie-backs 258
tiled floor, laying 270
tiles 129, 132
ceramic 86
flooring *see* flooring, tiles
kitchen 84, 85
mirror 130
quarry 269
terracotta 269
lumber
buying 212
sources 212
tips
brick 229
painting 235
plaster 224
plasterwork 227
wallpaper 249
wood 217
toilets 129
tongue-and-groove boards 216
towel rack 130
heated 130
Town House 65
traffic noise 119
transition points 176
tribal weaves 256
trimmings 256

Tupelo 214
twill 254

U
upholstery 265
uplights 286
utility room *see* room, utility

V
valance 261, 262
box 262
box-pleated 262
French-pleated 262
frills 262
vanity unit 128
vee-jointed 216
veneers 216
Venetian blinds *see*
blinds, Venetian
ventilation 29
bathroom 130
kitchen 87
one-room living 160
work rooms 141
veranda 177, 178
Victorian Gothic 196
vinyl *see* also paint
flooring *see* flooring, vinyl
wallcoverings *see*
wallcoverings, vinyl

W
wall
bracket fittings 286
partition 77
washers 286
wallcoverings 243
alternative 245
cork 245
felt 245
imitation suede 245
polysterene 246
using 246
vinyl 244
woven fabric 245
wallpaper 37, 243
assessing quantities 249
eighteenth-century 247
embossed 244
hand-printed 244
ingrained 244
machine-printed
nineteenth-century 248
period 247
seventeenth-century 247
twentieth-century 248
types 244
walnut 214
closet 117, 118, 119
warehouses 165
washes 237
whitewash 233
whitewood 214
William Morris 38, 246
Wimpole Hall 212
window
bay 280
corner 263
coupled 282
glass *see* glass,
window seat 121

windows 22, 45
French 16
sloping 263
tilting 263
wood 211
block flooring *see*
flooring, wood block
flooring *see* flooring, wood
floors, cleaning 219
in the kitchen 221
moldings 219
paneling 214
stopping 307
woodblock 107
woodchip 244
workrooms 135
see also budget ideas;
storage; style
dining room 138
garage 137
planning 138
shed 136
spare room 137
sunroom 138
work surface 75, 76, 85, 86, 128,
138, 221
worktable 138, 143